Art Journal Kickstarter

Pages and Prompts to Energize Your Art Journals

edited by
Kristy Conlin

NORTH LIGHT BOOKS
Cincinnati, OH
CreateMixedMedia.com

contents

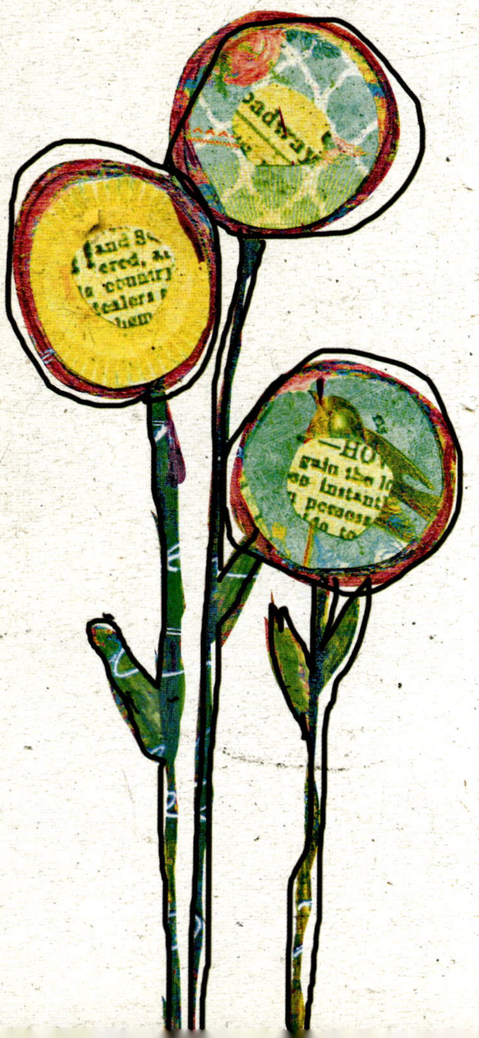

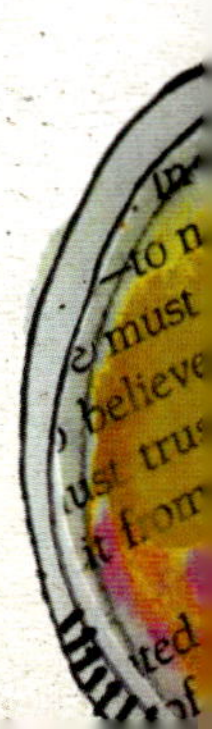

introduction

“In art journaling, anything goes.”

So says artist and *Art Journal Kickstarter* contributor Maureen Craddock (pages 108–109).

Truer words, I think, have never been spoken.

Let’s face it: I’m very fortunate to be able to work with some pretty top-notch art journalers—people like Seth Apter, Dina Wakley, Traci Bautista, Mary Beth Shaw and Gina Armfield just to name-drop a few. And I’m exposed on an almost daily basis to the work of numerous other artists, mixed-media artists who blow my mind with the work they produce and the materials they use.

But working on this book? Entirely new levels of mind-blowing. And inspiration to heights I can neither aptly nor articulately describe.

But I’ll try.

White correction fluid. Vintage book pages and sheet music. Fabric. Images cut from the pages of magazines. Gel pens. Silver leaf. Hand-carved stamps. Gel transfers. Maps. Metallic paint pens. Colored chalk. Sewing pattern paper. Wine labels. Tea and coffee. India ink. Dymo tape. Molding paste. Beet juice. Finger paints. Embossing powder. Kitchen tools. Encaustic wax. Sea foam. (Actual foam from the sea preserved on paper!) Gelli prints. Twigs. Waterslide decals. Beads. Glass glitter. Leaves. And of course acrylic paints, watercolors, markers, pens, pencils, colored pencils, various acrylic mediums and glazes, tapes, adhesives, pastels, crayons, inks, stamps, stencils, photos, stickers and any and all ephemera you can imagine and some you can’t.

Those are just some of the materials our 99 contributing artists used in creating the 151 art journal pages (created both in and outside of the journal itself) that grace the pages of this here, little book.

If those materials aren’t enough inspiration to get you started, perhaps the beautiful, fanciful, deep and meaningful, humorous, dreamy and heartfelt art will inspire you. *The Accidental Cat* (page 5), *Falling Flowers* (page 32), *Scent of a Lady* (page 64), *Chipped Nail* (page 80), *Be Patient* (page 88), *Blatherskite* (page 118) and *Patience* (page 136) are a few of my very favorite pages (although I really do love them all!).

Or maybe the words of wisdom, the personal experiences and stories, or the techniques and prompts will inspire you.

And that said, I leave you with these words from Natasha White (page 124):

“Every single day, do one thing, even a tiny, small thing toward your dreams. All those small things add up and, before you know it, you end up living with your dream every day.”

Best,
Kristy Conlin

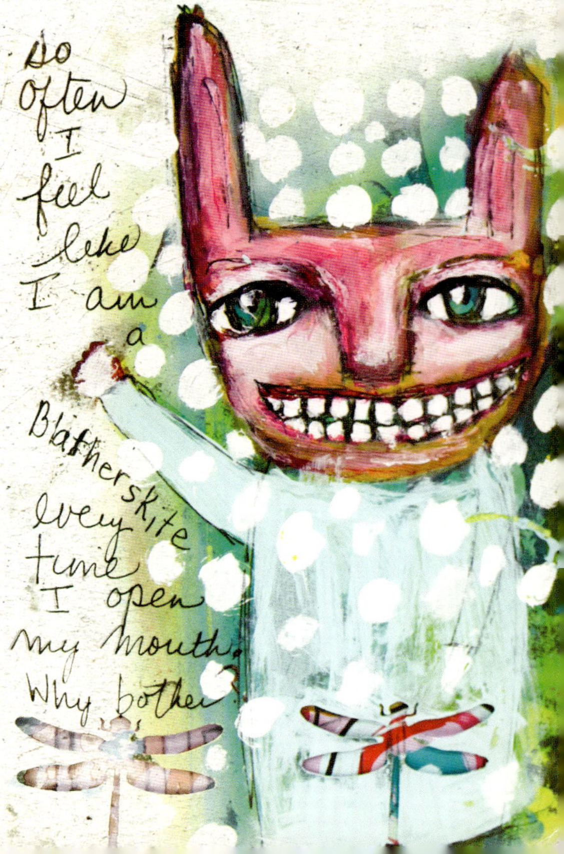

Nancy Belle

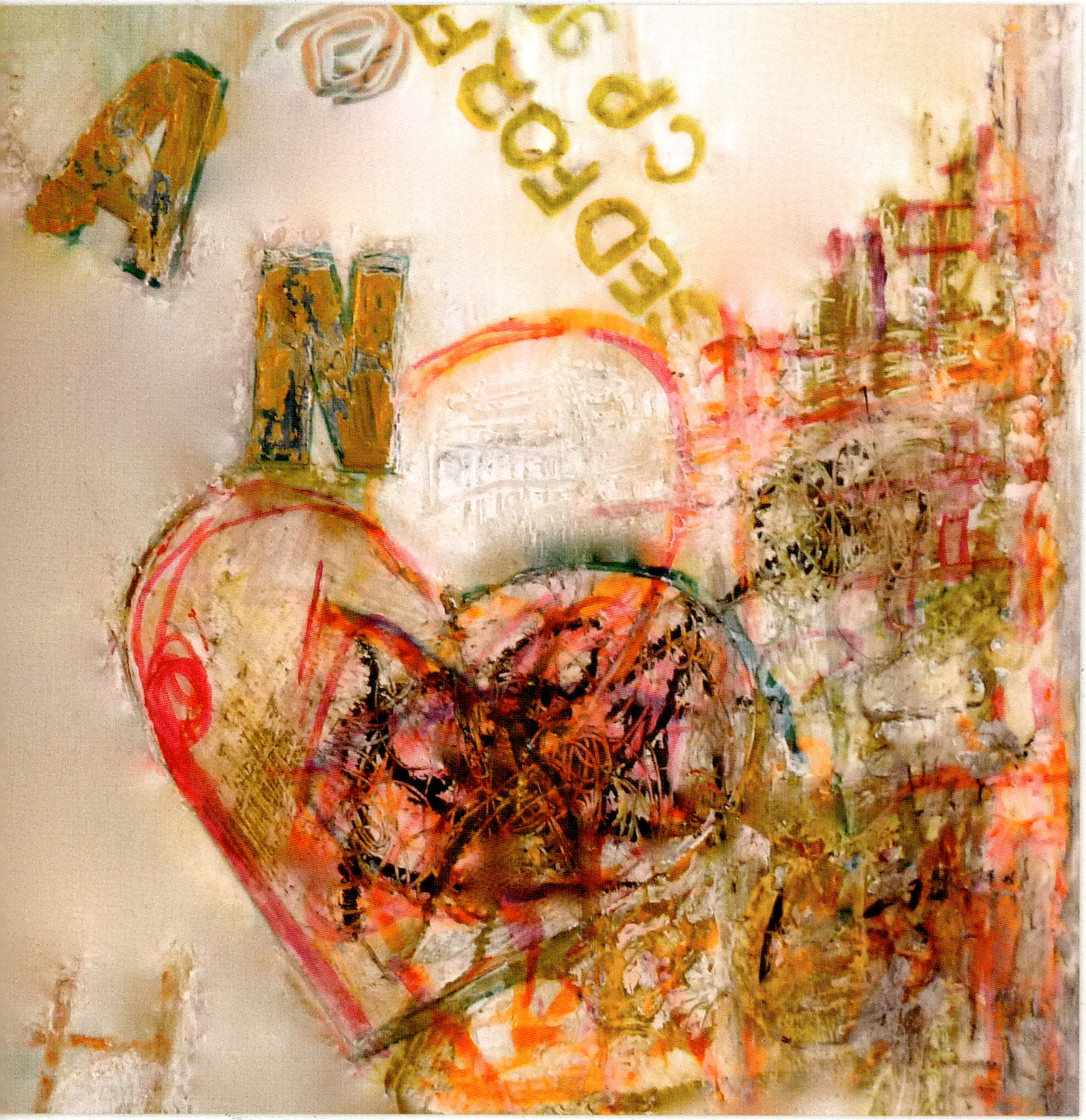

HEART SHADOW
Stationery, gel medium, ink, acrylic paint, white fluid correction pen, black marker

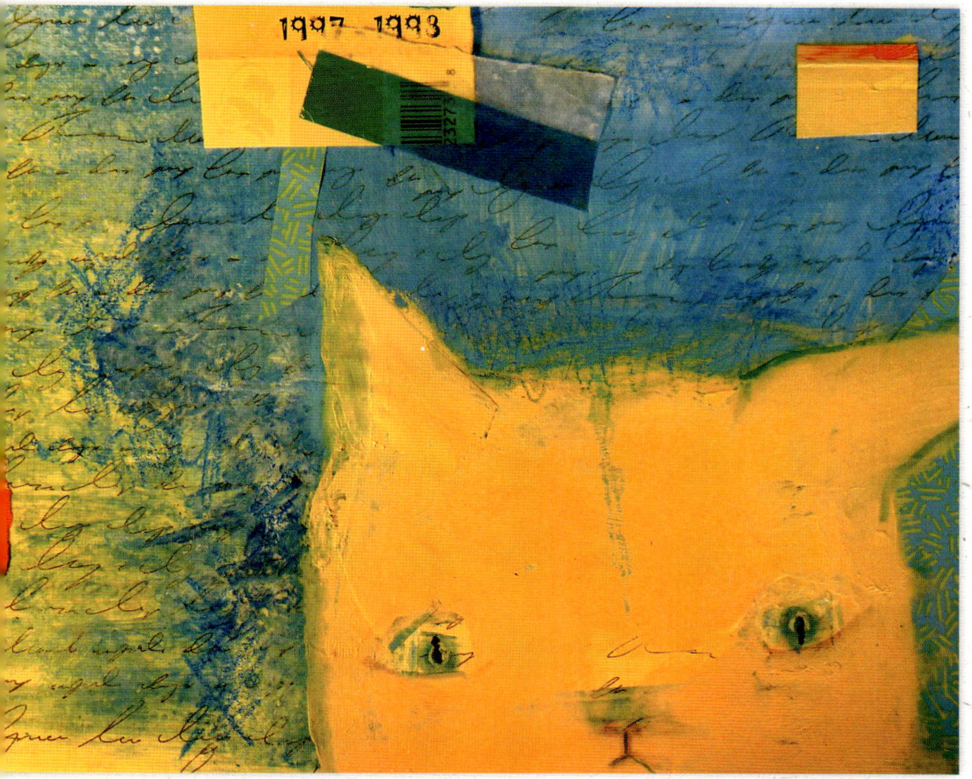

ACCIDENTAL CAT
Matte gel medium, paper, acrylic paint, collage ad scraps, date stamper

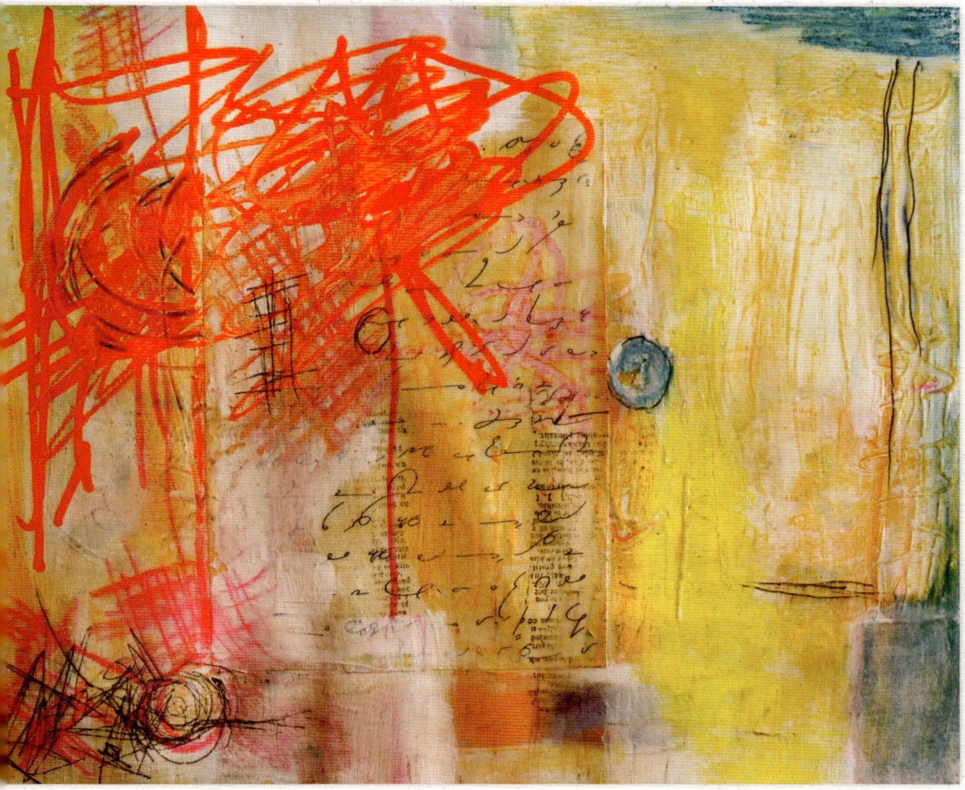

WRITE ME A LETTER
Old book, gel medium, acrylic paint, black ink

What was your inspiration for *Accidental Cat*?

The inspiration for *Accidental Cat* came to me out of the blue while I was working on another piece of art. I was working on top of a large sheet of paper, and I was not being very careful. There was a lot of paint spillover and, after a few minutes of painting, I noticed that my spill had formed the image of a cat's face. Needing a break from the piece I was working on, I immediately cut out the cat face and began defining the cat. It was exciting to create this cat piece so quickly and easily!

How did you come up with the title for *Accidental Cat*?

It was chosen for the obvious reason—because this piece happened purely by accident. I truly enjoy it when this happens!

Do you have an art journaling process?

I have no particular journaling process, and I go about my art journaling the same way I do my abstract art, in that I attempt to stay in the feeling of openness. I like using not only different sizes of journals, but on each page I attempt to have large and smaller images of texture and color, many times adding other paper collage.

What tips would you give to fellow art journaling artists?

When you are in doubt about composition, draw a square in the middle of your page. This is the area to stay out of with any important images. Align your important images with any of the four corners of the square, because the middle portion of your page is too obvious and distracting for the viewer.

Abigail LaShomb

What was your inspiration for this piece?

This piece was inspired by a friend who gave me the prompt, "the uniqueness and strength of women." The goal of the resulting image was to balance the modern view of female strength—namely individuality and the ability to *do it all*—with a more ancient view of female strength, one connected to nature and creation.

How did you come up with your title?

It connects humanity with nature (specifically the woman and the bird) and speaks to the subtle strength of the female archetype.

When and why did you start art journaling?

I kept a written journal during my high school years but fell out of the practice post-college. I was introduced to art journaling on the online crafting forum Craftster and decided to give it a try. I like the challenge of nonverbal expression and the creative outlet.

Do you have an art journaling process? If so, please describe it.

I try to create one journal page a month, inspired by whatever is relevant at the time.

What tips would you give to fellow art journaling artists?

Pick up little things everywhere. A bottle cap, a twig, even a trampled coin can trigger a bigger idea. You never know where inspiration will come from.

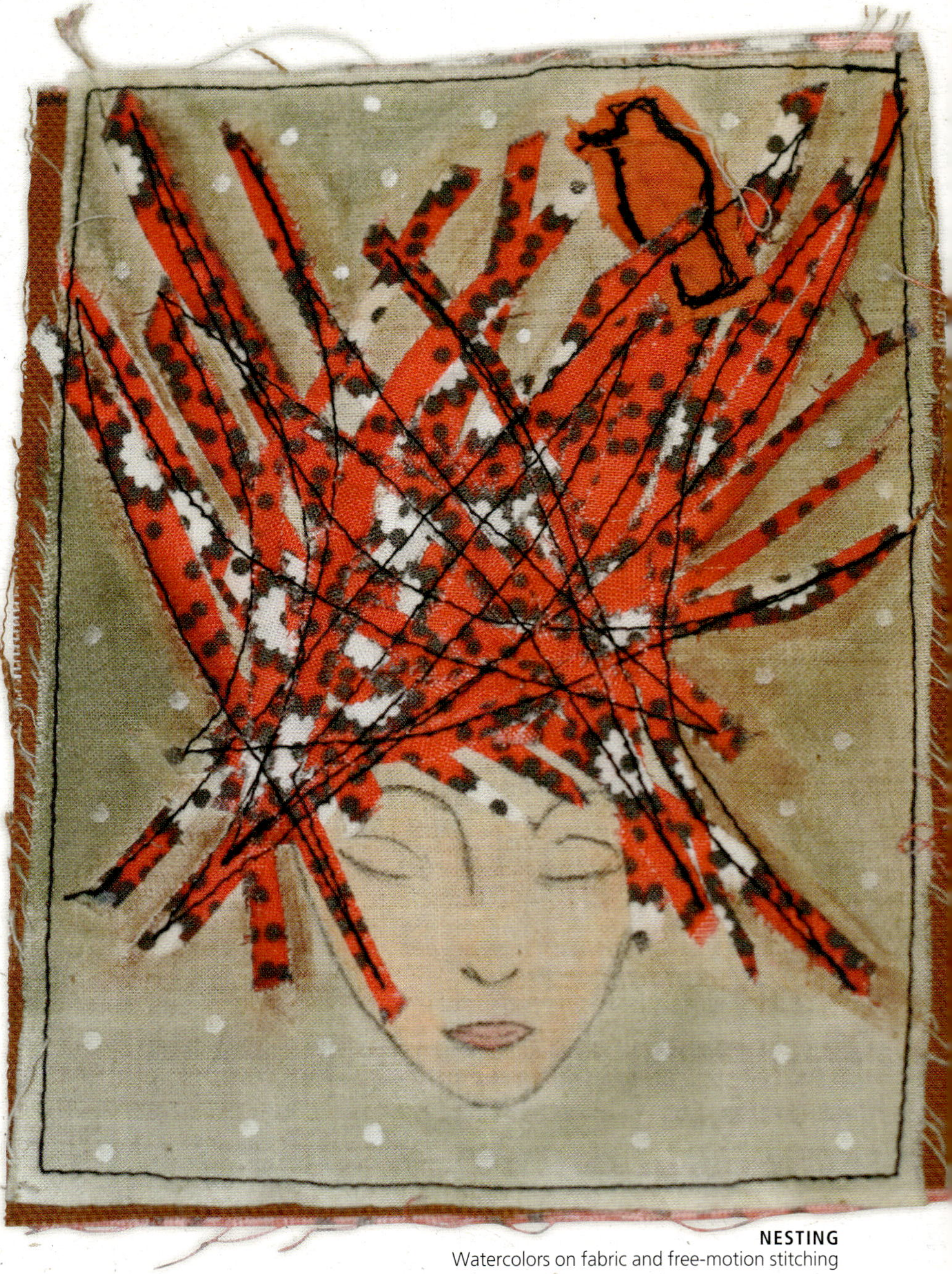

NESTING
Watercolors on fabric and free-motion stitching

Sharon Mathis

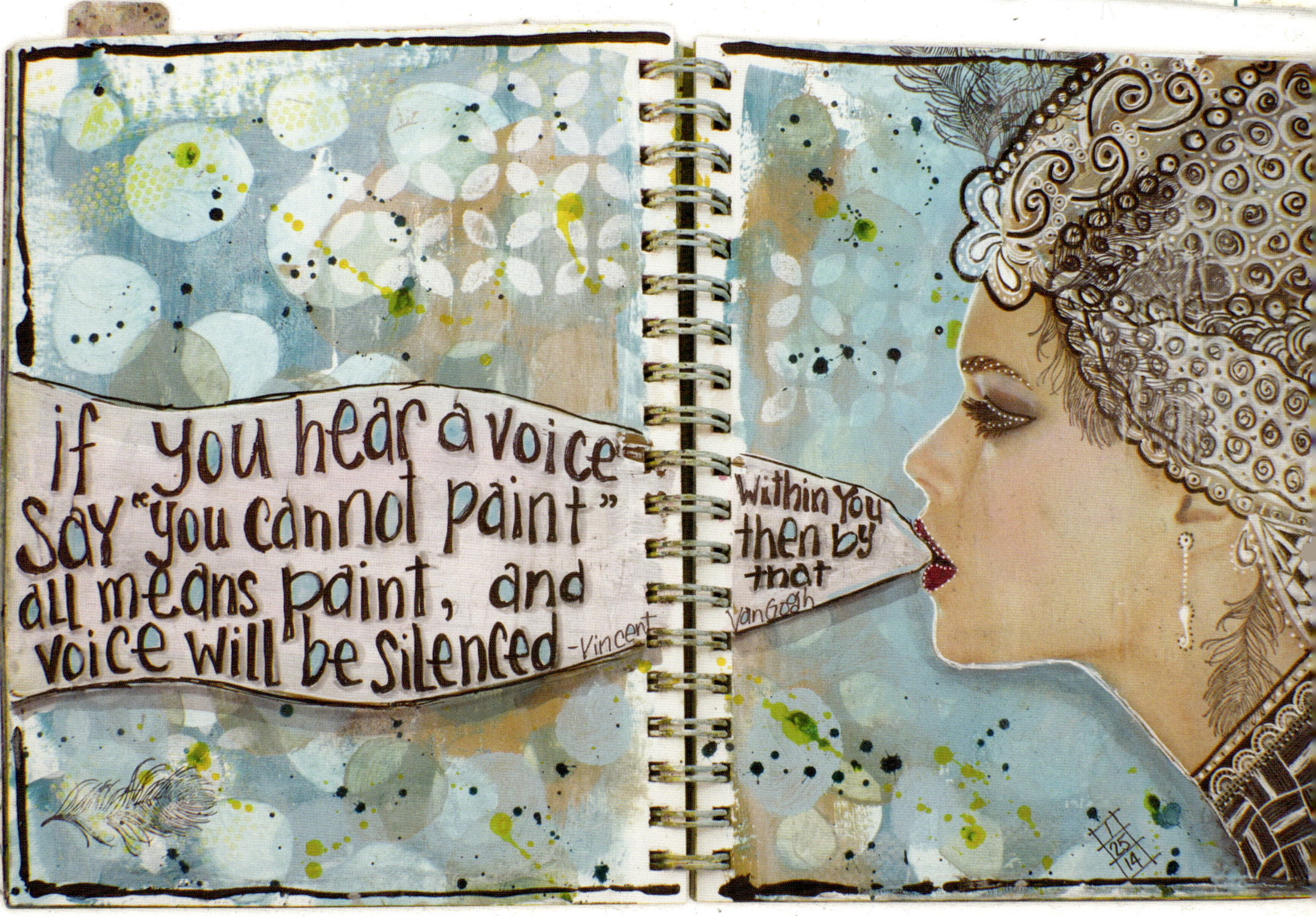

SHE SPEAKS
A face cut from an ad, cheapo liquid craft paints, various stencils, white pen, black Sharpie marker, gesso

What was your inspiration for this piece?

The inspiration for this piece was the quote from Vincent van Gogh about silencing our inner critic.

What interesting or unique techniques did you apply to this artwork?

I used the technique of reduction stenciling, where you apply paint, place the stencil over the wet paint and wipe away the paint with a baby wipe.

Are there any mixed-media artists who inspire you?

Julie Fei-Fan Balzer at BalzerDesigns.com. I love that she is a messy artist like me, and her bold use of color and patterns always makes me happy.

When and why did you start art journaling?

About three years ago, when my daughter gave me a book on taking ten minutes every day to do art.

What tips would you give to fellow art journaling artists?

Do a little something every day. If you don't like it, then layer over it.

> "*There are no mistakes in art,* ONLY CREATIVE OPPORTUNITIES."

Palma Rea

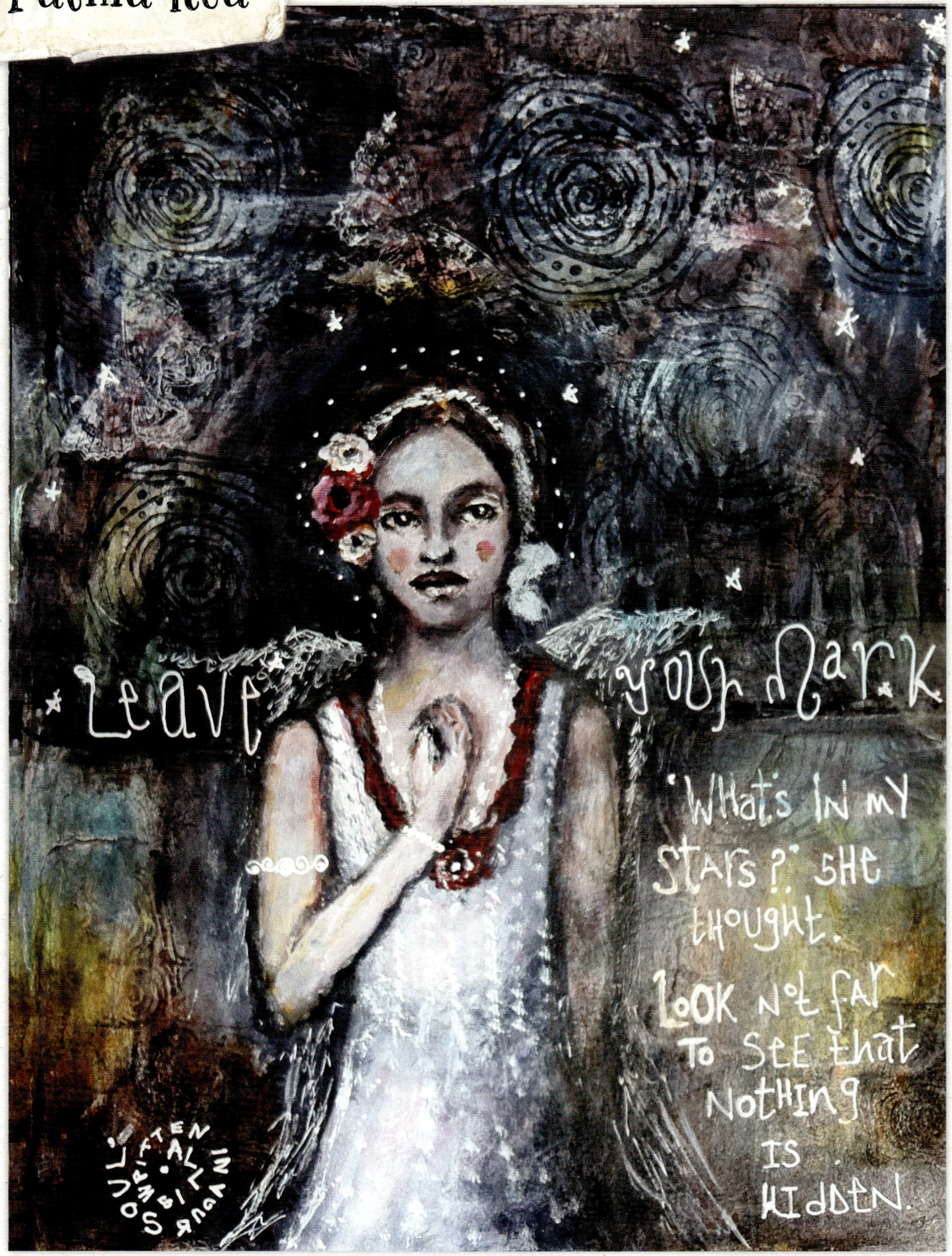

ALL IS WRITTEN IN YOUR SOUL
Acrylic paints, inks, gel pens, hand-carved stamp, black pencil

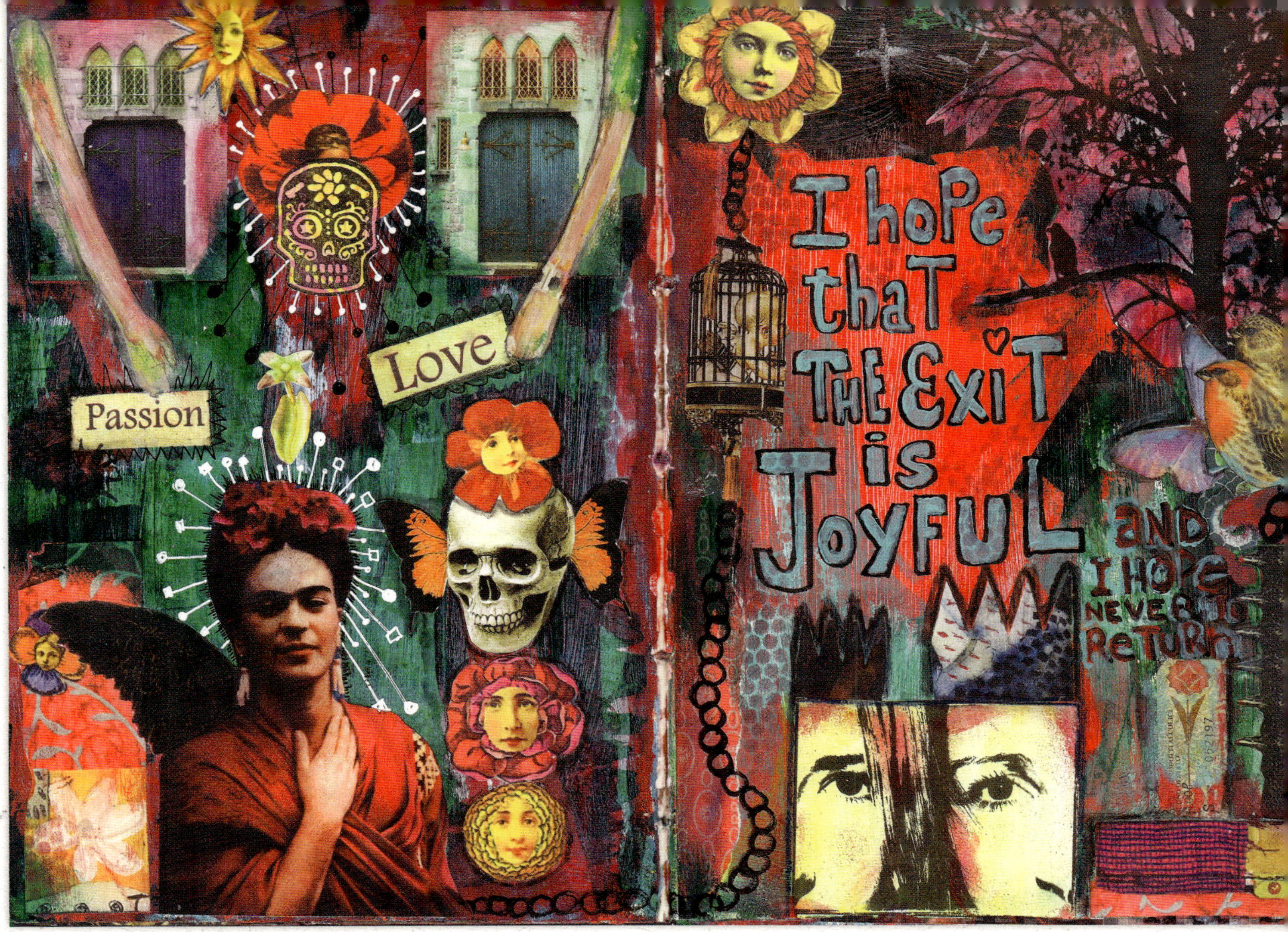

THE LOVES AND PASSIONS OF FRIDA
Collage, gel transfers, stencils, handmade printed papers, painting, prints

What was your inspiration for *All is Written in Your Soul*?

I was inspired by the soulful works of Misty Mawn. I really look forward to her online classes every year.

Do you ever give yourself journal prompts?

I occasionally use prompts, especially if they are out of my comfort zone. They become welcomed challenges as they not only help me to grow as an artist, but they keep my creative energy flowing.

When and why did you start art journaling?

I started about four years ago. My friend Nigel, who lives in another country, did circle journal swapping, and the idea of other artists working in a journal that I would get to keep on completion really appealed to me.

What tips would you give to fellow art journaling artists?

Journal for yourself! Many times I read about beginners who are afraid to show their work for fear of it not being good enough. It's your journal, so go wild in it and have no fear!

Also, journaling every day, if you can, is a healthy habit. This will improve your confidence and skills. And always explore!

"BY BEING A SOURCE OF INSPIRATION AND POSITIVE THINKING, BELIEVING IN ONE'S SELF AND FREELY SHARING—*your dreams will be sweeter.*"

Jenny Moed-Korpela

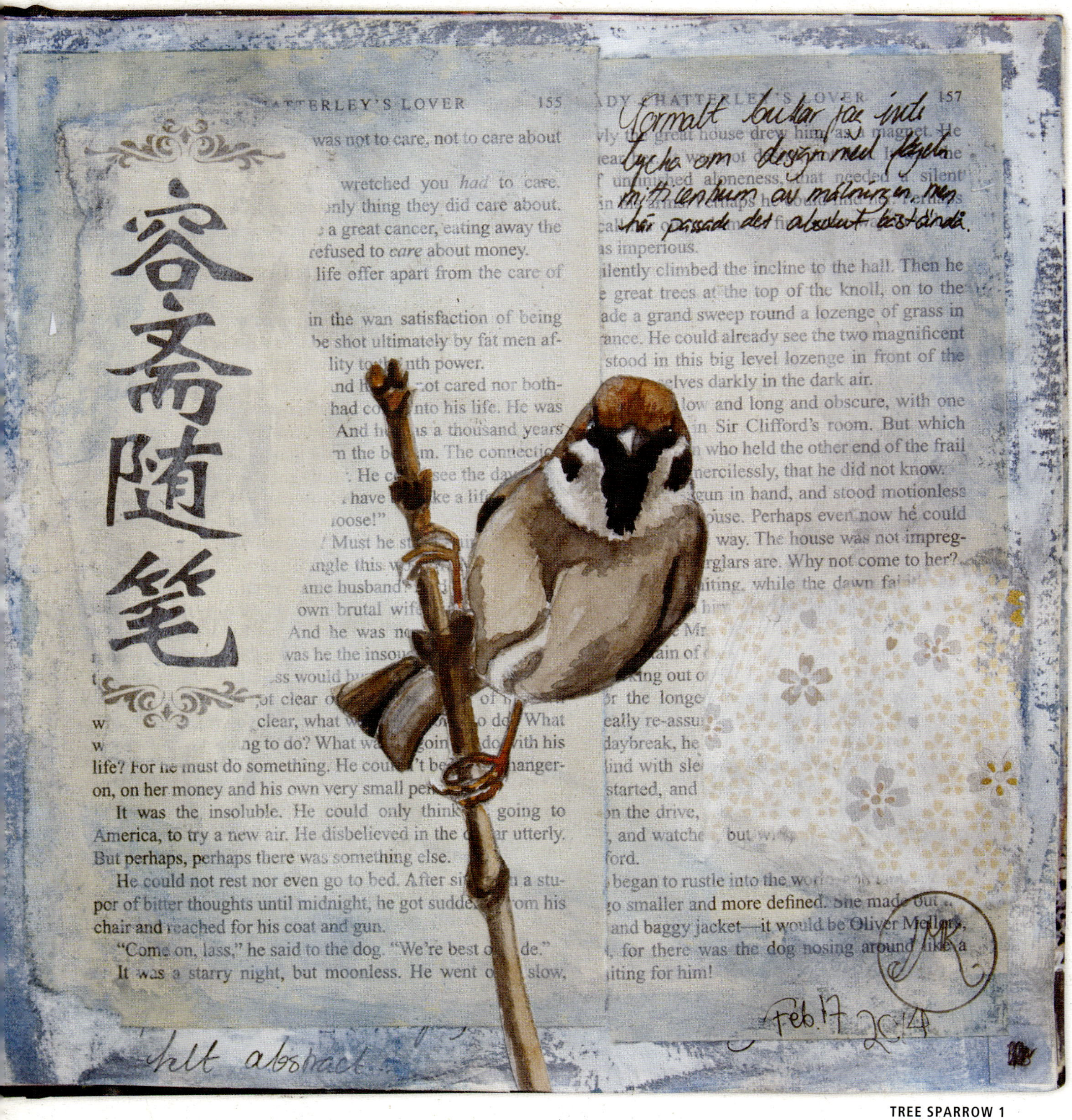

TREE SPARROW 1
Acrylic paint, spray bottle, bankcard, watercolor, gouache, adhesive

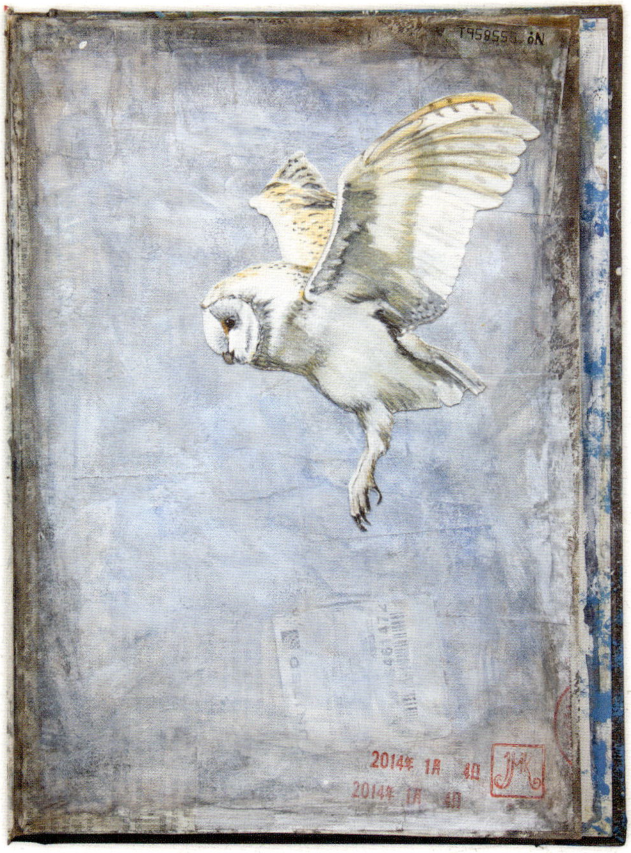

BARN OWL
Assorted pages, adhesive, acrylic gel, dry brush, acrylic paint, watercolors, gouache

What was your inspiration for *Light-vented Bulbul*?

My art journal is my safe place where I am allowed to do anything, play, experiment, try out new things and create without thinking. I am allowed to fail and learn from what does not work. My art has developed a lot through my journaling, and today I use mostly mixed media in my paintings. The flying bird silhouettes on this page reflect the freedom that art journaling is for me.

When and why did you start art journaling?

I have only been art journaling for about four years. In the beginning, my sketchbooks never filled up and I started my paintings without much planning. Often this led to me getting stuck halfway through creating, and I felt unsatisfied. One day I bought the book *Creative Awakenings* by Sheri Gaynor, and after looking up some of the artists online, I found a whole new world of art journaling. I never looked back. Now I paint as I journal, and every page is an inspiration to paint more.

"*Keep your heart open* TO THE WONDERS OF THE WORLD AND YOU WILL ALWAYS FIND SOMETHING TO BE INSPIRED BY."

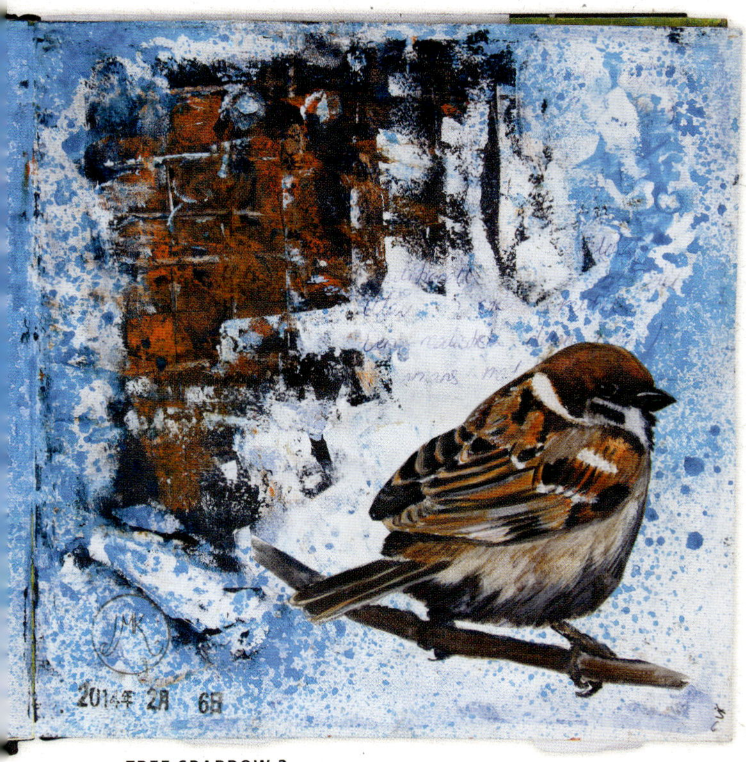

TREE SPARROW 2
Acrylic paint, spray bottle, bankcard, watercolor, gouache, adhesive

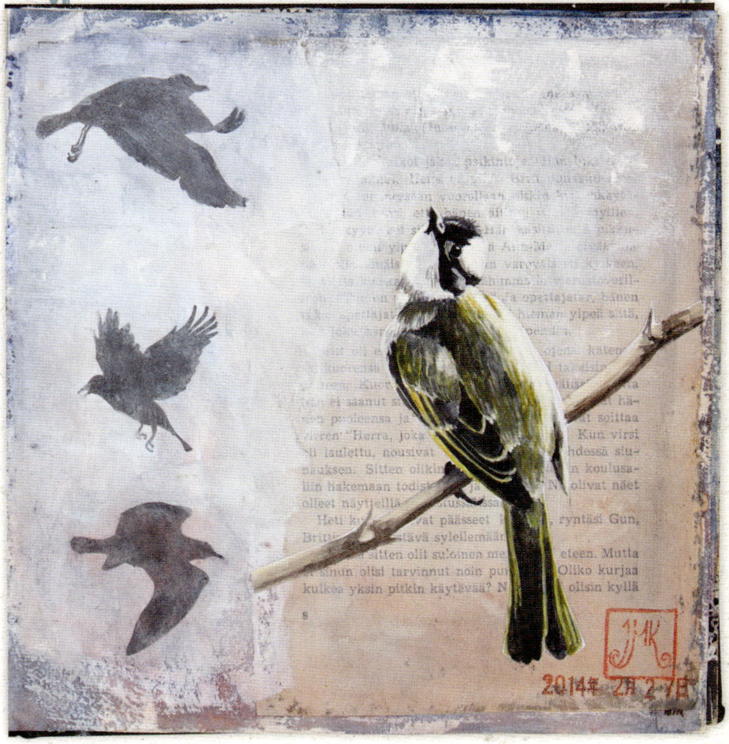

LIGHT-VENTED BULBUL
Acrylic paint, spray bottle, bankcard, watercolor, gouache, adhesive, mixed-media supplies

Amanda Judd

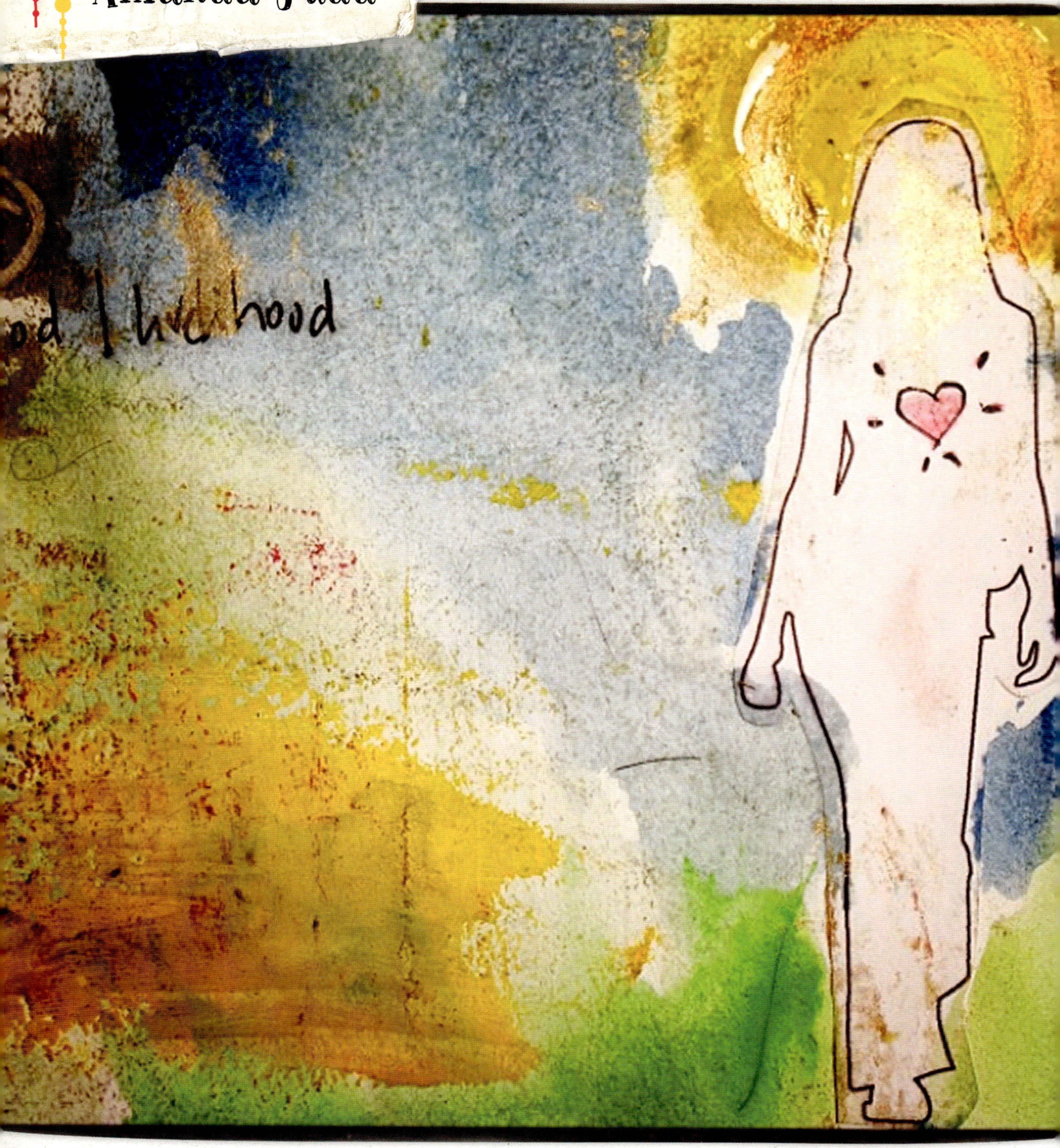

LEAD WITH HEART
Metallic paint, watercolor, acrylic, marker, digital print, gel medium

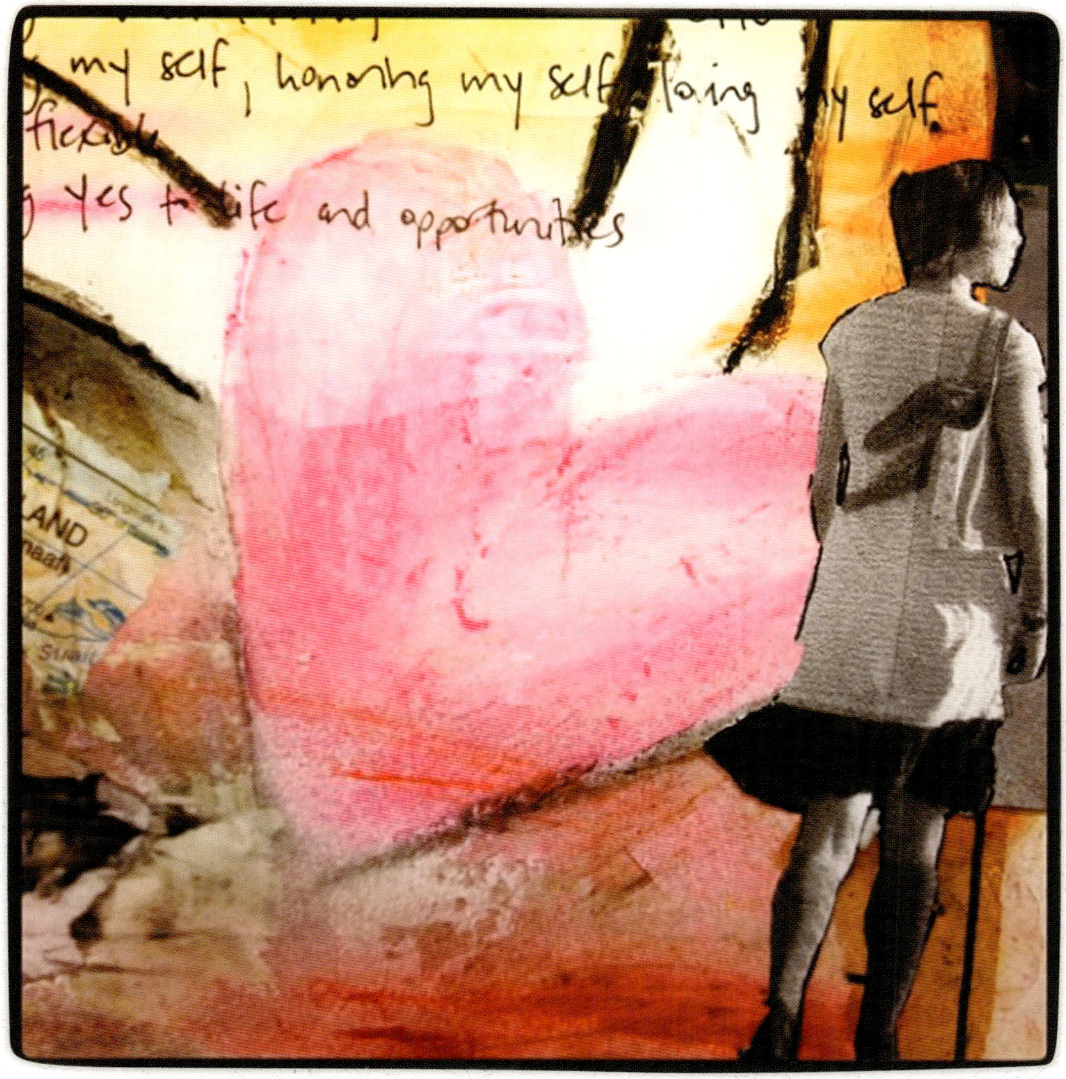

DIRECTION HOME
Pastels, gel medium, gesso, digital photographs, charcoal, map, sewing pattern, marker

How did you come up with your titles?

The same way the prince found Cinderella.

What was the inspiration for *Direction Home*?

Aligning with positive action.

What interesting or unique techniques did you apply to this artwork?

I used a self-reflective prompt to generate text.

Are there any mixed-media artists who inspire you?

Too many to name.

Do you ever give yourself journal prompts?

Yes, *Direction Home* came from a prompt that worked with identifying both destructive and positive choices.

When and why did you start art journaling?

Over five years ago, I was heavily into digital art making but I was hungry to touch what I was making, so I expanded into art journaling.

Describe your art journaling process.

It is spiritual practice. Art journaling is my yoga mat.

What tips would you give to fellow art journaling artists?

Be kind to yourself. Practice love. Let go. Play.

"*Love,* LOVE, LOVE!"

Denise Alloca

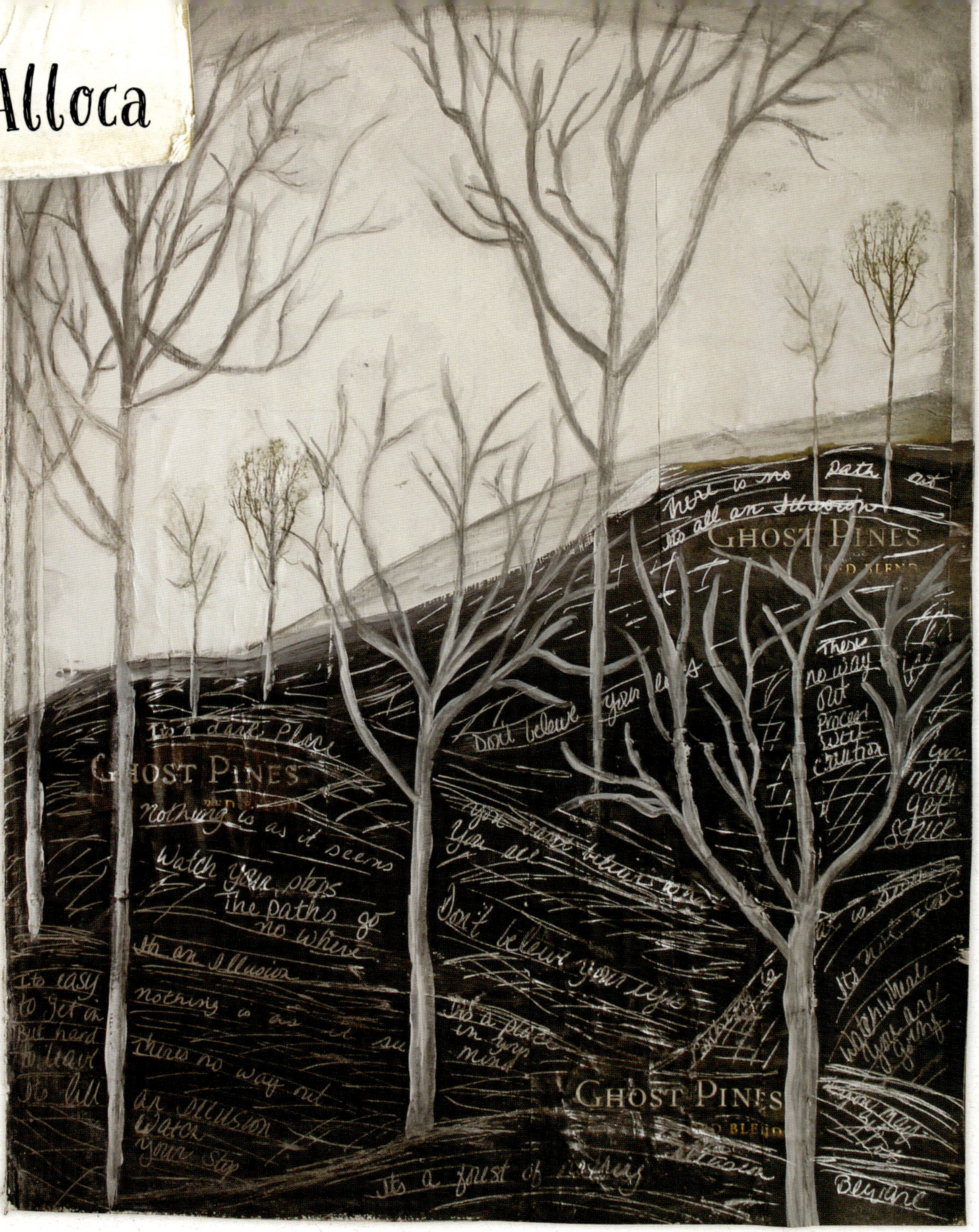

GHOST PINES
Wine labels, acrylic paint and mediums, water-soluble pencil, silver gel pen

What was your inspiration for this piece?

Inspiration for this piece came from the wine label *Ghost Pines*. The naked trees on the label, coupled with the fall season, allowed for an ominous yet cozy feel.

Are there any mixed-media artists who inspire you?

Mixed-media artist Jane Maxwell uses a combination of female figures and vintage materials to create her vivid, eye-catching work. I find this work captivating because the repetition gives an interesting pop art feel. Her up-cycling approach of using vintage commercial labels to give them a new life in an art form is very inspiring.

Do you ever give yourself journal prompts?

I like to refer to my art journal as a book of journal challenges. I ask myself, "What can I create from this idea or grouping?"

For example, the wine labels had powerful words and imagery. I wanted to expand on these ideas, so I prompted myself to make connections between names, ambiance or the meaning of something that I was using for inspiration.

Bernice Hopper

What interesting or unique techniques did you apply to this artwork?

I wrote with a waterproof pen and scraped a thin layer of modeling paste through a stencil. Because I don't clean my stencils, the pink ink that I had used previously spread onto the teardrops. I used a thin layer of blue acrylic paint over the whole page, painting around the teardrops. I added another layer of modeling paste and drybrushed the butterscotch acrylic paint over the top. Then I used a Thermofax screen and black and white acrylic paint to add the grasses. I printed the verse and colored the paper with Distress Inks before cutting up the words and gluing them to the page.

Are there any mixed-media artists who inspire you?

I am inspired by Dyan Reaveley and Dina Wakely.

Do you ever give yourself journal prompts?

I run quarterly art journal challenge blogs with prompts and use those in my own work.

When and why did you start art journaling?

My interest in art journaling grew out of attending workshops with Dyan Reaveley.

What tips would you give to fellow art journaling artists?

My tip is to play and not think too much. Just start a page and don't worry about what the finished product will look like.

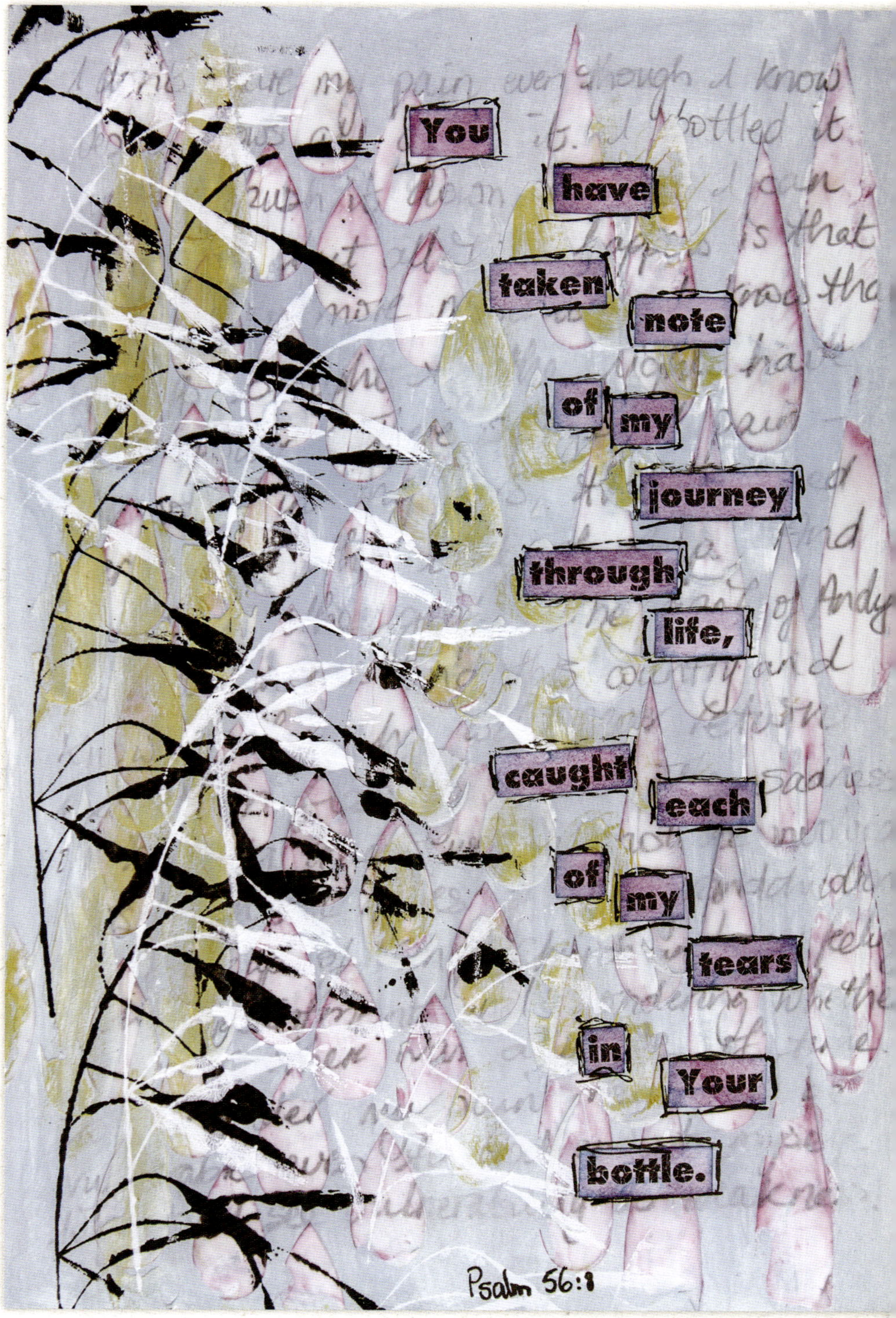

MY TEARS
Dylusions Journal, modeling paste, Crafter's Workshop stencil, waterproof pen, Ranger acrylic paint, Thermofax screen, Distress Inks

Carla Dixon

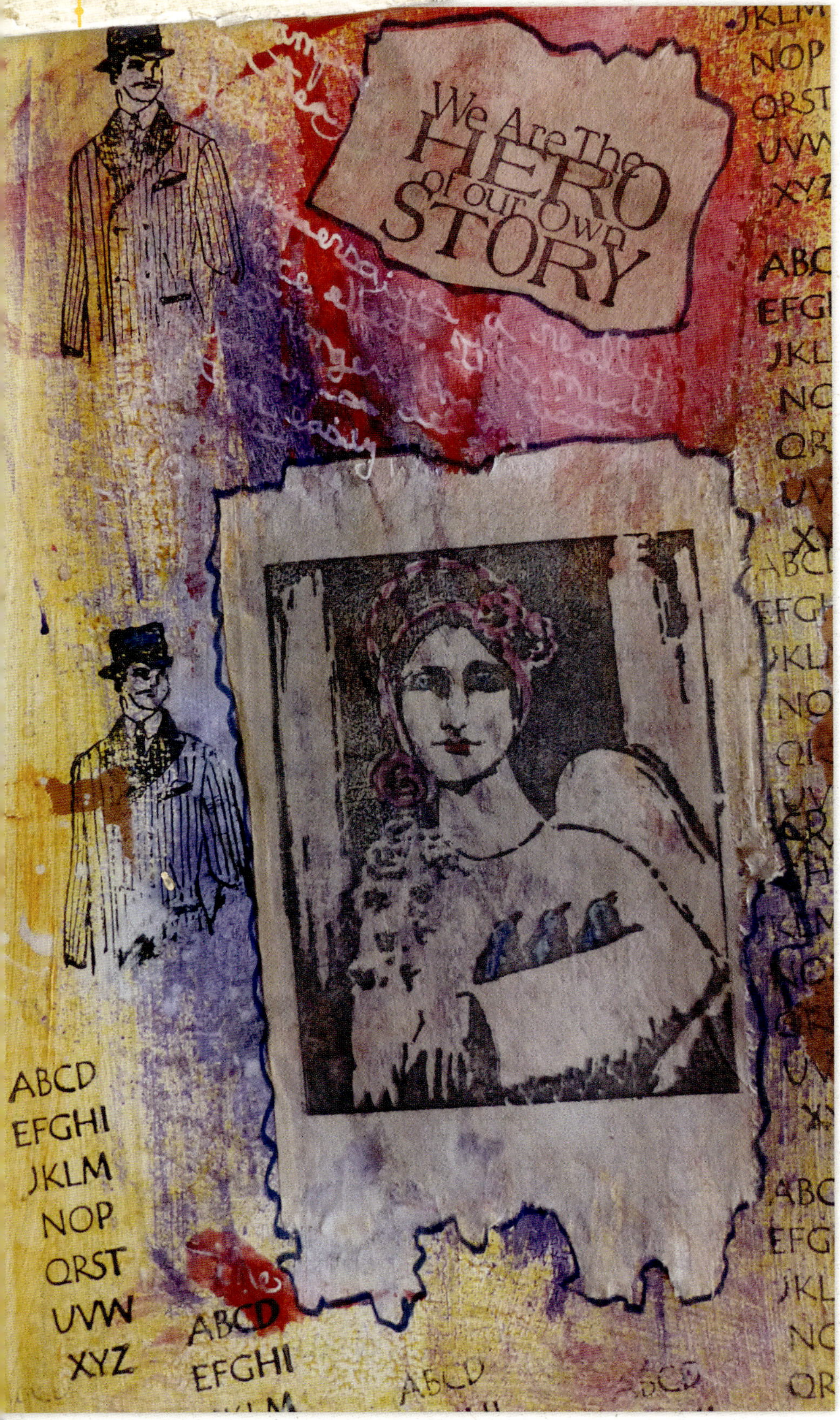

What interesting or unique techniques did you apply to this artwork?

I used dried tea bags with the leaves washed out. They are wonderful for stamping and layering on a journal page. Also, I stamped the portrait stamp on the dry tea bag paper, tore the edges and added a small amount of color to the image.

Are there any mixed-media artists who inspire you?

Some artists who inspire me are Pam Carriker, Dina Wakley, Roben-Marie Smith, Mary Ann Moss, Melanie Testa and Roxanne Padgett.

Do you ever give yourself journal prompts?

The only time I have used journal prompts is when collaborating with others. I love to do this because it allows me to make my own creative interpretations.

When and why did you start art journaling?

My first experience with art journaling was at a retreat I attended in Santa Fe, New Mexico in 2007. It took me several years to become consistent at it. Now it is either a daily or weekly effort.

What tips would you give to fellow art journaling artists?

Use what you have, learn from others and have fun.

WE ARE THE HERO OF OUR OWN STORY
Inks, markers, rubber stamps, tea bags, black and white pens

Anna K. Pasquale

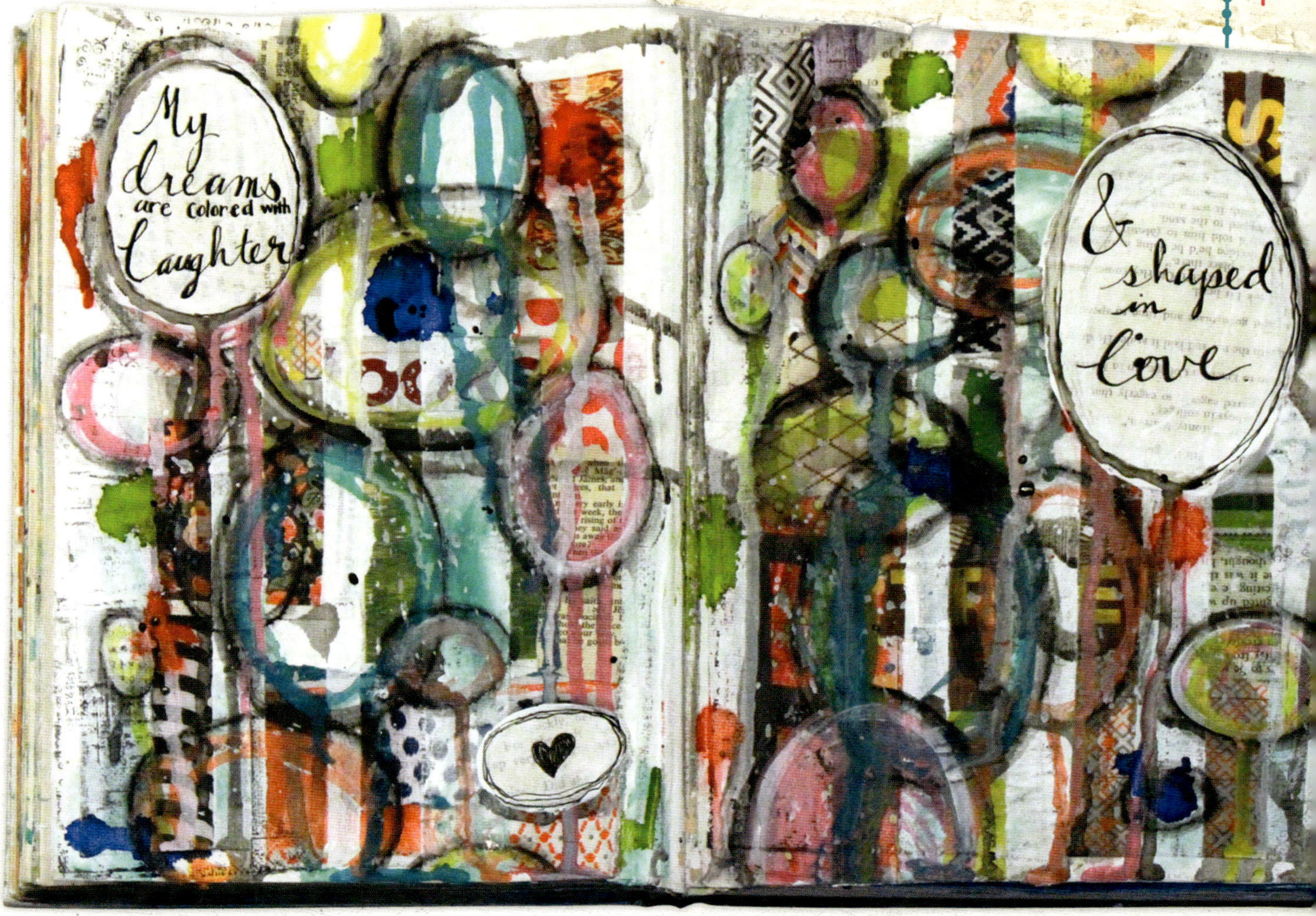

MY DREAMS ARE COLORED & SHAPED
Magazine clippings, acrylic paint, clear and white gesso, masking tape, vintage book pages, India ink, alcohol ink, Stabilo pencil

What interesting or unique techniques did you apply to this artwork?

Using masking tape and paint, I made stripes. I like the way they look behind the very organic shapes and drips on top.

Are there any mixed-media artists who inspire you?

Some artists I like are Jill Ricci, Donna Downey, Maria Pace-Wynters, Roben-Marie Smith, Lisa Congdon, Jenny Doh, Kelly Rae Roberts and many more.

Do you ever give yourself journal prompts?

I'm not sure if I'd call them prompts, but there are many times when I sit down to journal with a very specific emotion or image in mind.

Do you have an art journaling process?

I usually begin the same way: music, a prayer (as I draw in and release a deep breath) and then I dive in! I tape the seam of the pages and cover the pages with gesso. Then it's time to let go and create.

What tips would you give to fellow art journaling artists?

Allow your journal to be a judgment-free zone. Our art journals are meant for expression and experimentation, not perfection.

> "*Don't be afraid to make mistakes* BECAUSE THAT'S WHERE THE LESSONS ARE LEARNED AND GROWTH HAPPENS."

Barbara Giller

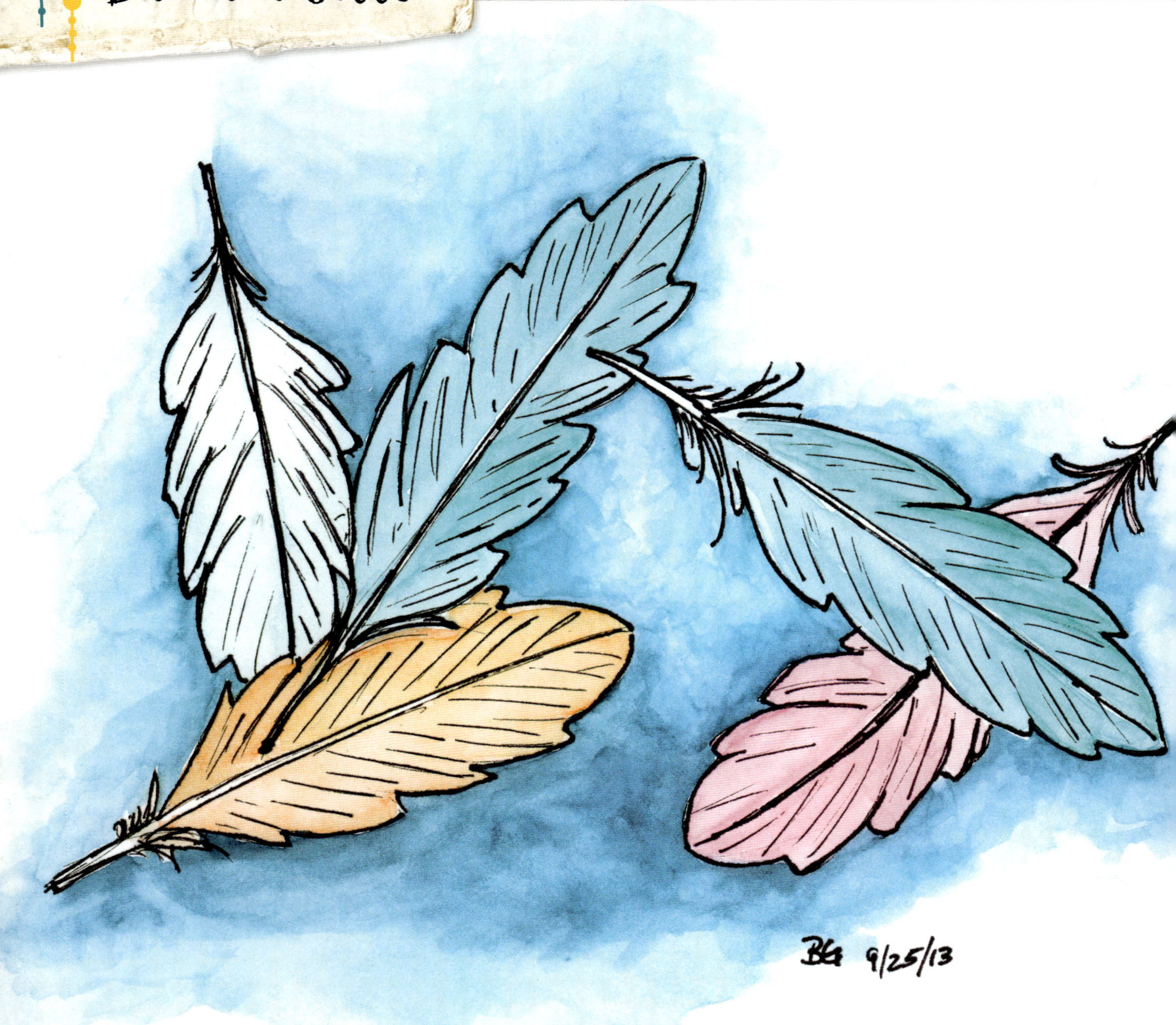

JOHN'S FEATHERS
Watercolor and ink pen

"*Have fun* WITH WHAT YOU PLAN TO DO, OR YOU WON'T CONTINUE TO DO IT!

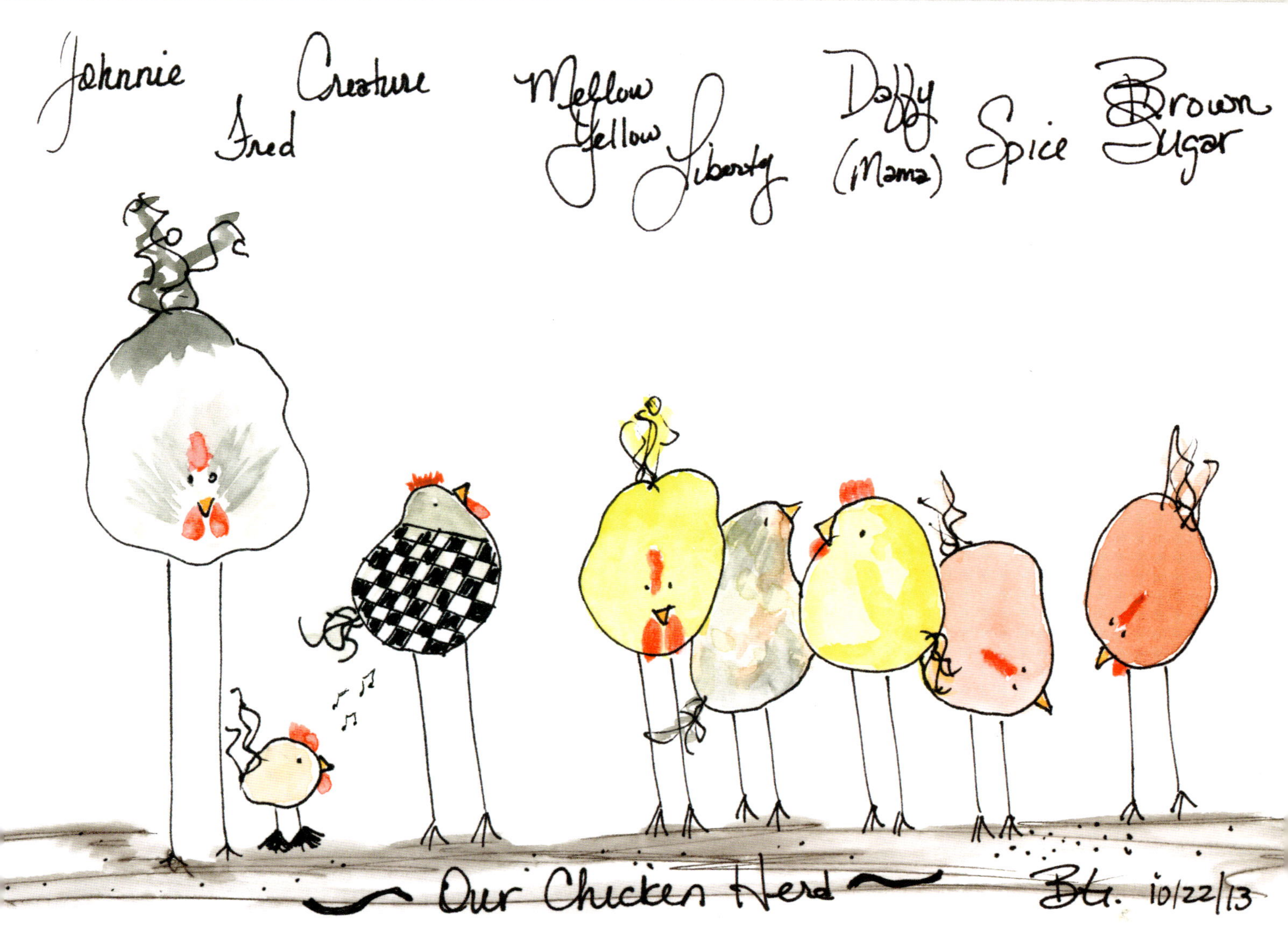

CHICKEN HERD
Watercolor and ink pen

What was your inspiration for *Chicken Herd*?

I was inspired by my chickens wandering around the yard on their normal morning hunt of weeds, seeds, bugs and spiders. All the while, totally ignoring my little rooster who thinks he's in charge of everything!

Do you ever give yourself journal prompts?

My journaling prompts are whatever I am doing or seeing when I sit down to do my morning pages.

When and why did you start art journaling?

When I found myself wanting to get back into art, I was disappointed in how I had lost *the touch* over the years, so I began journaling daily. I wanted to add some color, so I signed up for a local beginning watercolor class. I was horrid! As a result, I started playing in my journal instead of trying to *make art*, and I fell in love. Rarely a day goes by without my art doodling.

What tips would you give to fellow art journaling artists?

Get yourself a journal, some art supplies, whatever you are comfortable with. No need to spend a lot of money. Set aside a time of day for you to journal, and start playing and doodling. Eventually you'll find your inner child, and you should let him or her run amuck! Have fun with it or you won't continue.

Also, always sign (or initial) and date your work. Dating it is important so you can go back and see how much you have improved during your artistic journey!

Penelope Harris

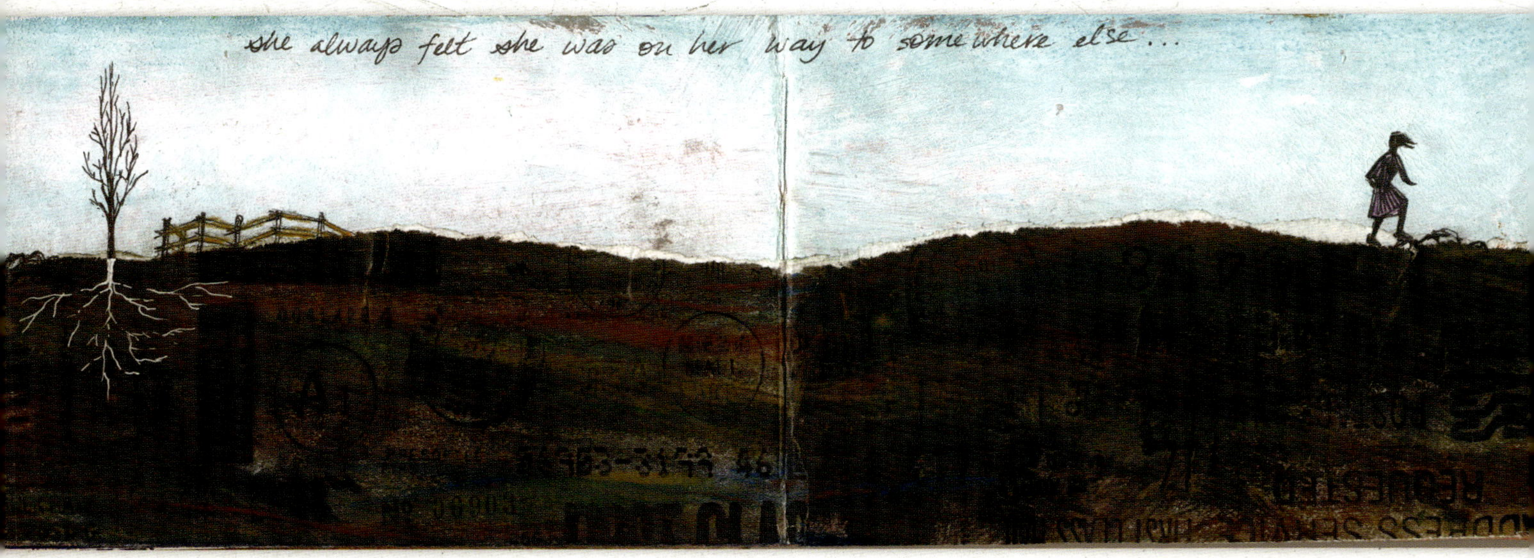

SOMEWHERE ELSE
Gesso, collage papers, mixed-media materials

What was your inspiration for this piece?

These pages began when I saw a rough landscape in the torn edges of a hand-painted catalog page. I imagined what someone crossing that landscape might feel: sometimes when we travel, we leave our roots behind.

Do you have an art journaling process?

My pieces often begin by juxtaposing ideas and materials. I begin by gessoing and collaging, then I skim my writing journal for thoughts with visual potential.

What tips would you give to fellow art journaling artists?

I advise beginners to start a journal where they don't judge how things look. Glue beautiful stuff in and figure out why you love it. Then replicate those elements in your own work in the same journal. The more you understand what sets you afire, the earlier you'll find your own unique voice.

Bunk *(Sarah Bunker)*

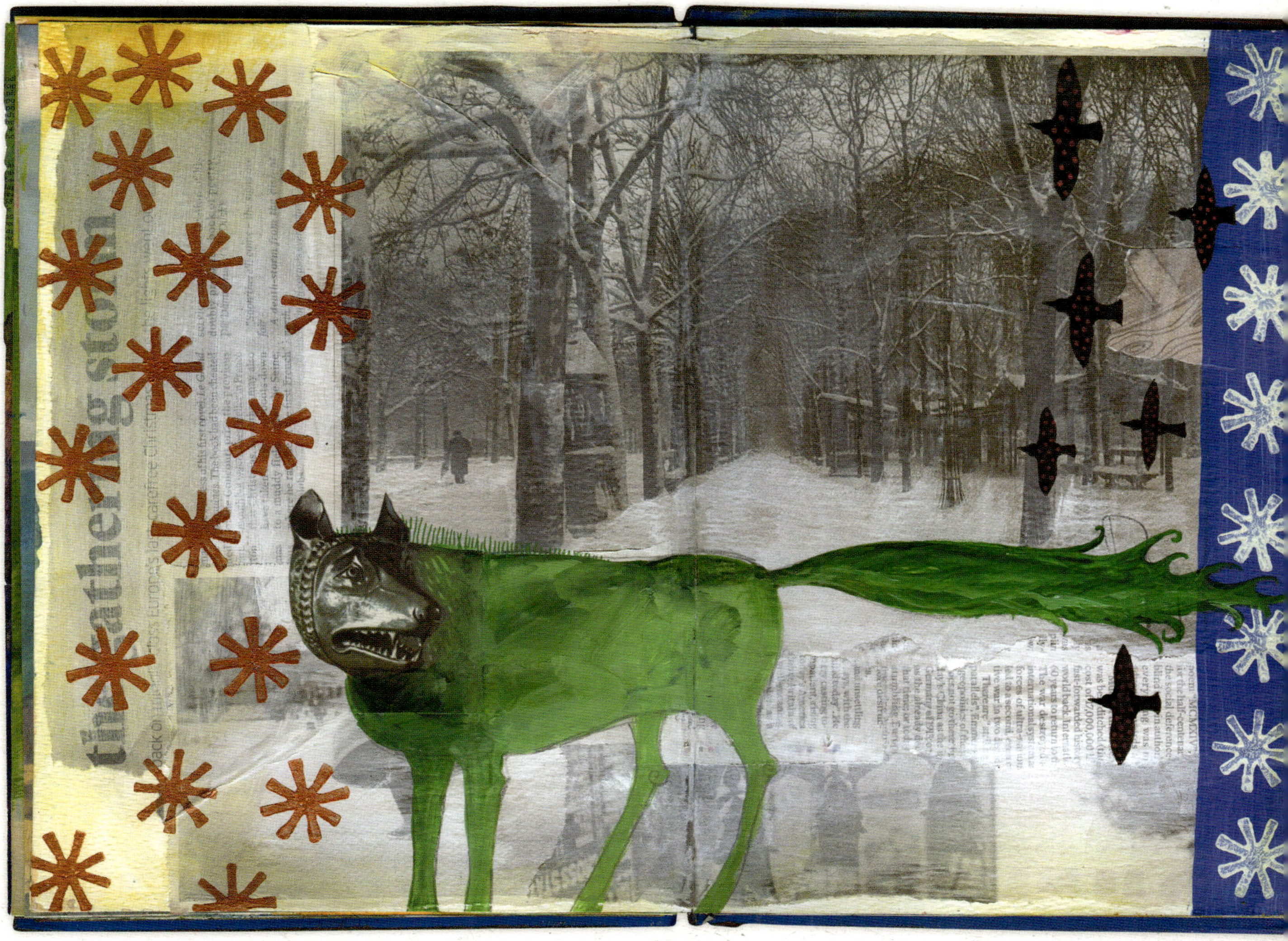

THE GATHERING STORM
Assorted paints, gesso, collage, stamps, pen

What was your inspiration for this piece?

The newspaper article in the background, which was about the beginnings of the First World War one-hundred years ago, was what got me started.

When and why did you start art journaling?

I've always drawn and had sketchbooks. For years they were simply observational, but then I started keeping notes and drawings about things I wanted to make. I came across Lynne Perrella's artist journals and sketchbooks and, since then, I've been journaling obsessively and teaching a little too.

Are there any mixed-media artists who inspire you?

The mixed-media artists who inspire me most are Orly Avineri, Juliana Cole, Brian Kasstle and Judy Paul.

Do you ever give yourself journal prompts?

I don't give myself prompts but, in a way, my materials are the prompts. When I start applying paint and collage elements, something begins to emerge. I am very influenced by nature, though, and animals, flowers and clouds usually appear somewhere. Sometimes I have an image that I want to get down on paper (usually a scene from a dream), and sometimes I use my journals as a way of working things out in my life.

Cindy Blevins

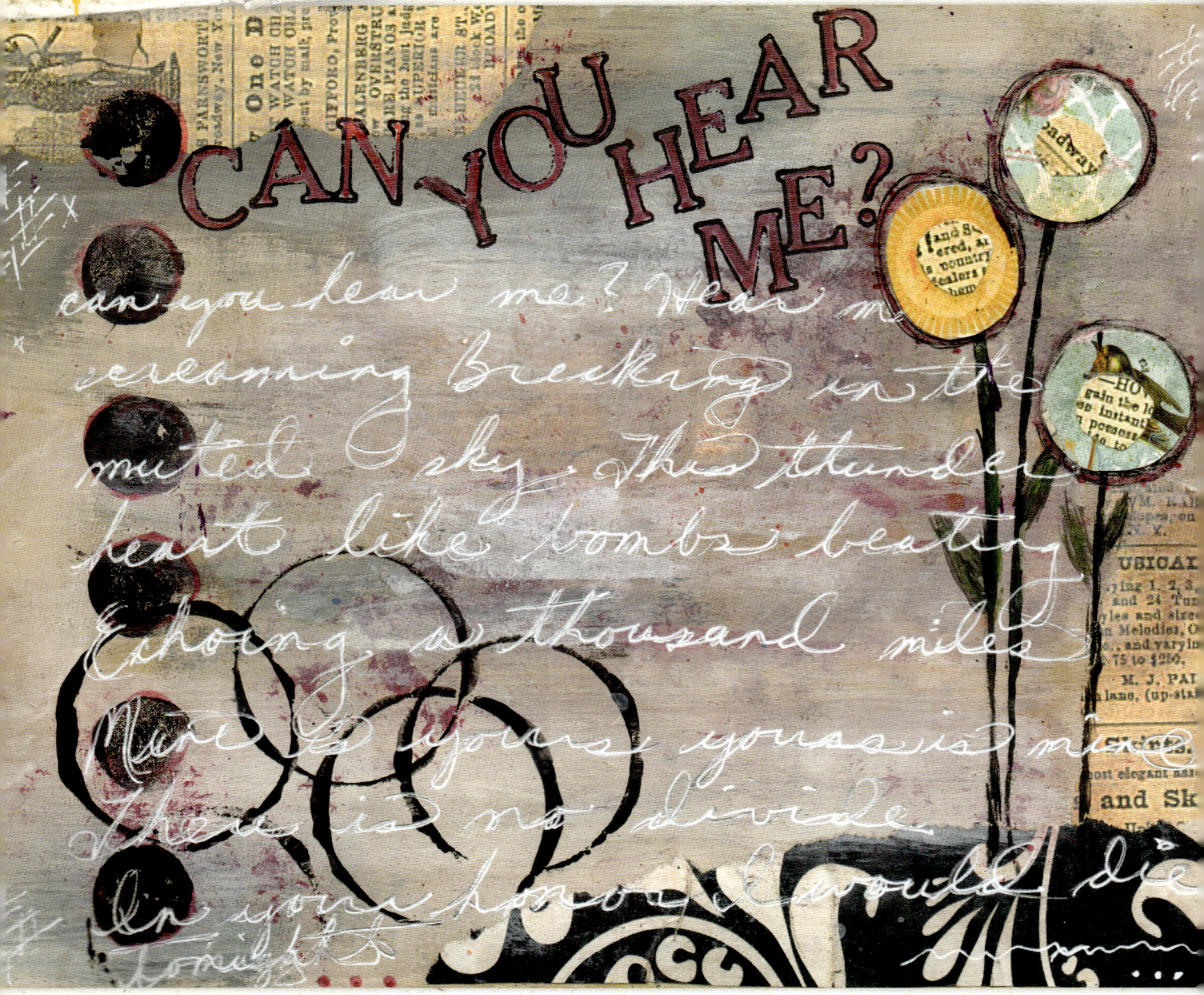

CAN YOU HEAR ME?
Acrylic paint, paper scraps, rubber stamps, pen

"AND THE DAY CAME WHEN THE RISK TO REMAIN TIGHT IN A BUD WAS *more painful than the risk it took to blossom.*"

— ANAIS NIN

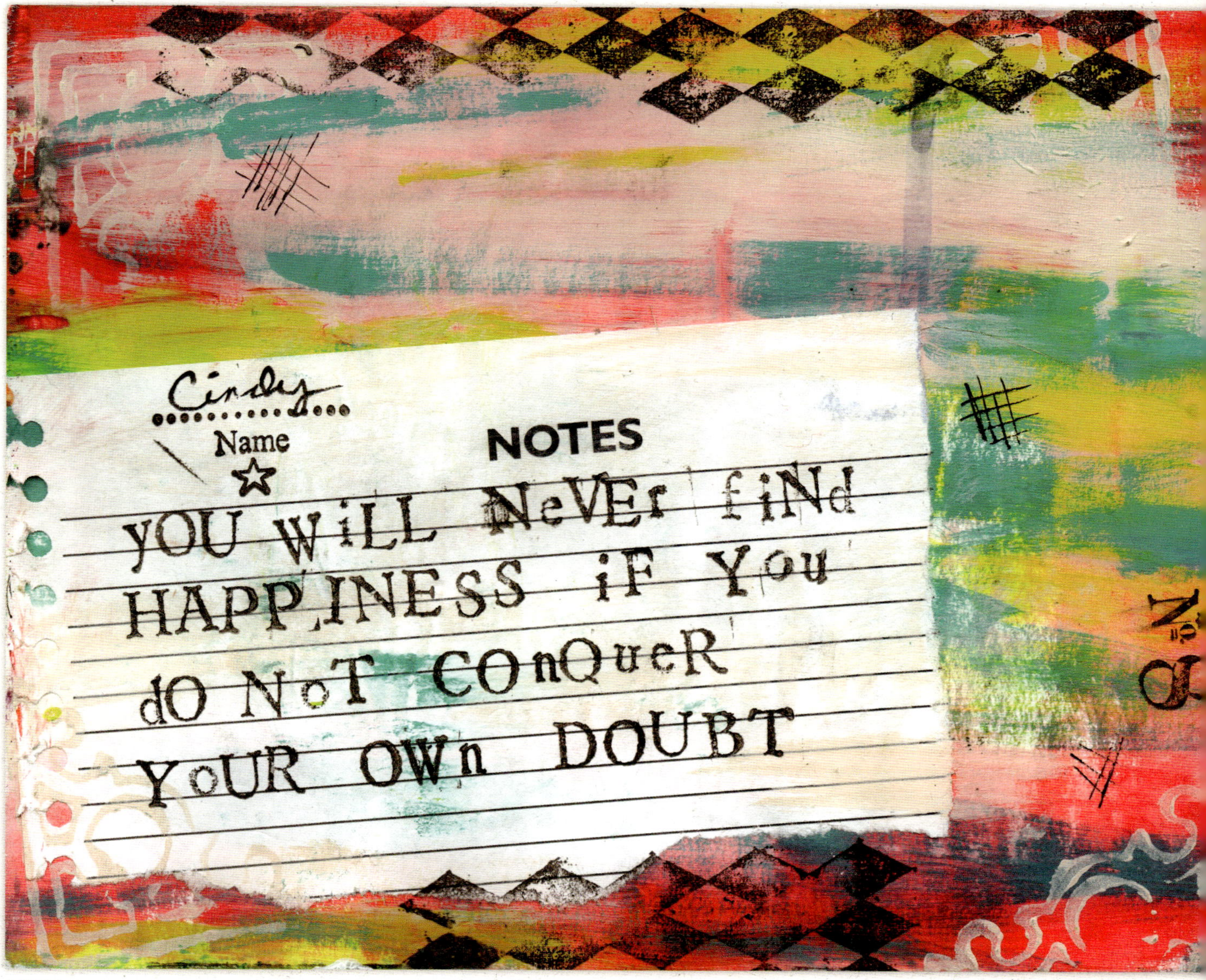

DOUBT
Acrylic paint, rubber stamps, pen

What was your inspiration for *Can You Hear Me?*

The frustration from not being given a chance to speak your side, opinion or feelings.

What interesting or unique techniques did you apply to this artwork?

I wrote my cursive words in silver pen, then went over them again with a white pen.

Are there any mixed-media artists who inspire you?

My daughter is an illustration major in college, and I have watched her do very brave things. She has inspired me to step out of my comfort zone.

When and why did you start art journaling?

I started four years ago. The most appealing thing for me is the freedom to use whatever materials I want.

Do you have an art journaling process?

I don't do art every day. I wait until thoughts build up inside my head, then I release them onto the page. It's the best therapy I have found. However, I do enjoy listening to music while art journaling.

What tips would you give to fellow art journaling artists?

Don't compare. Do your own thing, whatever it is that you love. Play.

Candace Lawlor

What was your inspiration for this piece?

This journal page was created as a reminder to myself that my hopes and dreams are important and deserve my attention.

What interesting or unique techniques did you apply to this artwork?

The texture in the background on this page was created using thin vintage book pages and a generous amount of glue so the pages would wrinkle.

Are there any mixed-media artists who inspire you?

Kelly Rae Roberts inspires me.

Do you ever give yourself journal prompts?

I do use journal prompts. I keep a sketchbook with me, and if I think about something I'd like to journal about, I write it down for later. I also challenge myself to journal about the hard stuff, like my fears and failures.

Do you have an art journaling process?

I usually have a few sketchbook pages lying around with color splashed on them that I grab for backgrounds. Usually my work goes from there, I literally reach for whichever color or product feels right in the moment.

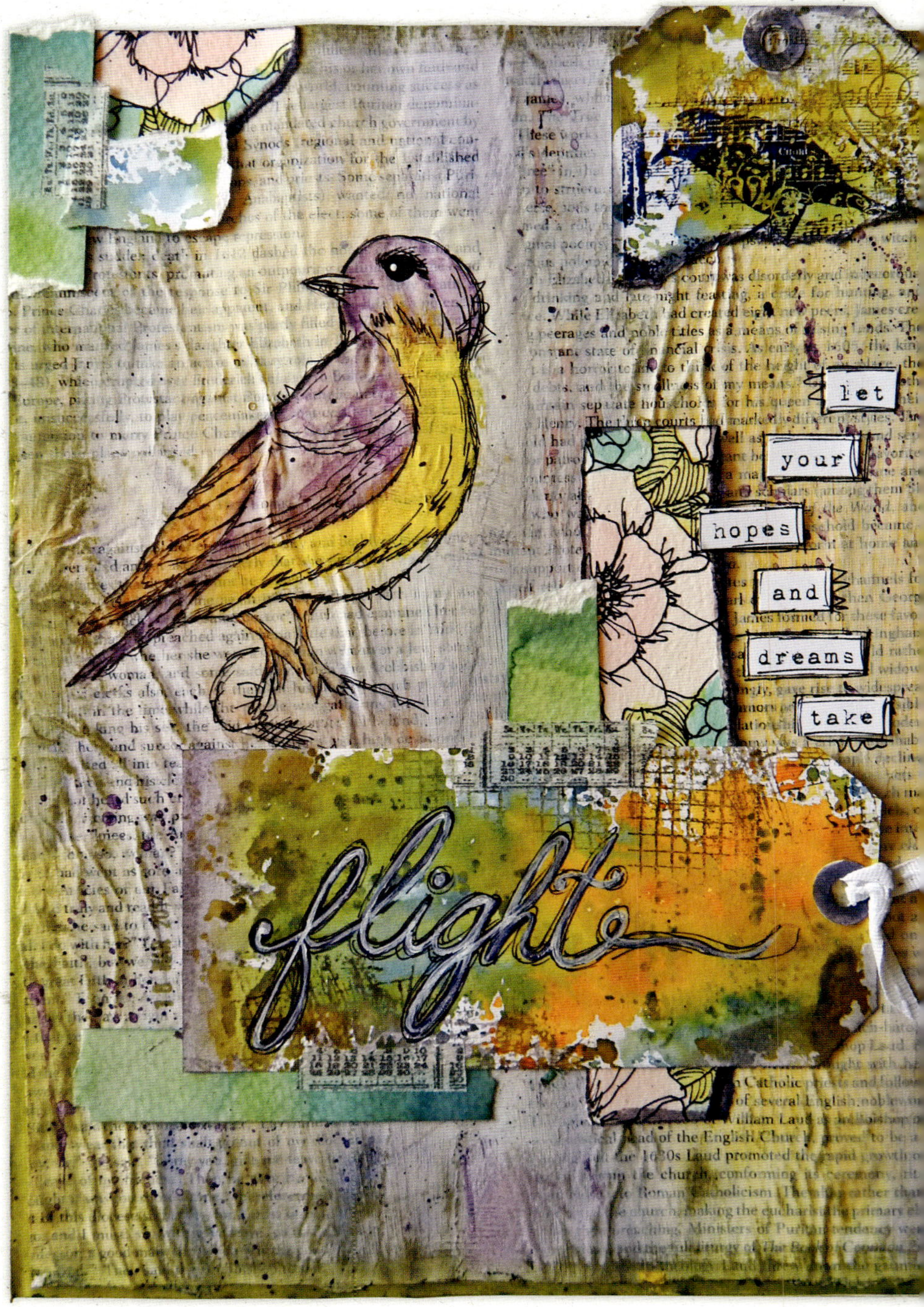

FLIGHT
Vintage book pages, dye inks, fluid acrylics, acrylic inks, archival inks, artist's pens, liquid watercolors

"DON'T LET FEAR OF JUDGMENT HOLD YOU BACK FROM BEING TRUE TO *who you really are.*"

Jean Marmo

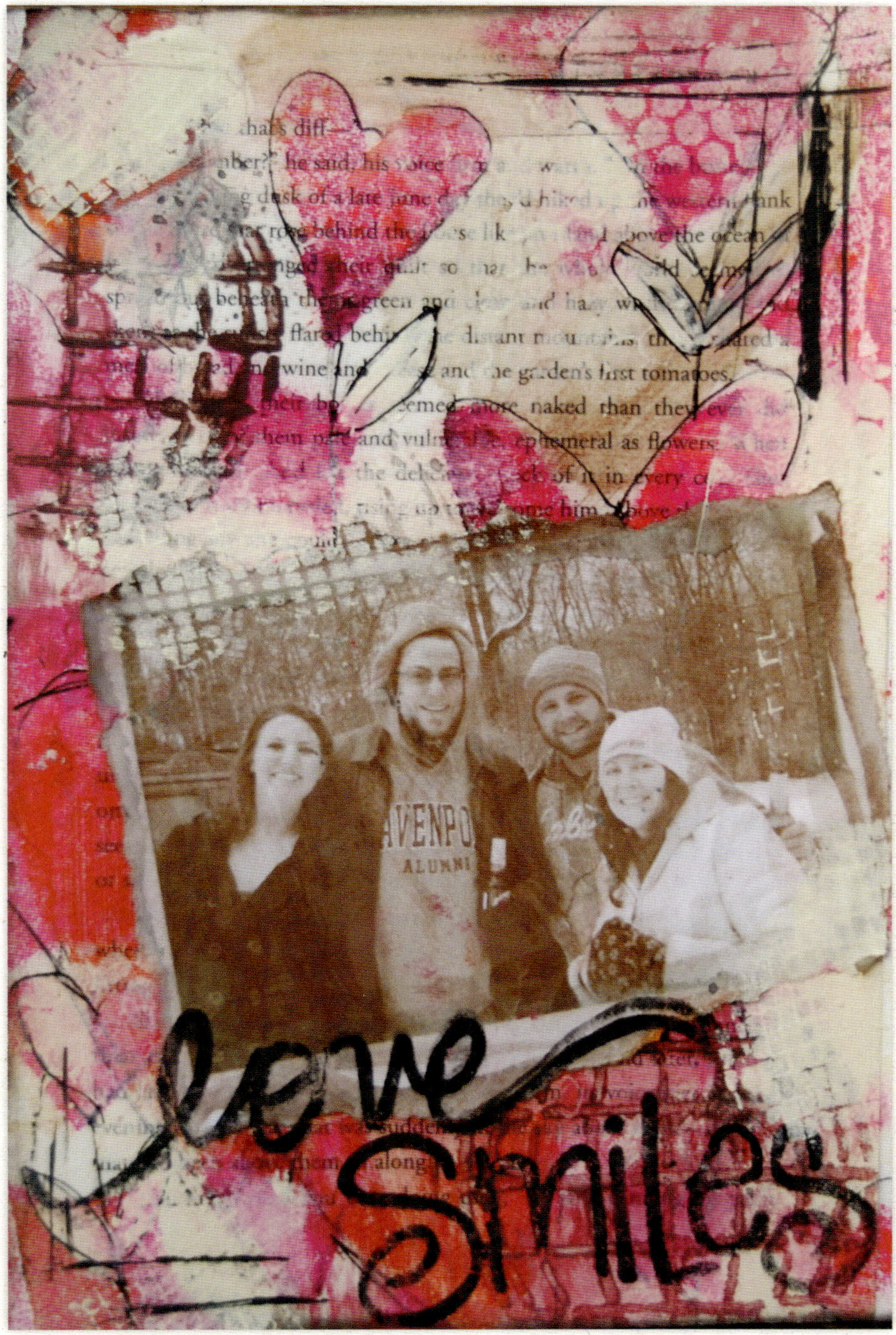

LOVE SMILES
Paints, stencils, doodles, stamps, photo

When and why did you start art journaling?

I have been a scrapbooker for many years, but only recently was introduced to the world of art journaling. At first, I was intimidated because I am not much of an artist. I can't paint or draw—but that's okay. Art journaling is about creating just for you!

Do you ever give yourself journal prompts?

Numerous online communities offer prompts, sharing and encouragement. I have begun adding mixed-media elements to my scrapbooking and, as in this piece, photographs to my art journal pages.

How did you come up with your journal page?

I have two adult children who each became engaged this year. I love having them home together and seeing them enjoy each other's company. It's wonderful to see them smile as they endure the family traditions, which I try to maintain.

> "*You are never too old* TO SET ANOTHER GOAL OR TO DREAM A NEW DREAM."
>
> — C. S. LEWIS

Gerit Nagel

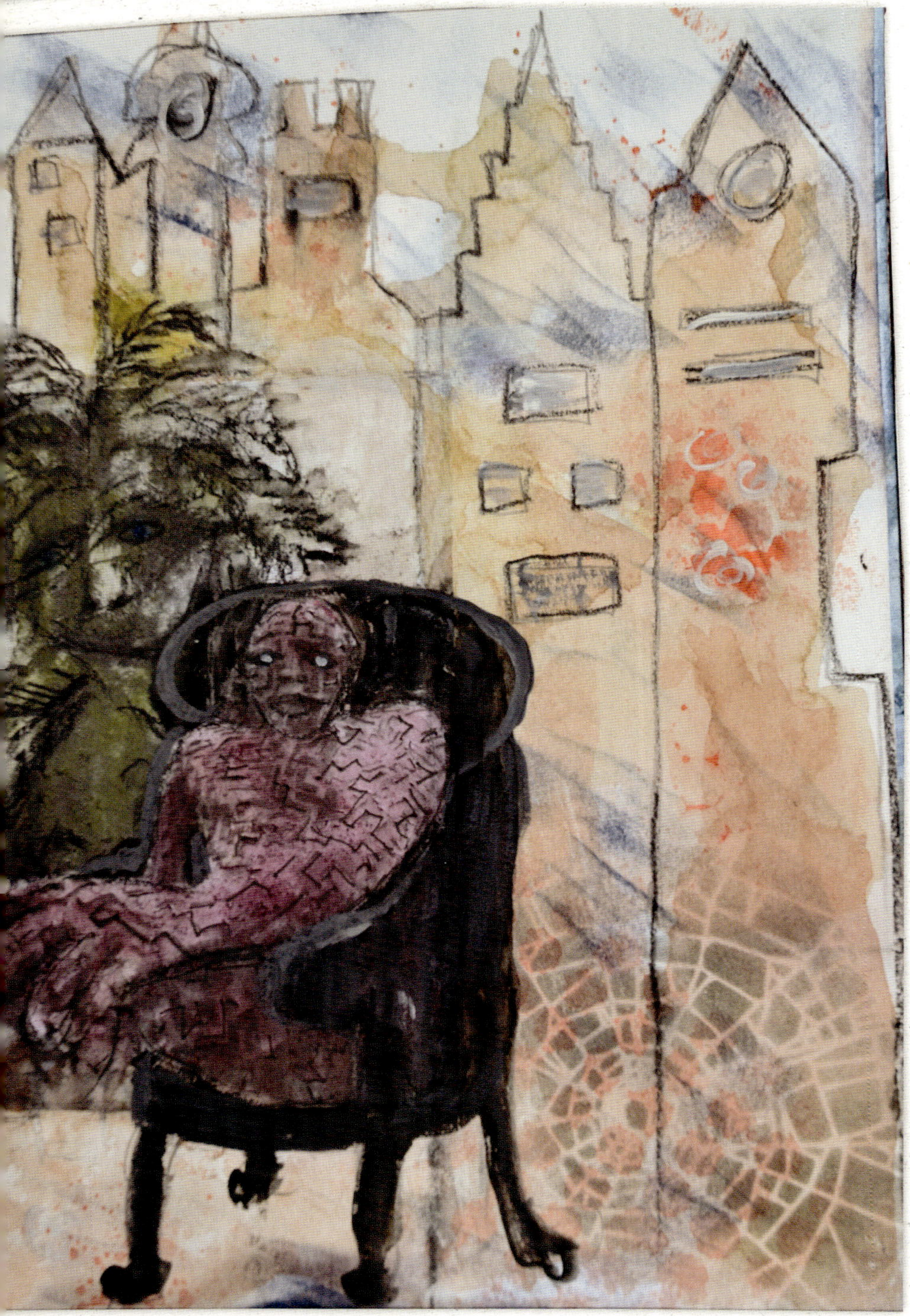

THE PALM TREE LADY
PanPastel, watercolor, Stabilo pen, Tim Holtz stencil

What was your inspiration for this piece?

I love to go in the field with my Nikon camera and take pictures. After thinking about how best to combine my passions—photography and art—I discovered that the best way to do it was through my journal.

What interesting or unique techniques did you apply to this artwork ?

I transferred one of my photos onto the journal page. Transferring an image is always a surprise; sometimes it works really well, and other times it's not so good—but you can always make something out of it.

Are there any mixed-media artists who inspire you?

I'm inspired by Michelle McCosh, Nathalie Kalbach, Anna Dabrowska and Dina Wakley.

How did you come up with your title?

I loved the end result, which made me think that she was dreaming about something.

Do you have an art journaling process?

Not really. I just get started and then see what happens.

Teri Mezzo Flemal

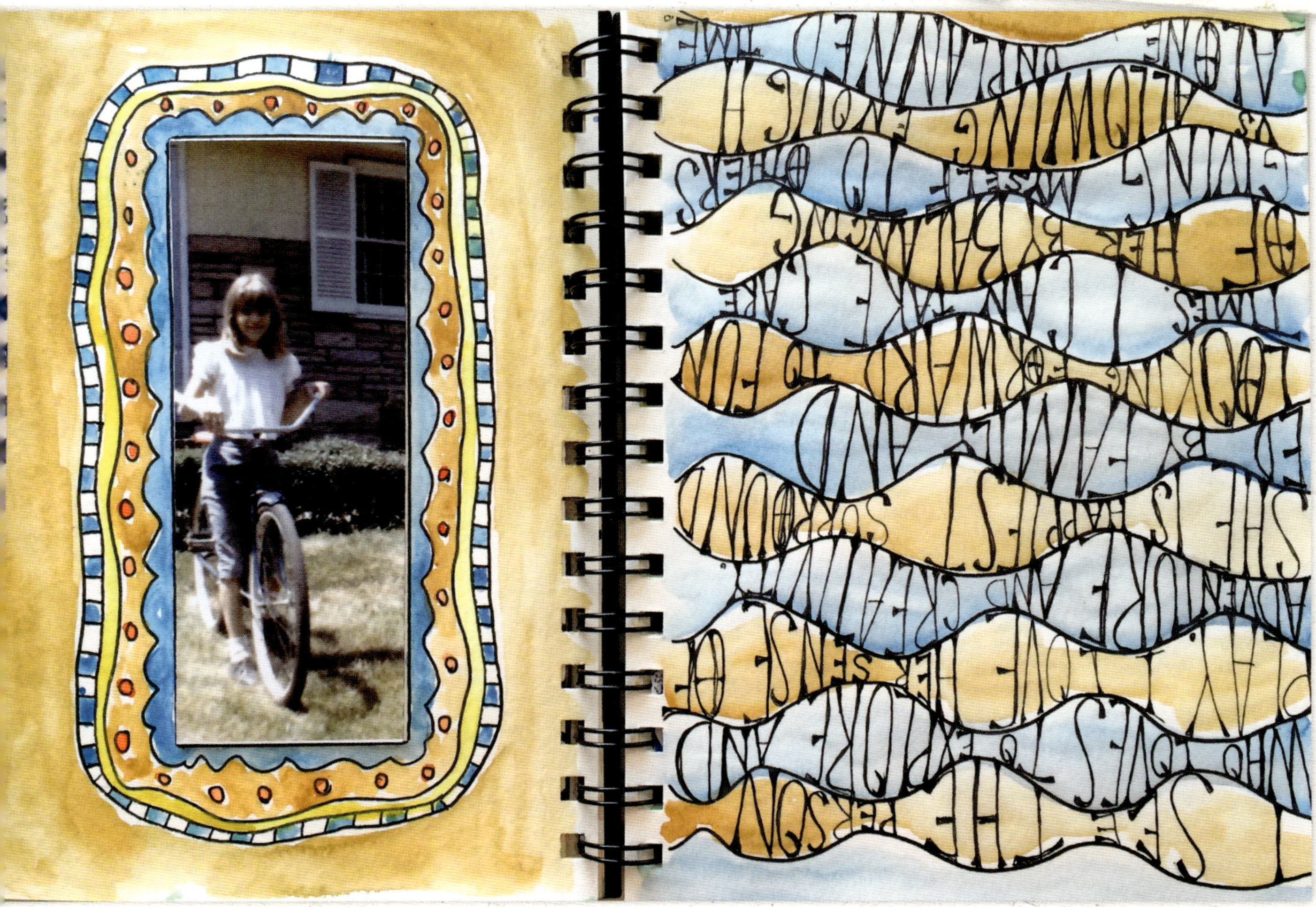

SUMMER OF '64
Vintage photo, gouache, black gel pen

What was your inspiration for this piece?

I was going through a box of old pictures and thinking about the hopes and dreams I had as a young girl. I was remembering exactly what it felt like to have the freedom of my new bike and the texture of the parched grass under my feet, along with blue skies overhead. I tried to bring those colors into the page background.

Are there any mixed-media artists who inspire you?

Mixed-media artists who inspire me are Martha Lever, Lori Vliegen and Misty Mawn.

Do you ever give yourself journal prompts?

I often give myself journal prompts. I think of them while I'm reading or listening to the radio or in conversation with friends, and something comes up that inspires me to write about that topic. People who say they don't know what to journal about just haven't practiced doing it enough; after a while, it becomes a very fulfilling daily practice.

Do you have an art journaling process?

I usually start with a quote, a photo or something related to my day, like a dream I had or something I'm grappling with, like a tough decision. (When I have absolutely nothing in mind, my go-to is making a list.)

> *"The illusion of perfection* IS THE ENEMY OF HAPPINESS AND CREATIVITY."

Colleen Mulligan Kline

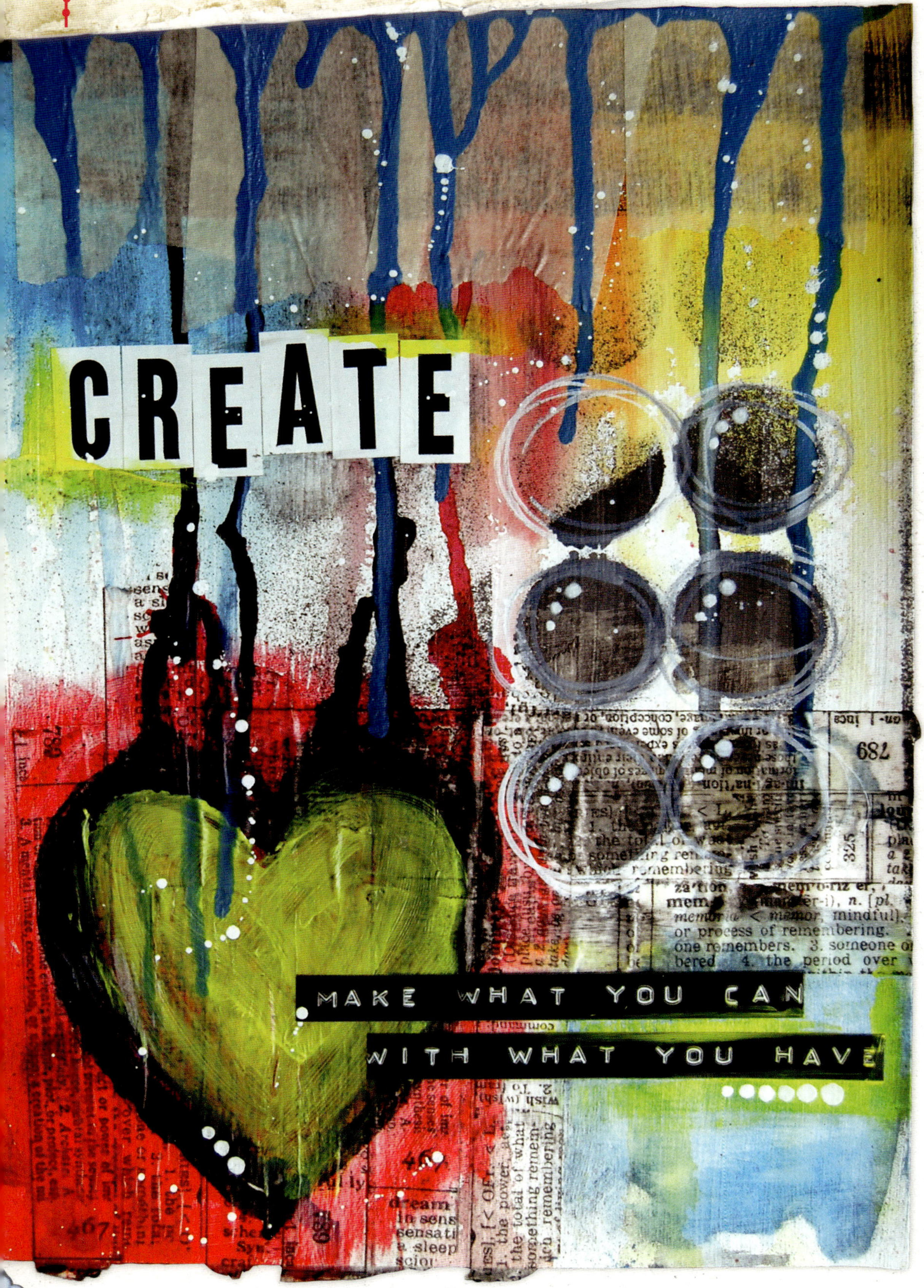

UNTITLED
Craft tape, acrylic paint, spray inks, India ink, letter stickers, paint pens, Collage Pauge, water, stencils, Dymo tape

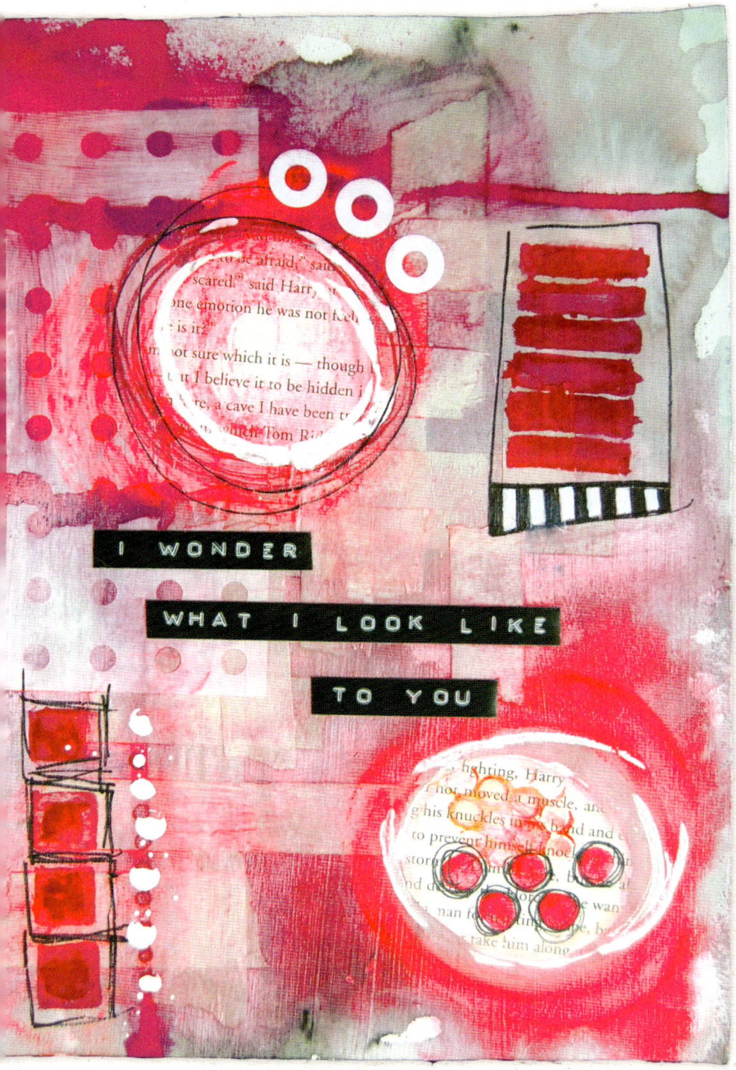

UNTITLED
Watercolor, acrylic paint, India ink, spray inks, masking tape, hole reinforcement stickers, sticker page scraps, paint pens, Collage Pauge, book pages, water, stencils, Dymo tape

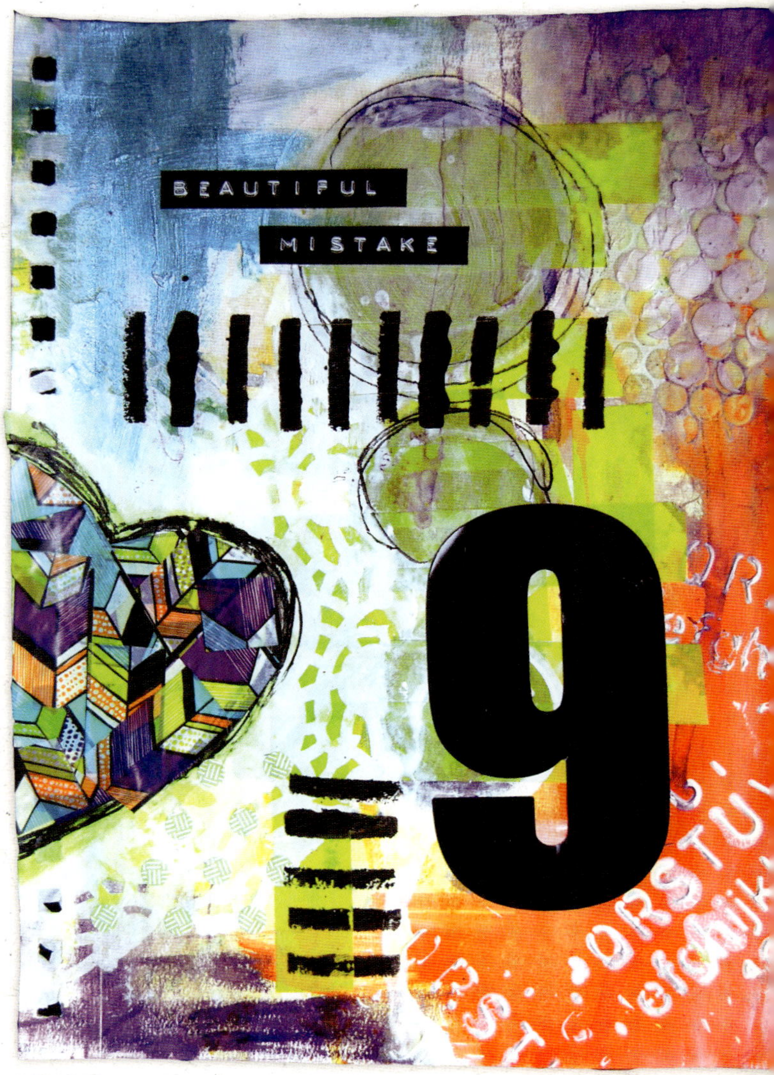

UNTITLED
Doily, modeling paste, acrylic paint, spray inks, India ink, Scotch tape, paint pens, Collage Pauge, water, stencils, Dymo tape, number sticker

Are there any mixed-media artists who inspire you?

The ladies I consistently follow and who inspire me to try different techniques are: Donna Downey, Roben-Marie Smith, Julie Fei-Fan Balzer, Nathalie Kalbach, Magda Bolinska, Kristin Peterson and Belinda Fireman.

What is the title of your piece?

I have not yet begun to title my works.

Do you ever give yourself journal prompts?

No, my prompts come from seeing works from artists whom I admire and trying to figure out their techniques and incorporate them into my own work.

When and why did you start art journaling?

I began journaling in early 2013 when I was inspired by the art journaling phenomenon. I started researching on Pinterest, Instagram and watching YouTube videos to teach myself this therapeutic and creative release.

Do you have an art journaling process?

No, not really. I start by thinking of a color palette and a background. The rest is just playing!

What tips would you give to fellow art journaling artists?

If it interests you, just do it!

Cindy Angiel

"*Draw from your well* ON THE INSIDE AND YOU'LL BE PLEASED WITH WHAT APPEARS ON THE OUTSIDE."

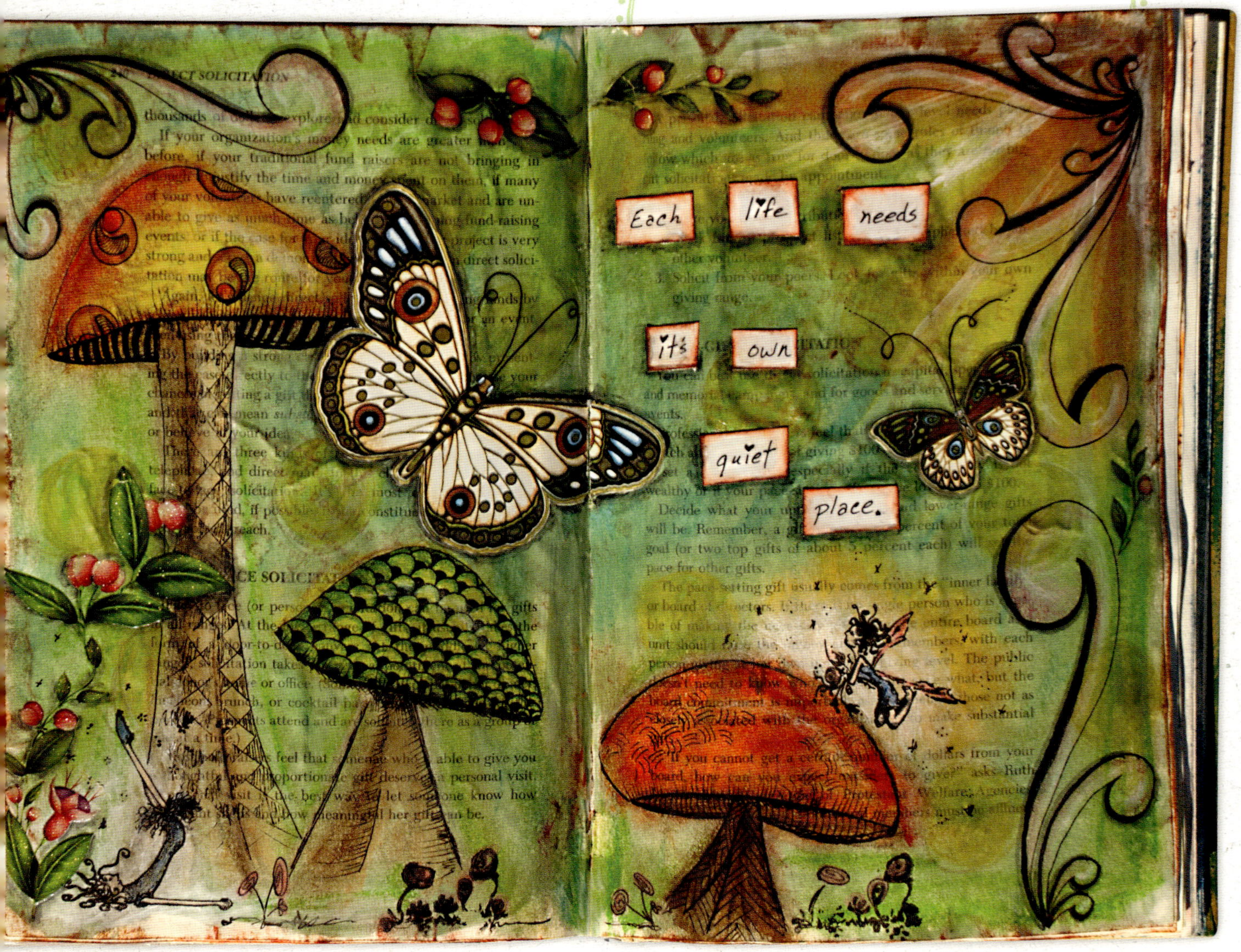

EACH LIFE NEEDS A QUIET PLACE
Pastels, book pages, pattern art, stamps, stickers, rub-ons

What was your inspiration for this piece?

I was inspired to create on a day when I was seeking a quiet place to meditate and heal my body. My favorite place to rest is in my garden, so I fantasized about fairies, which moved me into a state of relaxation and childlike happiness. The butterflies in this piece represent freedom—flying away from pain, toward comfort.

How did you come up with the name of your artwork?

It references the tiny living things found in a garden (and the imaginary creatures too).

Do you ever give yourself journal prompts?

Using a prompt or phrase to start a project helps me string together thoughts as I seek out colors and elements to use.

What tips would you give to fellow art journaling artists?

Let your pages grow naturally as your spirit moves you without forcing things to look a certain way. Also, if you're using another artist's work for inspiration, draw colors, shapes, themes or the spirit of the piece rather than trying to duplicate their pages.

Terry Garrett

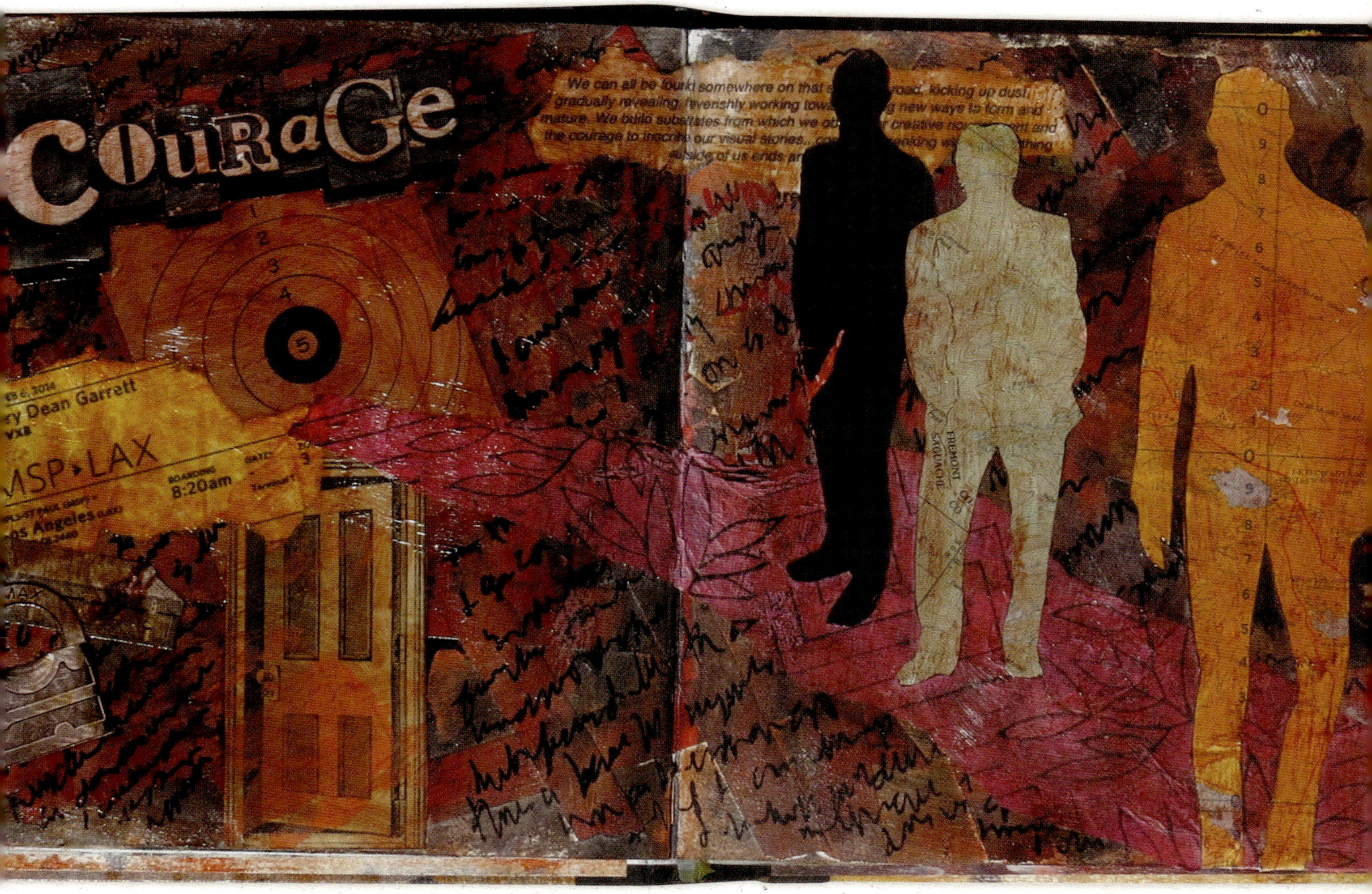

COURAGE
Acrylic paints, acrylic markers, tissue paper, ephemera

What was your inspiration for this piece?

The inspiration for this journal spread was one of celebration. I had just returned home from a trip to California. I had not flown in thirteen years and had not traveled alone for a very long time, but this was representative of me moving past my fear and taking the trip.

Are there any mixed-media artists who inspire you?

There are several mixed-media artists who inspire me. Orly Avineri opened my eyes to a new approach to journaling. Also, I want to mention the work of Tom LaBadia, Brian Kasstle, John Arbuckle, Jacki Long and Irene Rafael.

Do you have an art journaling process?

Of late, the process I use in my journaling is to open my journal to a blank spread. Then I go to my box of paints, pick out colors I am drawn to and start journaling. Often, I have no idea where I am going to go with a spread.

What tips would you give to fellow art journaling artists?

Tips I'd give those starting in journaling are to do this for you and trust in your own intuition.

Darby Casey

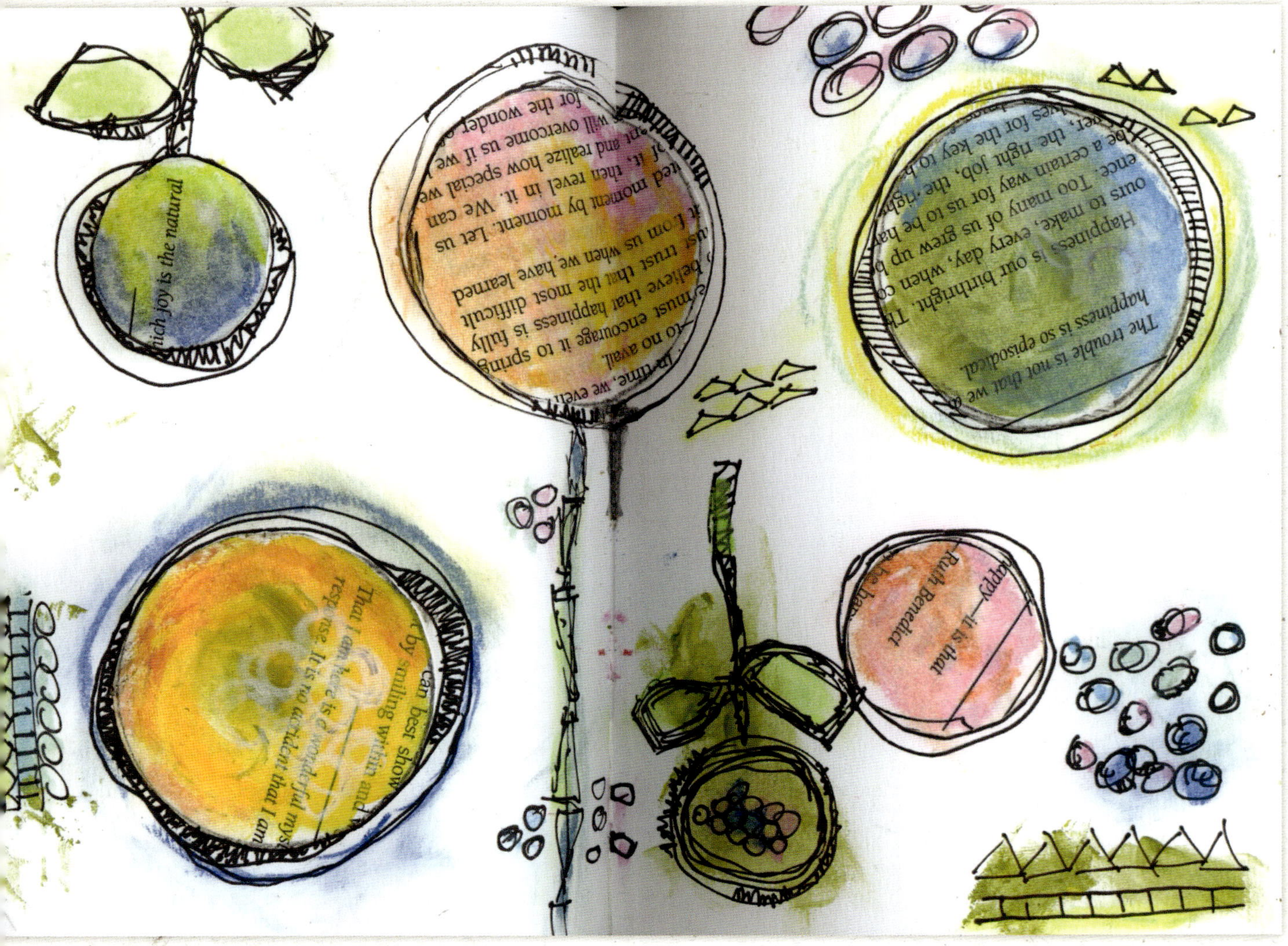

FALLING FLOWERS
White paper, acrylic paints, credit card, book pages, adhesive, oil pastels, black Sharpie

What was your inspiration for this piece?

This piece was inspired by a carefree day during which I watched *Alice in Wonderland*.

Are there any mixed-media artists who inspire you?

I find myself inspired by Nukuzu, Sabrina Ward Harrison, Dina Wakely, Jason Craighead, Dominique Fortin and countless others.

How did you come up with the title?

Within the piece, some of the flowers on the page are upside down. I imagined being Alice falling, with flowers falling all around me, feeling happy and light and ready to see where I was going to land.

What tips would you give to fellow art journaling artists?

Allow yourself to make a mess and "ruin" a page, because often it can free you to discover a new way of seeing and creating.

> "*Put your goals out there* WITH INTENTION AND CREATIVE PASSION, AND CONTINUE TO DO SO EVERY DAY."

Lea DeCosta

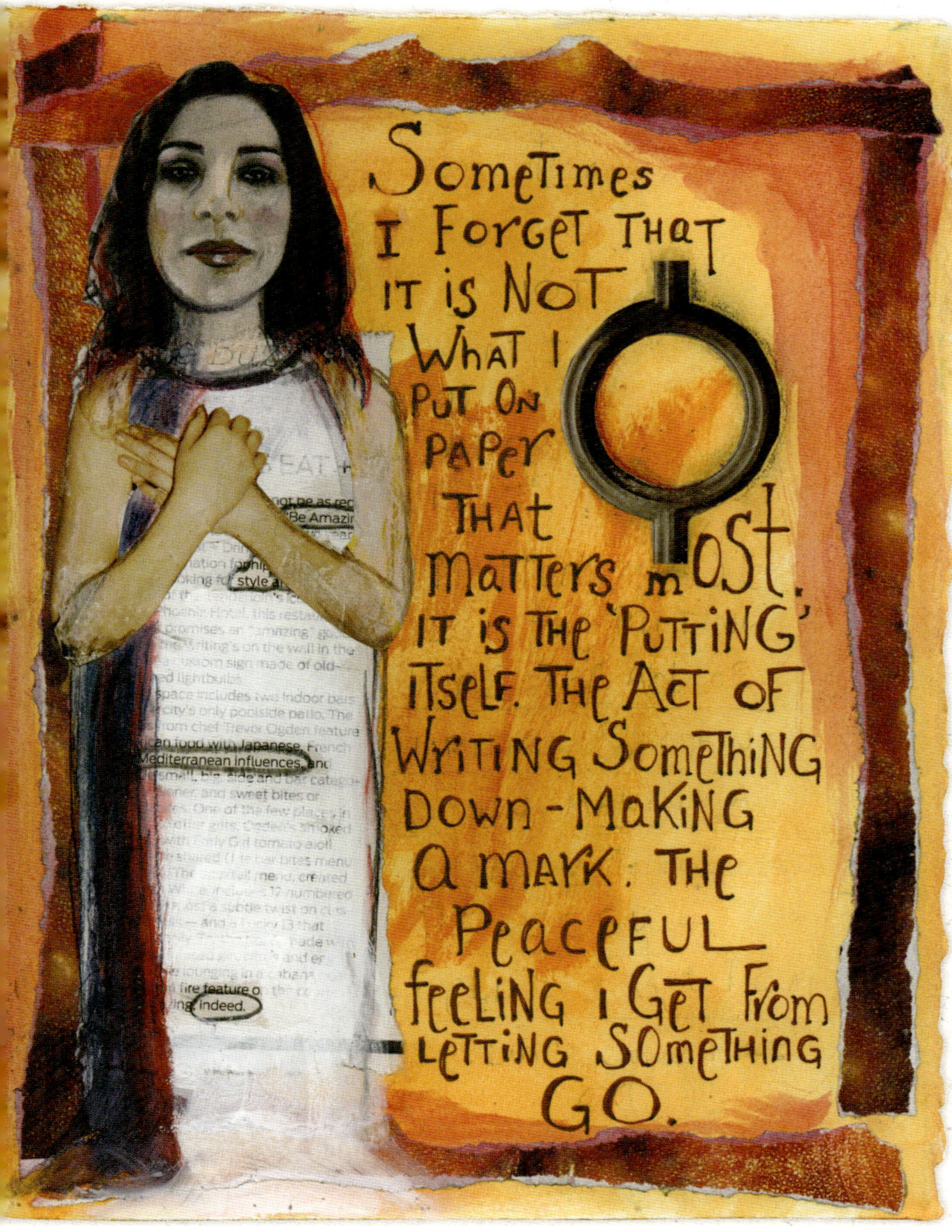

SERENITY
Watercolor paints, hot press watercolor paper, matte medium, magazine pages, photo, newspaper, gesso, colored pencil, water-soluble wax pastel artist crayons, permanent ink marker

What was your inspiration for this piece?

This image is from a journal I made while trying to sort through some very difficult things. I created a journal as a way to work through the sadness I was experiencing, figure out what to do next in my life and move on to a more positive place.

What interesting or unique techniques did you apply to this artwork?

Because my intentions for this journal were so personal, I decided to use actual images of myself.

Are there any mixed-media artists who inspire you?

I am constantly inspired by other mixed-media artists and creative people of all kinds. One of my favorite things to do is flip through a book such as Seth Apter's *The Mixed-Media Artist*, because there are so many wonderful artists and works to discover all in one spot.

Also, while I am always adding new names to my list of favorites, two of my current inspirations are the incredible art journalist Teesha Moore and Austin Kleon.

Do you ever give yourself journal prompts?

I use prompts only if there is something specific I am trying to accomplish.

When and why did you start art journaling?

I started art journaling very recently, only about a year and a half ago.

Belinda Spiwak

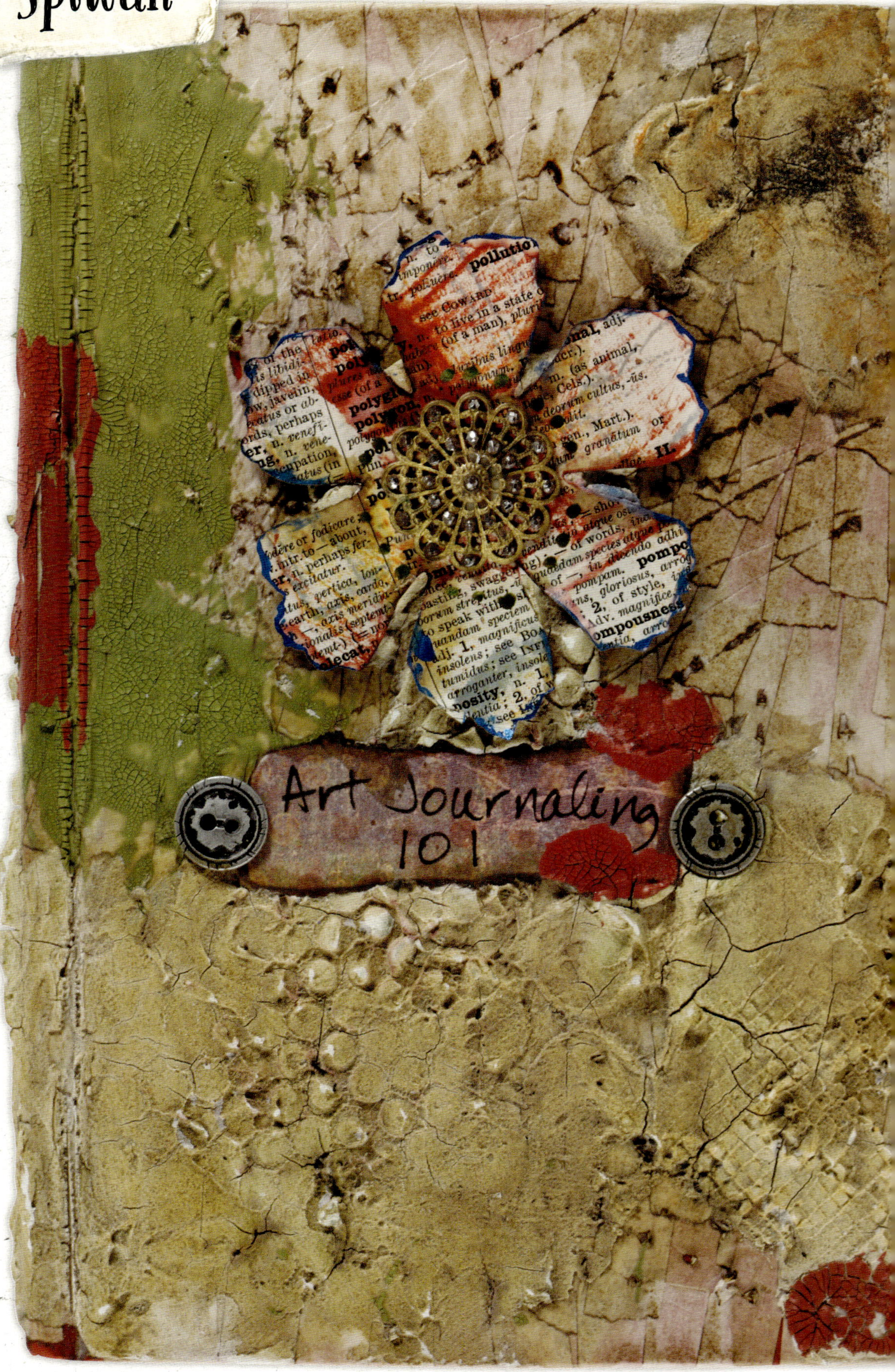

ART JOURNALING 101
Masking tape, rubbing stamp pads, acrylic paints, crackle, flower embellishment

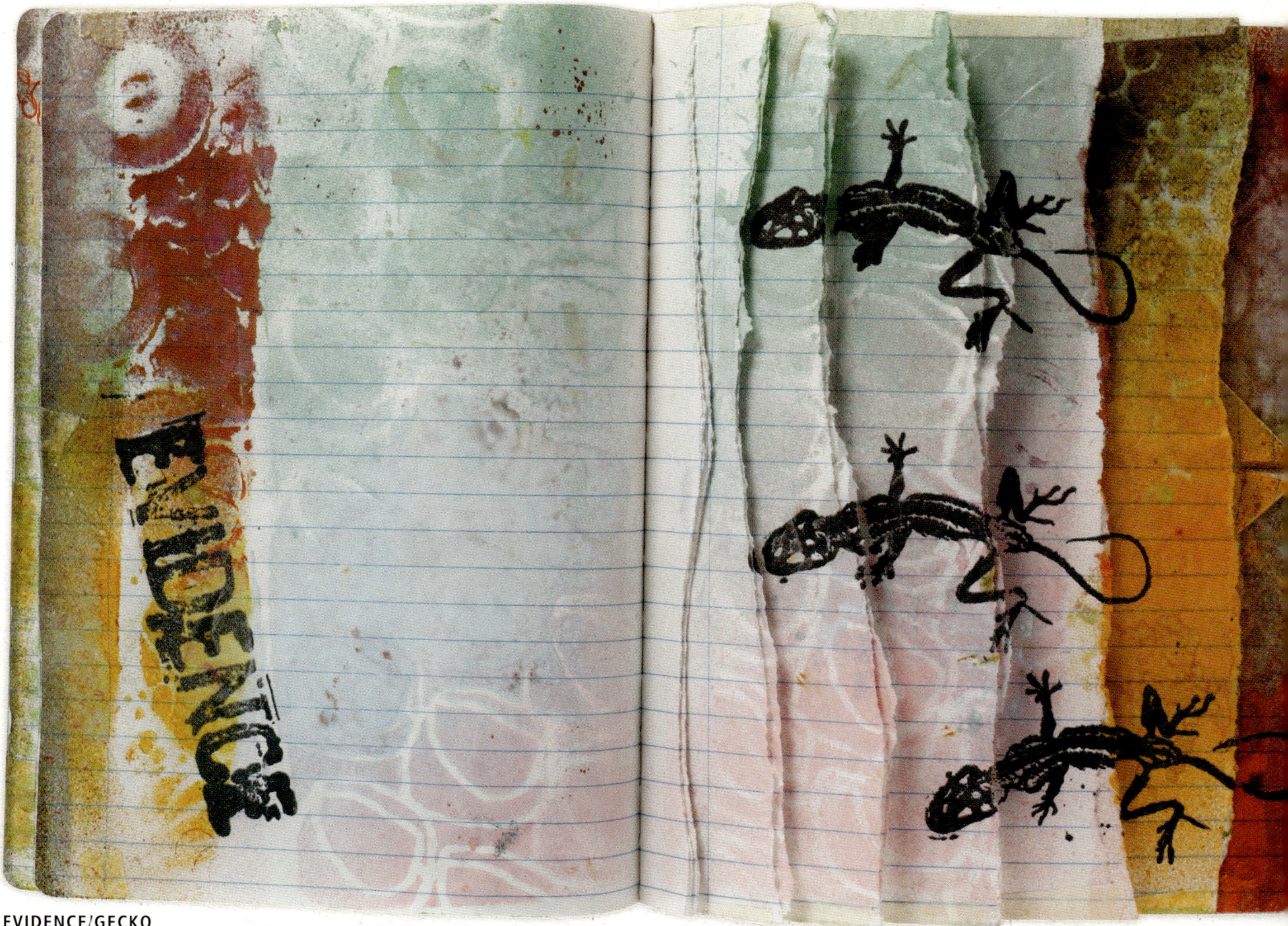

EVIDENCE/GECKO
Acrylic sprays, acrylic ink markings and writing, stenciling, stamps

What was your inspiration for *Art Journaling 101*?

This was my sample art journal shown as a model for my fifth-grade students. I used it to show my students how to use simple techniques to create their own art journals from recycled hard-covered books.

Do you ever give yourself journal prompts?

At random times I give myself journal prompts. Some of these prompts are on strips of paper that I tape to my journals. When I'm stuck and need something to write, I like the lock of the random prompts on the strips.

When and why did you start art journaling?

This whole idea started so students would be encouraged to write more in my school. Also, I had just gotten a bunch of new stencils that I wanted to try. I created a set of composition notebook art journals as a reward for my school—one for each grade level.

Do you have an art journaling process?

Although I have been art journaling in one form or another for thirteen or so years, I have no real process except in the initial physical structure (so it will last longer). As an artist, I enjoy the randomness of art journaling as it comes to me.

> "*Creativity knows no bounds* WHEN YOU CREATE FROM YOUR HEART."

Debra Ann Terry

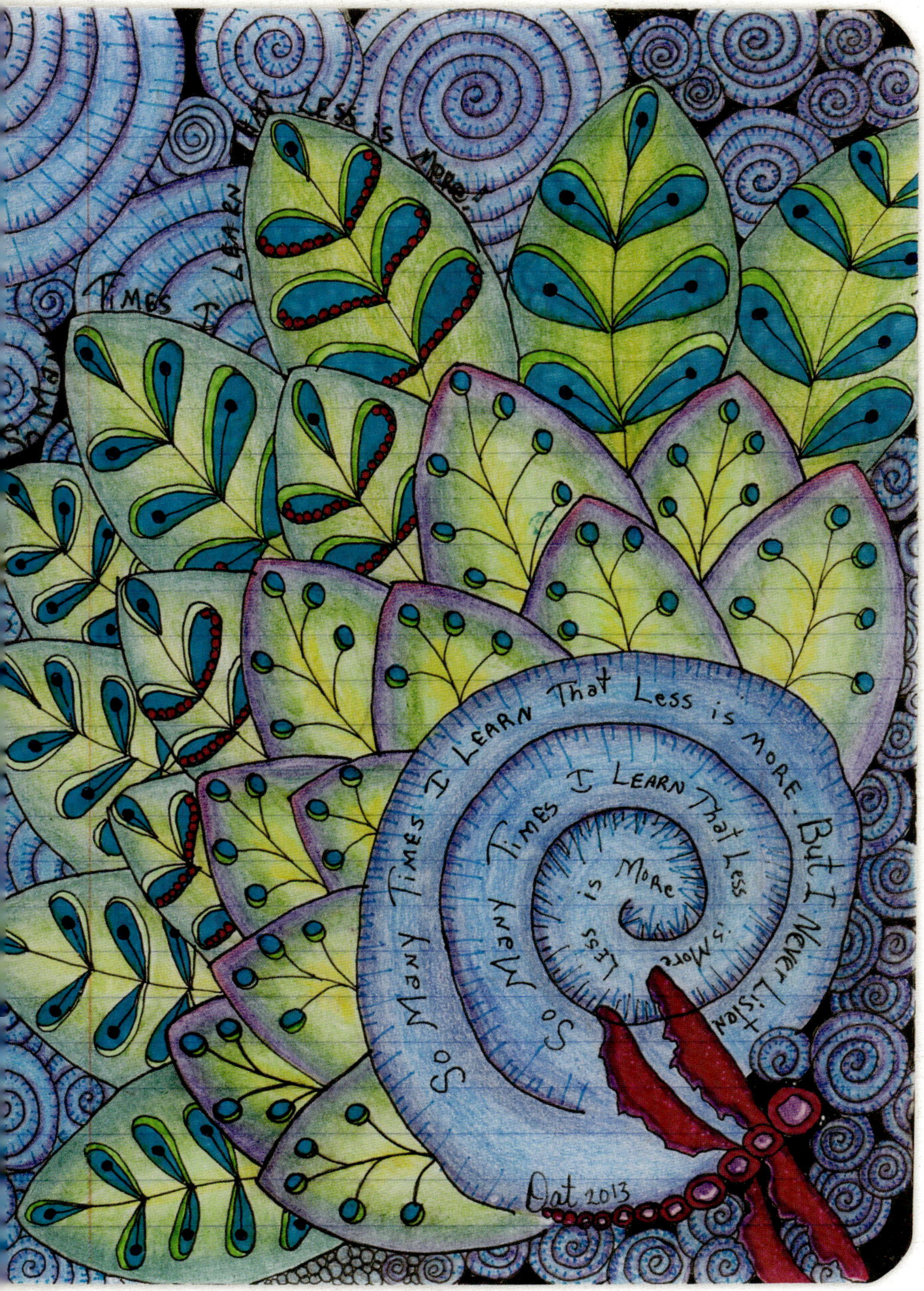

LESS IS MORE...EXCEPT WHEN IT ISN'T
Composition book, colored pencils, marker

What was your inspiration for this piece?

I love to draw details. The more intricate, the better. I often have to remind myself that less is more—white space can be just as important as the details and color. After all, the eye needs a place to rest. But then again, I usually just shrug off that little bit of common sense and happily continue to add detail and color.

What interesting or unique techniques did you apply to this artwork?

My art journal is a composition book. With this piece I did not try to block out the lines on the page. Instead I made them a part of the artwork.

Are there any mixed-media artists who inspire you?

Oh yes! I would have to mention Rach0113, Teesha Moore and Vicky Papaioannou—all of whom can be found on YouTube.

Do you have an art journaling process?

Lots and lots of daydreaming before anything hits the page.

What tips would you give to fellow art journaling artists?

Play. I use my art journal to remind myself to play. There are no mistakes in my art journal, just opportunities to grow and learn.

Jessica T. Kovan

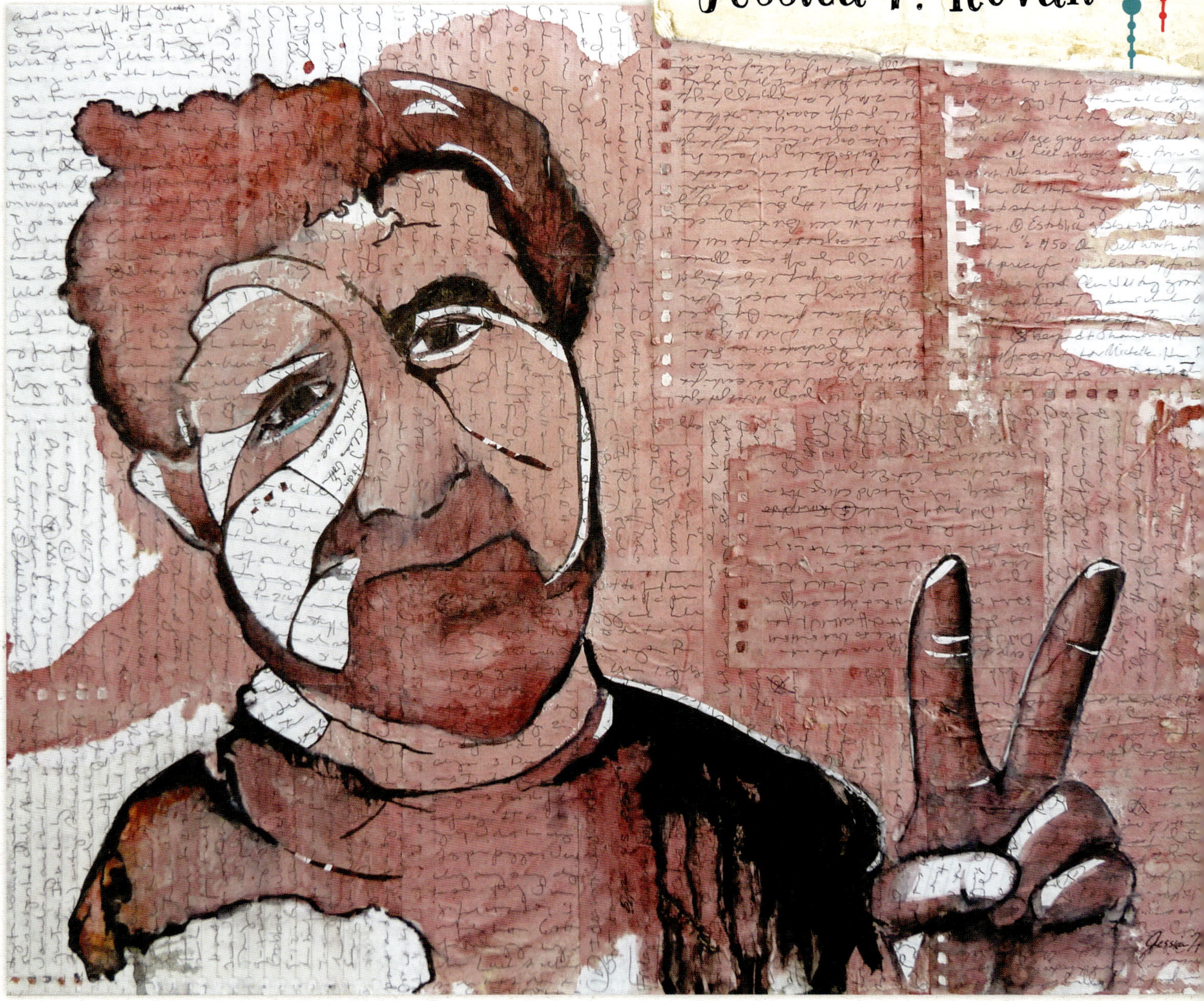

THE BEETNIK
Journal pages, beet juice, acrylic paints

Do you have an art journaling process?

I journal every morning and love to use my journal pages in my artwork.

What was your inspiration for this piece?

I created the beginning of *The Beetnik* while making Thanksgiving dinner. I had just cooked beets and was looking down at the beauty of the beet juice, then stopped what I was doing. I ended up randomly covering a canvas with my journal pages and poured the beet juice onto the canvas. Art took priority over the preparation of the meal! After much staring and with the addition of a little acrylic paint and some cut-up journal pages, my husband's image emerged from the beet juice.

"*Know yourself,* BE DARING, DO GOOD WORK AND TRY NOT TO WORRY. FOLLOW YOUR DREAMS WITH COURAGE."

Dianne Bishop Carey

What was your inspiration for this piece?

This was one in a series of mixed-media journal pages in which I explored how I see myself, how others see me and my many roles.

What interesting or unique techniques did you apply to this artwork?

Various painted papers were collaged onto the border, including finger-painted designs that I did with my grandchildren.

Are there any mixed-media artists who inspire you?

Lynne Perrella, Nina Bagley, Cathy Johnson, Randel Plowman and Jane Davies are just a few names.

Do you ever give yourself journal prompts?

I have found inspiration on the Internet, in books and in magazines. I enjoy ancient or ethnic art and find the motifs and designs in various periods throughout art history to often be the prompt I need to get started on a journal page. Kandinsky, van Gogh, Native American, Egyptian, medieval and Asian art are some of my more favored themes. An old art history book gives an endless supply of journal prompts!

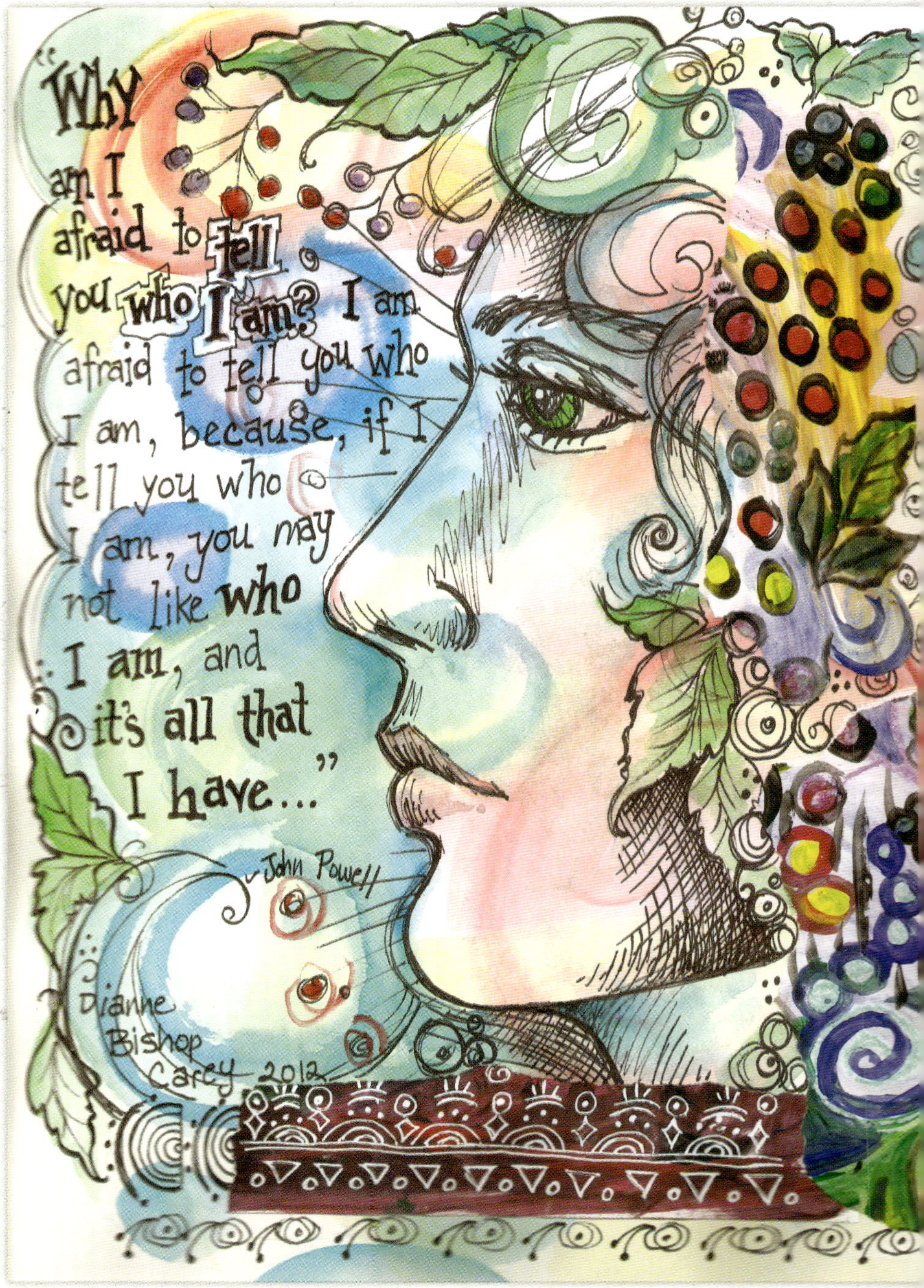

WHO I AM
Watercolor, Sharpie pen, finger paints, craft glue, white gel pen

"TO CREATE ONE'S OWN WORLD IN ANY OF THE *arts takes courage.*"
— GEORGIA O'KEEFFE

Eila Anttila

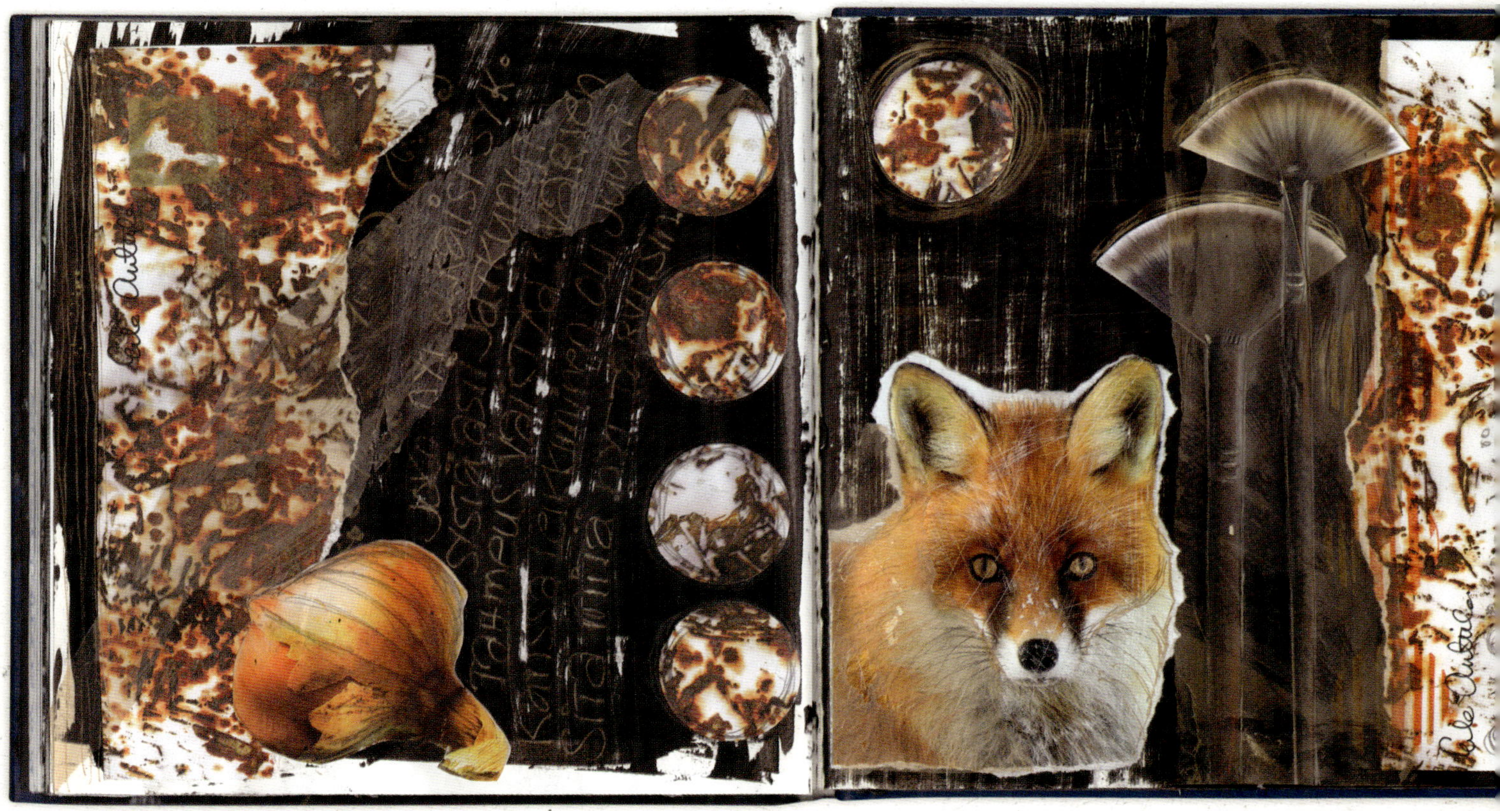

LOVELY COLORS
Assorted papers, mixed-media supplies

What was your inspiration for this piece?

I attended an art class called Sweet Colors where we made printing and dyeing experiments with waste materials.

What interesting or unique techniques did you apply to this artwork?

I covered a photo paper with wet onion skins, and the result was a fantastic rust-patterned sheet.

What materials did you use for this piece of art?

I found the fox and onion images from junk mail, and I scanned and printed two watercolor brushes. The background is a used book, which I painted with black gesso.

When and why did you start art journaling?

I started art journaling in 2009. I wanted to express my thoughts and feelings in a visual way, having kept a written journal ever since my childhood.

> "*Experiment, practice and share,*
> AND YOU WILL LEARN WONDERFUL THINGS!"

Dawn Howell

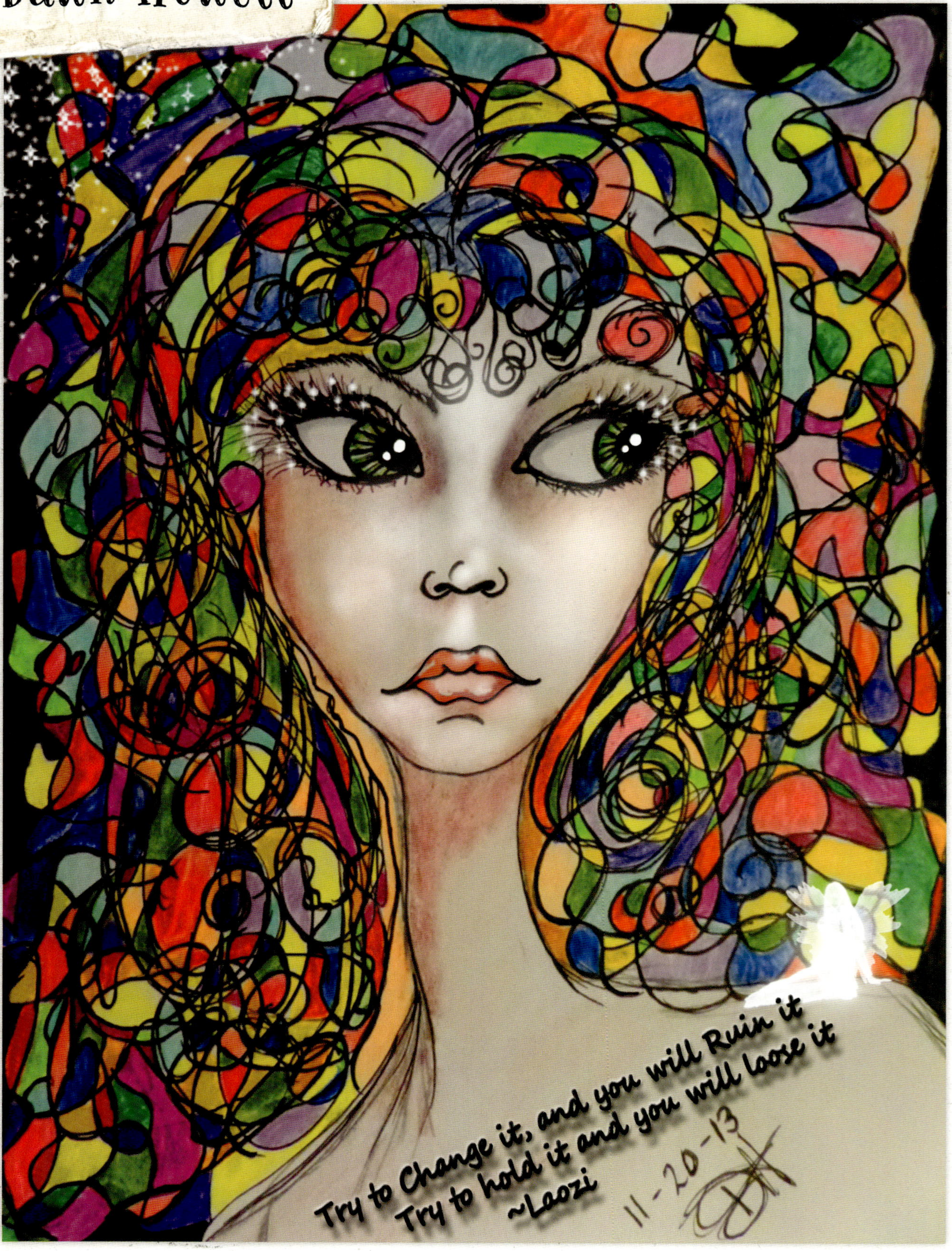

WISDOM
110-lb. (234gsm) Georgia-Pacific cardstock, Ticonderoga SenseMatic mechanical pencil, Faber-Castell Pitt Pen medium tip, Prismacolor Scholar 60 count for hair, Prismacolor Premier Portrait set for face, stencil for fairy

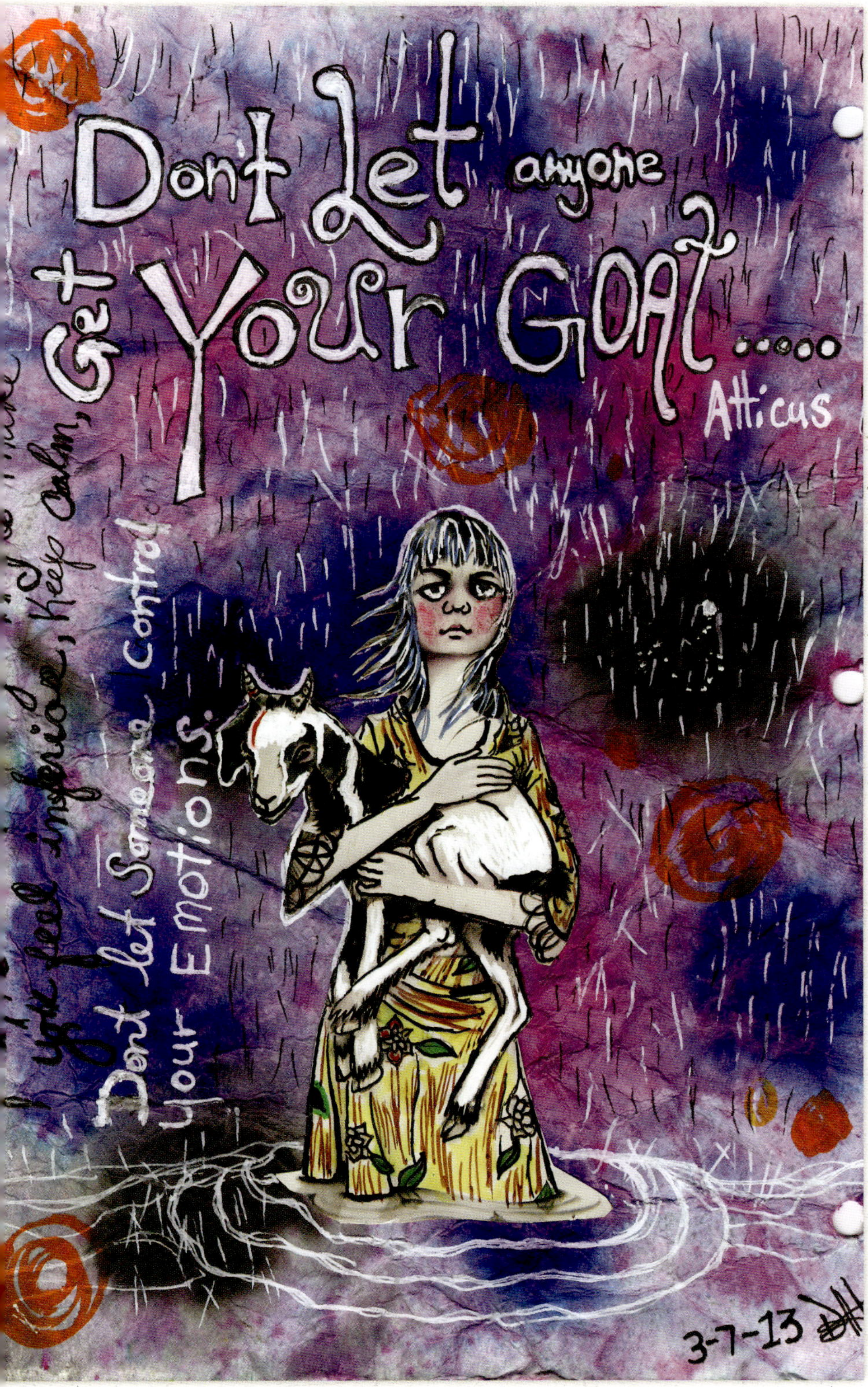

GET YOUR GOAT
Canson 140 (300gsm) watercolor paper, Dylusions spray ink, Faber-Castell Pitt Pen medium tip, Uni-ball Signo for white highlights and writing, Crayola markers

What interesting or unique techniques did you apply to this artwork?

With *Get Your Goat,* I crumpled the page and then added some spray ink before going over it with some Ranger Distress ink. This gave the background a really cool weathered effect.

Are there any mixed-media artists who inspire you?

Jennibellie because she uses a lot of recycled materials.

Do you ever give yourself journal prompts?

Yes, when I need that boost during an artist's block, my niece will give me a prompt that we both have a week to complete. It's usually a combination of two or three animals, or two to three descriptions. An example would be: coffee deprived + drunk dialing.

When and why did you start art journaling?

As a teen I wrote in a diary, but someone read it. This so horrified me that I couldn't bring myself to ever reveal another inner thought ever again, no matter how many journals I bought. Then one day I saw a YouTube video that was about art journaling, and I was forever hooked!

Do you have an art journaling process?

Many evenings as I watch television, I will sit and just color in pages or glue scraps down.

> "*Leaving a legacy full of art will* SURELY PIQUE A FUTURE GENERATION'S INTEREST MORE THAN JUST A DIARY OF WORDS ALONE."

Frieda Oxenham

What was your inspiration for this piece?

Scottish winters are long, dark and cold, so when I saw the quote, I had to use it.

What interesting or unique techniques did you apply to this artwork?

I over-stencilled the page but created calm by using hand-cut face silhouettes to tame it.

Are there any mixed-media artists who inspire you?

I'm inspired by Julie Fei-Fan Balzer.

Do you ever give yourself journal prompts?

I regularly cut out phrases or words from newspapers and magazines to get me going.

Do you have an art journaling process?

I work in stages, one day painting the page, on another day adding collage, then stencilling, etc.

What tips would you give to fellow art journaling artists?

You're the boss in your own journal and you only need to please yourself.

"Just start playing!"

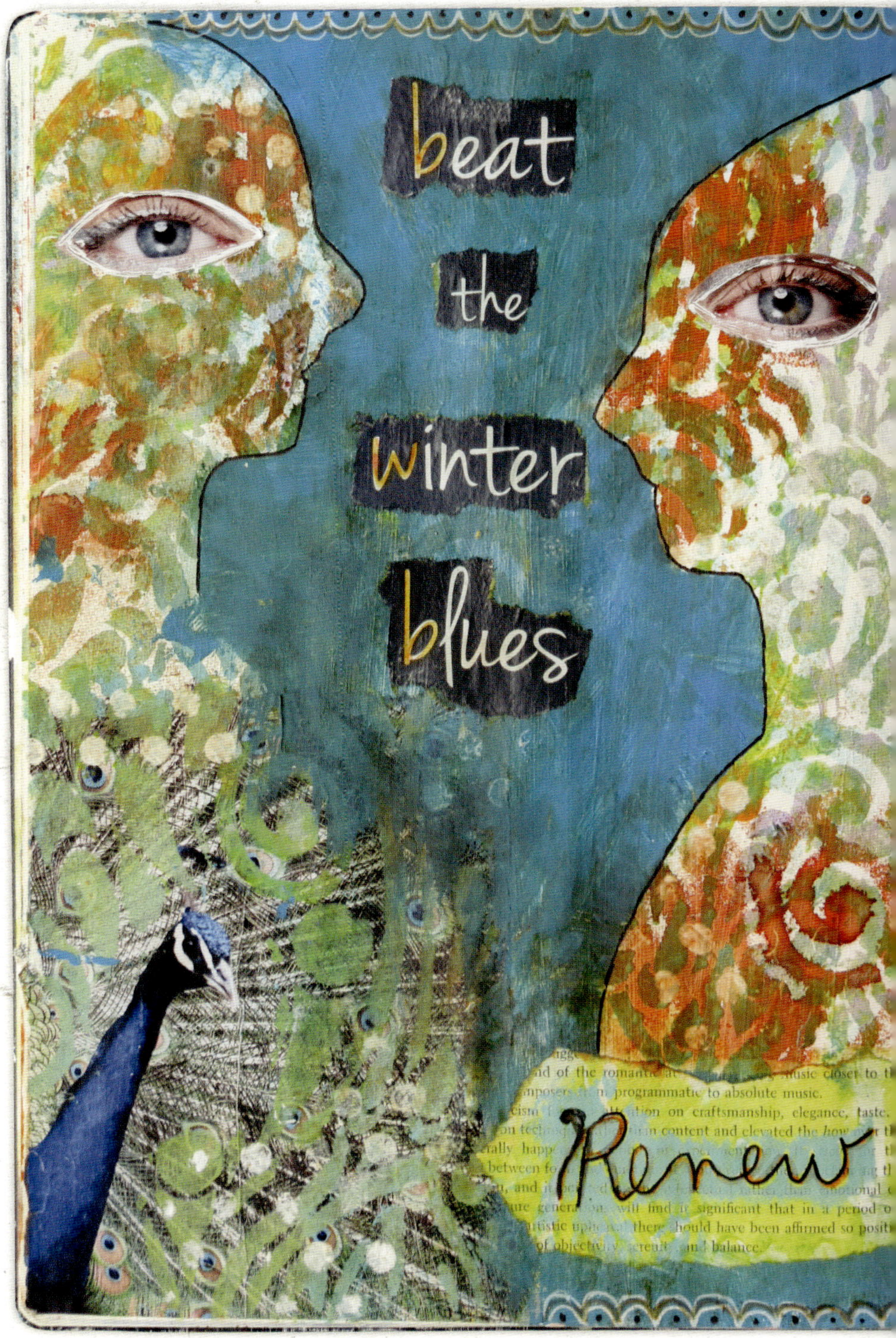

BEAT THE WINTER BLUES
Stencils, cutout words and images, acrylic paints

“ART JOURNALING IS A PERSONAL PROCESS OF DISCOVERY—*be fearless in your exploration!*”

Tristina Dietz Elmes

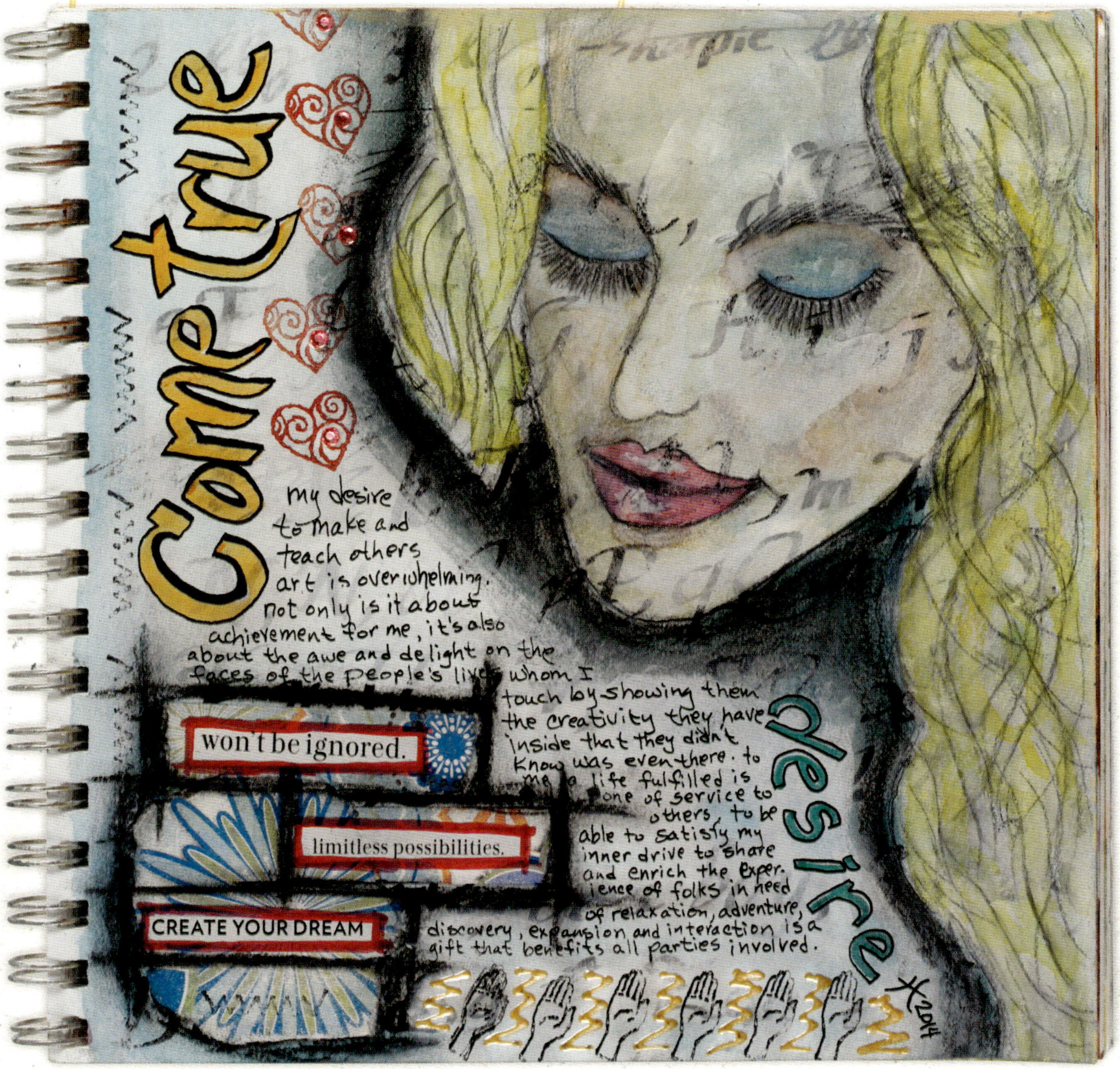

DREAMS COME TRUE
Assorted papers, gesso, pencils, charcoal, Letraset Aqua-Markers, artist pens

What was your inspiration for this piece?

I was inspired to create this journal page by words and images found in a Victoria's Secret catalog. They compelled me to express a strong desire to share my passion for making art and teaching art to others.

Are there any mixed-media artists who inspire you?

Julie Fei-Fan Balzer for her classes on faces and stamping, and Mary Beth Shaw and Seth Apter for their lessons on layering. Also, a YouTube video by Jane “Danger” Davenport inspired me to try the fantastic Letraset watercolor markers, which are perfect for enhancing journal pages on the go.

How did you come up with your title?

It was a reminder to myself that with passion, commitment and drive, I can fulfill my desire to build a creative art-based business, which will support my family and enrich many others' lives along the way.

Do you ever give yourself journal prompts?

I'm usually prompted for the subject of a journal page by thumbing through interesting papers, old books (my favorite is a dictionary that's older than me rescued from a library sale), magazines, postage stamps and photographs.

Deborah Hunter-Davis

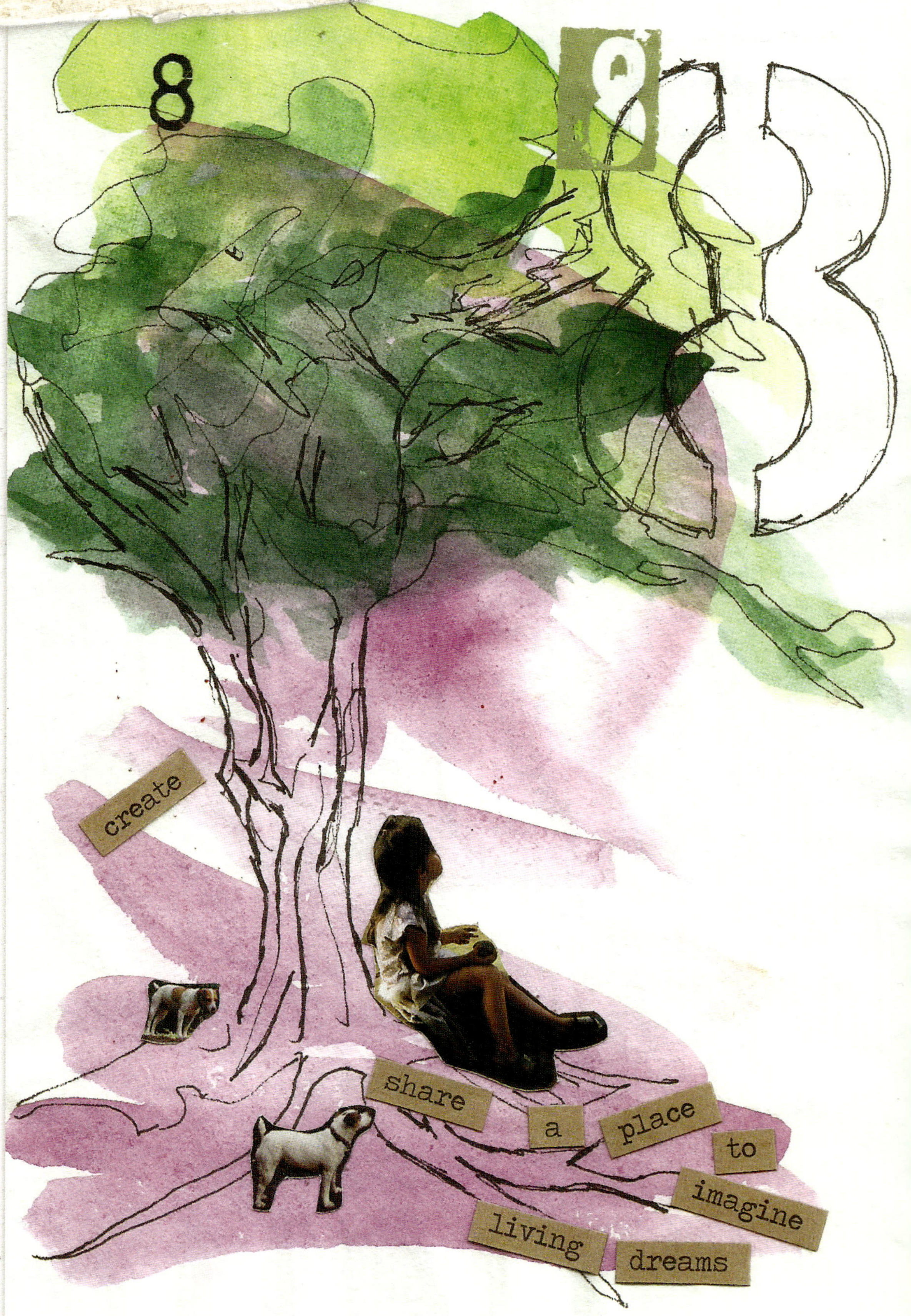

DAY8
Ink, watercolor, pen, collage materials, rub-on letters, handmade paper

What was your inspiration for *Day8*?

My inspiration for *Day8* was a story that my good friend, Jane, tells about being raised near an old oak tree that still stands in the backyard of her family home in Mobile, Alabama. She talks about sitting in the branches and on the roots of the old tree, telling it poems and stories, and singing songs.

Do you ever give yourself journal prompts?

I find that it's helpful to begin a piece with a prompt, but I don't always use this process. Also, I don't think it crucial to the piece to stay with the prompt if something else comes to mind once the work is started.

Do you have an art journaling process?

I am quite loose with my journaling process because it is just easier for me to work on the fly. I will begin a piece by lightly sketching in the larger elements of the composition, then laying down a wash in watercolor. If I want to keep working, I will blot the page and continue. However, most times I will let this dry for a few hours while I consider other parts of the composition—whether or not I want to add type, collage elements, etc.

What tips would you give to fellow art journaling artists?

One tip that was really helpful to me was to stay loose and avoid getting bogged down with the technical aspect of creating the piece. Journaling is an excellent way to experiment with mediums on a small scale.

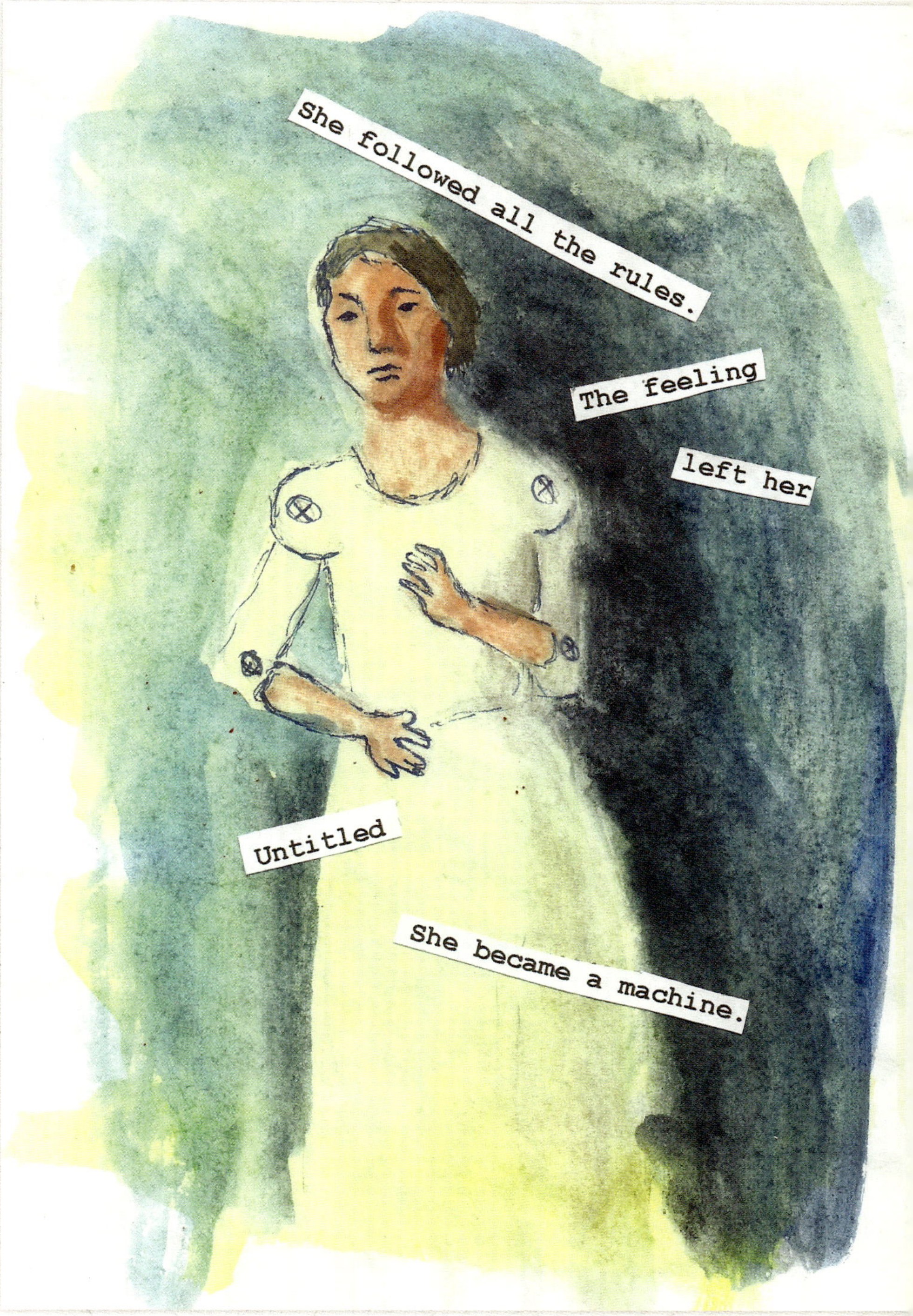

DAY25A
Ink, watercolor, pen, handmade paper

Gayle Price

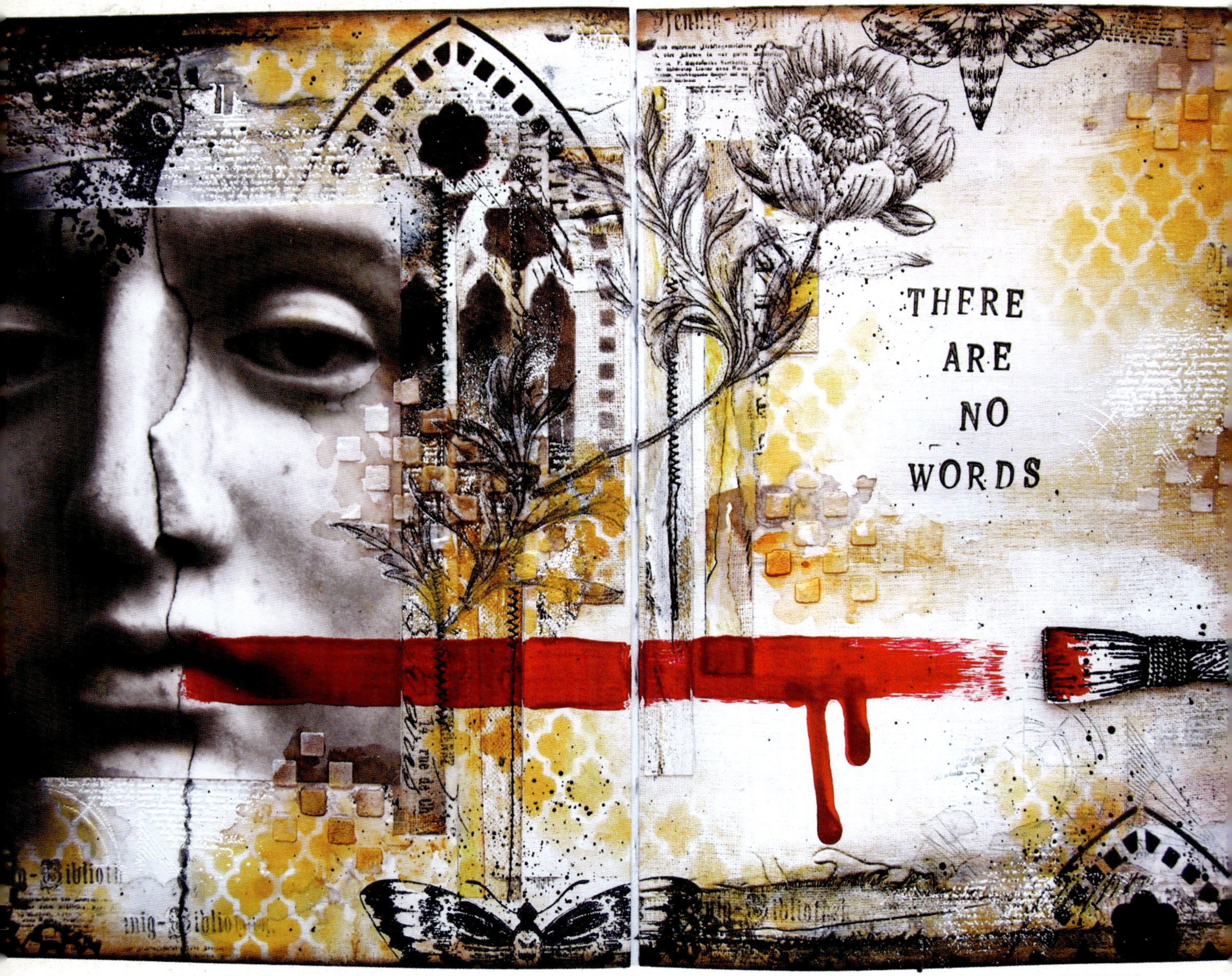

NO WORDS
Gesso, paint, inks, stamps, masks, paper napkins, texture paste, machine stitching, embossing

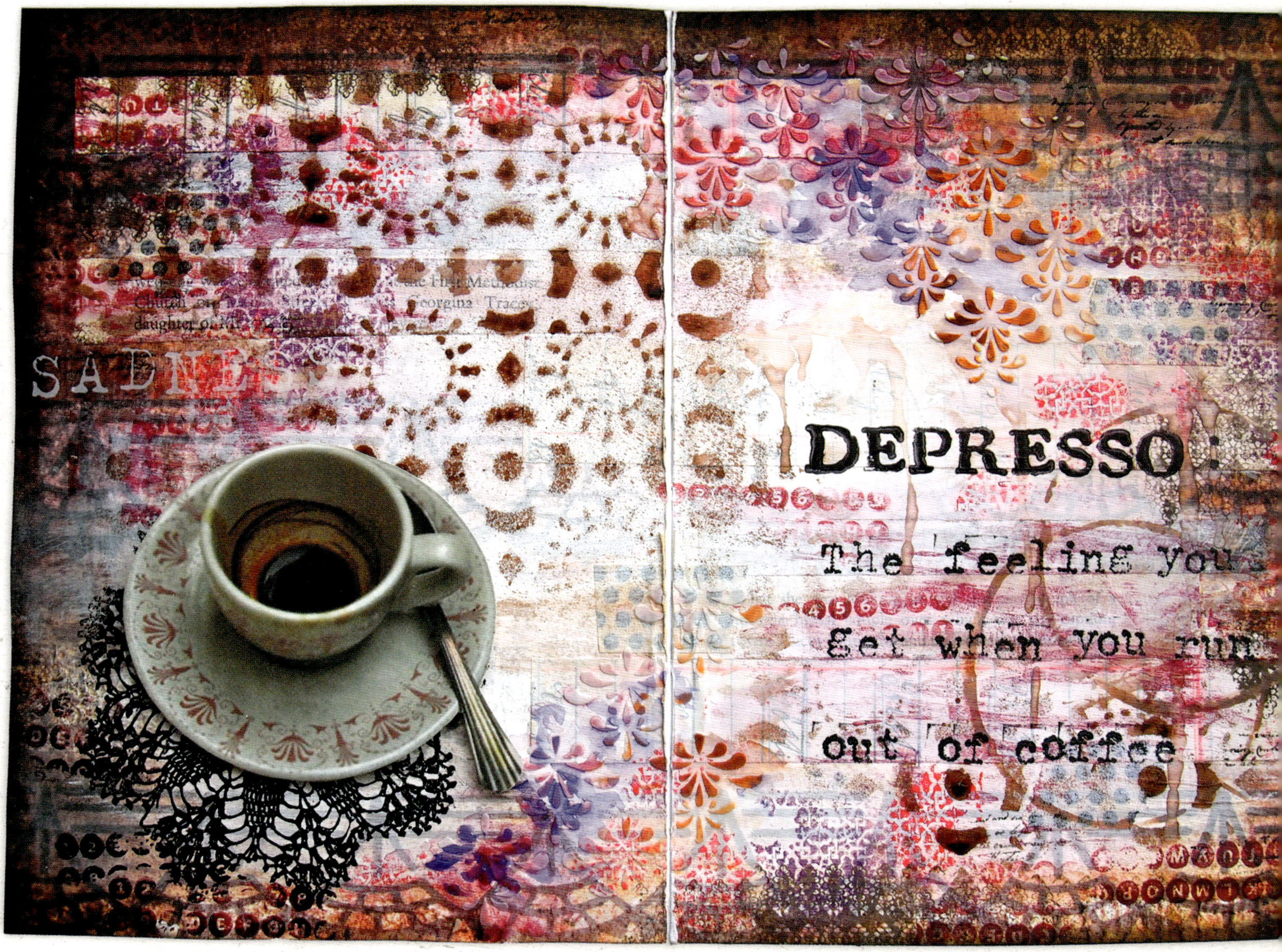

DEPERESSO
Stamps, masks, inks, texture paste, embossing powder, watercolor paint

What interesting or unique techniques did you apply to *Deperesso*?

Instead of sticking the coffee cup flat onto the page, I used 3-D tape to raise it, then outlined it with a gray watercolor pencil. This gave it a shadow, creating a more three-dimensional effect.

Do you ever give yourself journal prompts?

Quotes, lines from movies and songs, and memorable passages from books are, for me, great inspiration prompts for art journal pages.

Do you have an art journaling process?

My art journaling process always begins with the emotion, the sentiment, the situation or the story that I want to express. I then search for personal photos, magazine pictures or images from the Internet that resonate or relate to my idea. Sometimes I draw my own images, and sometimes there are no images at all—just words, colors, patterns and textures.

The application of mediums to my page is quite spontaneous and random. I have no preconceived idea of what I want the page to look like when it's finished.

What tips would you give to fellow art journaling artists?

Do not overthink things. Express yourself on your page, using what feels right for you, and not what you see others do. Make your page as simple or as complex as it needs to be in order to express what you want to say. Lose yourself in the process. The pages you will love the most are the ones you'll admire when finished—but you most likely won't remember how you did them.

Ann Renee Lighter

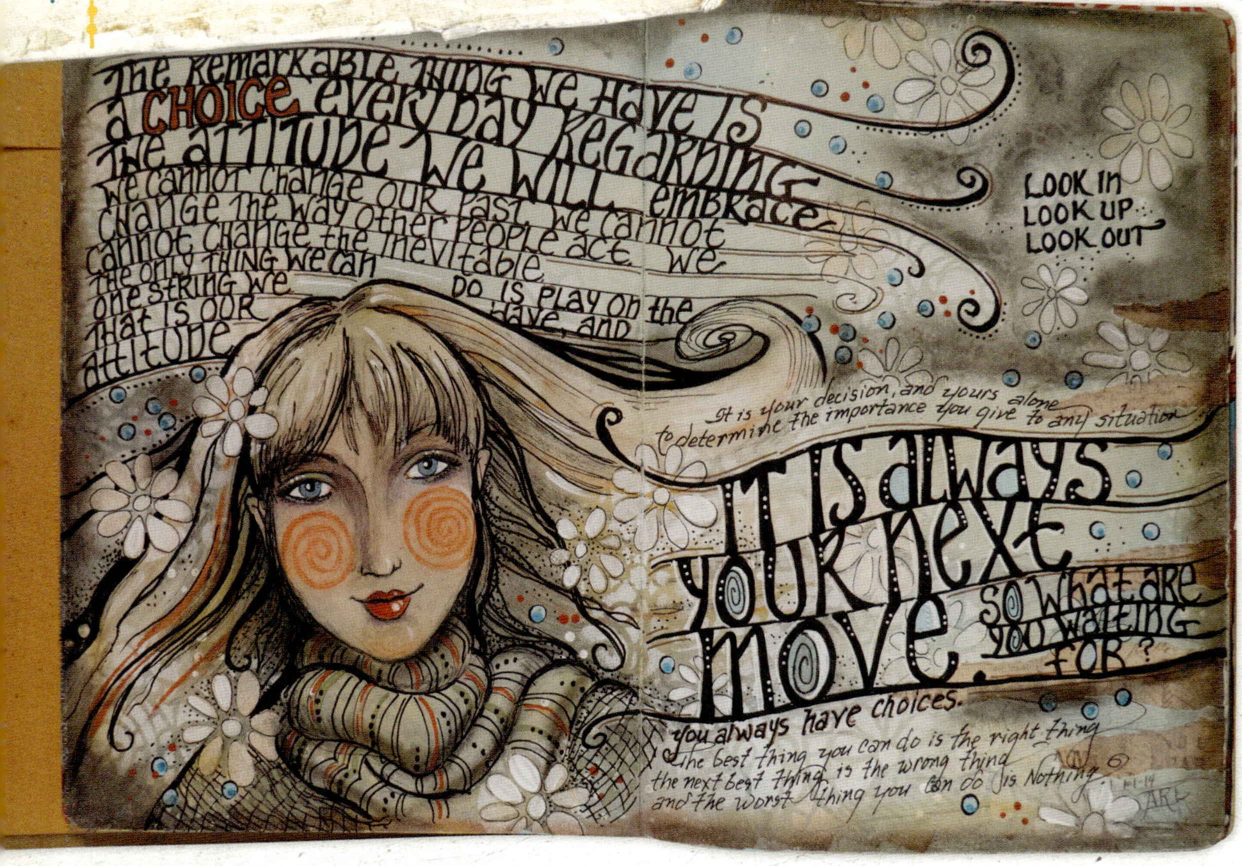

ATTITUDE
Acrylics, black pens, acrylic paint pens, water-soluble oil pastels

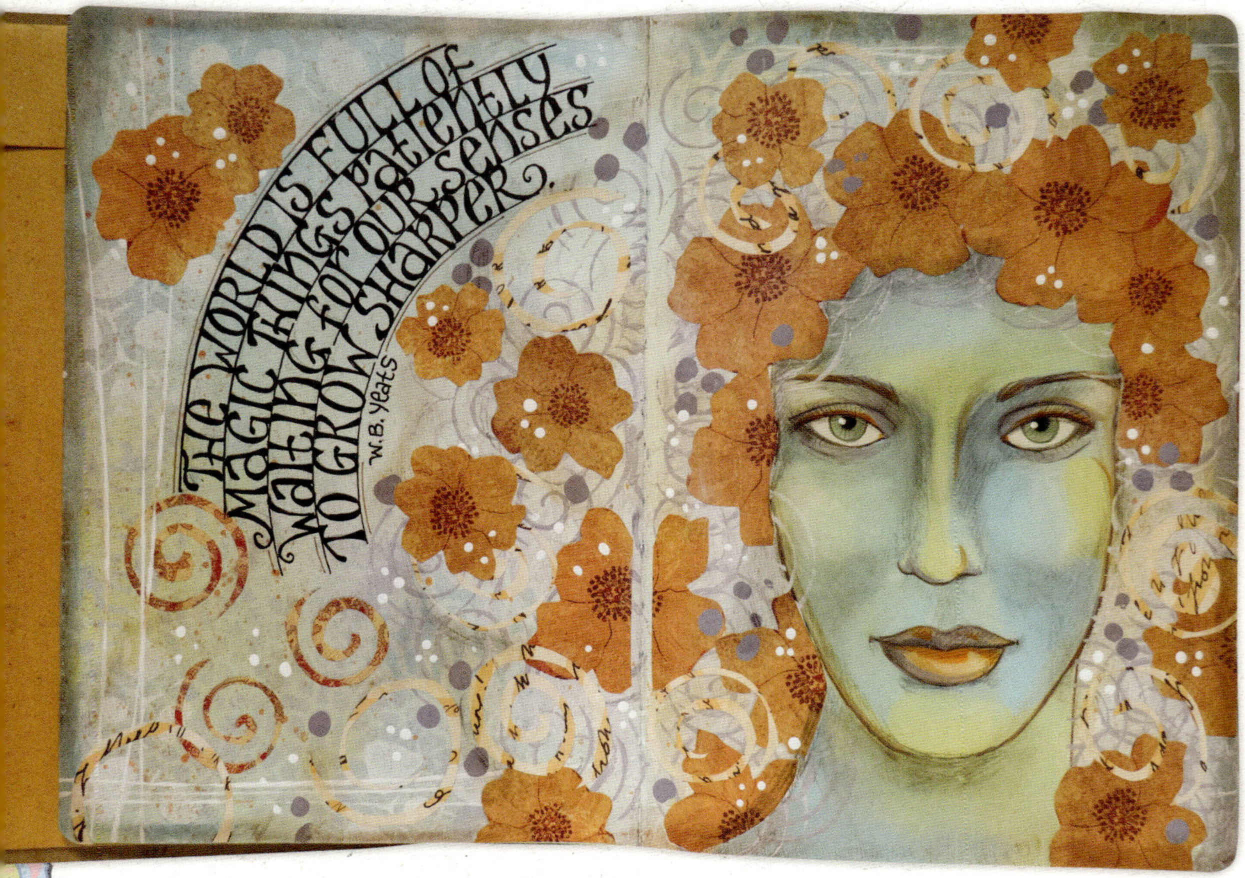

MAGIC
Kitchen utensil (stamping), acrylic paint, collaged embellishments

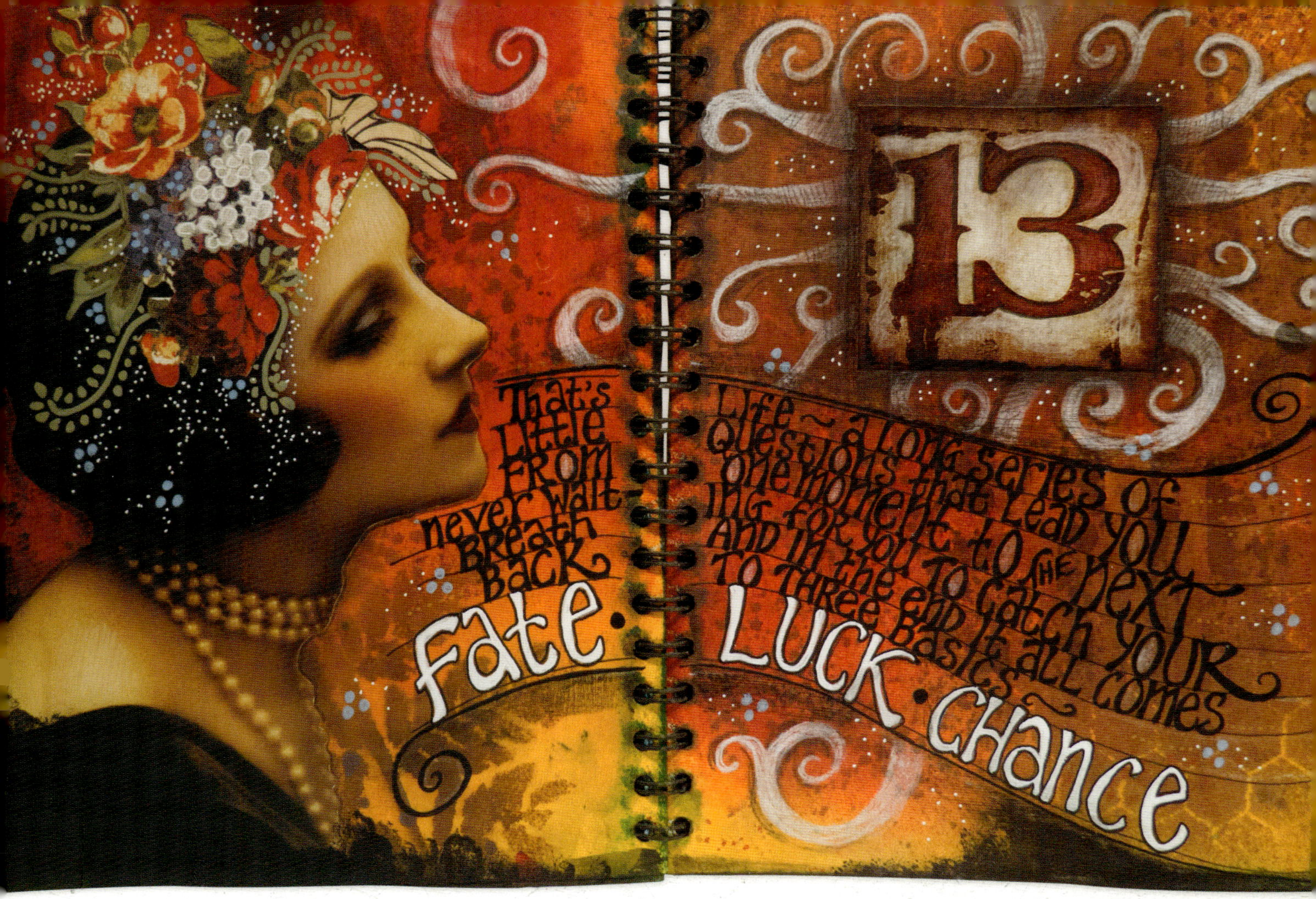

FATE
Colored inks, paper collage with matte medium, acrylic pens, colored pencils

What was your inspiration for *Magic*?

I've always loved the painting *At the Moulin Rouge* by Toulouse-Lautrec with the lady with the lovely green face in the lower right-hand corner of the work. So when I was painting this face, it seemed right to make it green. The rest evolved once the face was finished.

What interesting or unique techniques did you apply to this artwork?

For one of the background layers, I used a kitchen utensil to stamp spirals with acrylic paint. It's fun to experiment with markmaking using unexpected objects. I also cut spiral shapes and flowers out of paper and collaged them onto the piece.

Are there any mixed-media artists who inspire you?

I'm inspired by so many artists, some of whom directly influence my work: Teesha and Tracy Moore, Andrea Matus deMeng, Michael deMeng, Jane Davies, Anne Bagby and Lynne Perrella.

Do you ever give yourself journal prompts?

Usually I let the pages evolve as I work. I enjoy working intuitively and try not to overthink what I'm doing. It's more fun that way.

What tips would you give to fellow art journaling artists?

Work freely, let things happen spontaneously and don't be afraid to try something new. The beauty of the art journaling process is that it becomes your playground to experiment.

> "ALLOW UNEXPECTED THINGS TO HAPPEN ON YOUR PAGES AND *be genuine in your expression.*"

Jeanette C. Montero

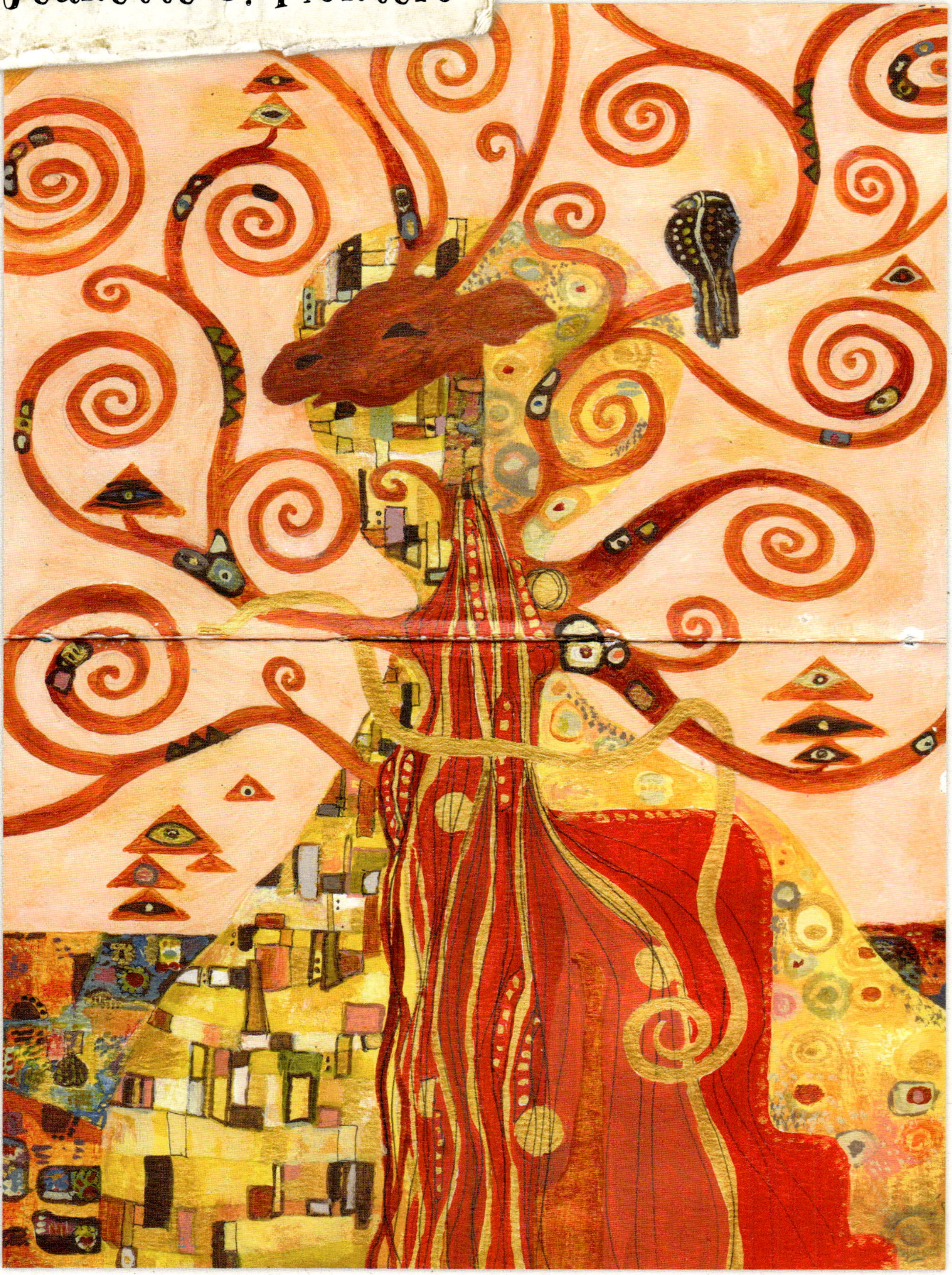

CARNAVAL
Acrylics, pencil, ink

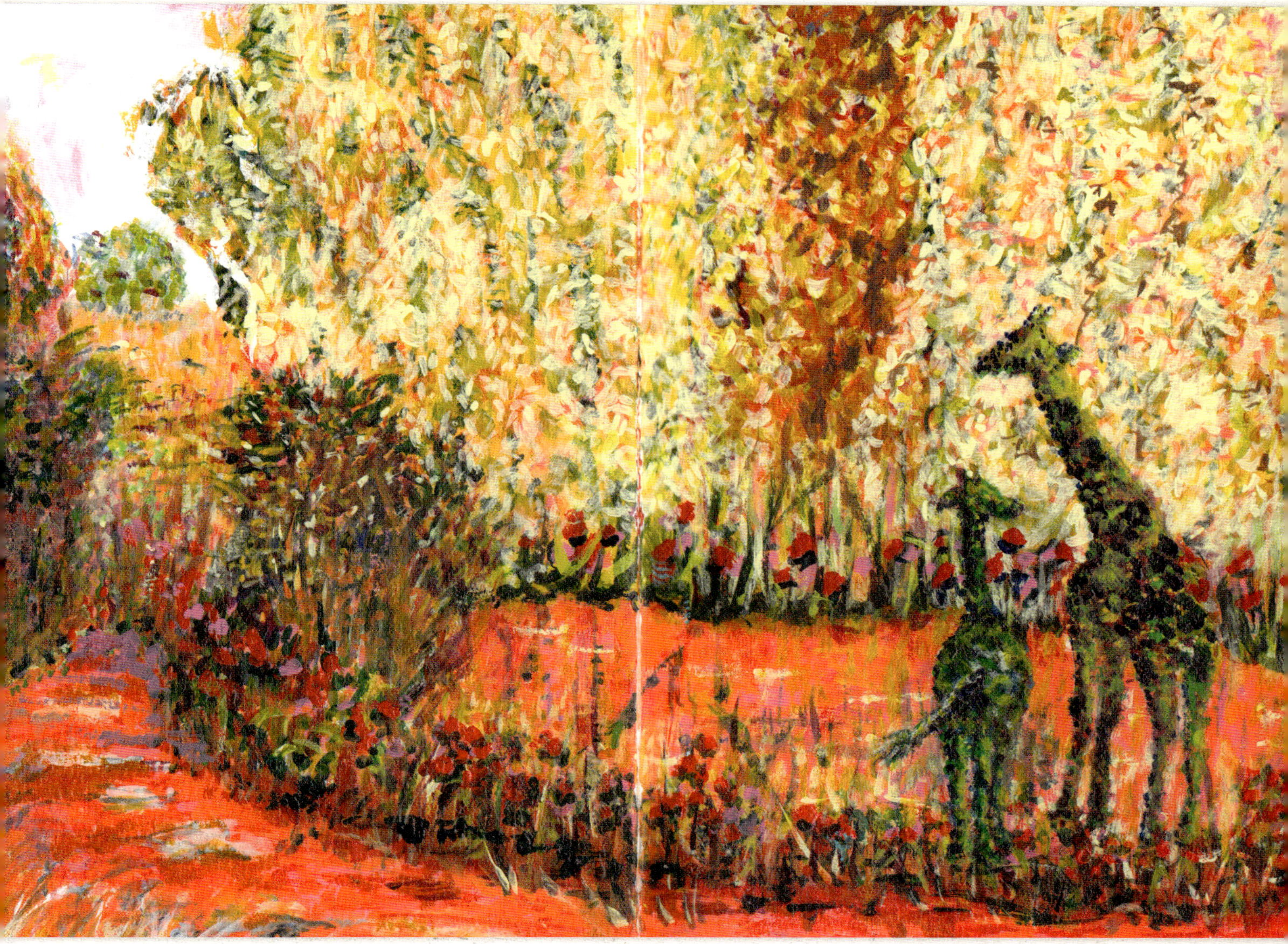

MOTHER MAY I?
Acrylics

What was your inspiration for *Carnaval*?

This piece is one in a series of giraffe paintings I did in the style of my favorite artists. I wanted to learn new techniques that I could apply to my own work. The highly ornamental patterns, symbols, spirals, swirls, bright colors and gold accents are reminiscent of Gustav Klimt's work and remind me of the flamboyant Carnaval!

When and why did you start art journaling?

I only recently started art journaling because I usually paint with the intention of gifting it to someone. Since I only have so many friends and relatives I can give my art to, it makes sense to journal. It's a great place to work out the ideas in my head and, since I have the option to share it or not, there's less pressure to come up with something perfect.

What interesting or unique techniques did you apply to *Mother May I?*

I tried to recreate the sense of peace and calm evident in most of my favorite Monet paintings. Art journals are the perfect place to try out new styles and the techniques of artists I admire.

"*Art is not just about what you created,* BUT WHAT YOU LEARNED AS YOU CREATED IT."

Jeanne Brickman

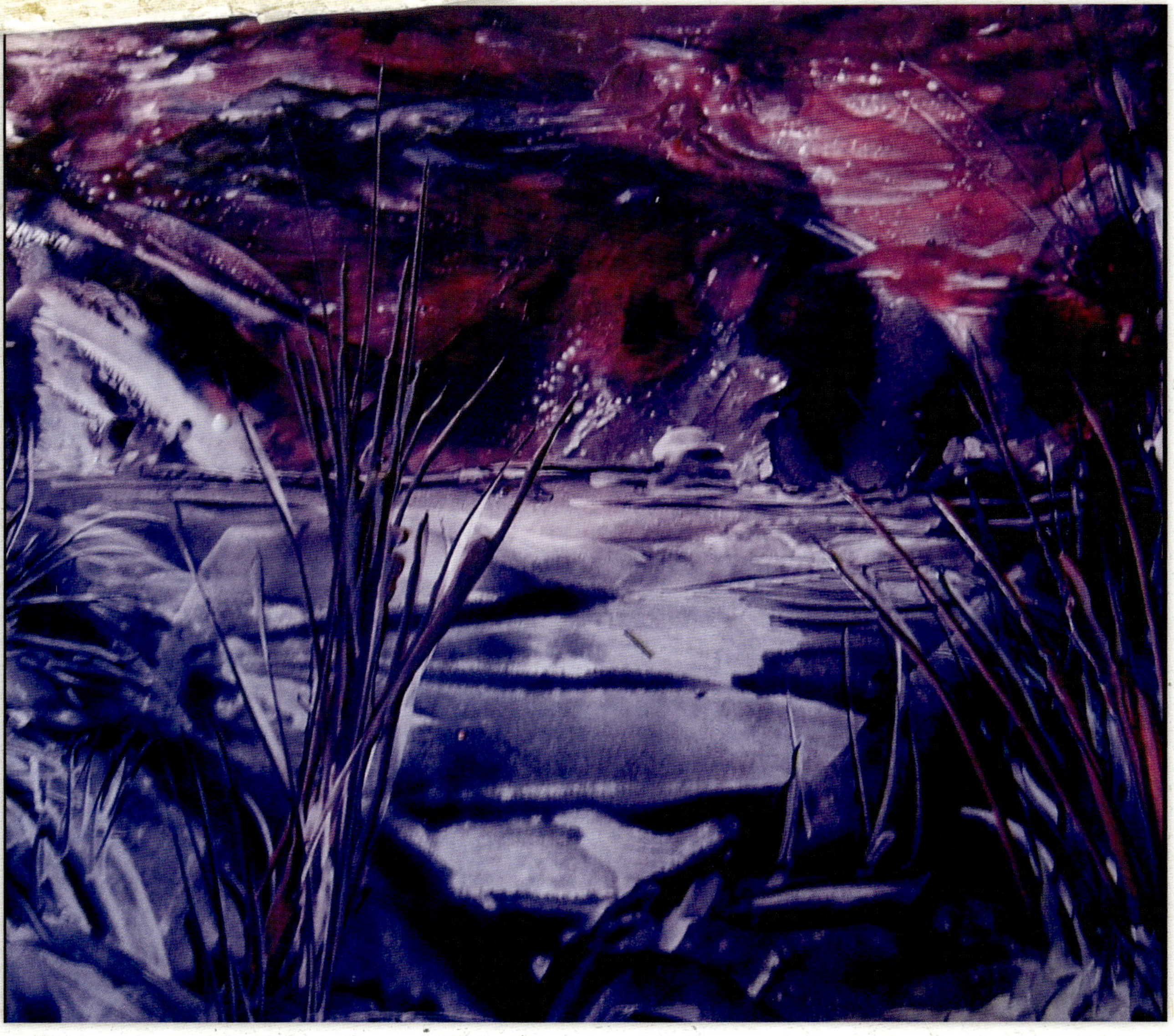

MY WORLD
Encaustics, wax, heat tools, knives, assorted paints

What was your inspiration for this piece?

I was inspired to do *My World* while enjoying an early morning in Rhinelander, Wisconsin. I have always loved landscapes, and the beauty around me took my breath away. Also, purple is my favorite color, and my love of fantasy landscapes lifts my heart and mind.

Do you ever give yourself journal prompts?

I love the idea of journal prompts; they do help to get the ideas turning in the mind. Also, I usually jot down my dreams and then expound on them. Those can be my journal prompts too.

> *"There is no wrong in art,* JUST EXPRESS YOURSELF FOR YOU."

When and why did you start art journaling?

I started art journaling about a year ago because I loved creating art and wanted it all in one book so I could look through and enjoy the moment again and again.

What tips would you give to fellow art journaling artists?

Just let the ideas flow and go with it. Sometimes one word will lead you on an amazing journey.

Delfina Zapata

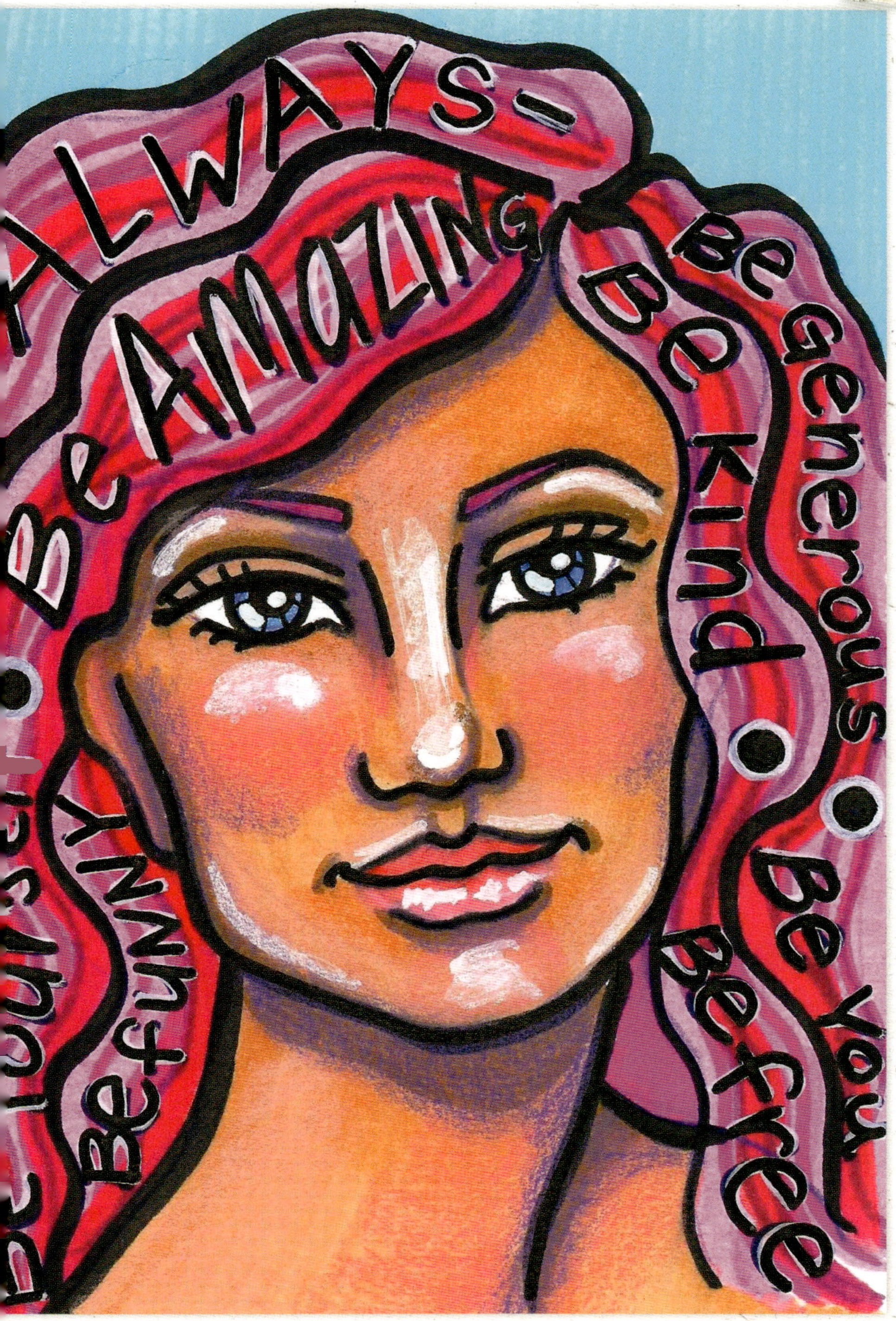

What was your inspiration for this piece?

My inspiration was the idea of positive affirmations.

What interesting or unique techniques did you apply to this artwork?

I used colored pencil and opaque white marker over Copic marker and regular markers.

Are there any mixed-media artists who inspire you?

There are many! Jane Davenport, Tamara Laporte, Julie Fei-Fan Balzer, Kathy Cano-Murillo, Tim Holtz and so many more inspire me as an artist.

Do you ever give yourself journal prompts?

Sometimes, but most of the time it comes from my head or my heart.

Do you have an art journaling process?

I sketch it out and then, on bigger pieces, I work on the background. Then I work on my character because ninety percent of the time, I'm drawing a person or figure.

JUST BE
Drawing journal, pencil, regular markers, colored pencils, Copic marker, opaque white marker

"I JUST WANT TO *make beautiful things,* EVEN IF NOBODY CARES."

Sherry Pollack

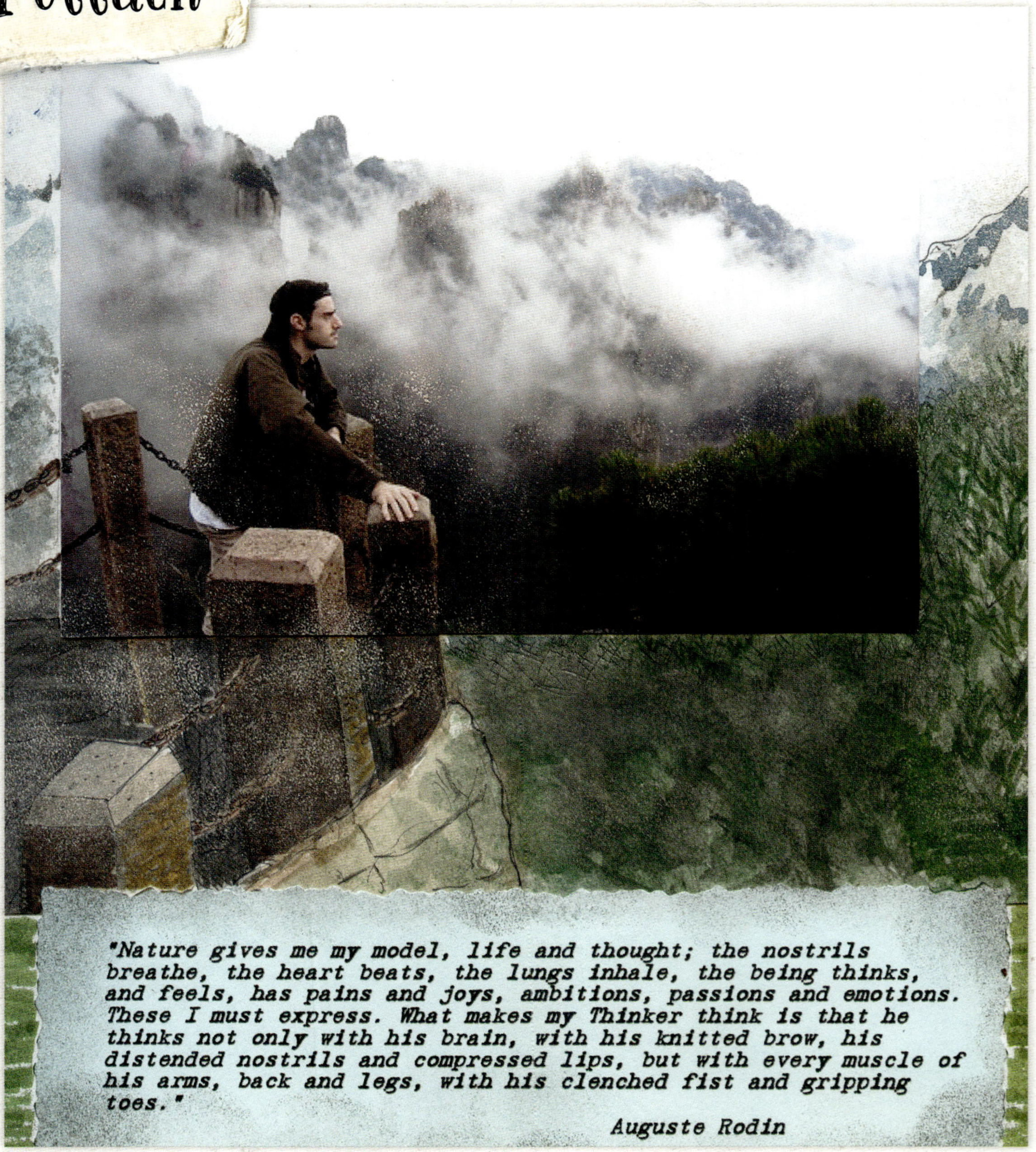

THE THINKER
Pen, watercolor, markers

What was your inspiration for this piece?

The Thinker was inspired by the photo of my son sitting pensively on a Chinese mountaintop. His pose immediately reminded me of Rodin's sculpture.

What interesting or unique techniques did you apply to this artwork?

With pen, watercolor and markers, I extended the photo onto the surrounding page and added the very fitting Rodin quote.

When and why did you start art journaling?

I discovered art journaling after retiring several years ago, through a local Artful Journaling class that I've been taking ever since. Art journaling has become integrated into my life, leading me happily down other artistic paths such as digital art, mixed media, drawing, lettering and book art.

What tips would you give to fellow art journaling artists?

As a child, you didn't care whether your artistic creations were good. You simply enjoyed the process. Art journaling can help you reconnect with that creative spirit.

Patricia E. Van West

What was your inspiration for this piece?

I was inspired by a windswept day at the ocean.

What interesting or unique techniques did you apply to this artwork?

I covered a wash of watercolor with sea foam from the beach. The texture in the painting is the dried foam.

How did you come up with the title?

I was swept away by the beauty of the day.

When and why did you start art journaling?

I started painting and art journaling in 2008 because I wanted a visual way to express myself. Art journaling allowed me to use pieces of paintings that didn't work as a whole. *Swept Away* is part of a larger painting; I turned the rest into one-of-a-kind bookmarks.

Do you have an art journaling process?

I alter books from garage sales and turn them into my art journals. *Swept Away* is in a book titled *Fantasies.*

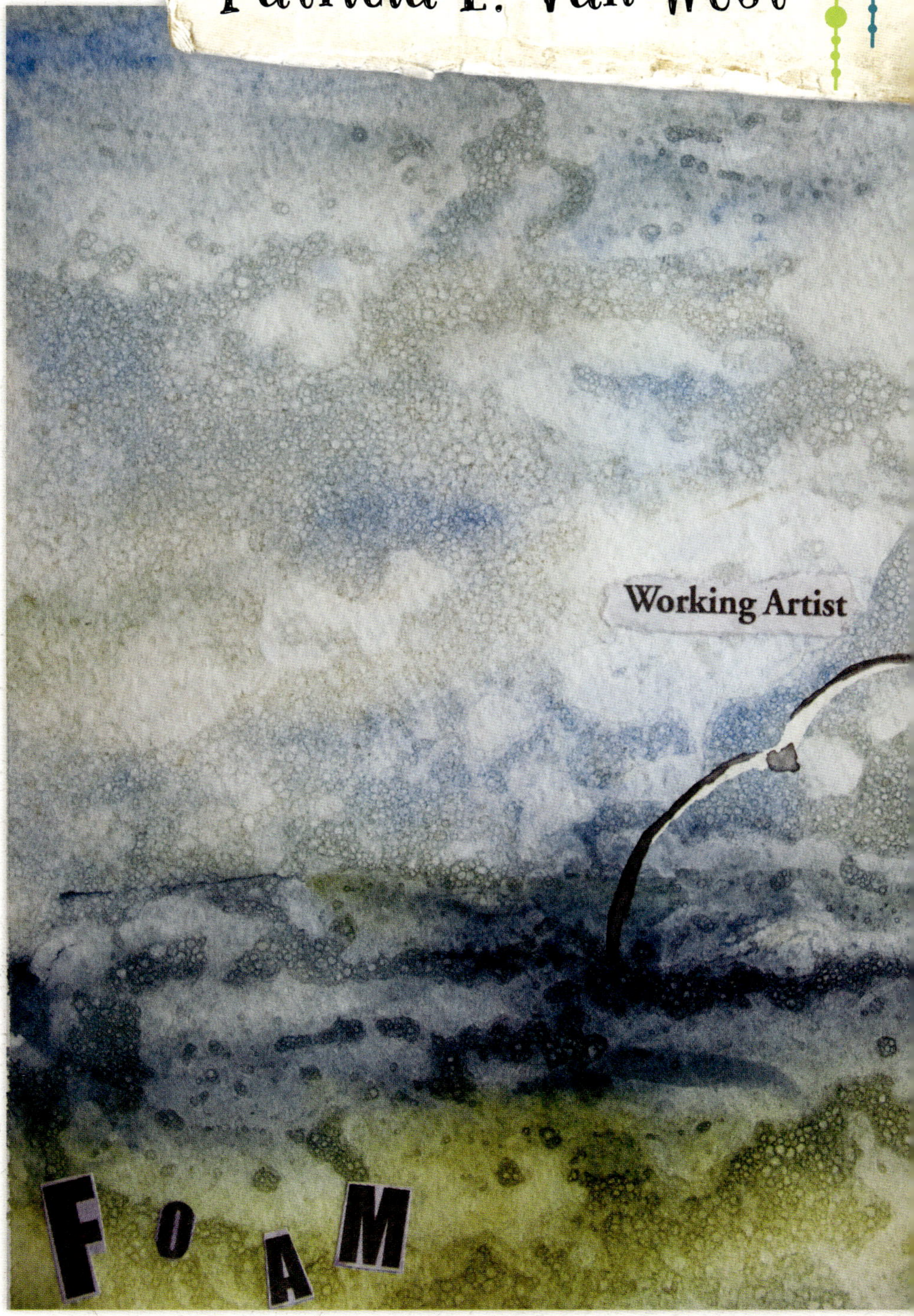

SWEPT AWAY
Watercolors, sea foam, magazine text

> "LOCK YOUR LOGICAL/PRACTICAL/ CRITICAL SELF IN THE CLOSET AND *let your creative/playful/ imaginative self out."*

Joanna Grant

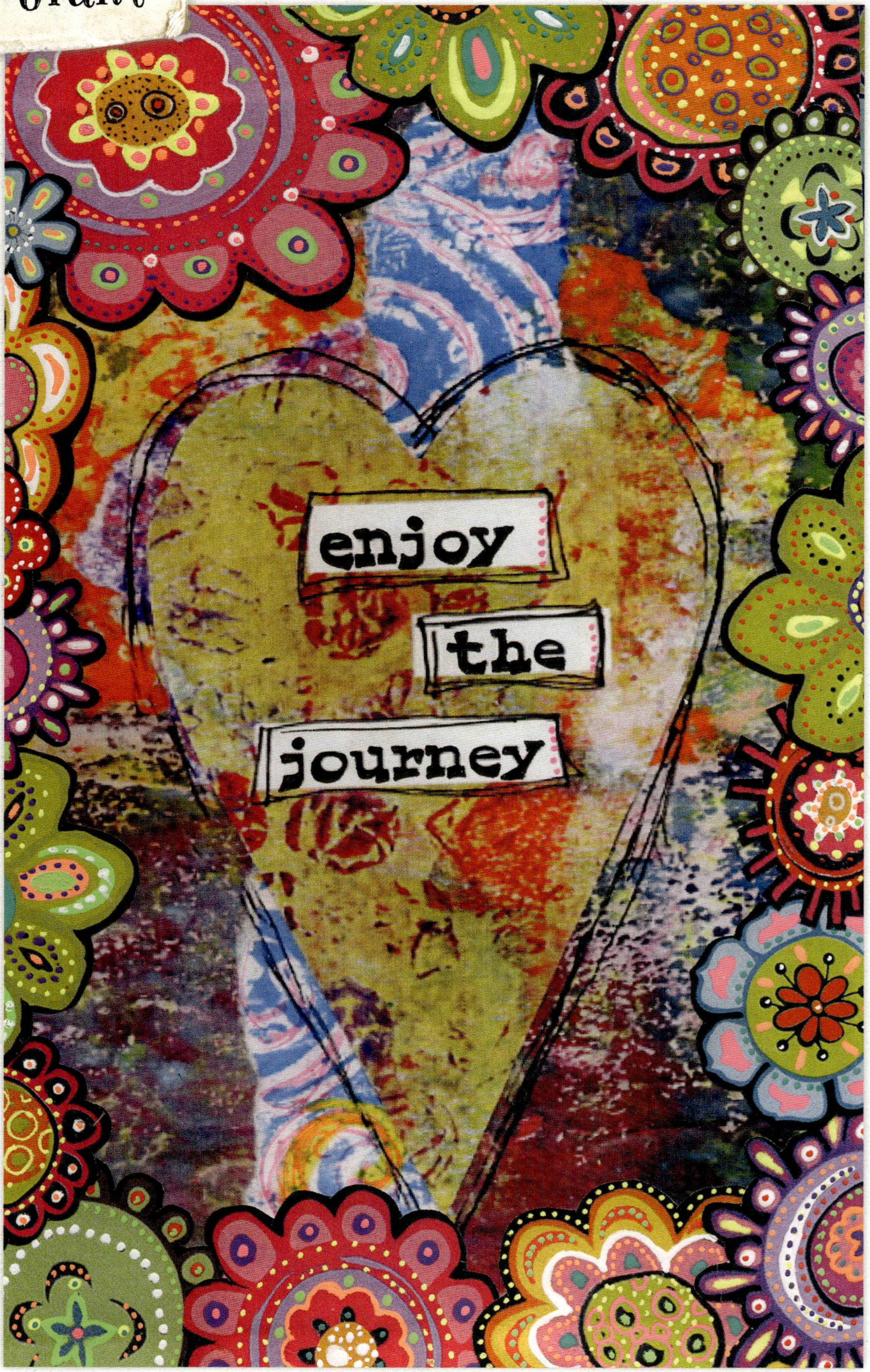

ENJOY THE JOURNEY
Gelatin prints, collaged pages, gel pens, markers

What was your inspiration for *Two Hands*?

As with most of my art, whether mixed-media, collage or art journals, I am often inspired to start a piece in order to use up recycled materials or scraps I end up with after making other art.

What interesting or unique techniques did you apply to this artwork?

This page has a background of monoprints from my gelatin printmaking, which were enhanced with more acrylic paint and a bit of stenciling. The hands were gelatin prints that I really disliked, so I glued some netting that had metallic flowers screen printed on it (recycled material) over the hands. The quote was printed on copy paper, cut out and distressed with inks and paint before being glued on the page.

Do you have an art journaling process?

I don't use a regular process for art journaling, other than to incorporate as many recycled or found elements as I can. When I'm art journaling, I just start working and see where things go.

What tips would you give to fellow art journaling artists?

My advice to new art journalers is to not waste time comparing what you are doing to others' works. You are on your own journey, and it is just as important and just as good as anyone else's.

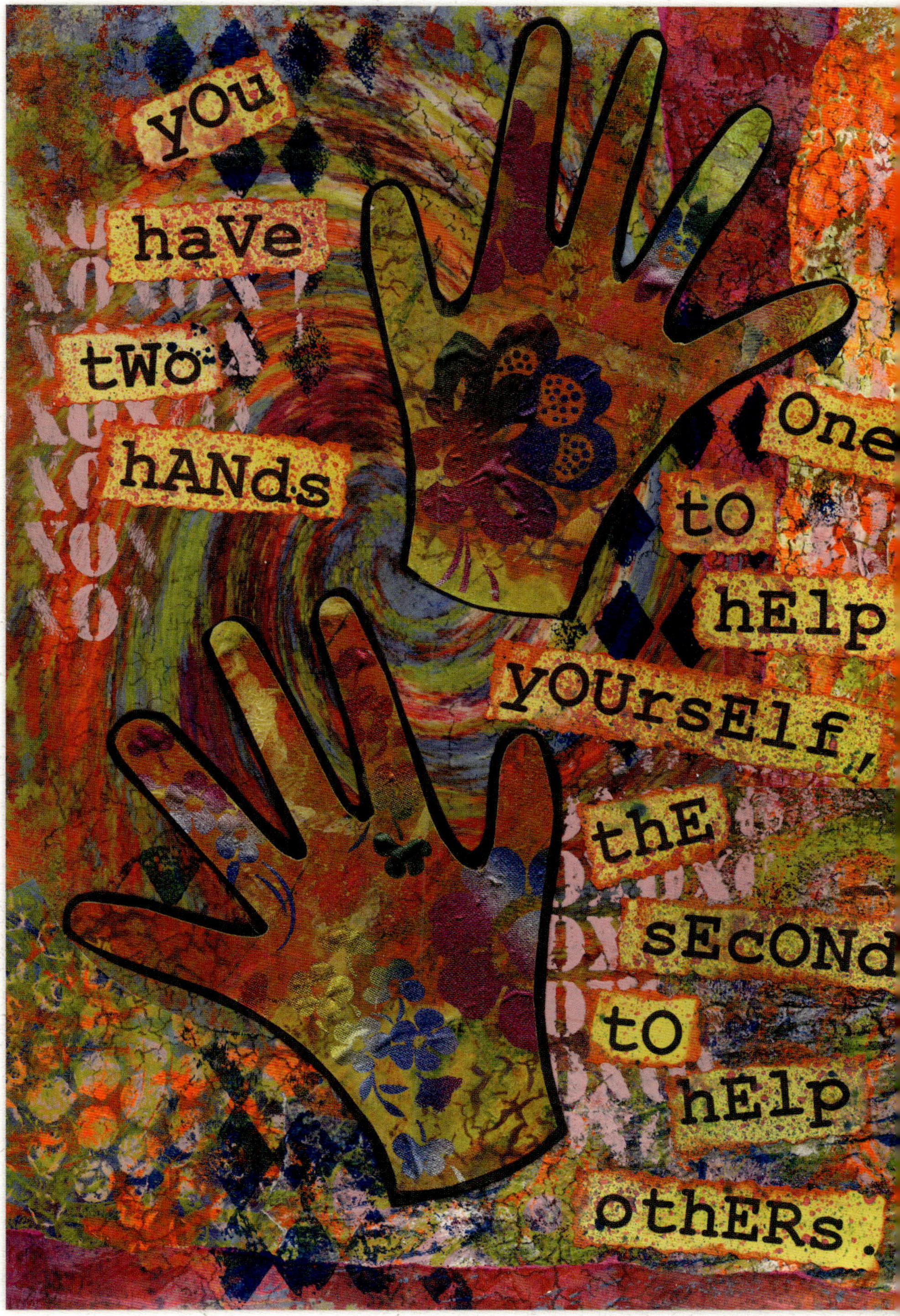

TWO HANDS
Monoprints, acrylic paint, stencils, gelatin prints, metallic flowers, copy paper, inks, adhesive

"*Always find time for your art,* EVEN IF IT IS JUST A FEW MINUTES STOLEN FROM YOUR BUSY DAY."

Julia Antica Dean

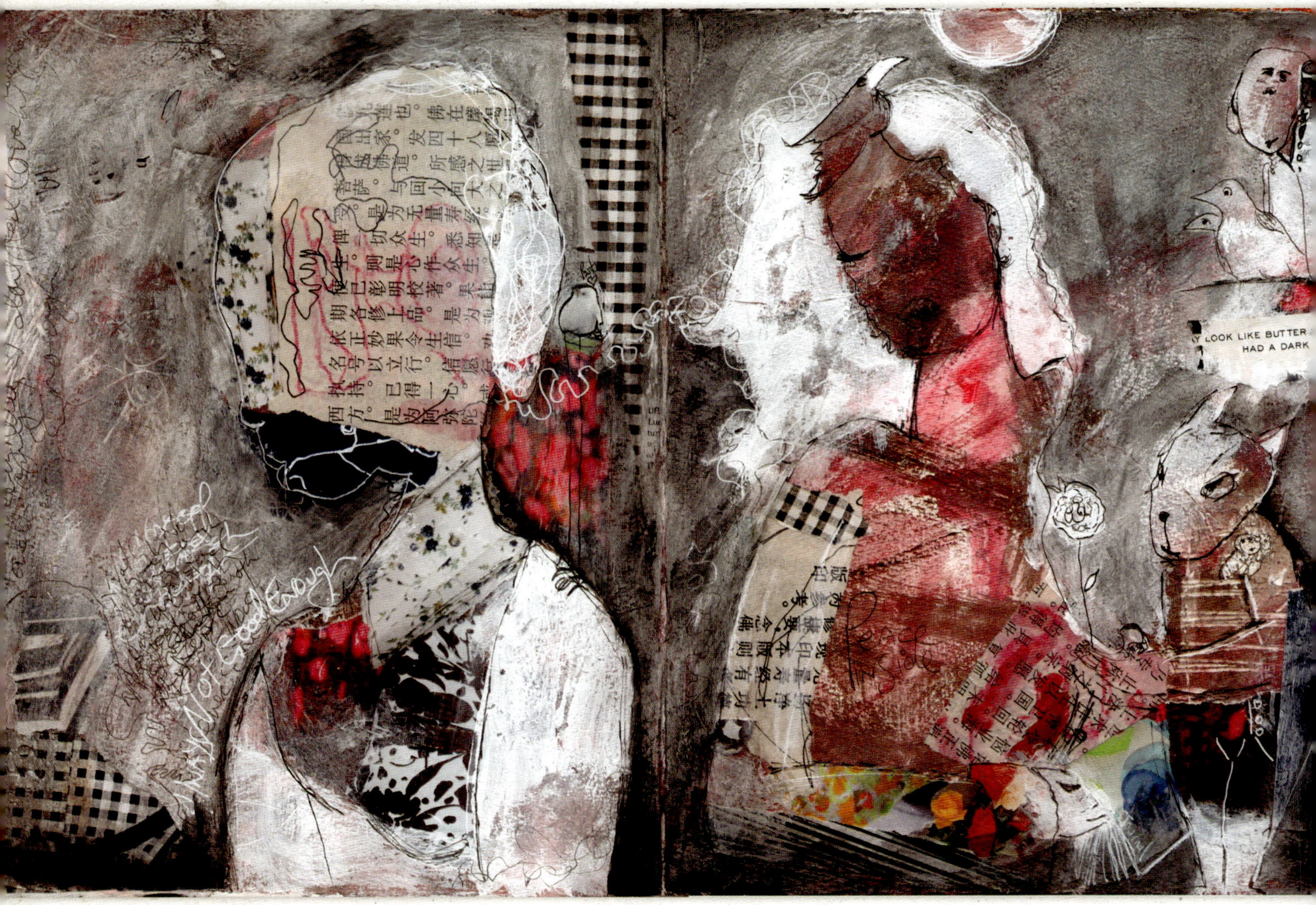

GREY DAYS
Gingham-patterned paper, collaged pieces, assorted pens, assorted paints

What was your inspiration for this piece?

I am always inspired by the weather of the day, but this piece came after a disagreement with a friend. I felt bad about not being my most loving self with her.

Do you have an art journaling process?

I start my journaling in the morning. After a cup of tea, I sit and meditate and look out into my garden. I watch the trees, look at the sky and, if it's a wintery day, I feel the cool air at the window.

Are there any mixed-media artists who inspire you?

I'm inspired by Flora Bowley, Orly Avineri, Monet, Bill Scott, Mel McCuddin and Amadea Bailey.

What interesting or unique techniques did you apply to this artwork?

I always add my little white sparrow, because it is my art sign or symbol. My grandson, in a dream, said the name "Gallivant," and when I looked it up, I found that it described a little white sparrow which in turn is described as someone who is detailed, likes small objects, shy, introverted, etc.—it just fit the way I like to do my art so perfectly!

Karen Bearse

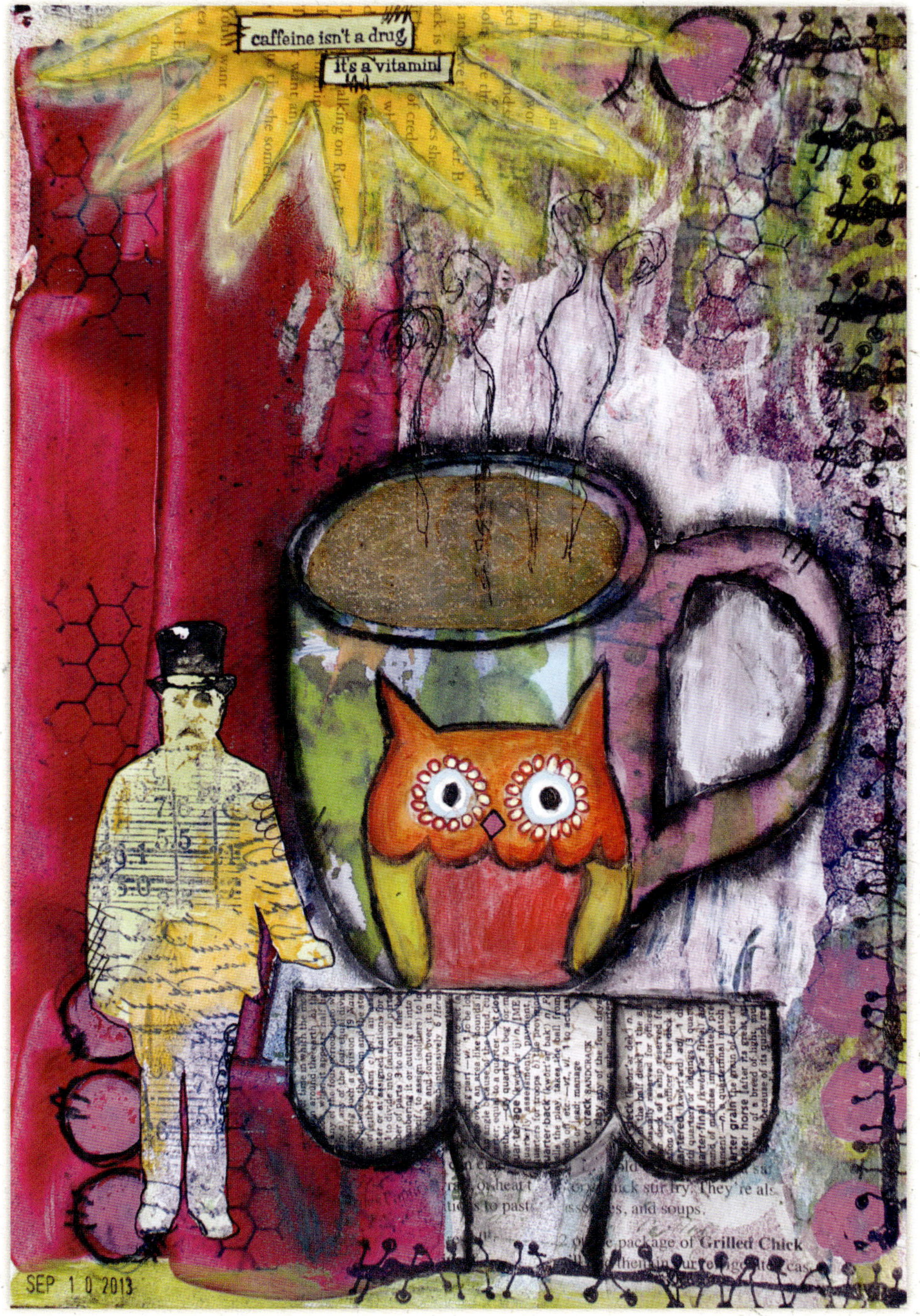

What was your inspiration for this piece?

The inspiration for my page was a challenge to draw my new coffee cup.

When and why did you start art journaling?

Starting out as a scrapbooker, I loved all things inky and that gradually moved me into the world of art journaling.

Are there any mixed-media artists who inspire you?

I am inspired by artists like Donna Downey, Tim Holtz and many others.

Do you have an art journaling process?

My process in designing a page usually starts as a product-based idea. As a teacher, I like to take a product and find a new and unique way to use it. Practicing in an art journal is the perfect way to discover new techniques.

What tips would you give to fellow art journaling artists?

Anyone can make beautiful art journal pages; it just takes practice, practice and patience.

COFFEE, PLEASE JEEVES
Acrylic paints, distress stains, markers, Moleskine sketchbook

“THE BEST INTENTIONS ARE GREAT, BUT YOU HAVE TO ADD HARD WORK TO *make your dreams come true.*”

Stephanie Trice

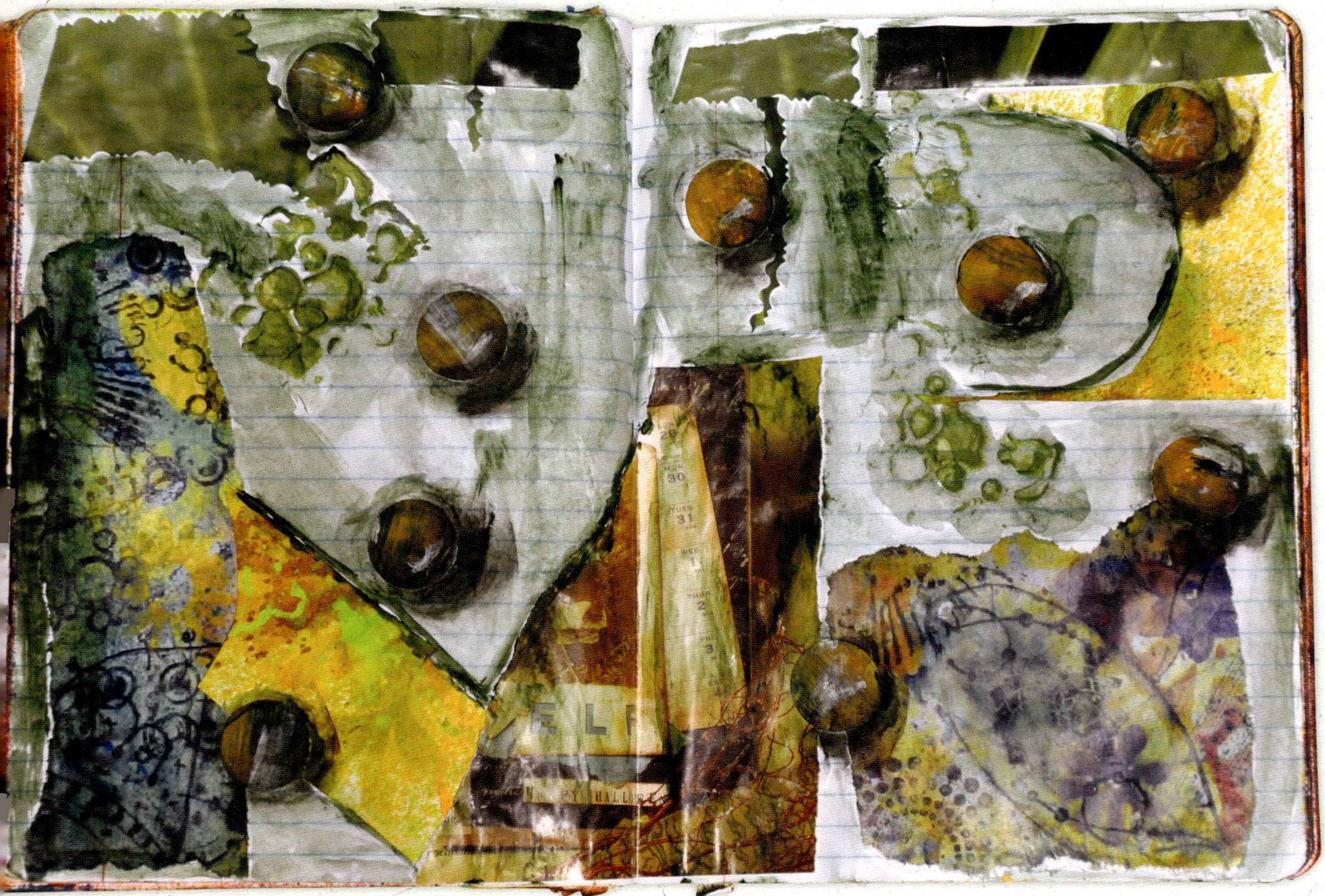

STUDY IN GREEN
Acrylic paint, paper, molding paste

What was your inspiration for this piece?

My inspiration for this piece was experimenting to get some dimension on circles, like I had seen in works by Roben-Marie Smith and others.

What interesting or unique techniques did you apply to this artwork?

In this piece, I used copies of my other artwork for some of the papers and also some scraps I had laying around. I also liked using the fun scissors to get shaped edges on some of the magazine paper I used.

Do you have an art journaling process?

I work a lot on 5" × 7" (13cm × 18cm) paper because I don't think an art journal has to be bound. Plus, I enjoy trying new things. I think you have to learn to be okay with the fact that not everything is going to be great art. Some of it is just really bad, but that does not mean you don't enjoy the process or learn something from it.

"YOUR JOURNAL, *your rules.*"

Carol Marion

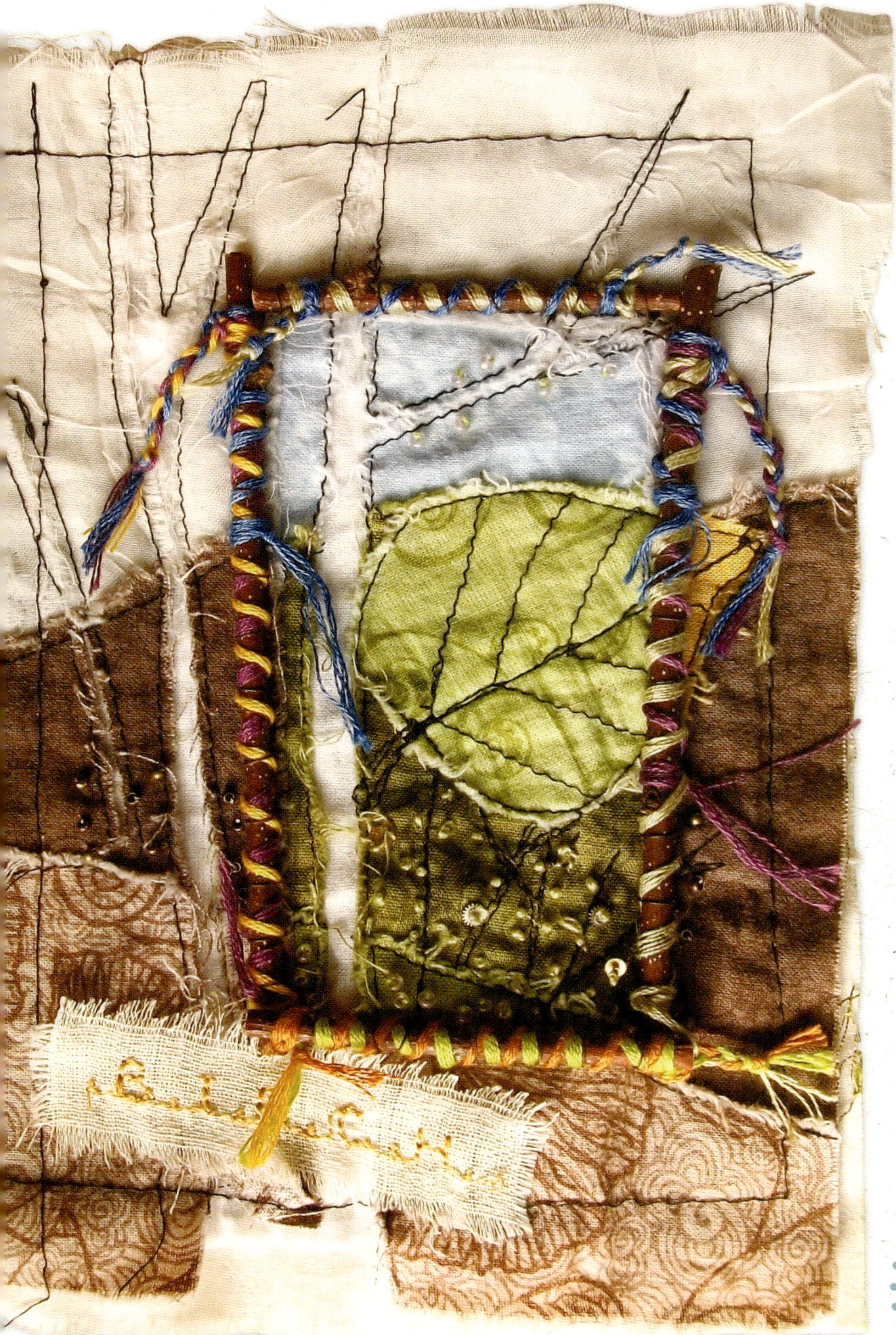

SPRING WINDOW
Fabric, machine stitching, beads, birch twigs

What interesting or unique techniques did you apply to this artwork?

I used a modified reverse applique technique. I layered up fabrics, covered with a muslin top layer, machine stitched the pattern and cut to reveal the sandwiched fabrics. The window is framed with birch twigs wrapped in embroidery floss. I added some scattered beads, and the edges were left raw at the request of my partner.

Do you have an art journaling process?

I like having an already partially painted area to start the process. Paint-splattered protective paper, gel prints, pages where I've cleaned my brushes, some color and pattern to start the process. I open a random page and start drawing. I like pastels, colored pencils, fine line markers and embellishments of embroidery floss, paper beads and fabric.

What tips would you give to fellow art journaling artists?

Keep journals everywhere—in your car, your bag, by your chair or bed—anywhere you get inspired. And don't judge; just get something on paper. This is your journal, your life—have fun with it.

> "NOTHING IS TOO SMALL, TOO BIG, OR TOO ORDINARY TO JOURNAL ABOUT. *Just get it on paper!*

Julia Crucil

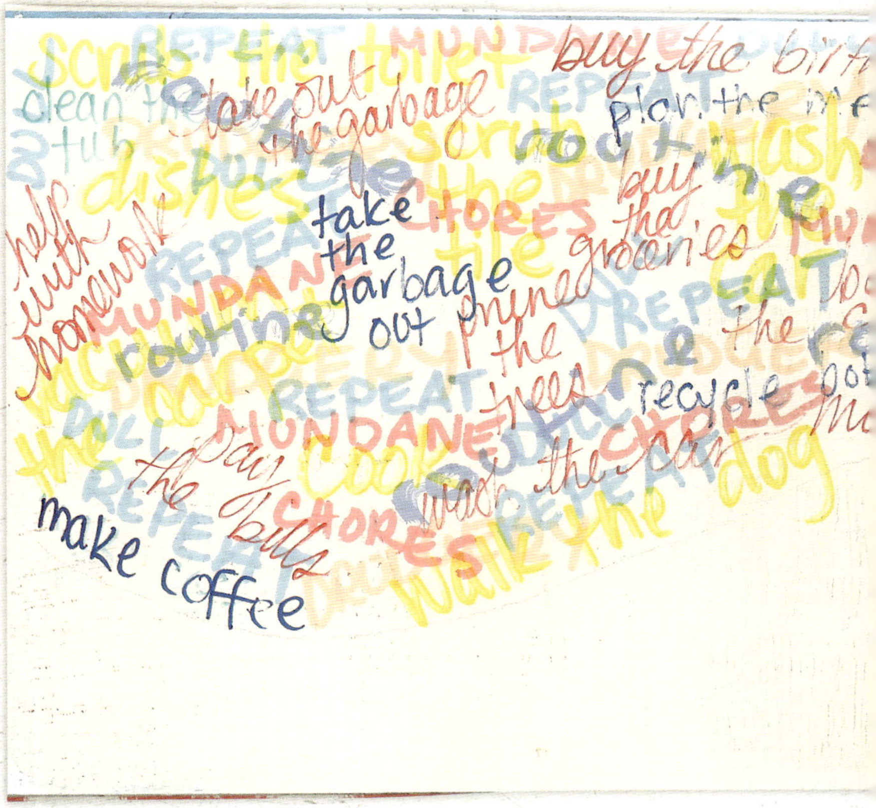

THE HOUSEWIFE
Acrylic paints, craft paints, assorted papers, assorted ephemera, calendar, adhesive

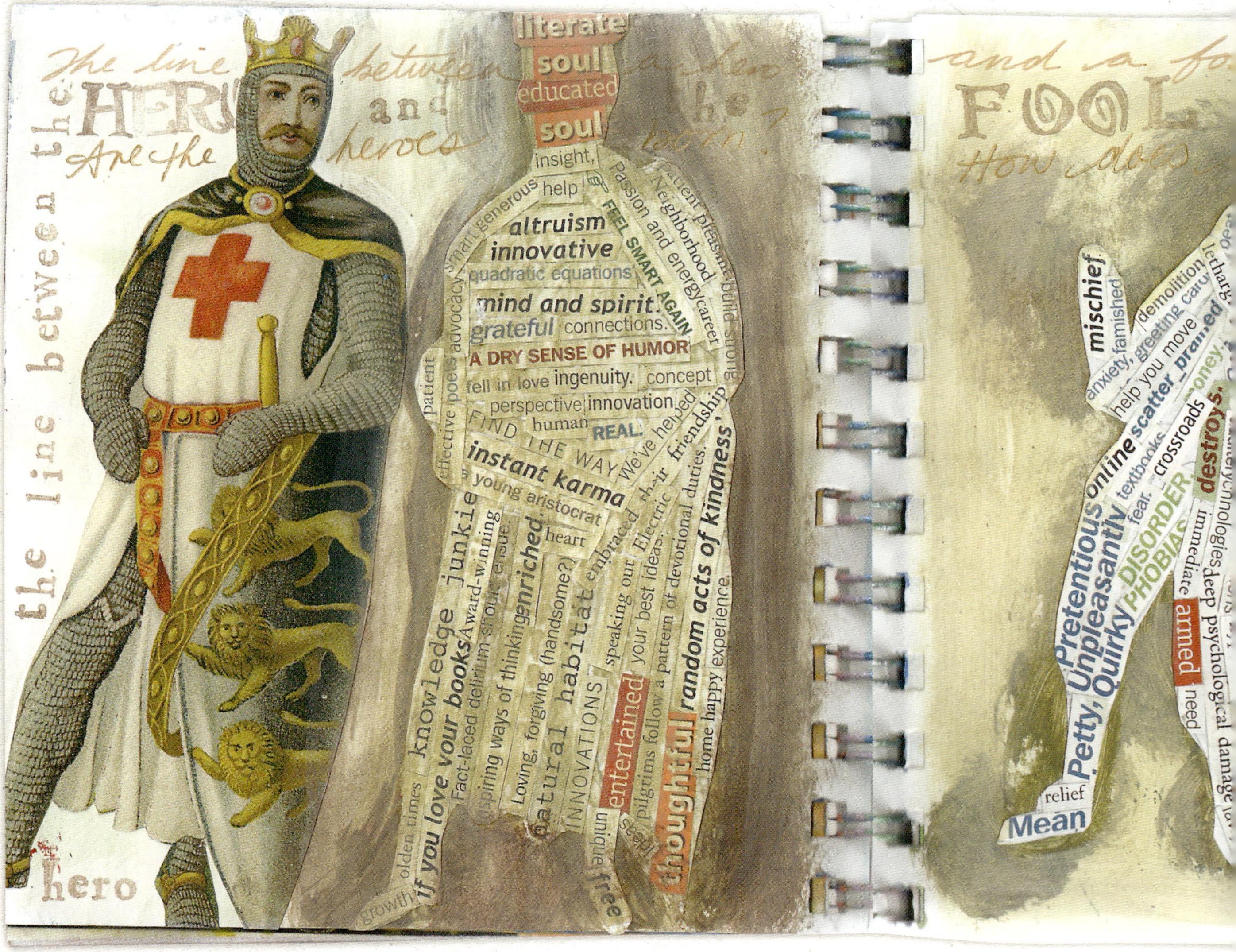

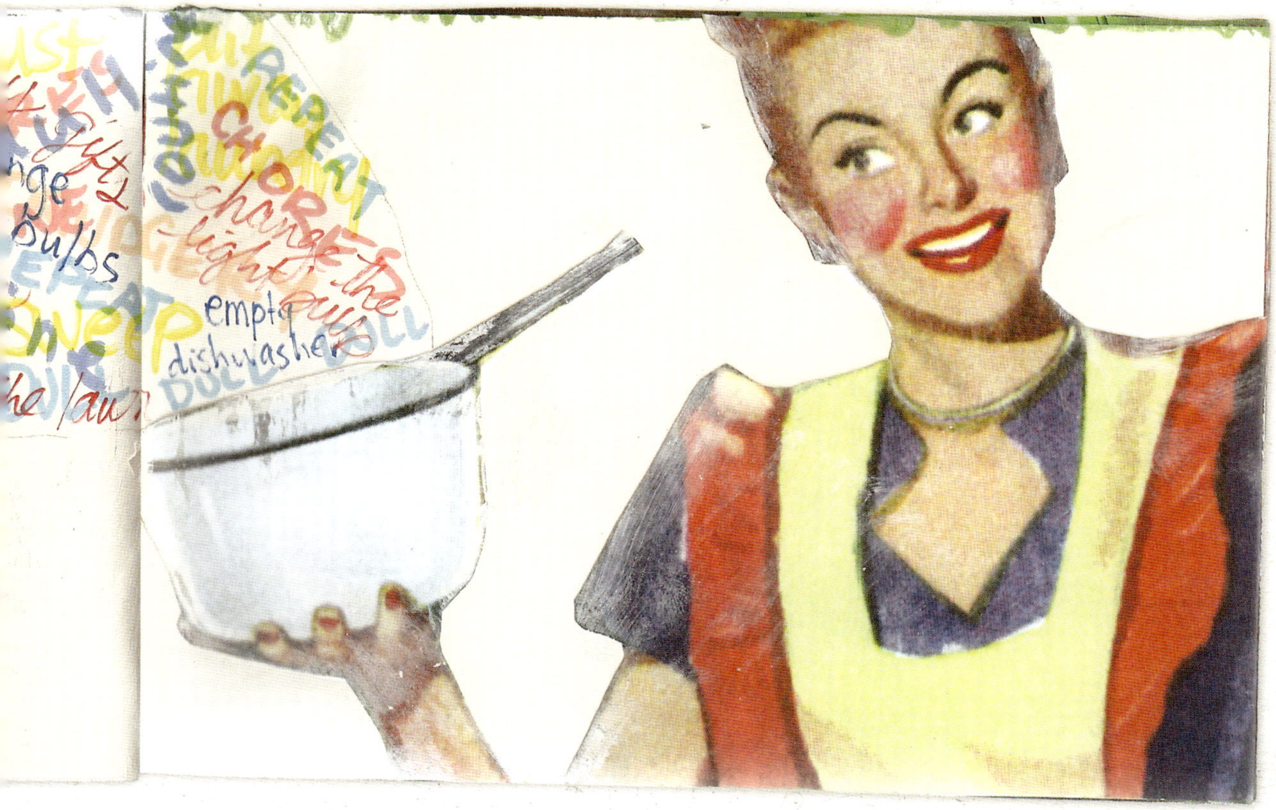

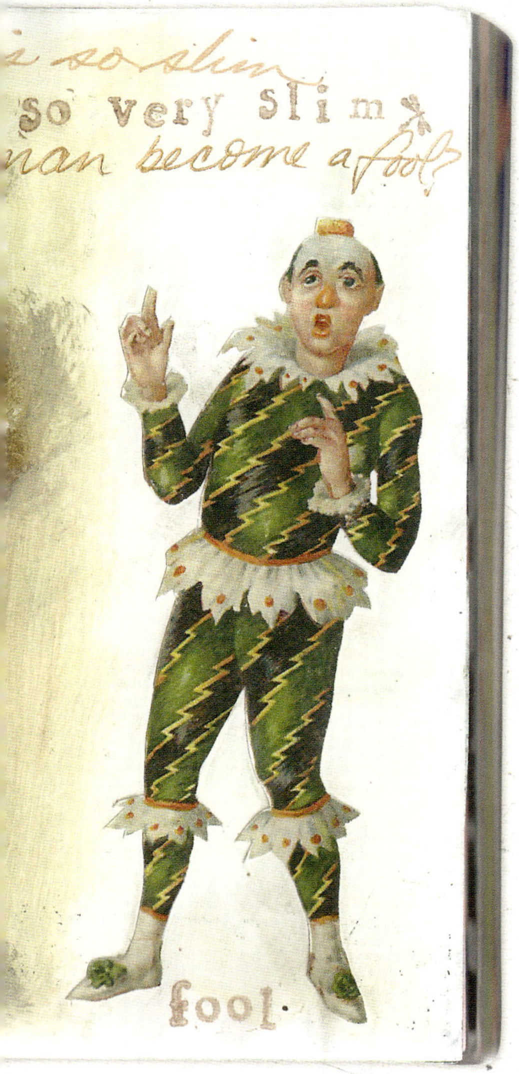

Do you have an art journaling process?

The process I use for art journals is fairly consistent. I usually do a page at the end of a workday in order to empty my brain of all the little bits banging around in there. I paint the background in a light wash of acrylic or craft paint. Then I dig through my collection of found papers, catalogs, dictionaries, textbooks, magazines and ephemera looking for the pieces that fit a theme or idea that is niggling at me.

When and why did you start art journaling?

I use my art journals as part of a creative process to work out ideas and play with imagery or text.

What was your inspiration for *The Hero and the Fool*?

My stepson was about thirteen years old when he was anguished with his first crush. It occurred to me that young boys growing up are caught in a complicated place between romantic notions of chivalry and mass-media messaging that is anything but slow and kind. Hence the text, "The line between a hero and a fool is so slim."

I made this collage from images in an old textbook, acrylic paint, rubber stamps and text added with gel pens. Snippets of magazines form the shadow figures. I later used this imagery in a larger screenprint entitled *Thirteen,* which examines notions of masculinity and the roles boys grow into.

THE HERO AND THE FOOL
Old textbook, acrylic paint, rubber stamps, gel pens

Katherine Jeanne Wood

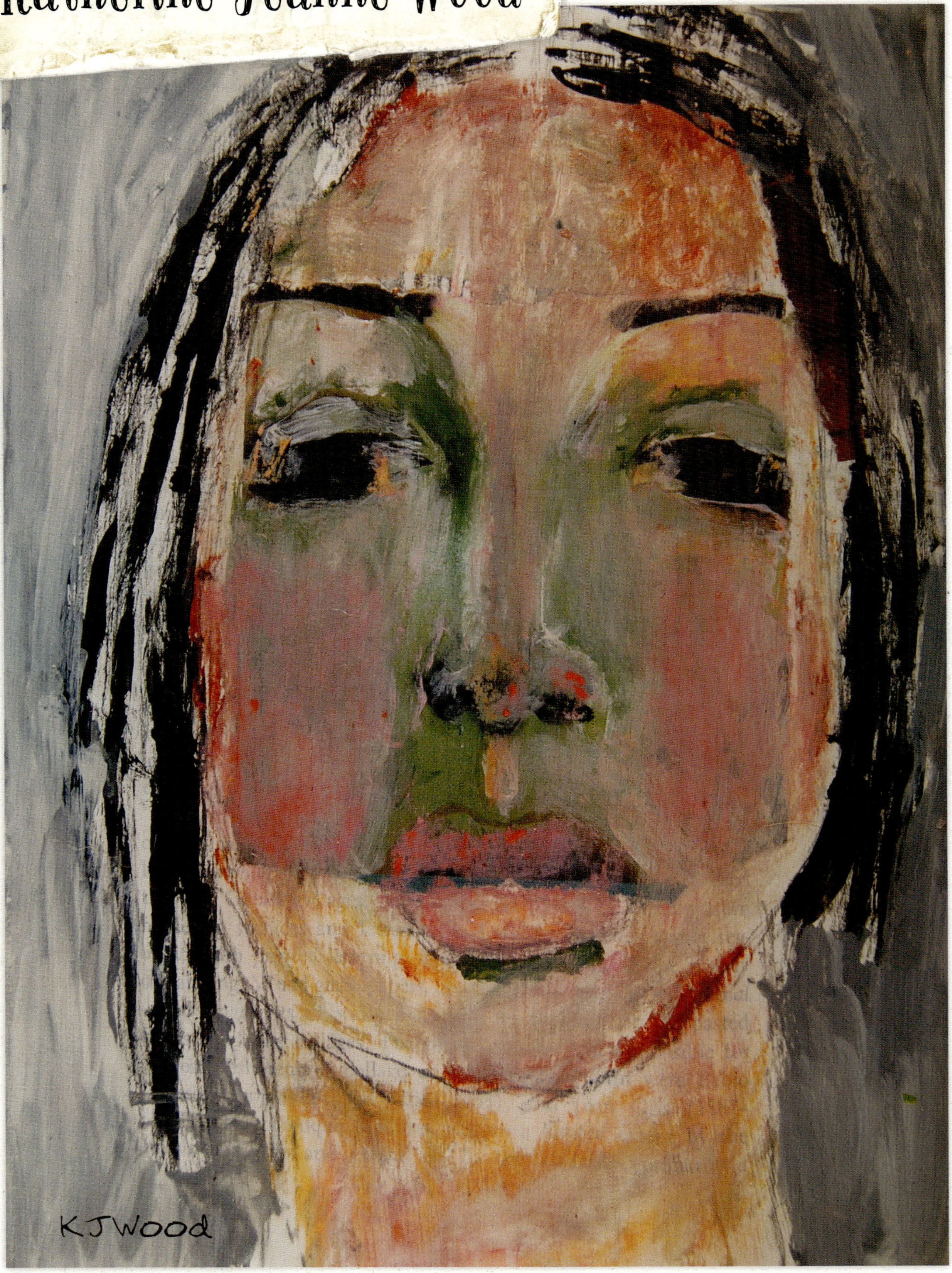

SCENT OF A LADY
Magazine cutout, Stabilo pencil, acrylic paint, pastels, chalk

What was your inspiration for *Scent of a Lady*?

My inspiration for this piece came from a song I was listening to at the time titled *Scent of a Lady* by Scomber.

What interesting or unique techniques did you apply to this artwork?

This page started with a magazine cutout of eyes, a nose and half a mouth. I glued it down on my page with gel medium and then got to work painting. I drew in the mouth, forehead and hair with a Stabilo pencil.

Next, I added pastels. I was concentrating on her facial expression, as I usually do when I'm painting portraits. I mainly focus on painting emotions.

Are there any mixed-media artists who inspire you?

I'm inspired by Misty Mawn, Jane Spakowsky, Alisa Burke, Wanda Marie Miller, Bridgette Guerzon Mills, Orly Avineri, Sarah Ahearn Bellemare and Judy Wise.

Do you have an art journaling process?

Some of my pages start as backgrounds. I get some paint or collage paper down on the page, so I'm not staring at a blank page anymore and go from there. I work intuitively, so whatever happens happens in the moment. If I don't like the direction a page is taking, I grab some black paint and paint over the original work. Or I glue some collage paper on top and keep going.

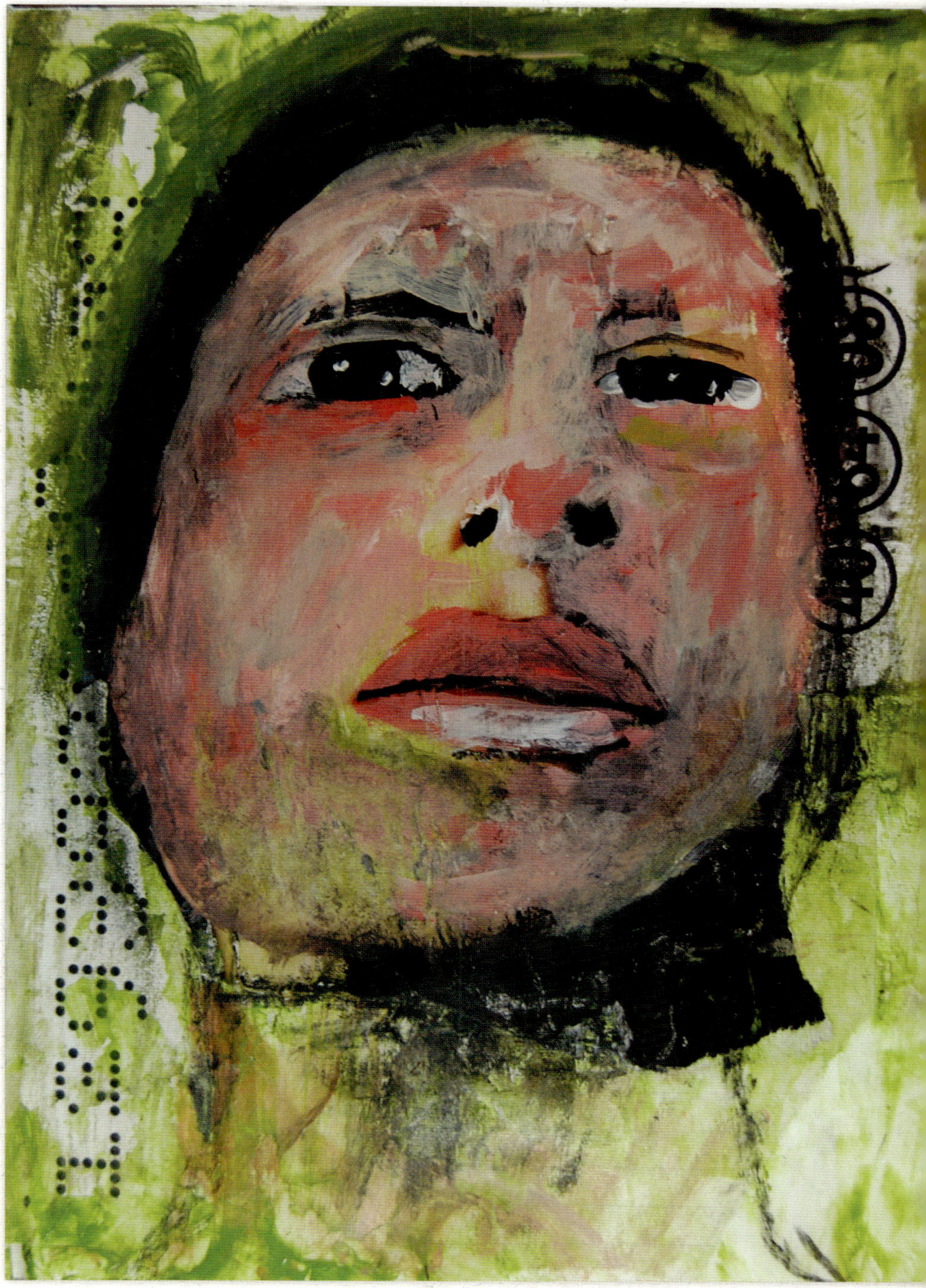

POWER IN NUMBERS
Magazine cutout, gel medium, collage papers, acrylic paint, pastels, chalk

Linda Sedgley

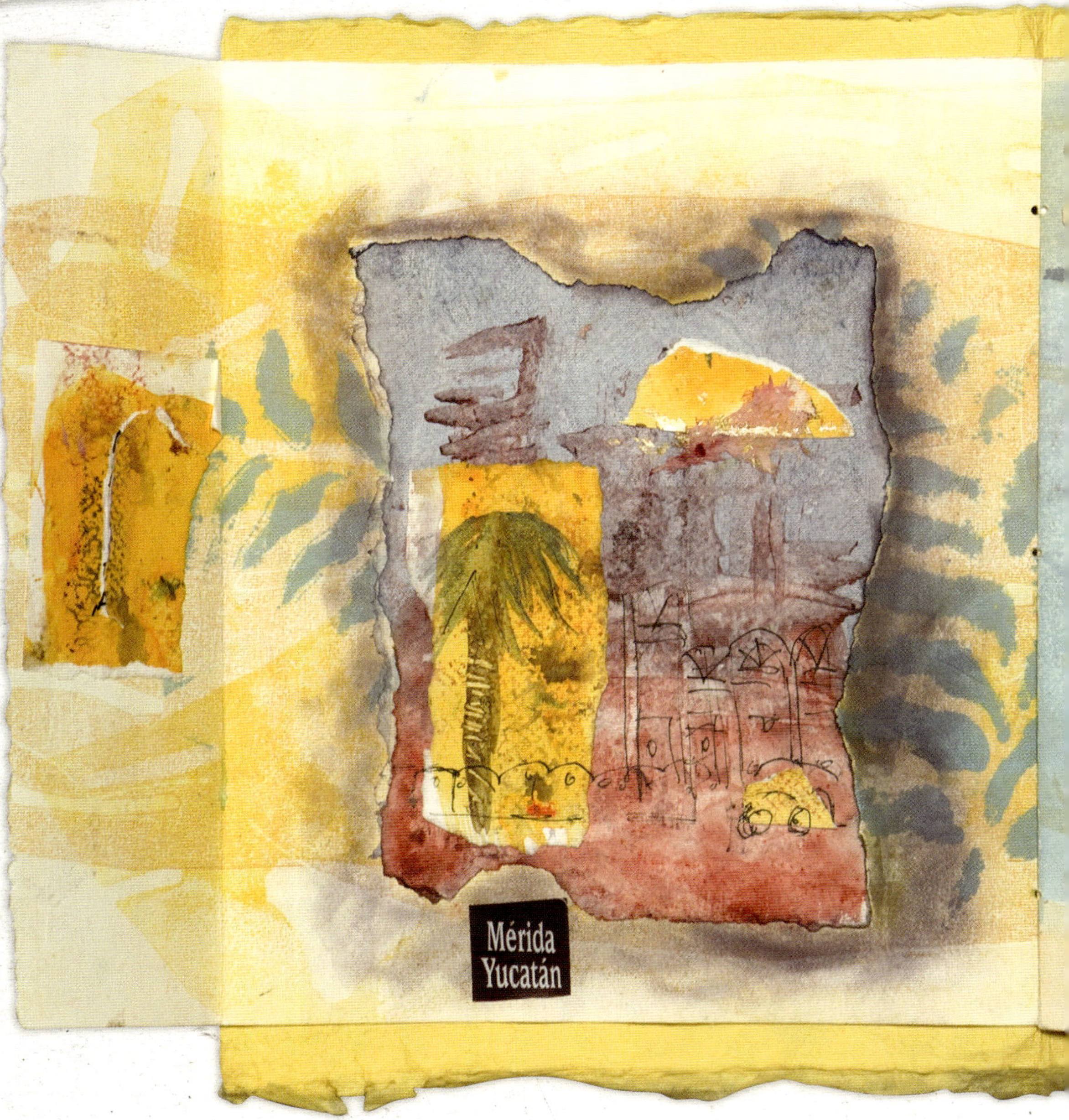

YUCATAN
Assorted papers, paints, Nori paste, brayer

What was your inspiration for this piece?

This is one page from my Mexican travel journal.

What materials did you use for this piece of art?

Using a printing press, pages are printed with stencils and background colors on 22" × 30" (56cm × 76cm) Stonehenge paper.

Are there any mixed-media artists who inspire you?

I assembled and bound the journal using Teesha Moore's YouTube video as a guide.

Do you have an art journaling process?

I sketch and paint on watercolor paper that I tear into small pieces and collage into the journal with Nori paste and a brayer. I add writing, collage and sketches. Finally, it is wrapped portfolio style in coordinating paper and ribbon.

What tips would you give to fellow art journaling artists?

I've been legally blind for ten years, yet I manage to find new ways of seeing every day and don't let my disability get in my way. Find your way of seeing.

Lisa L. Cyr

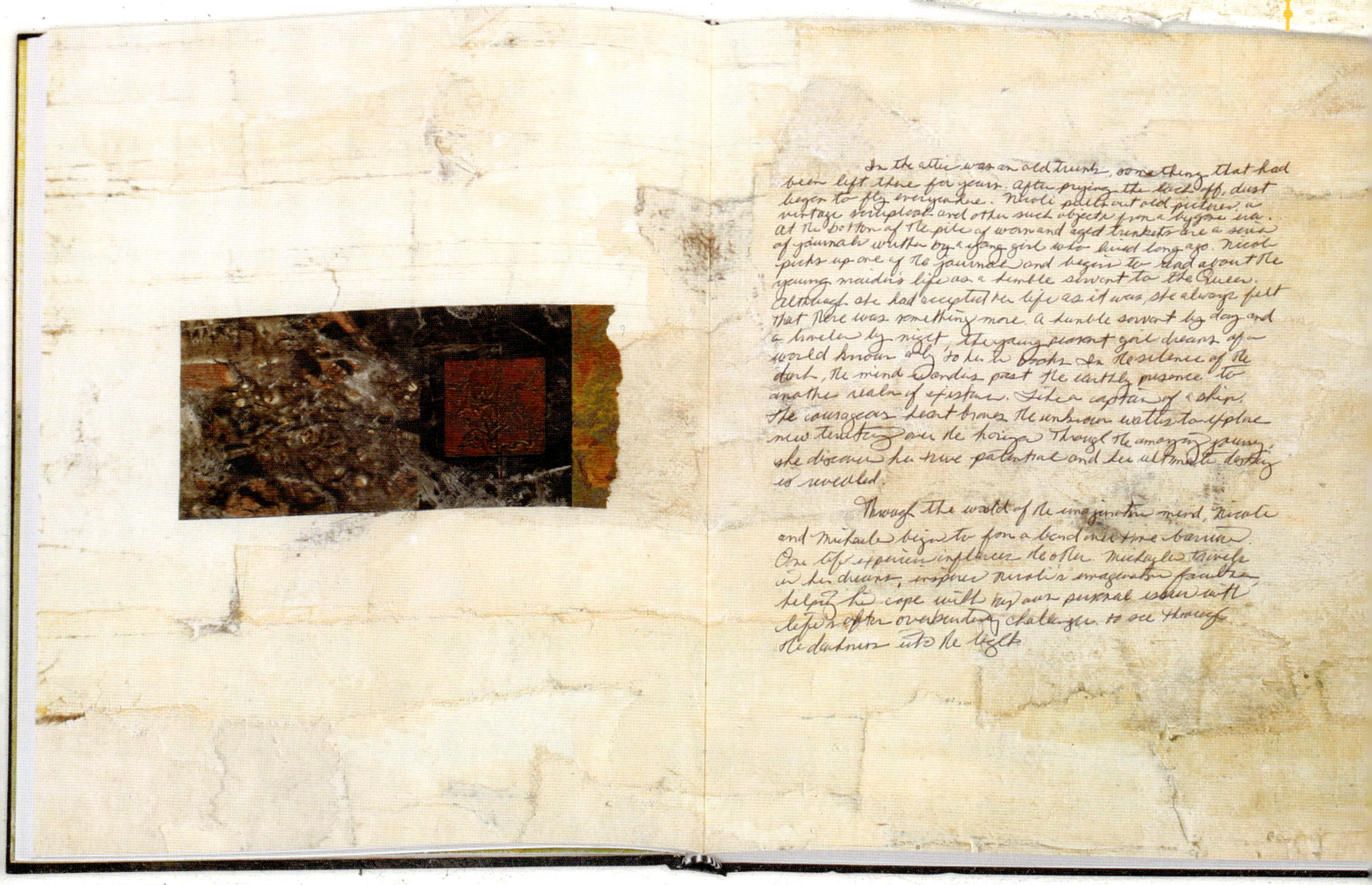

BETWEEN THE WORLDS
Acrylic, mixed-media materials, journal pages

How did you come up with your title?

My lyrical, multilayered composition reorganizes, overlaps and juxtaposes abstract elements to illuminate an underlying concept about a subconscious inner journey into worlds unknown. Disparate, visually dynamic and tactile elements come together to create meaningful relationships that impose the power of suggestion, transcending the image beyond the sum of its parts.

A square portal, door or gateway appears in a transformative, free-flowing spatial continuum, symbolic of unearthly travel. The viewer is given a hint as to the destination of the quest by the abstract scene to the right of the composition.

What interesting or unique techniques did you apply to this artwork?

The journal spread employs several mixed-media techniques, including collage of aged newsprint papers, ink dissolving and blotting techniques, debossing into gel medium, drybrushing and the painting of handmade paper.

"OBSERVE, CONTEMPLATE, IMAGINE, THEN SEE ANEW—*to interpret is to transform.*"

Liubov Kadyrova

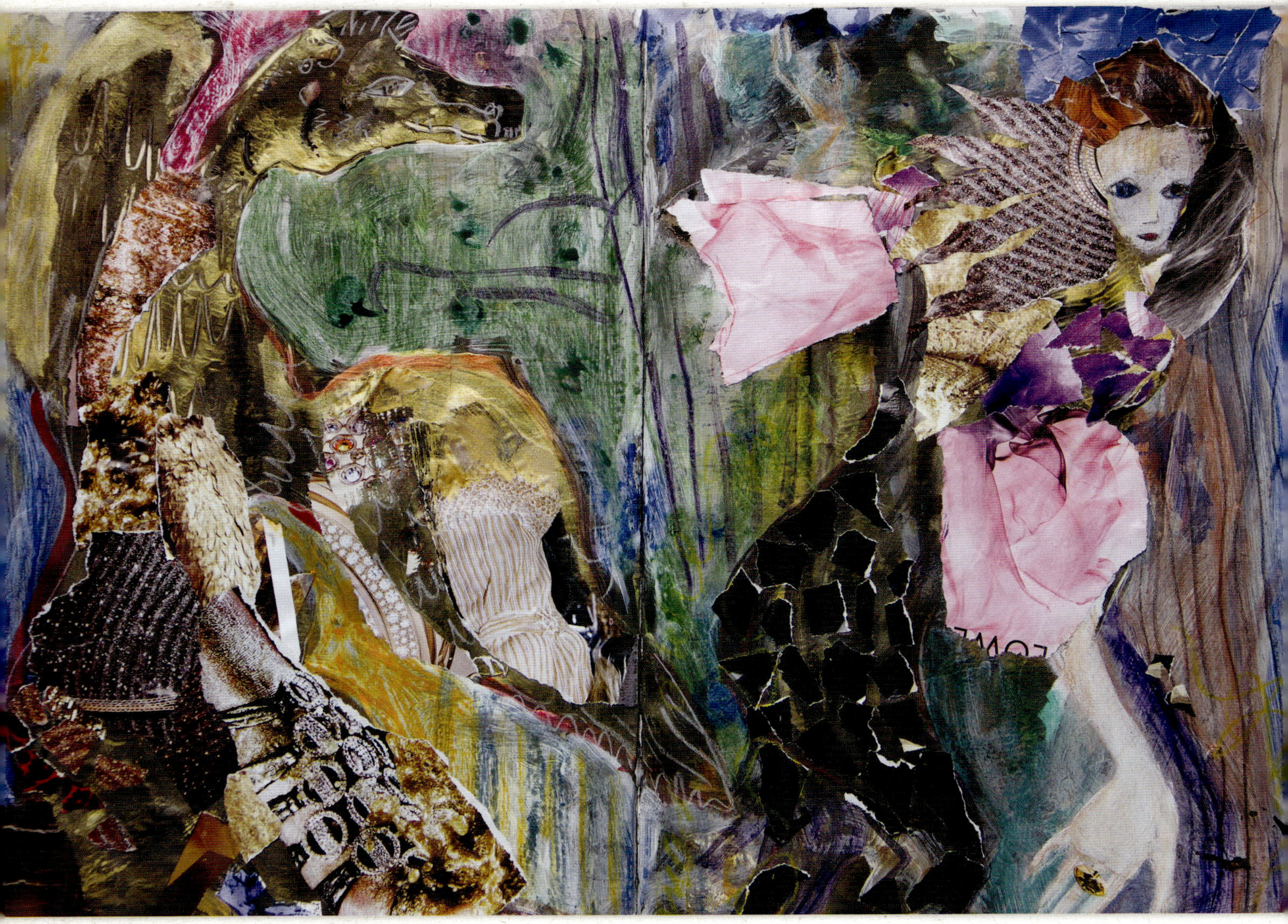

THE PRINCESS AND DRAGON
Fashion magazines, paint, glue, white gesso, color pencils, A3 notebook

What was your inspiration for this piece?

Old fairy tales.

What interesting or unique techniques did you apply to this artwork?

I used paper cuttings like a paintbrush, describing form and volume, blocking negative and positive areas.

How did you come up with your title?

I love fashion magazines. This particular season had a lot of silver and gold shiny, sparkly dresses, which looked like a knight's mail or dragon scales.

Do you ever give yourself journal prompts?

I would like to say that my favorite prompt is *what if?*

When and why did you start art journaling?

I started in 2002.

What tips would you give to fellow art journaling artists?

Enjoy doing it!

Mandy van Goeije

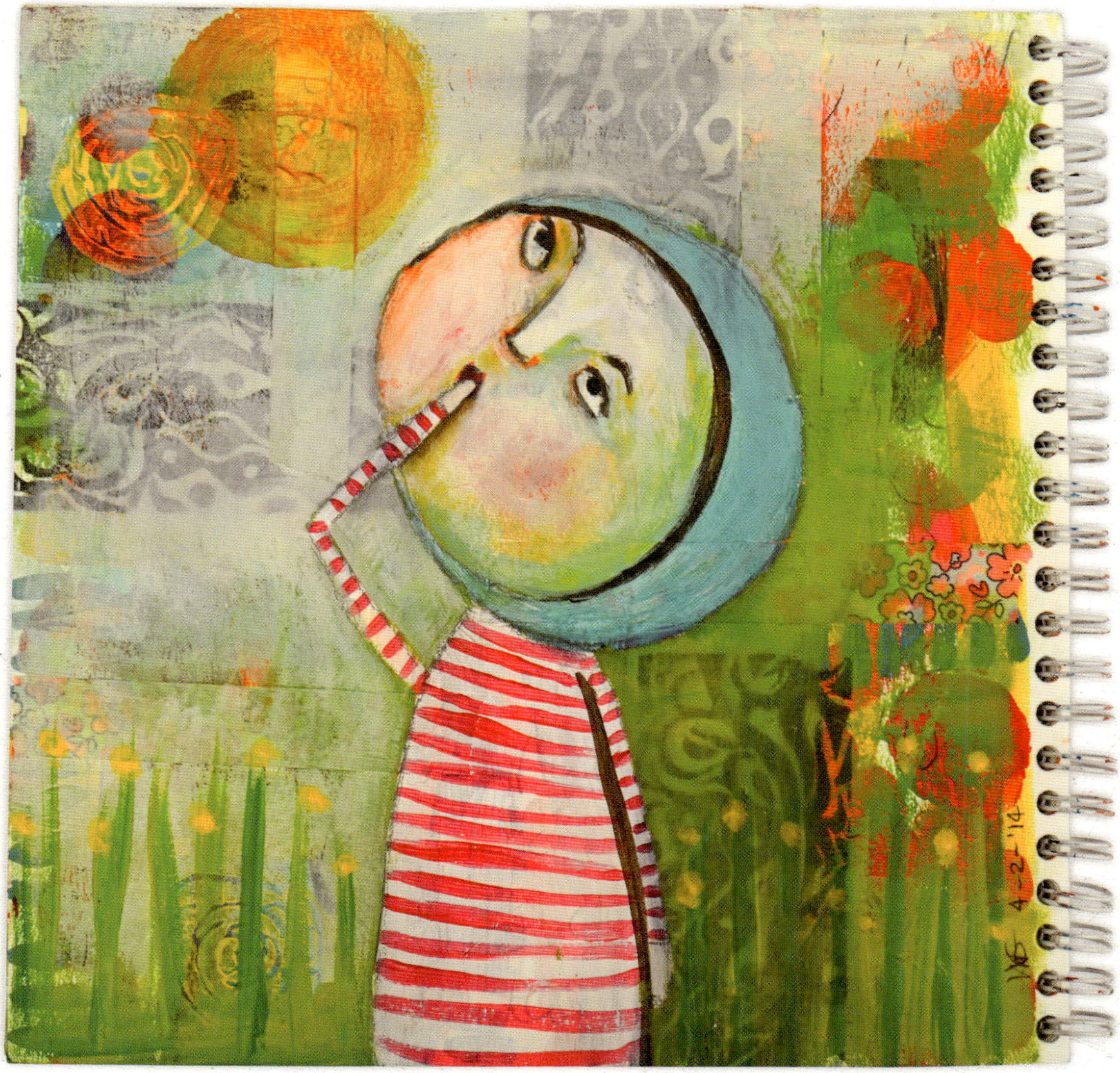

DISCOVERY
Ballpoint pen, hand-carved stamps, hand carved stencils, washi tape, gel medium and paper scraps for collage, HB pencil, Golden fluid acrylics, Amsterdam acrylics, cotton cloth, make-up sponge, Winsor & Newton gesso, Caran d'Ache Neocolor II crayons, Winsor & Newton Designers gouache

What was your inspiration for this piece?

An important discovery I made about my life inspired me to make a page about a discovery as bright as the sun. I found inspiration for the technique and style in a mixture of the many mixed-media artists I follow.

What interesting or unique techniques did you apply to this artwork?

For this page, I used quite a few hand-carved stamps and homemade stencils. I love the rose stamp I made. Right beside the sun, I stamped it with yellow paint and at the bottom left of the page, I stamped it into wet paint, lifting some of it so it shows more delicately.

Are there any mixed-media artists who inspire you?

My journal pages are sometimes heavily inspired by new artists who I discover and study such as: Kaatje Vermeire, Elke Trittel, Ofra Amit, Karen O'Brien, Mitsi B., Melissa Sauk, Misty Mawn, Nathalie Nayer, Bebe Butler and Erin Faith Allen.

What tips would you give to fellow art journaling artists?

Ignore your inner critic, hard though that can be.

"*Illustrate* YOUR LIFE!"

Kristin Peterson

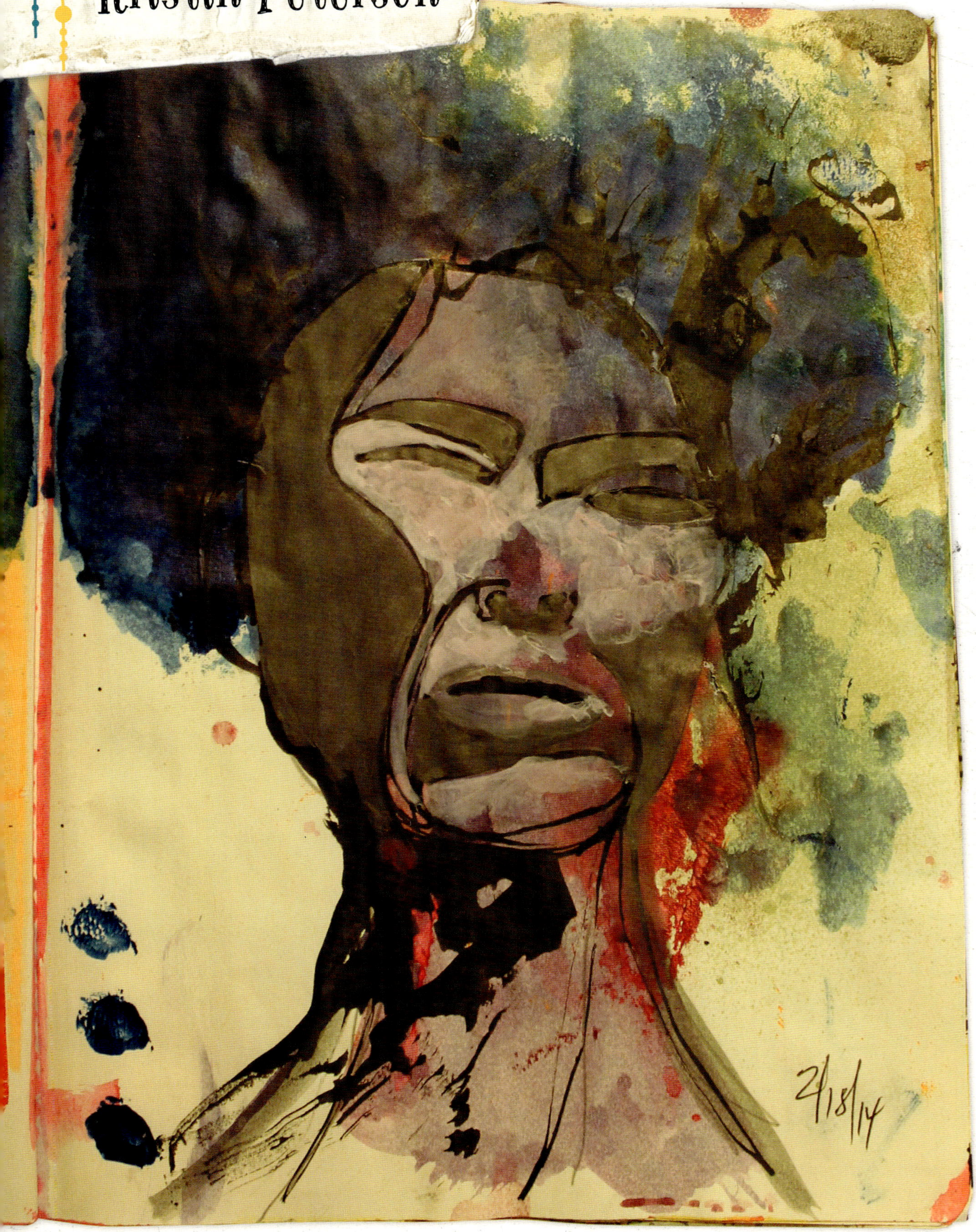

FACE #18
Golden High Flow acrylics, black and white gesso, India ink

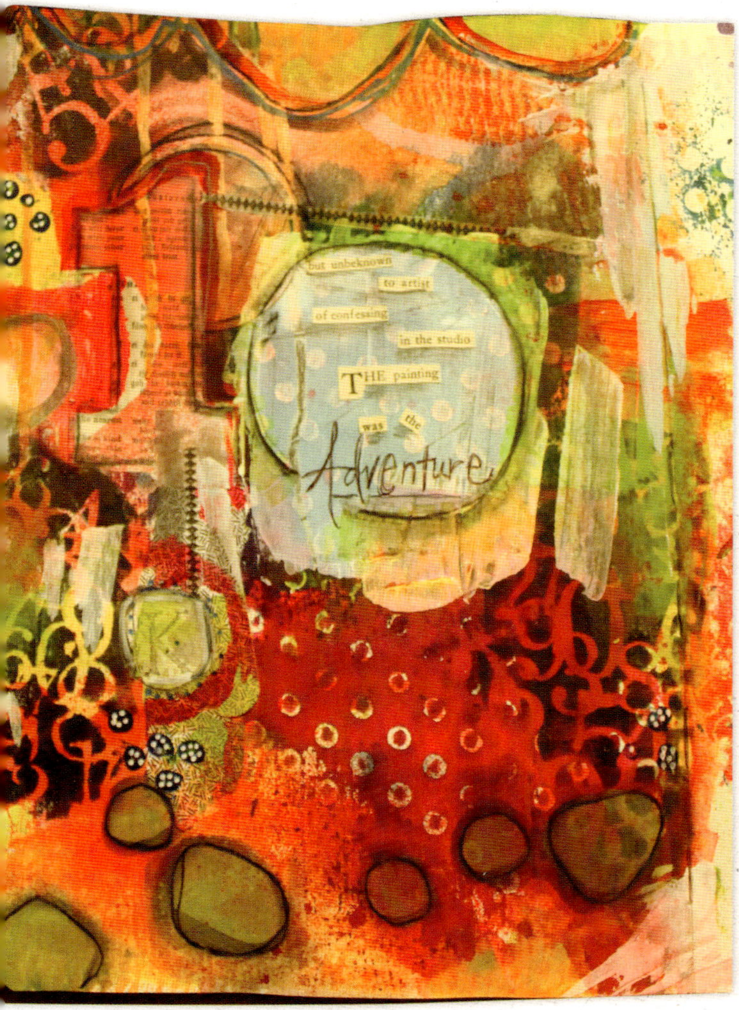

ADVENTURE
Acrylic paint, spray inks, stencils, book paper, book words, Stabilo pencil

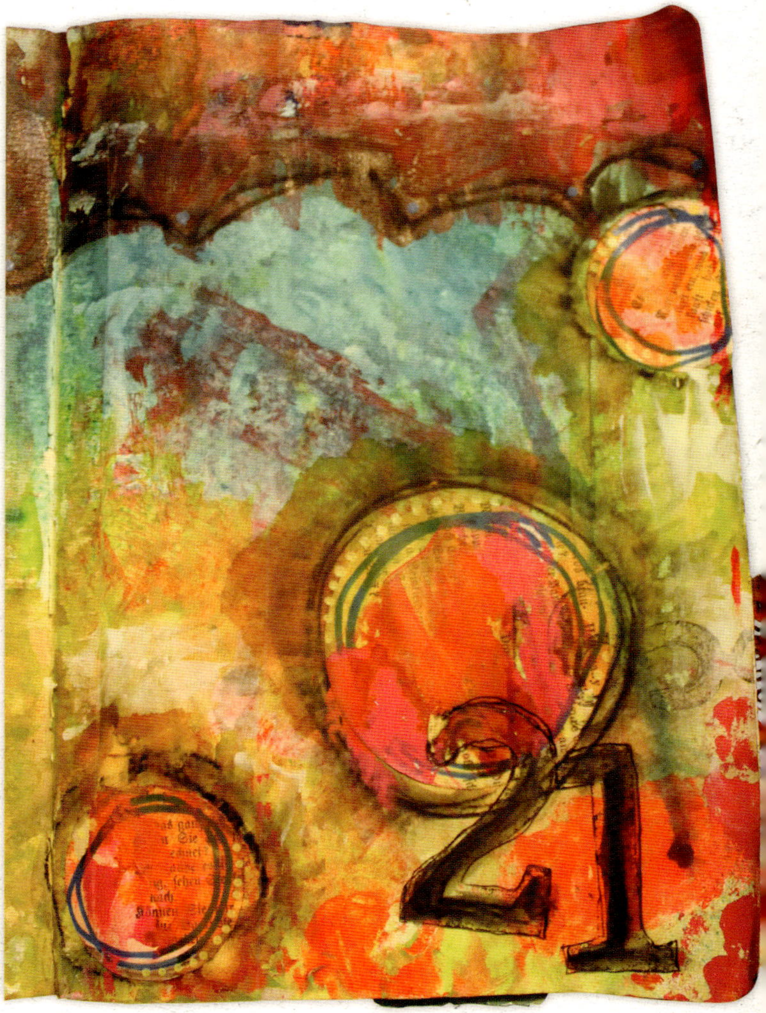

21 SECRETS
Acrylic paints, homemade stencils, book paper, Stabilo pencil, number stamps

What was your inspiration for *21 Secrets*?

My journal page was created while I was participating in 21 Secrets LIVE! The *21 Secrets* page was created after I had watched a live video from an inspiring artist on journaling.

What interesting or unique techniques did you apply to this artwork?

This piece embodies my sense of style in that it's colorful and vibrant—and a bit on the messy side.

Are there any mixed-media artists who inspire you?

I am inspired by many mixed-media artists. My current list of inspiration comes from Roben-Marie Smith, Kate Crane and Dina Wakley.

Do you ever give yourself journal prompts?

These pages were based on prompts. However, I have several other art journals and tend to simply play or try new techniques in those.

Do you have an art journaling process?

I don't really have a true process when it comes to art journaling. I work simply based on what I am attempting to create. If I feel like the paper needs to be gessoed before I work, I will gesso the paper—but not always. Sometimes it's about not being consistent.

What tips would you give to fellow art journaling artists?

My tip would be that your art journal is yours, and it does not necessarily have to be shared or conform to what you think art journaling has to be. The art journal is for you to play and create without any outside comments or judgment. Your art journal is the place for you to ask yourself, "I wonder what would happen if I did this?" Then try that.

Maz Hawes

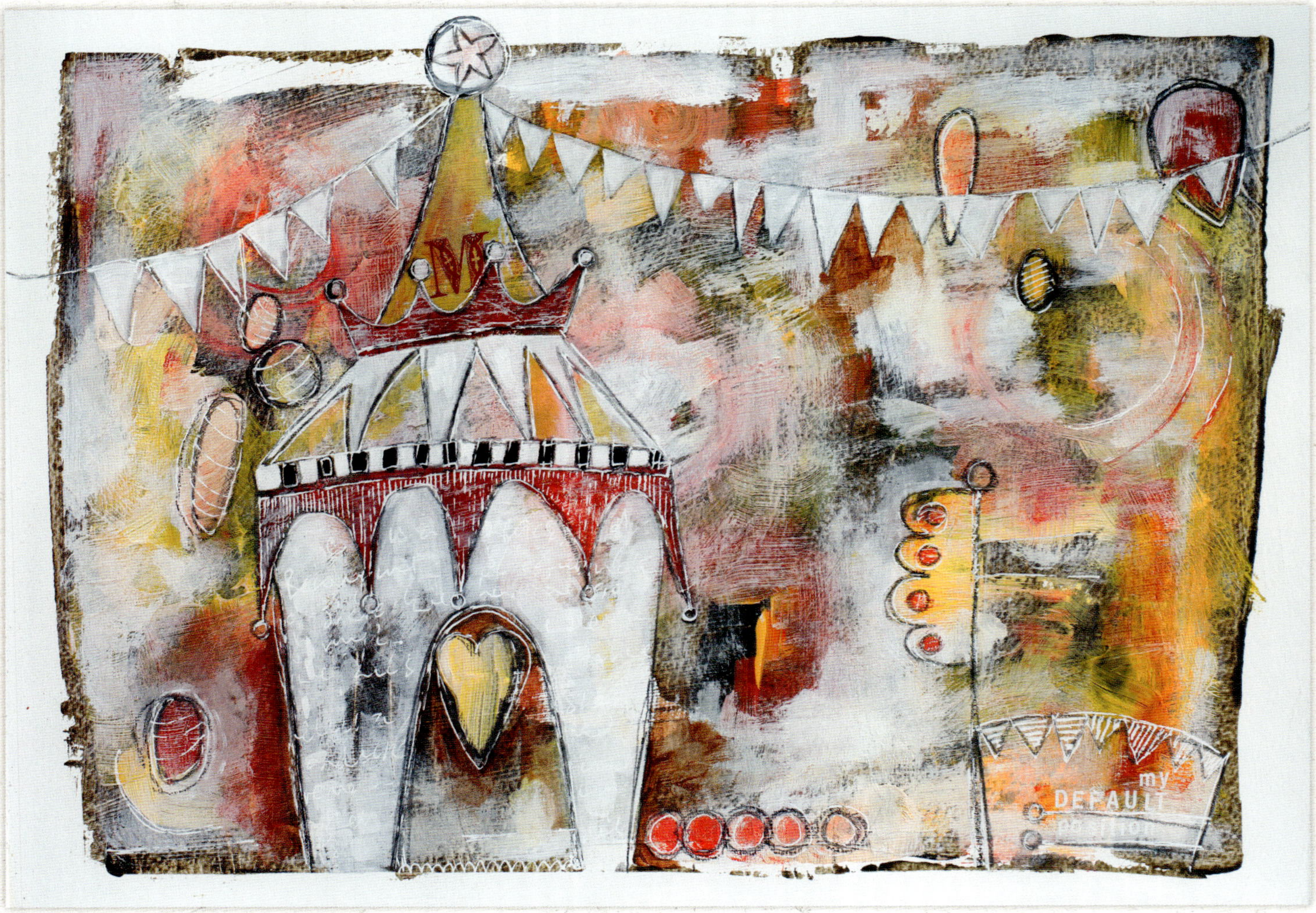

MY DEFAULT POSITION
Acrylic paint, graphite pencil, Letraset, white ink rollerball

What was your inspiration for this piece?

I'd been pondering whether happiness was still my baseline emotion or whether I had defaulted back to blame, frustration and other negative emotions. I believe a positive mind-set is something we have to constantly exercise, like a muscle.

What interesting or unique techniques did you apply to this artwork?

Layers—lots of lovely layers. Building up layers of paint until my intuition sees something emerge. I had no idea when I started what was going to appear.

How did you come up with your title?

In general, I'm intrigued by the study of positive psychology and the search for well-being and happiness as a goal. But there was a specific scene in the television show *The West Wing*, when the president asks his director of communications what he's so happy about. The director replies, "Happiness is my default position." I just love this quote!

Do you ever give yourself journal prompts?

I keep a notebook with me at all times and write down snippets of articles I read, phrases from books or poetry and bits of conversation. I dip back into the notebooks for inspiration. My journal pages almost always start with words.

Stacy Spangler

What was your inspiration for this piece?

I was inspired to create this piece while working on my monthly devotion at a women's shelter as an art project for the women.

How did you come up with your title?

I came up with this because of the women I work with at the local women's shelter. They bravely leave behind their past and find the shelter and hope they need to build a new life.

When and why did you start art journaling?

I started art journaling regularly about five years ago when I started selling my artwork. My art journal helps me to record things that I can use for inspiration when creating a painting. It also gives me a safe and inexpensive place to express myself and try new things.

What tips would you give to fellow art journaling artists?

I would recommend my fellow art journaling artists to get connected online (Facebook, Instagram, etc.) to learn and share new techniques and ideas. Don't be afraid to ask other artists how they create something or what product they used—most are more than willing to share.

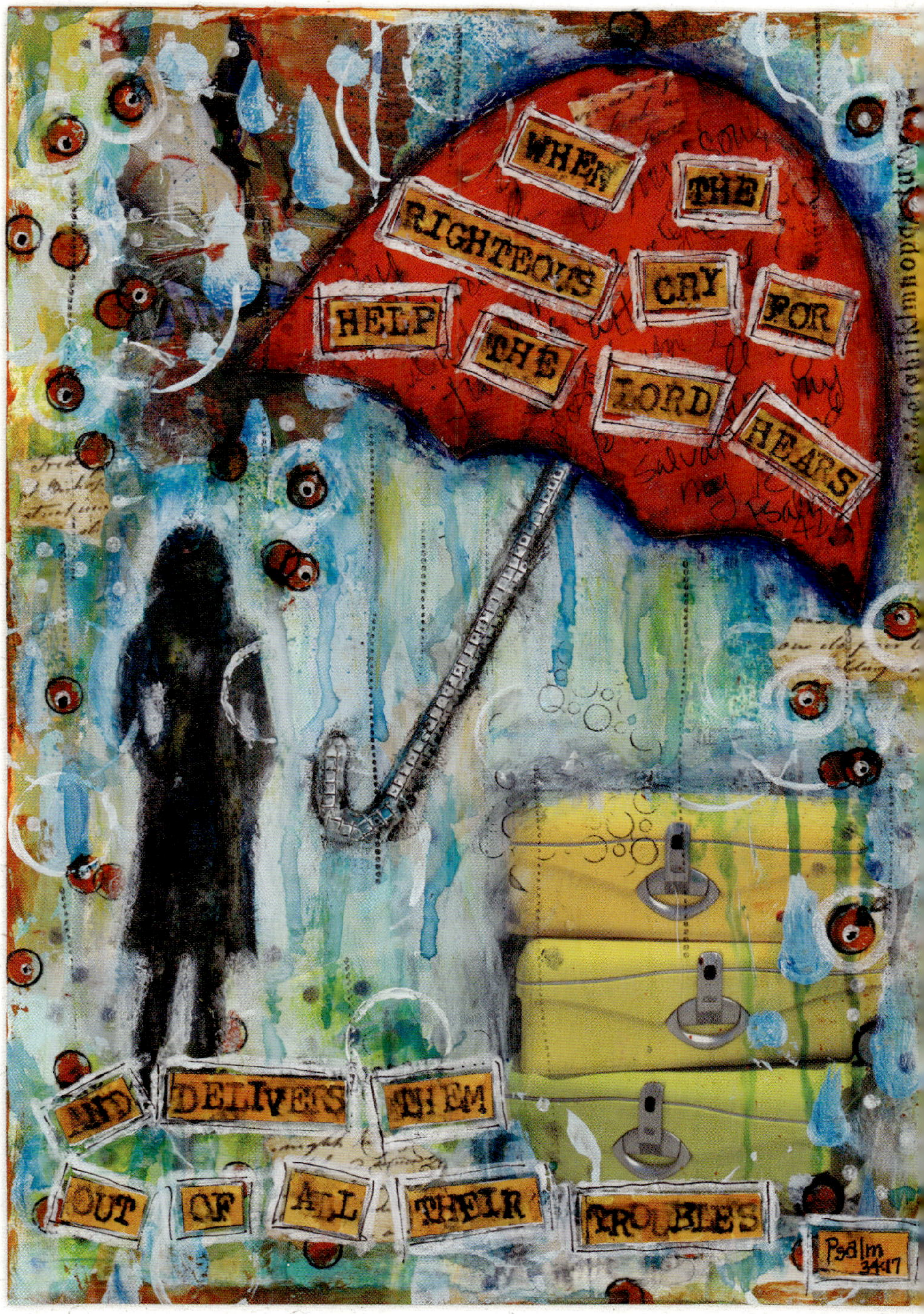

LETTING GO
Acrylic paint, ink, Gelatos, gesso, gel medium

Molly Alexander

What was your inspiration for this piece?

I was inspired by the song lyrics written along the border of this piece from a song by Christy Nockels called *For Your Splendor*. It talks about how our beauty comes not from the outside, but from the deep seeds planted in us.

What interesting or unique techniques did you apply to this artwork?

This actually resulted from a "happy accident" situation. I had glued a dictionary page to my journal page and didn't like how it was taking the watercolor, so I started to peel it off, which left the ink from the back side of the page on the watercolor paper. I liked the texture it left, so I did my drawing on top of the print.

What tips would you give to fellow art journaling artists?

The biggest thing I can pass on to fellow art journaling artists is not to expect perfection in your journal. Define how you will be using it (as a diary, as a place to try new techniques or lettering, etc.), and just go for it. It will never be perfect, and it is definitely a place to be transparent, especially with yourself.

> *"Your story* IS WORTH TELLING."

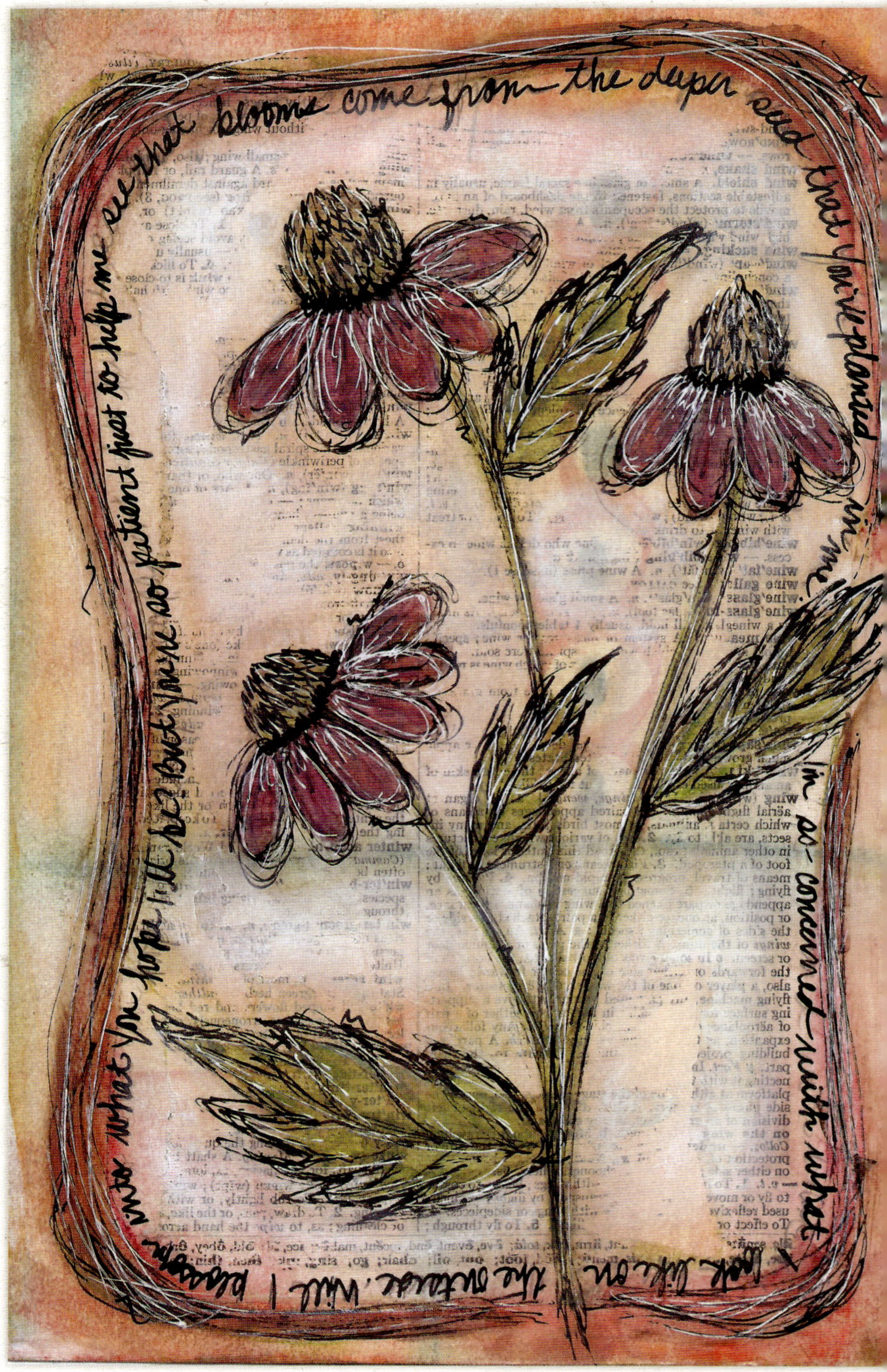

CONEFLOWERS
Pencil, watercolors, ink, assorted papers

Kara LC Jones (MotherHenna)

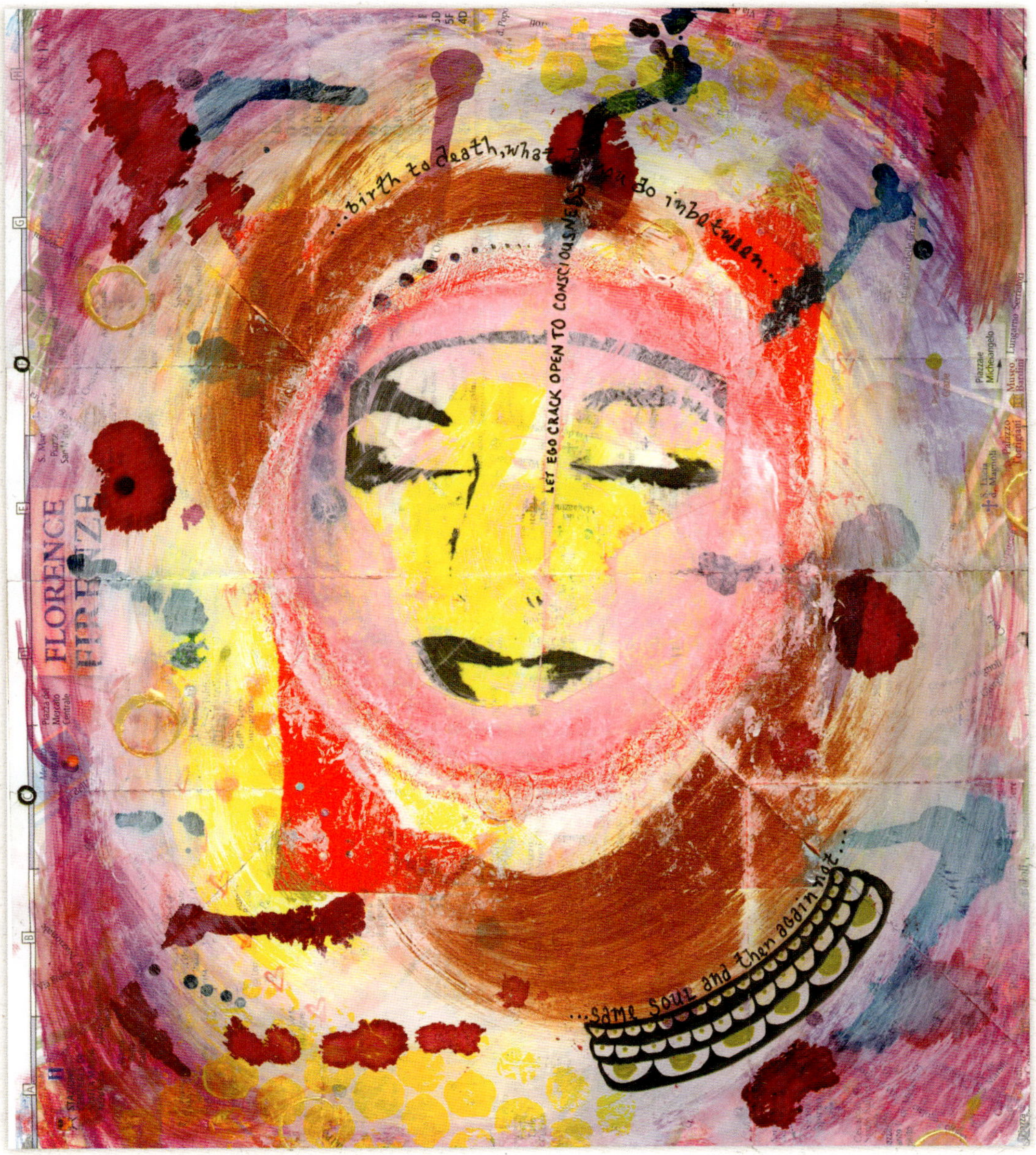

TRANSPARENT SELF PORTRAIT
Altered fold-out map, mixed-media materials

> “IT’S A PRACTICE, *not a perfect.*”
> — YOGI MEKOSUN

What was your inspiration for this piece?

I had an interesting fold-out map of Italy that I wanted to use to explore family lineage and my place within that lineage. So I began altering the map with self-portraits, photo transfers from old family albums and lots of mixed-media techniques.

Do you have an art journaling process?

My art journal process is not really formalized, except that I do have one sort of ritual around creating them. I never have just one journal—I always start four to six art journals at once. This way, I have them spread out all over my studio and I can work the layers on one, set it aside to dry, but continue to make art by starting another layer in another journal, set that one aside to dry, start another, and on and on.

What tips would you give to fellow art journaling artists?

My only tip for people is to just keep working the page. There are no mistakes, even when you make a mistake. It’s all a practice, not a perfect.

Robyn Wood

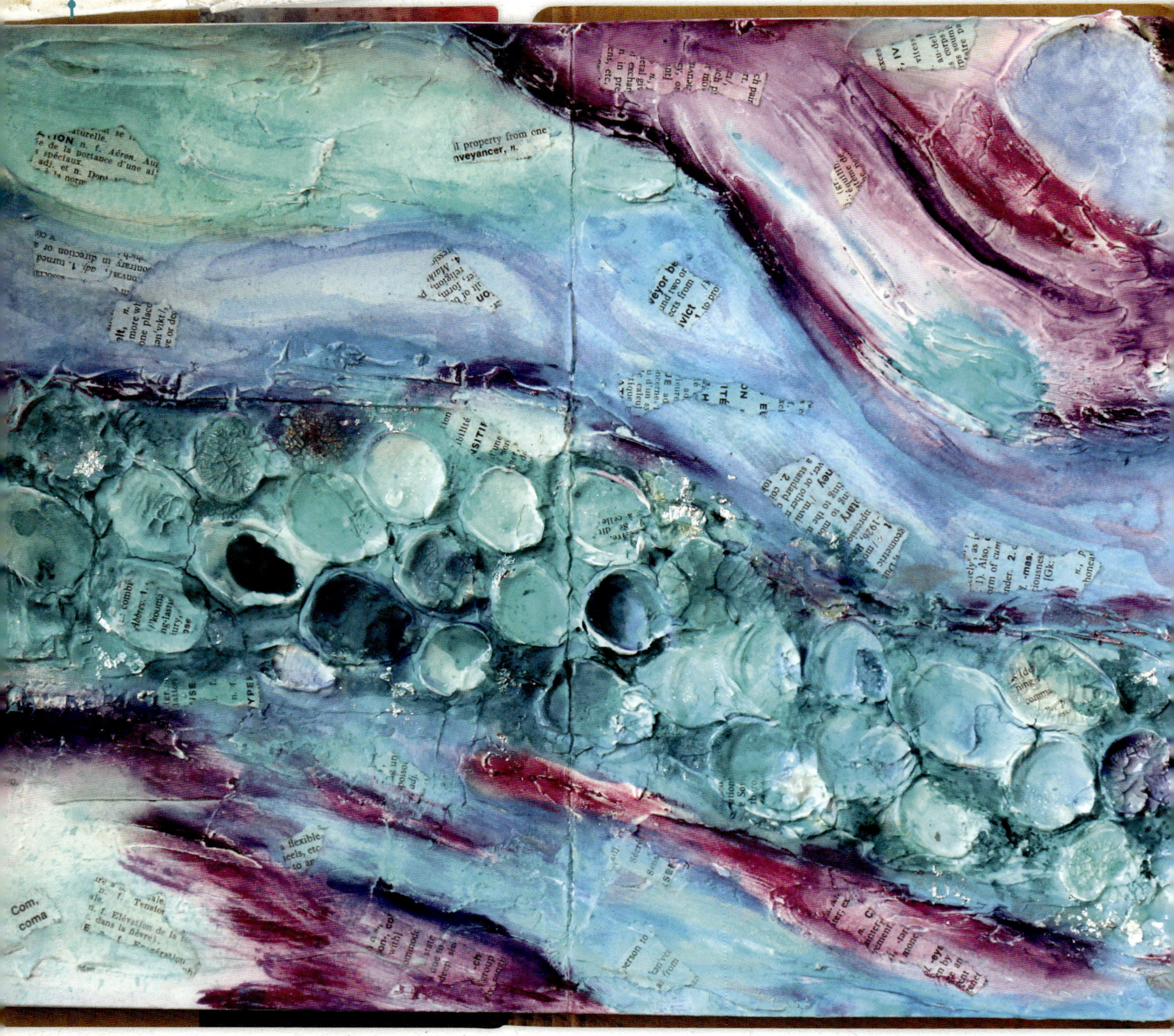

A RIVER RUNS
Texture paste, dictionary paper, pouring medium, Distress crackle paint, Gelatos, acrylic inks and paints, glass glitter, silver leaf

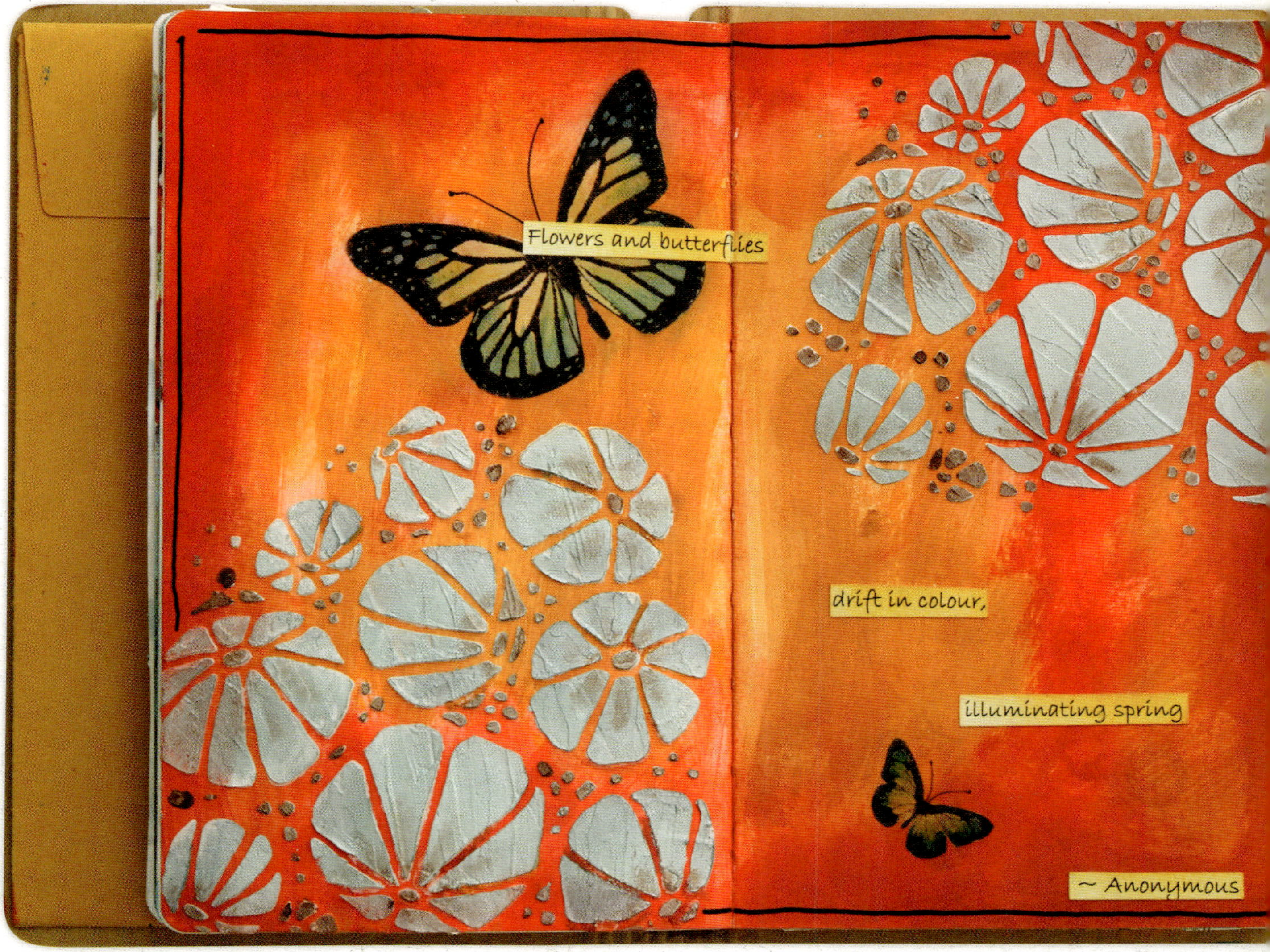

DRIFT IN COLOUR
Darkroom Door stamps, Artistcellar pod stencil, texture paste, Stewart Gill Metamica paint, Distress paints, Copic marker

What was your inspiration for *A River Runs*?

My hometown is spread around a sprawling, dynamic, beautiful tidal river, and it constantly inspires me.

Are there any mixed-media artists who inspire you?

The work of fellow Australian Jane Davenport as well as Seth Apter, Marjie Kemper, Donna Downey and Christy Tomlinson give me constant inspiration.

How did you come up with the title for *A River Runs*?

It came to me after I laid the initial texture and had started to add color. It looked like a river flowing around a tide pool.

Do you have an art journaling process?

I'm not a "get your feelings out onto a page" type of art journaler. To me, art journaling is a way of experimenting with no real aim in mind—pure play. Instinct takes over and the placement of color, images and texture happens without a lot of thought. I rarely create to a plan.

What tips would you give to fellow art journaling artists?

Keep playing and experimenting with techniques and ideas. Take whatever classes, online or in person, that are available to you and connect with others in the mixed-media community. Allow yourself to be inspired by others and take inspiration from wherever you find it. Remember that there are no rules!

Normajean Brevik

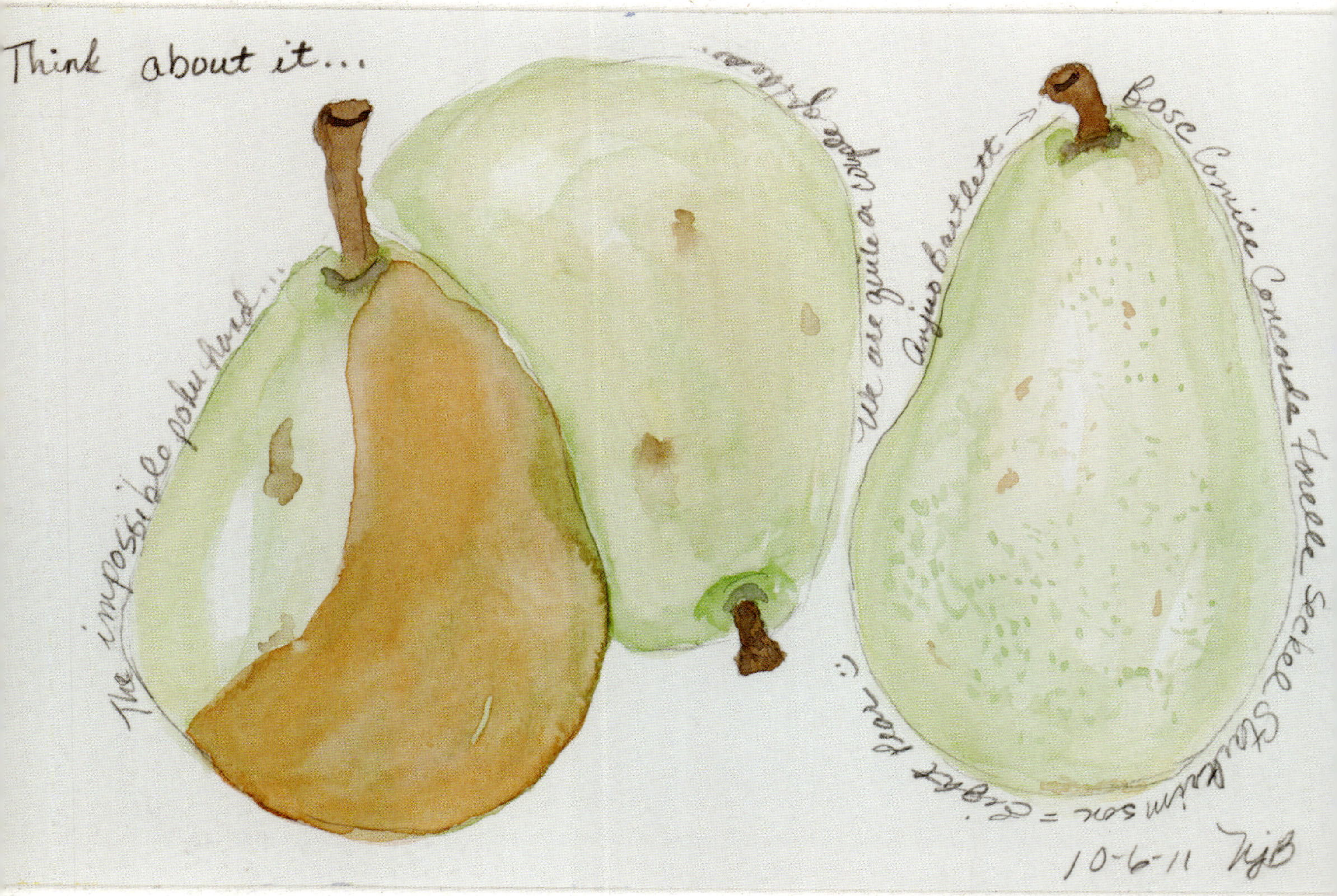

THE IMPOSSIBLE POKER HAND
Watercolor paper, assorted paints

What was your inspiration for this piece?

I draw and watercolor things from everyday life in my journal, and these happened to be on my kitchen counter. Perhaps it's because I don't always have the most elaborate subject matter, but I like to add a bit of whimsy and humor to my journal pages in the text that I add.

Are there any mixed-media artists who inspire you?

Vickie Lowe is a watercolor artist whose work I admire.

How did you come up with your title?

My attempt at humor—three pear/pair.

Do you ever give yourself journal prompts?

Not journal prompts as much as finding humor, poetry or commentary about everyday subject matter.

Do you have an art journaling process?

Not a process as much as an art mantra: Art everyday. I often use my journal as a warm-up for a bigger project or as an easy way to chronicle my vacations and journeys.

Joy Bathie

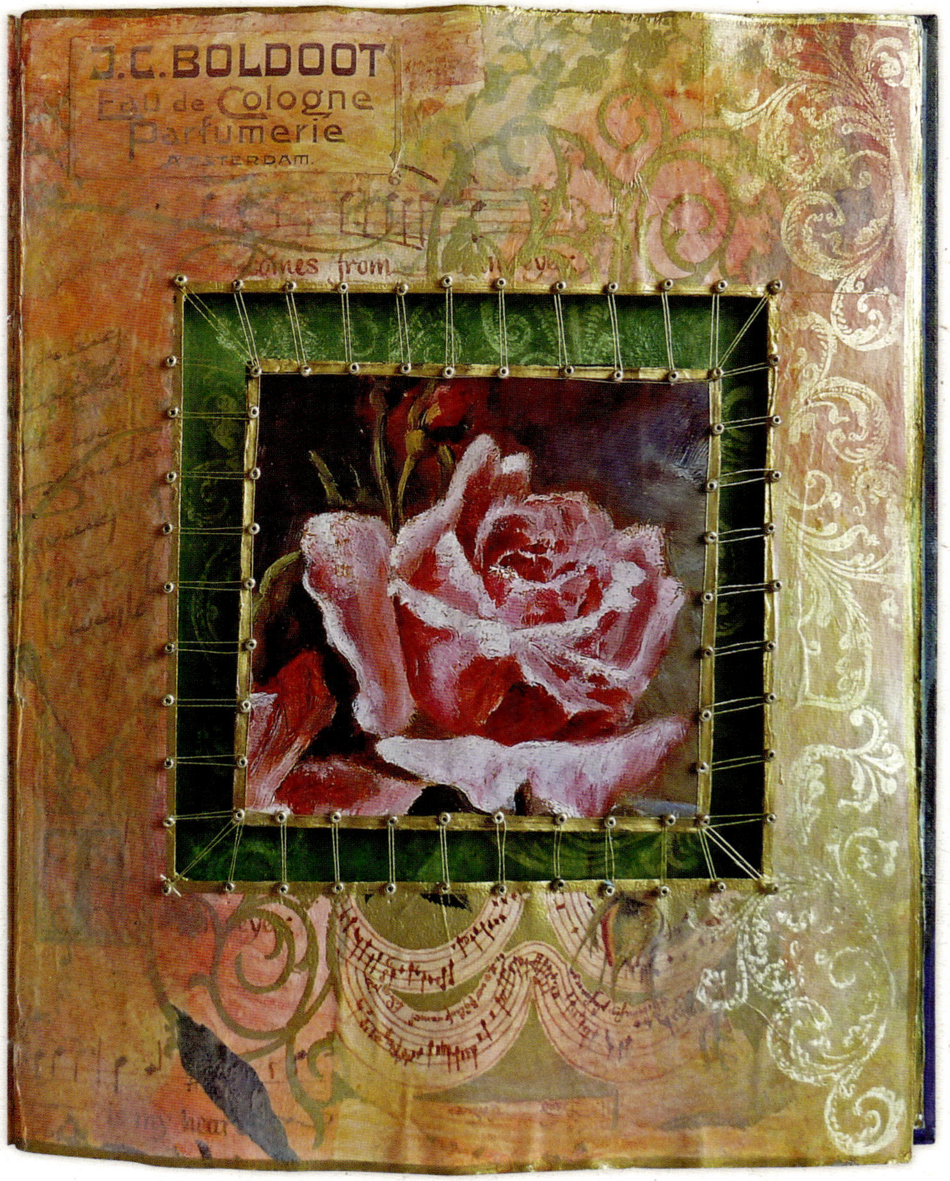

ROSE
Journal pages, acrylic paints and varnish, rubber-stamped images, tiny beads, gold thread

What was your inspiration for this piece?

The inspiration for my journal page was the beauty of the rose, which I wanted to focus on in a manner that would complement the delicacy of the bloom.

What interesting or unique techniques did you apply to this artwork?

Text, music and other images were printed onto tissue paper. Then I glued them into place with gel medium, blending the images into the painted background. Various rubber-stamped images were then added, some using metallic gold paint instead of ink. Several layers of soft color washes were brushed over the whole page and a final coat of acrylic gloss varnish, to seal and protect, allows the golden gleam of the stamping to shine through. This gives an almost brocade-like effect. The rose panel was suspended in the window with fine gold thread secured by tiny gold beads.

Are there any mixed-media artists who inspire you?

I'm inspired by Ann Baldwin, Beryl Taylor, Jacqueline Sullivan, Carol Nelson and Ann Bagby.

"*What would life be like* IF WE HAD NO COURAGE TO ATTEMPT ANYTHING?"

— VINCENT VAN GOGH

Jill Hejl

"Whatever your dreams are, START TAKING THEM VERY, VERY SERIOUSLY."

— BARBARA SHER

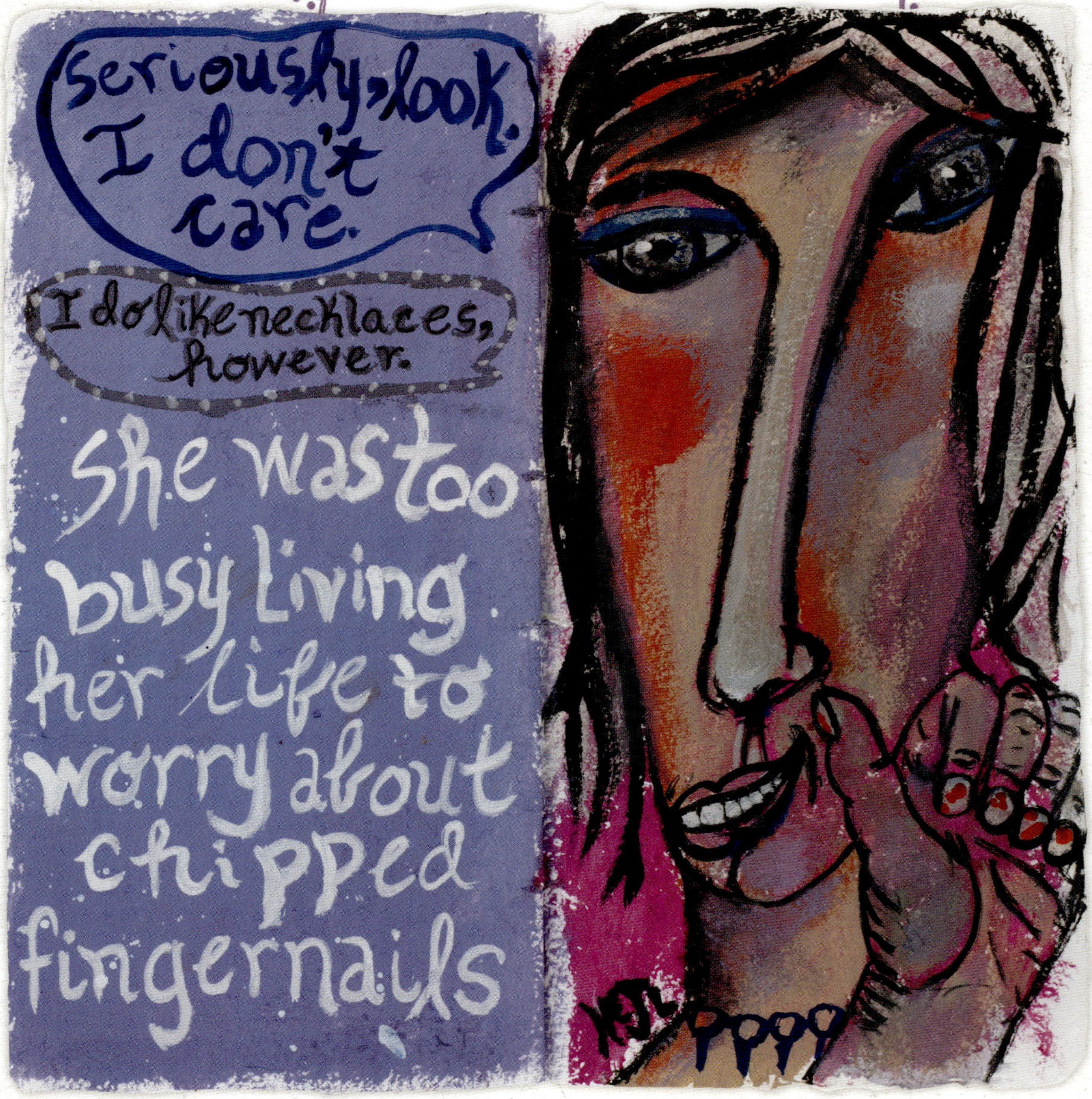

CHIPPED NAIL
Acrylics and ink on heavyweight, textured watercolor paper

What was your inspiration for this piece?

It was inspired by a conversation that I overheard in a checkout line. Two women were discussing the importance of always having well-manicured fingernails. I looked down at my paint-splattered hands and nails and thought that was the best manicure of all.

Do you ever give yourself journal prompts?

I don't use journal prompts. My art journaling is based on everyday events—things I've pondered, read, seen or heard—or they emerge from paint splattered on a page and the image I see in it.

Are there any mixed-media artists who inspire you?

I feel drawn to Orly Avineri's work. I aim for the same open, free-flowing, emotional style that she employs.

What tips would you give to fellow art journaling artists?

My best piece of advice is to become attuned to the inspiration around you and the feelings within you. Feel things deeply—no emotion is bad. Express it all and don't worry about being perfect.

Sara Naumann

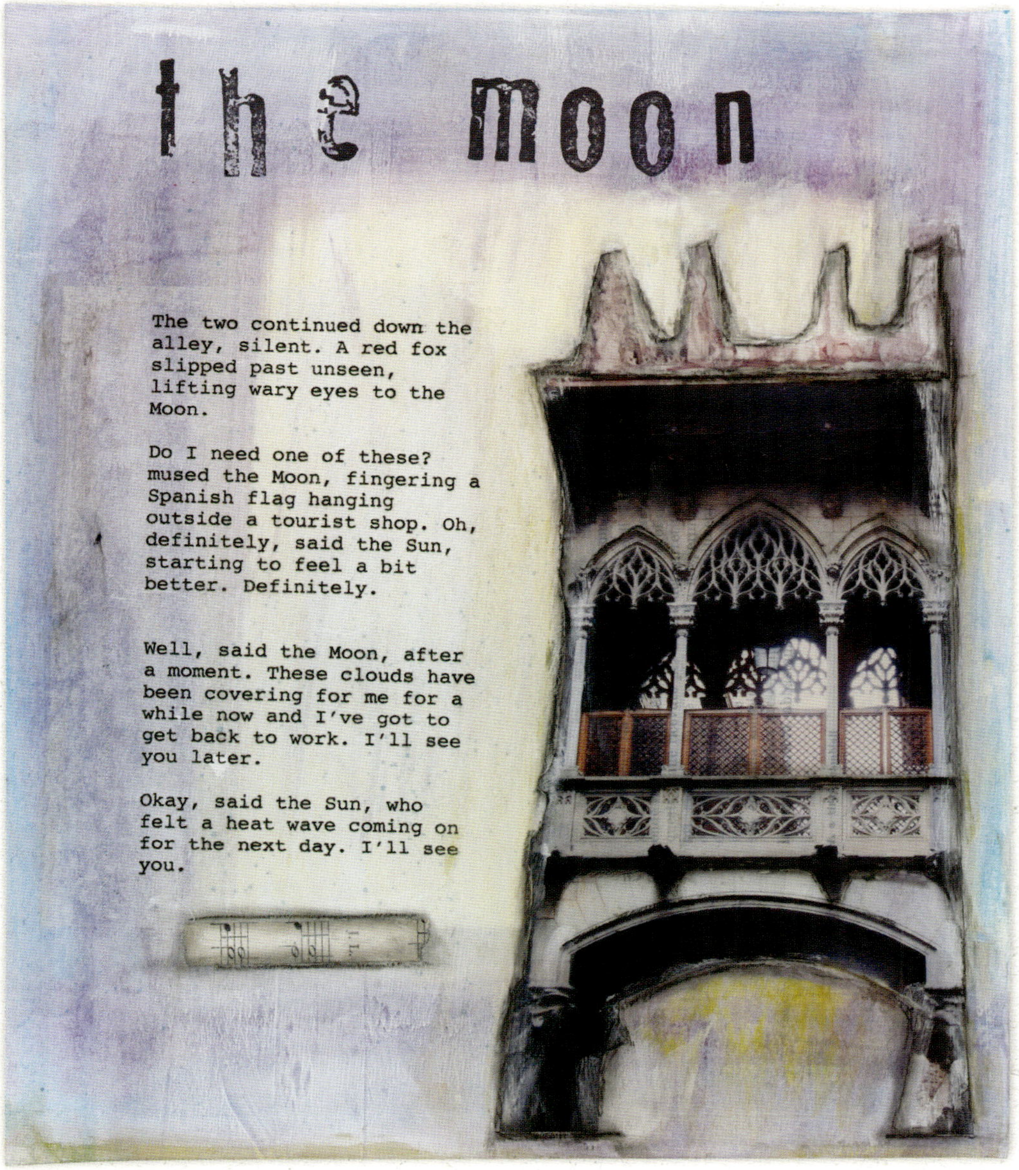

BETWEEN THE SUN & THE MOON
Stamping, Lazertran Waterslide Decal Paper (to transfer the photo), Gelatos, Mod Podge

What was your inspiration for this piece?

Travel gives my art journaling a different perspective, often inspiring me to write short stories or vignettes rather than traditional journaling. This story was inspired by the beautiful and mysterious alleys and streets in Barcelona's Old Town.

What interesting or unique techniques did you apply to this artwork?

I do a lot of writing on my journal pages—a lot—and the trick is always how to fit it on without overcrowding the page. So I typed my journaling and printed it onto white tissue paper, which I collaged onto the colored background.

How did you come up with the title?

It simply relays an imaginary conversation between the two. Where else would they meet but in an alleyway in Barcelona?

Do you ever give yourself journal prompts?

I have lots of journal prompts to keep me writing regularly. Sometimes it's a theme or a place or an experience or one I've read or just had in my head for a while.

Melissa Johnson

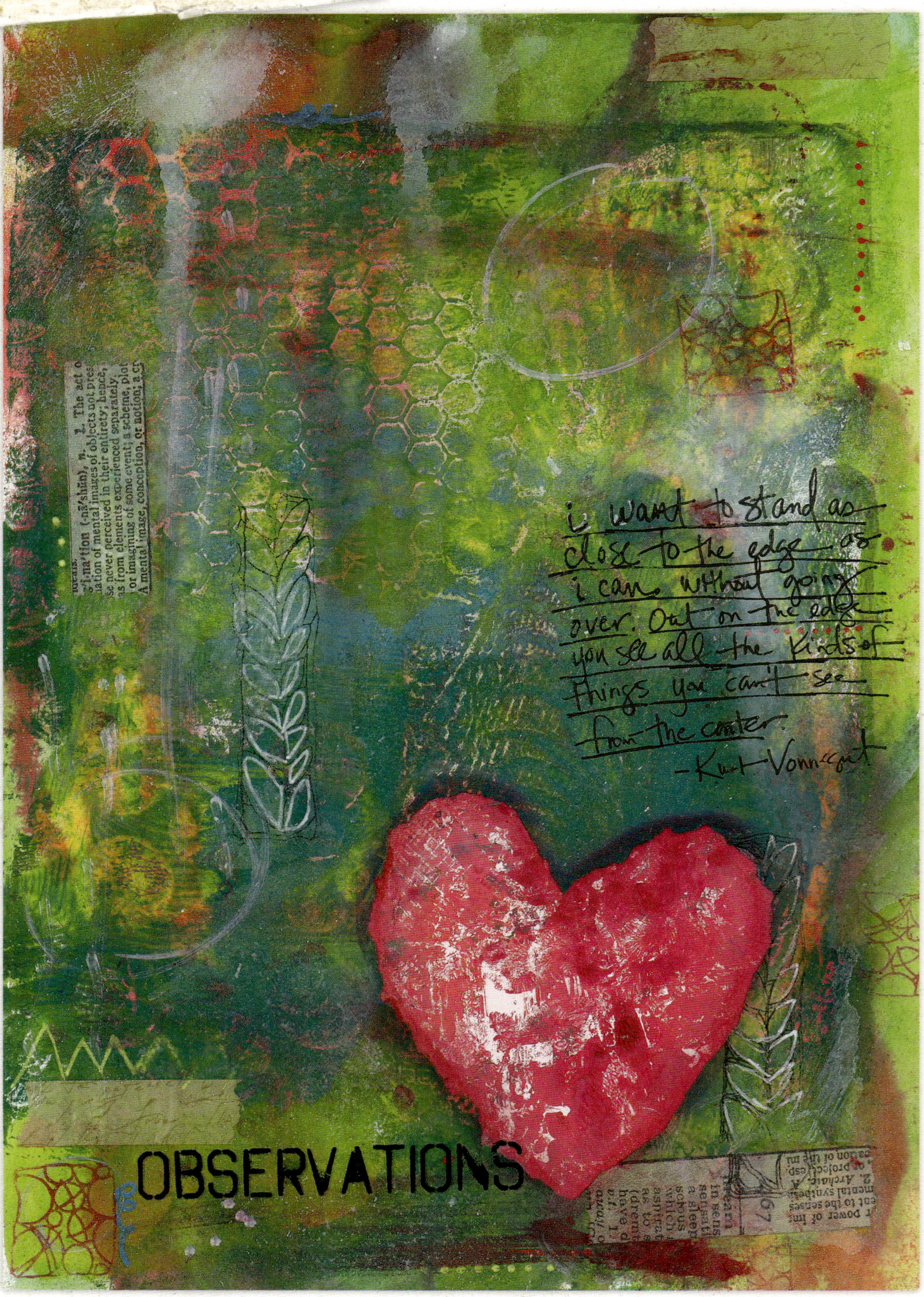

OBSERVATIONS
Stencils, paints, washi tape, doodles, stamps

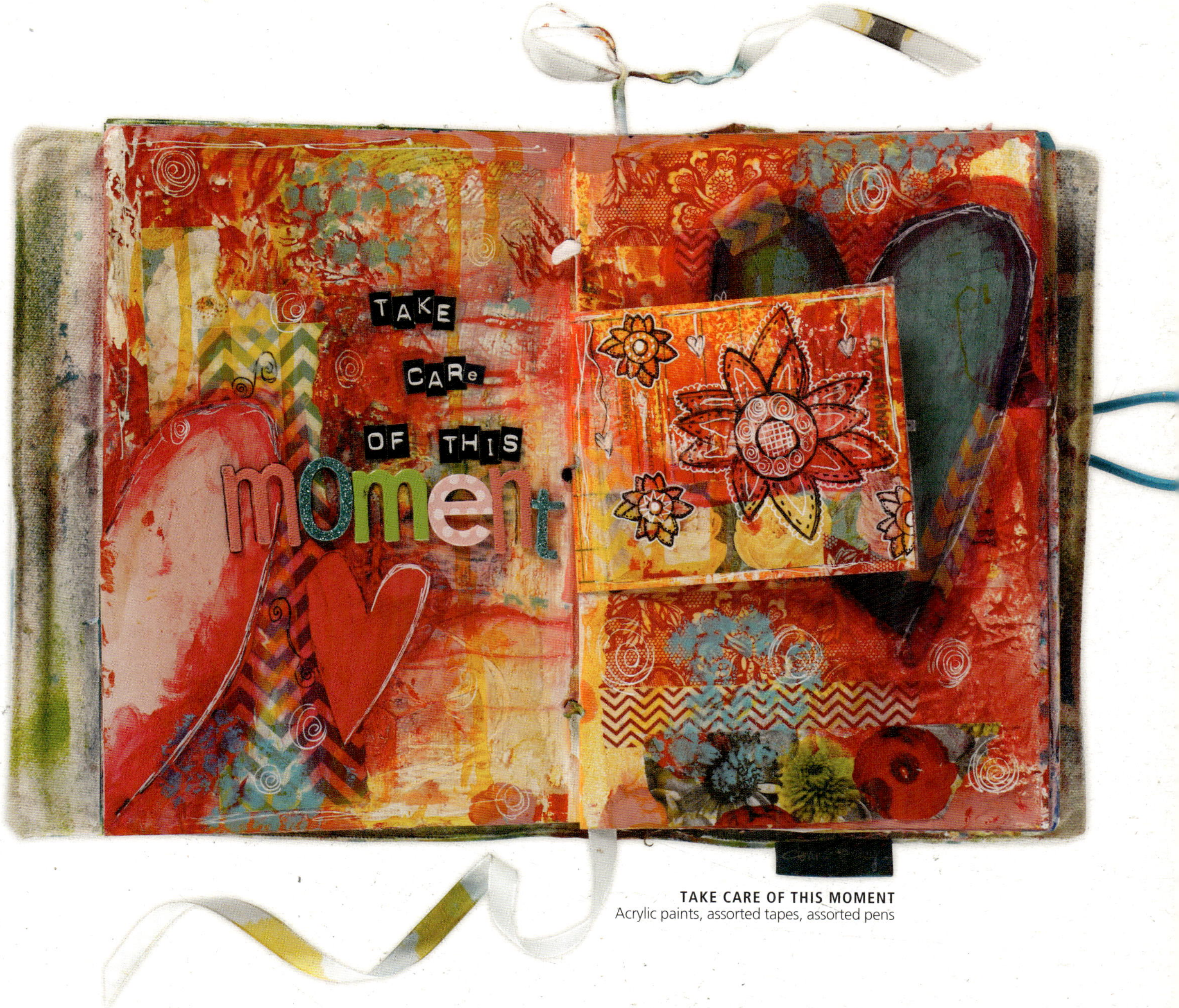

TAKE CARE OF THIS MOMENT
Acrylic paints, assorted tapes, assorted pens

What was your inspiration for *Observations*?

My inspiration for this piece came from my stash of Gelli printed scraps and premade backgrounds.

Do you ever give yourself journal prompts?

I love collecting meaningful quotes to use as prompts in my journals.

Do you have an art journaling process?

My process for creating is pretty random. I just grab things that I like and start playing! I like to listen to music while I work; it gets the creativity flowing. Having several ready-made backgrounds makes it easy to jump right in and get a page completed—no scary, blank white page!

What was your inspiration for *Take Care of This Moment*?

My inspiration for this page came from my love of bright colors and hearts. To create texture, I scratched into the wet acrylic paint and built up layers with collage and washi tape. I added a lot of dimension by shading the hearts with big brush-tip pens and then smudging with my finger. I also used stamps and created doodles with a white gel pen.

Are there any mixed-media artists who inspire you?

I was first inspired to art journal by Christy Tomlinson's fun, brightly colored style—she continues to inspire me!

Seth Apter

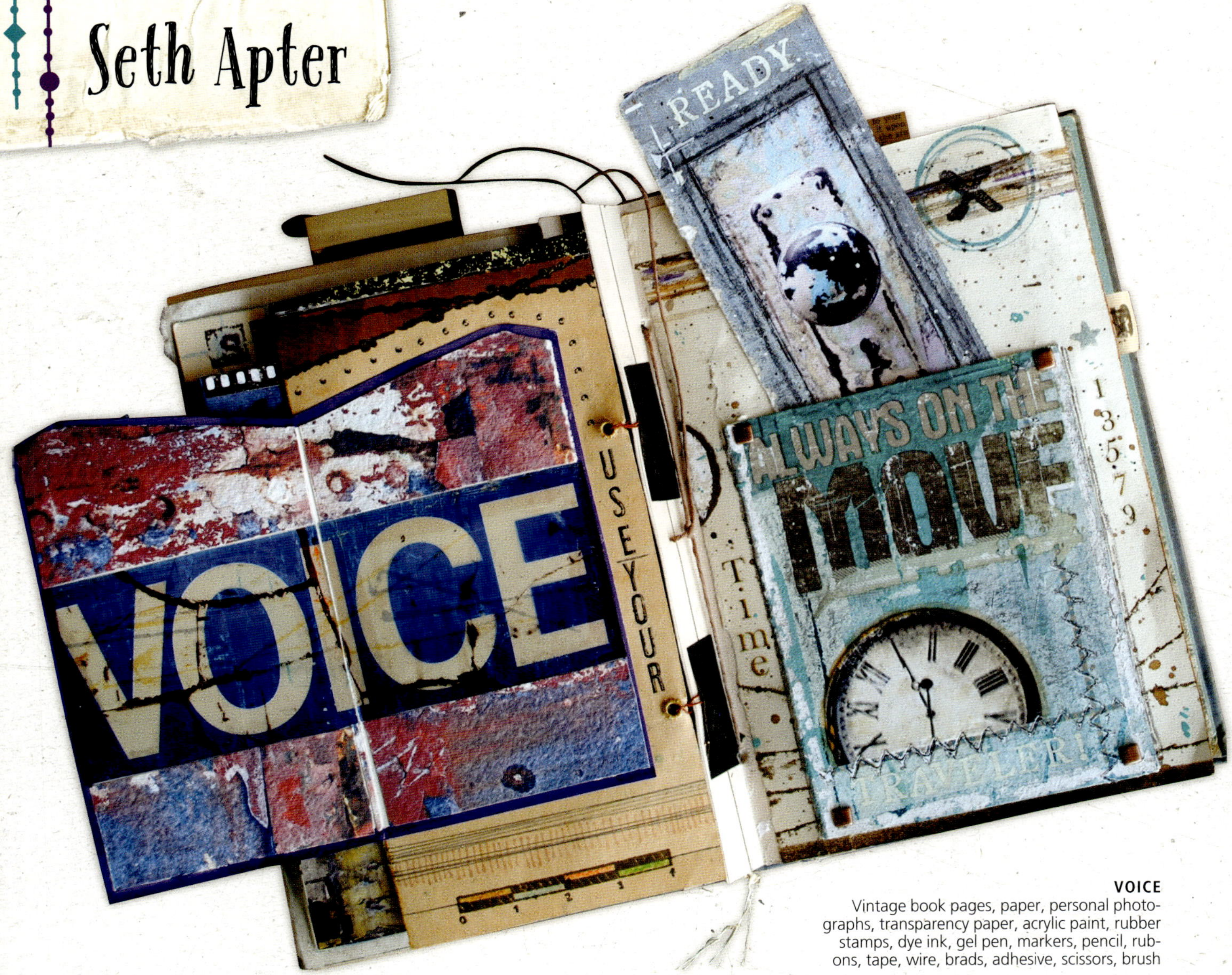

VOICE
Vintage book pages, paper, personal photographs, transparency paper, acrylic paint, rubber stamps, dye ink, gel pen, markers, pencil, rub-ons, tape, wire, brads, adhesive, scissors, brush

What was your inspiration for this piece?

These pages were inspired by the fact that I have come to a time in my life where I am feeling confident to express myself and ready to embrace every opportunity and adventure that comes my way. For me, journaling is one of the most personal forms of expression in art.

Are there any mixed-media artists who inspire you?

In terms of art journaling, two mixed-media journal artists come to mind as strong inspirations: Dan Eldon and Orly Avineri. I admire both of these artists for their ability to express their souls through journaling in such an honest, raw and real way.

> "*We create our world* WITH EVERY CHOICE WE MAKE."

How did you come up with the title?

The title is *Voice* and reflects the meaning behind this journal spread. I am in a place in my life where my voice is expressed and can be heard, leading to opportunities that I'm ready to embrace.

What tips would you give to fellow art journaling artists?

There are no rights or wrongs when it comes to art journaling. Speak your truth on the pages. Use your journal as a place to create one-hundred percent for yourself. Do not feel obligated to journal every day but, rather, be comfortable with journaling when you feel the need.

Boo Giannini Martin

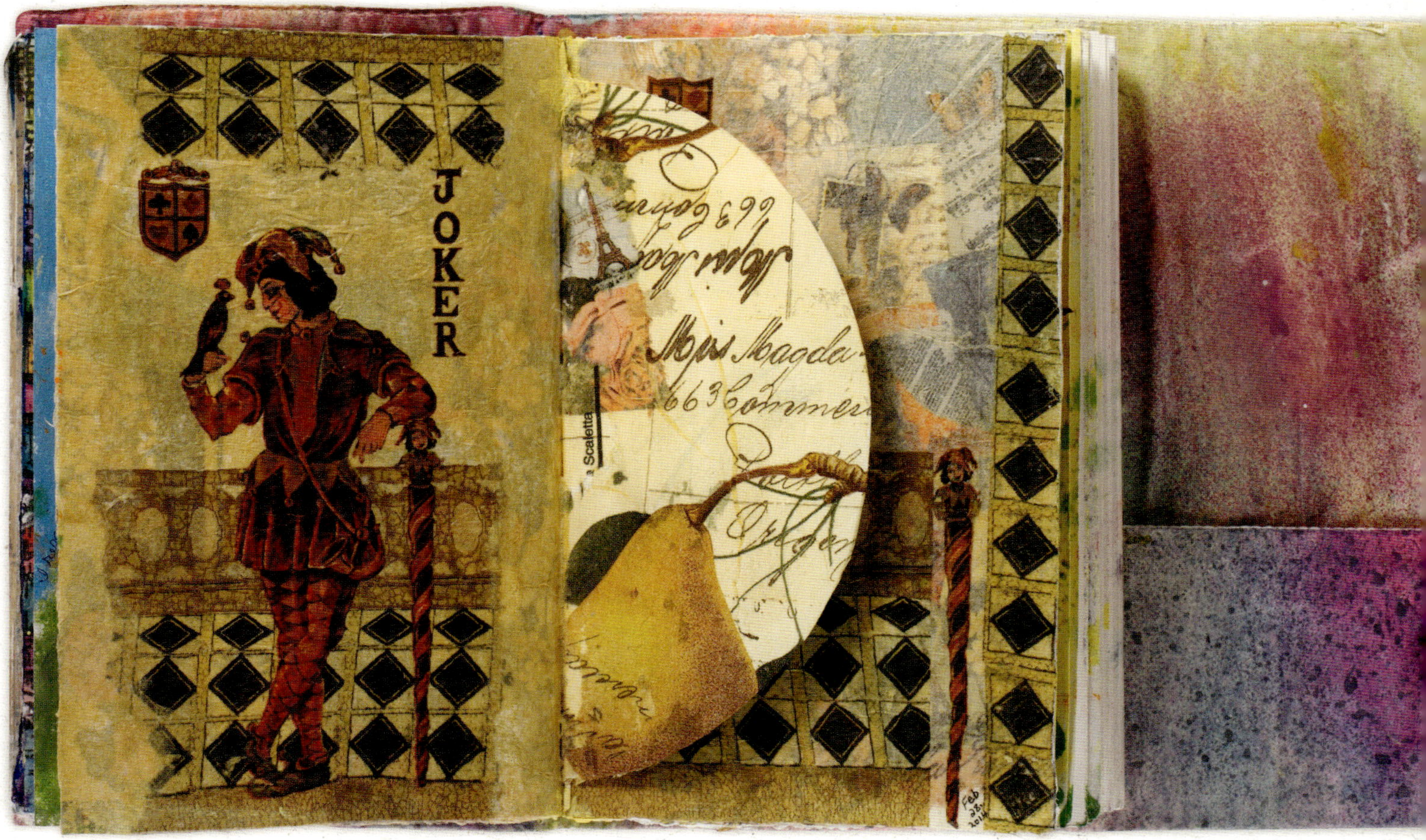

REMINISCENT
Paper napkins, deli paper, matte medium in a T's Crafty Ways Handmade Art Journal

What was your inspiration for this piece?

Play was the inspiration for this piece. I just wanted to play. I also like to use whatever is on my worktable at the time. I had several paper napkins in my table stash because I was sending them to a friend as happy mail.

What interesting or unique technique did you apply to this artwork?

Layering is what made this piece unique. I started this page by collaging four different napkins.

Are there any mixed-media artists who inspire you?

I'm inspired by Frances Papillon, Carolyn Dube and Donna Downey.

Do you have an art journaling process?

My way of art journaling has no rules. I love no rules. My art journals are more about the art and less about the journaling (i.e. written words). I let the paint and paper speak to me—they lead me.

"*The act of creating* IS MORE IMPORTANT THAN THE WORK OF ART."

Sharen Chatterton

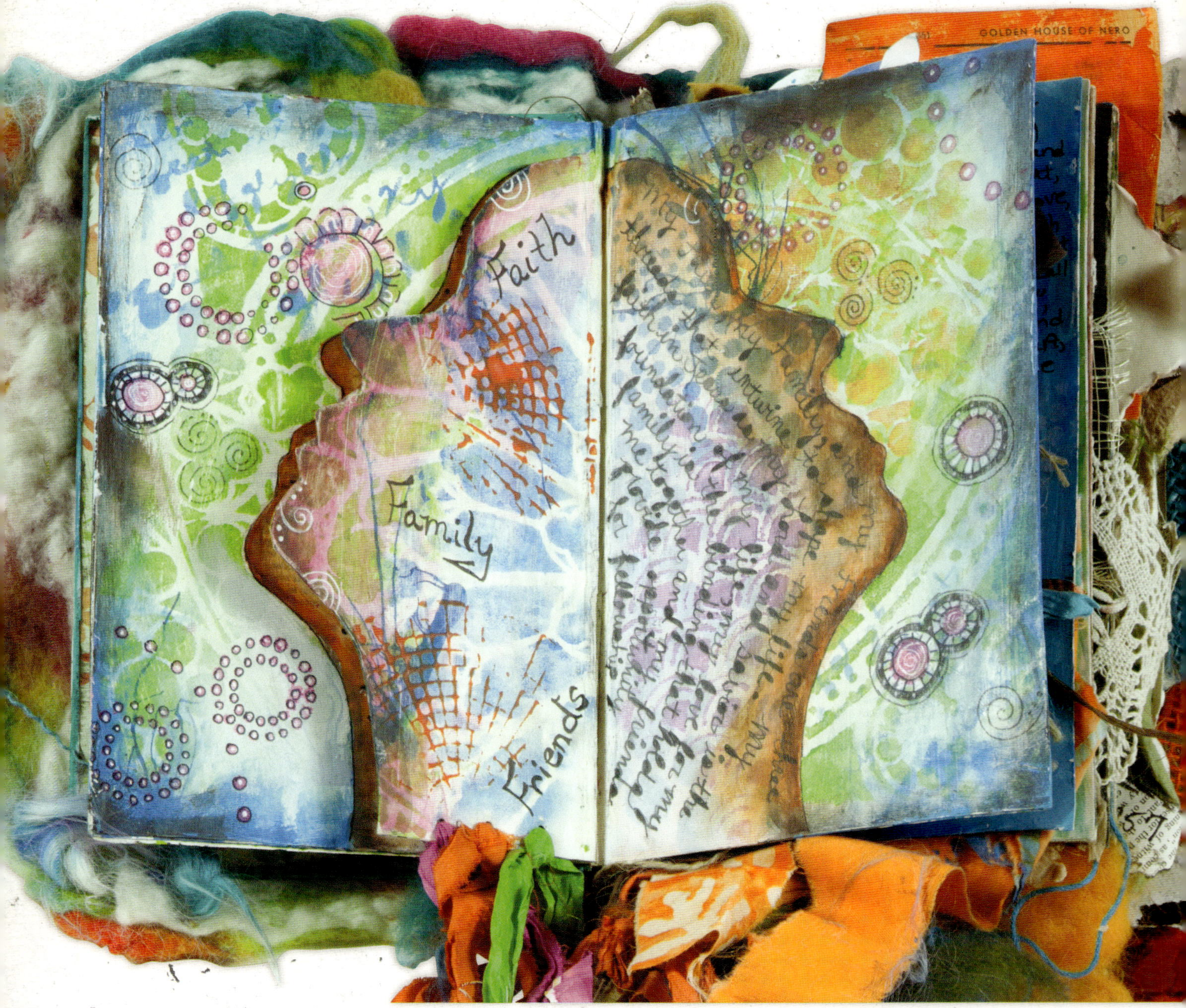

THE THREADS THAT SHAPE ME
Acrylic paints, acrylic inks, stencils both made and purchased, gesso, Neocolors

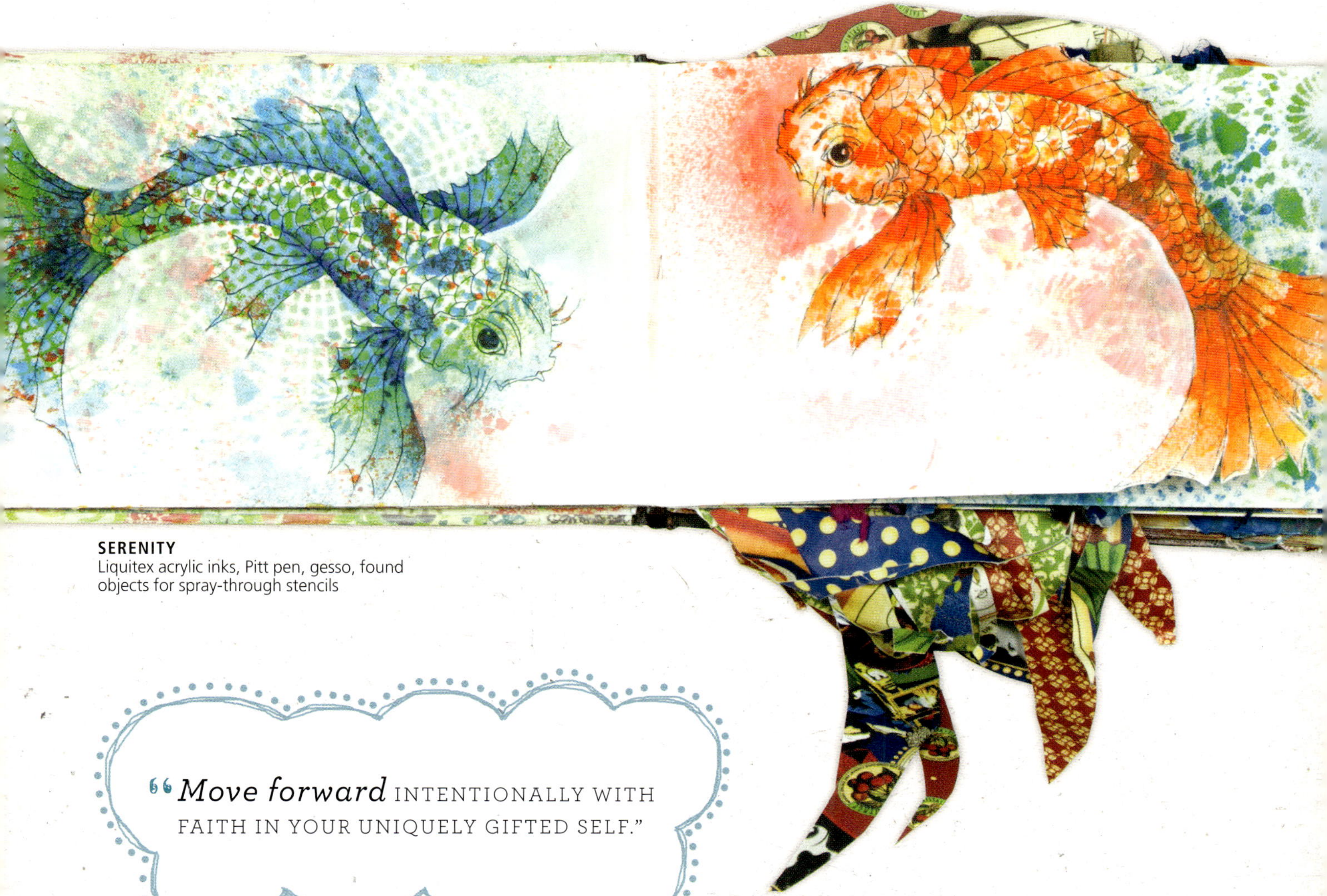

SERENITY
Liquitex acrylic inks, Pitt pen, gesso, found objects for spray-through stencils

> "*Move forward* INTENTIONALLY WITH FAITH IN YOUR UNIQUELY GIFTED SELF."

What was your inspiration for *Serenity*?

My koi pond in our side yard inspired this journal page. It has several butterfly koi in it. Every morning and evening I go out to the pond and, just like clockwork, as soon as I walk up to the edge, the koi swim up, wanting to be fed. It is such a peaceful time for me, just watching them glide through the water; truly each is a work of art. I was inspired to portray those peaceful times in my journal.

Are there any mixed-media artists who inspire you?

I love the work of Pamela Underwood and Jane LaFazio.

When and why did you start art journaling?

I have been journaling for several years now. I started journaling to have a place to experiment with different techniques. My journal pages were created without expectations of creating a canvas piece. It was so freeing for me; it opened up a whole new world beyond the graphite, acrylic and watercolor artist. I then became a mixed-media artist.

What tips would you give to fellow art journaling artists?

I always tell my students to step out of their comfort zone, loosen up, choose colors that you would not normally choose, place an image in an unusual way and do something that is original to you.

Sharon Denney-Parcel

What was your inspiration for this piece?

Please do not laugh, but my inspiration was the pineapple and the pomegranate. I had cut them out of a magazine and as I looked at them, I thought, "nice dress!"

What interesting or unique techniques did you apply to this artwork?

For the background, I applied an acrylic wash to one large sheet of hot-pressed watercolor paper. It was applied in swatches of color, then I rubbed the excess off with a paper towel. Afterward, I cut it to size for my journal.

Are there any mixed-media artists who inspire you?

Teesha Moore has provided me with so much inspiration. I love her quirky, odd Zetti style of journaling.

How did you come up with your title?

I have to tell myself to be patient constantly!

"WHEN YOU STOP FEARING FAILURE—
you will start being an artist."

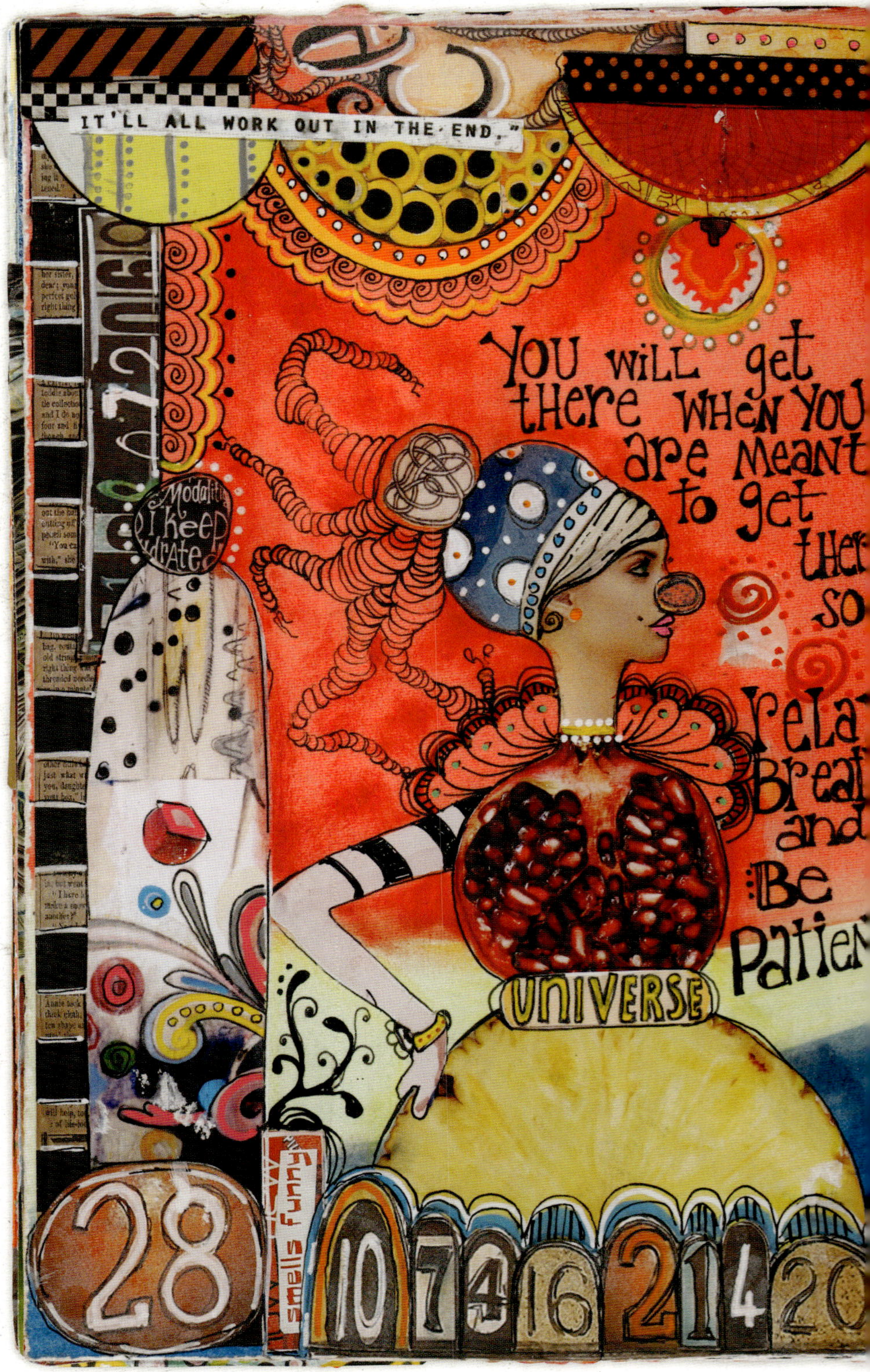

BE PATIENT
Matte gel medium, magazines, collage art found on the Internet, Pan Pastels, paint pens, black markers

Melinda Newlin Tshudy

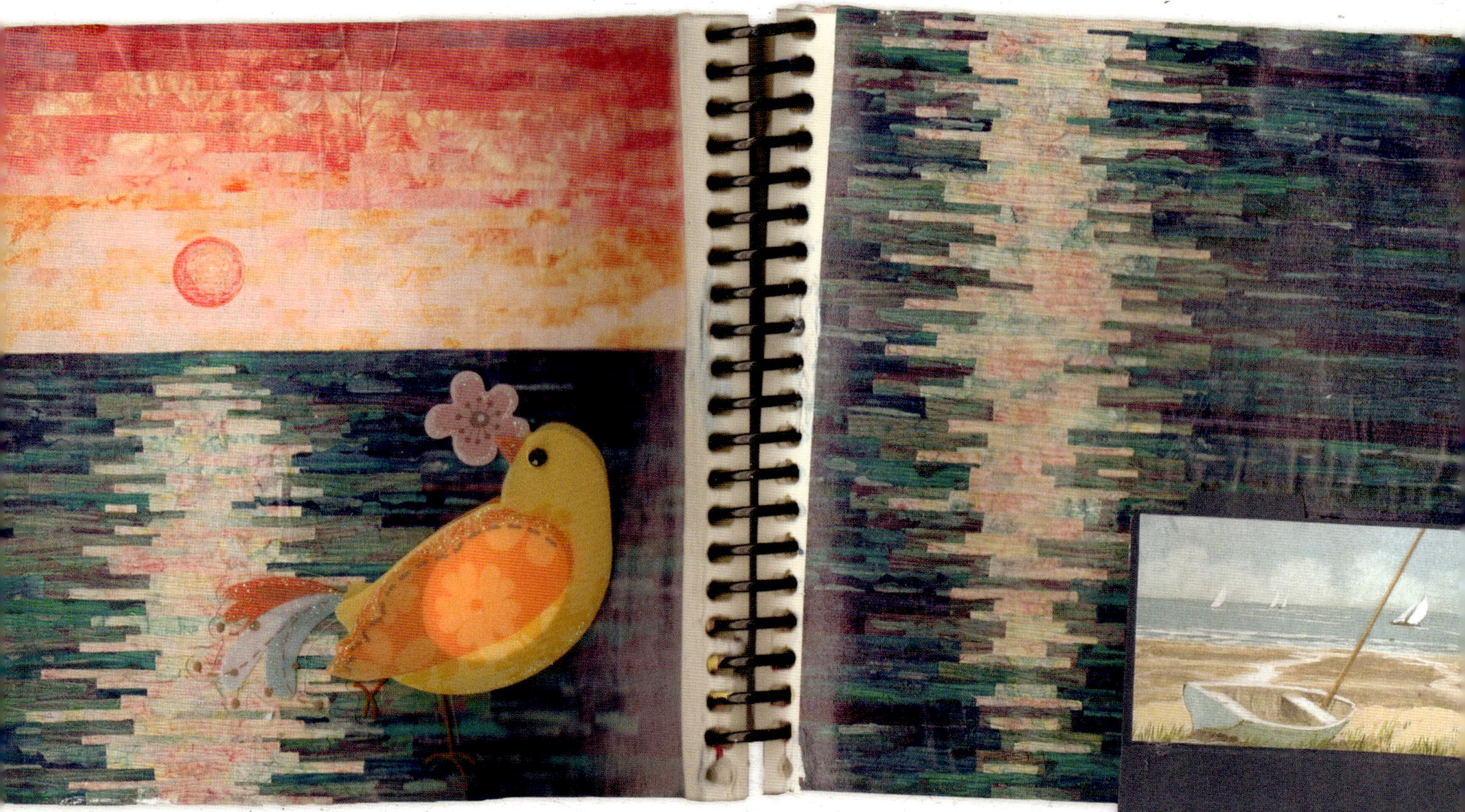

SEA JESUS MINI JOURNAL
Stickers, magazine pictures, glue sticks, tacky glue, Anna Griffin peacock sticker, store finds, yard sale finds, cut-up greeting cards, Graphic 45 paper, vintage photo images, stash scraps

What interesting or unique techniques did you apply to this artwork?

For this journal, I was determined to use what I already had on hand. My mini journal used to be a recipe book which I found at a yard sale.

Are there any mixed-media artists who inspire you?

I'm inspired by Elizabeth Bunsen, Carolyn Saxby and Shauna Lee Lange.

Do you ever give yourself journal prompts?

Yes, my prompts are my emotions of the day, from situations I find hard to handle. I create from the negative feelings; then life becomes positive again.

When and why did you start art journaling?

I watched my dad create color scheme layouts for homes he decorated by pulling together paint colors, fabric colors and pictures of furniture—it became second nature to me. Also, my mom's beautiful flower gardens are extremely inspiring. I started to scrapbook in the seventh grade, but it wasn't until after I was thirty-five when I started art journaling. It was a way of using both my parents' creative forces together to create my own style.

"WE MUST FIGHT THROUGH OUR DARKEST MOMENTS WITH *our brightest paints.*"

Ruth S. Levy

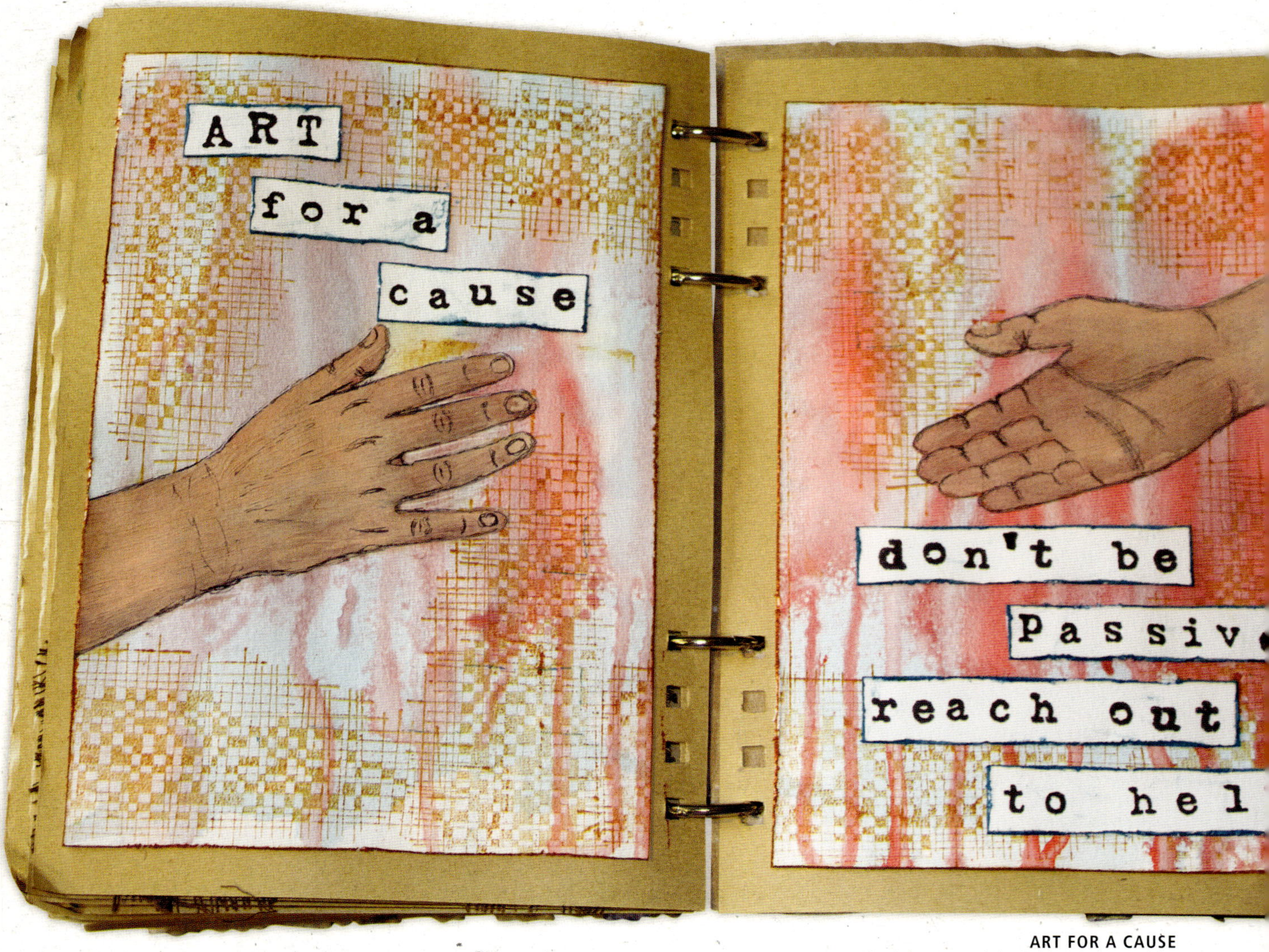

ART FOR A CAUSE
Sennelier ink, Distress ink, Golden Artists acrylic, black marker, archival ink

What was your inspiration for *Art for a Cause*?

My art journal pages are often mirrors of my feelings, whether it be happiness or frustrations, sometimes only a word or a cry-out. This one was made especially to try to get the attention of others, to move people to do something—it was a protest against passive behavior. I am a believer. I believe that somehow we can make the world a better place.

Are there any mixed-media artists who inspire you?

I'm inspired by Carolyn Dube, Julie Fei-Fan Balzer and Jessica Sporn.

Do you ever give yourself journal prompts?

Sometimes I follow prompts, but other times I need my freedom in art journaling. Art journaling is pretty much like having my own diary, with the difference being that here I put my memories or thoughts or feelings down in an image. For me the image is very important; it can be abstract or figurative, but in my art journals, I always express myself through the first picture that comes into my mind, and it's always generated by my daily life.

What tips would you give to fellow art journaling artists?

A lot of people are scared about beginning on a white page—to open that brand new journal and put the first stain on it. Well, my advice is simple: Keep a journal around the work table.

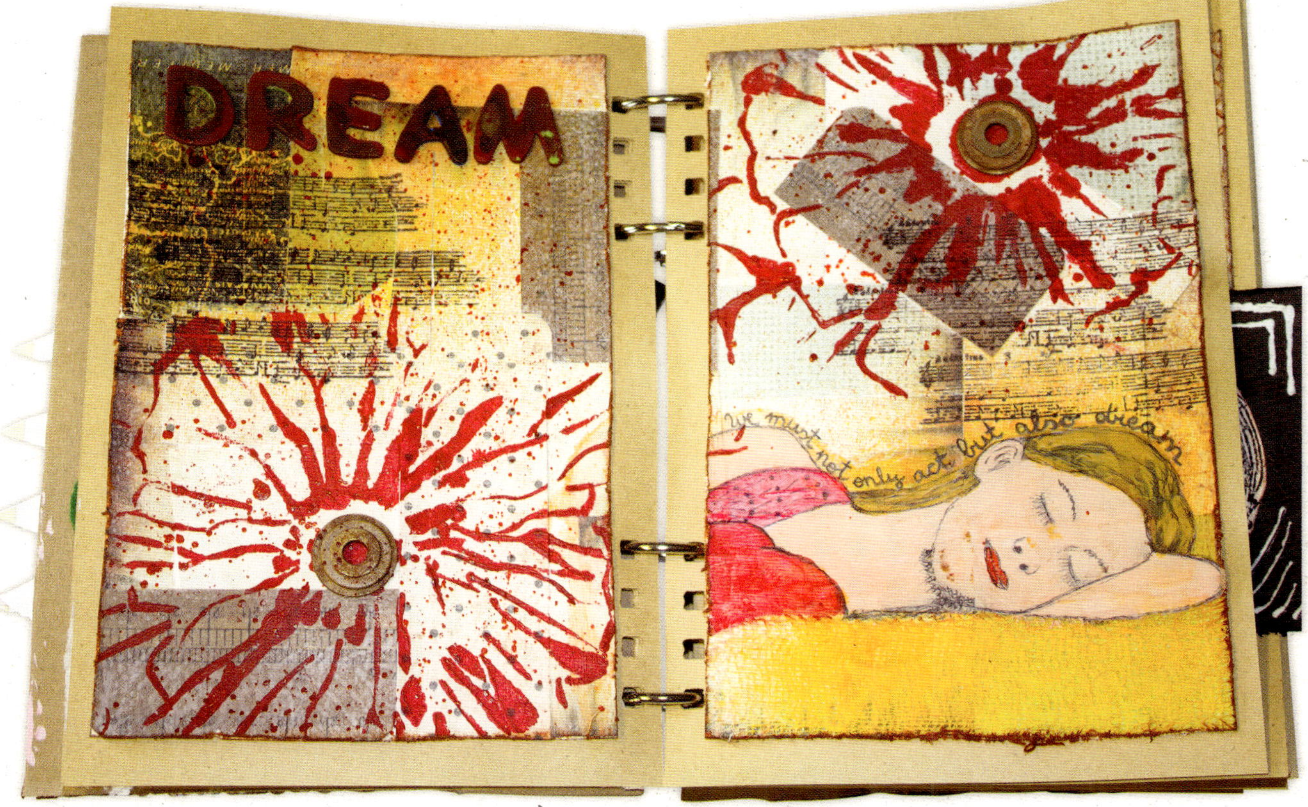

DREAM
Leftover paper pieces, gesso, Dylusions ink, Golden Artists acrylic, black marker, archival ink, self-altered washers

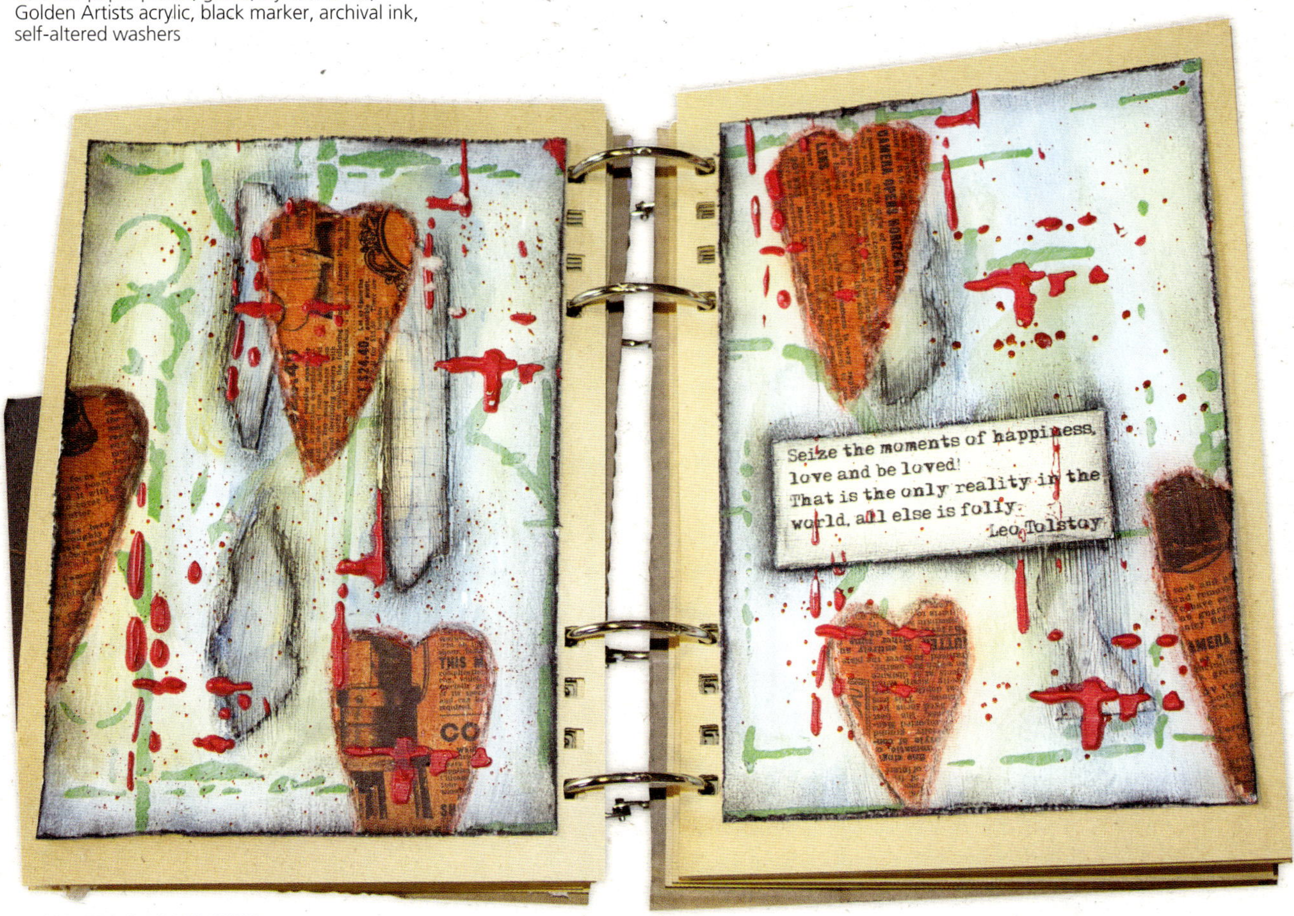

MOMENTS OF HAPPINESS
Gesso, Golden Artists acrylics, paper collage, old newspaper, modeling paste, charcoal, sepia chalk

Kay M. Reist

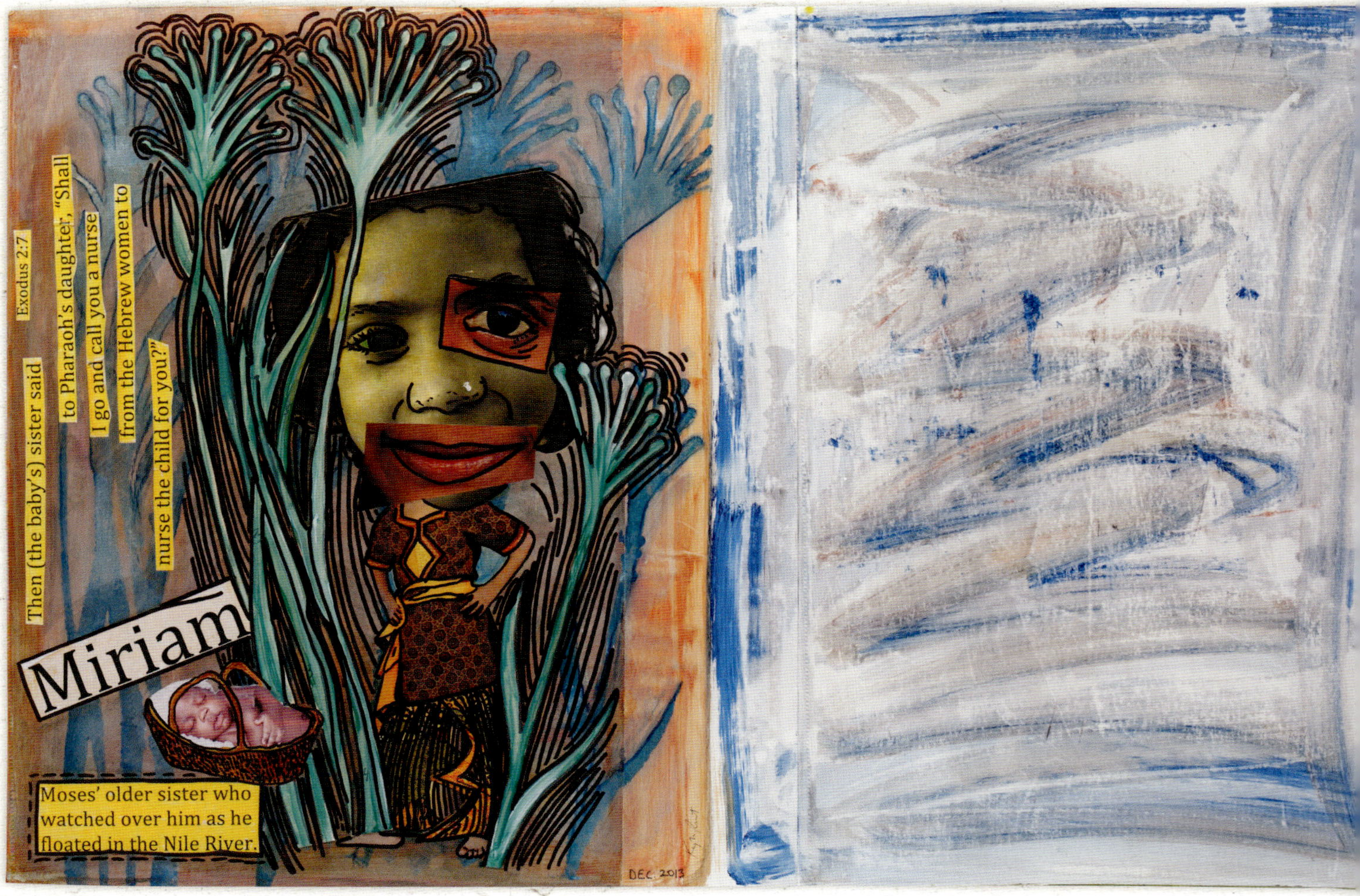

MIRIAM EXODUS 2:1–10
Mixed media

What interesting or unique techniques did you apply to this artwork?

I made a papyrus stencil out of poster board; after stenciling the image, I decided to add the positive image of the stencil directly to the composition. Layering the media created depth in the piece.

Do you ever give yourself journal prompts?

I like to work with themes, themes that have meaning to me. I have also realized that researching individual topics and subjects is something that takes me into the art zone.

I've worked with themes that include everything from documenting the year I was born to my fourth-grade year to different artists' styles.

What was your inspiration for this piece?

This piece is from a journal that illustrates characters from the Bible. No one really knows what they looked like, so I can be as creative as I want!

Tammy Murdock

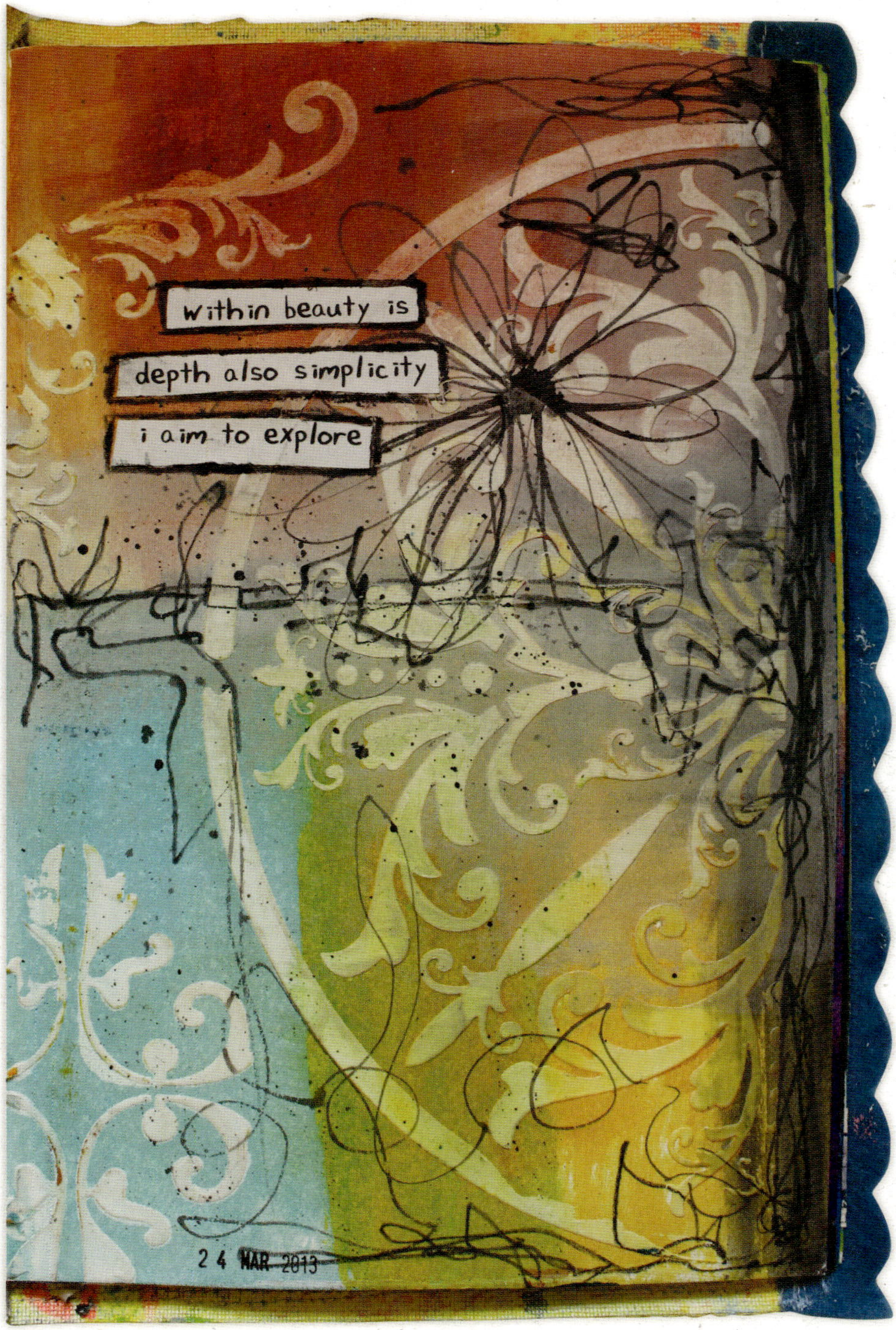

HAIKU
Golden paint, molding paste, stencil, Stabilo All pencil

What was your inspiration for this piece?

This piece was inspired by my love for supplies. This is what happens when molding paste finds itself on a desk when stencils are nearby. I started out with an uncommon color combination (for me) before getting pulled back into my familiar blue when I felt trapped by the warm colors.

Are there any mixed-media artists who inspire you?

I'm inspired by Magaly Ohika, Flora Bowley, Teesha Moore, Roben-Marie Smith, Joanne Sharpe—I could go on for days!

Do you ever give yourself journal prompts?

I often start out with the intention to give myself journal prompts. I will randomly open up a book but then get distracted. Mostly I fall back on using my supplies and recent things I have read.

What tips would you give to fellow art journaling artists?

My art journaling tips would be to do some research. Use a kind, gentle voice with yourself. When viewing other artists' work, try not to let the comparison monster rear its ugly head and stop you in your tracks. Back away from the computer and discover your own style!

Paula Hagar

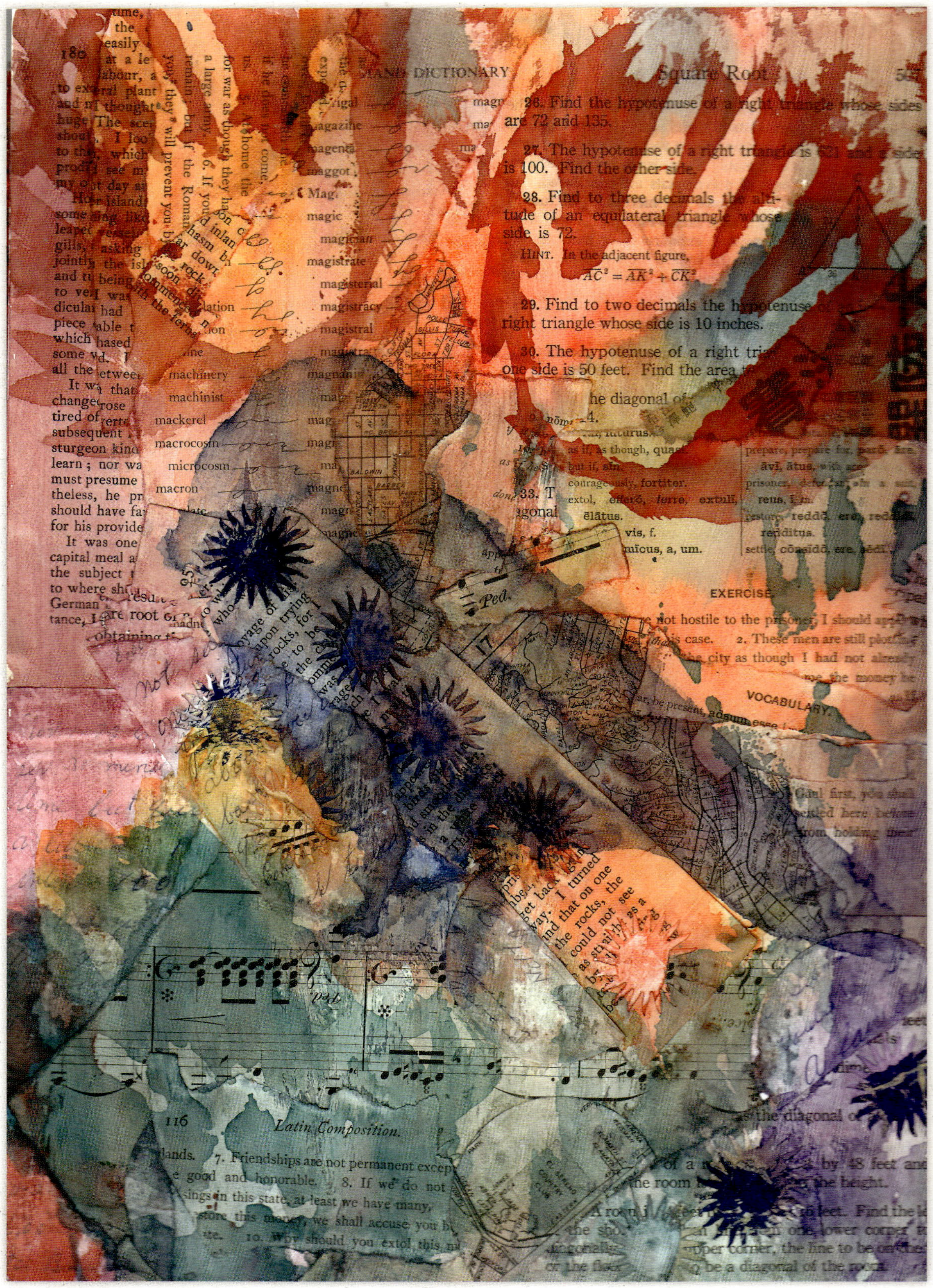

BIRD IN HAND
Old textbook paper, watercolor paint, stencils, 140-lb. (300gsm) watercolor paper

“A VISION CAN NEVER COME TO LIFE IF IT STAYS IN YOUR HEAD. *Give life to your vision.”*

— JANICE EARHART

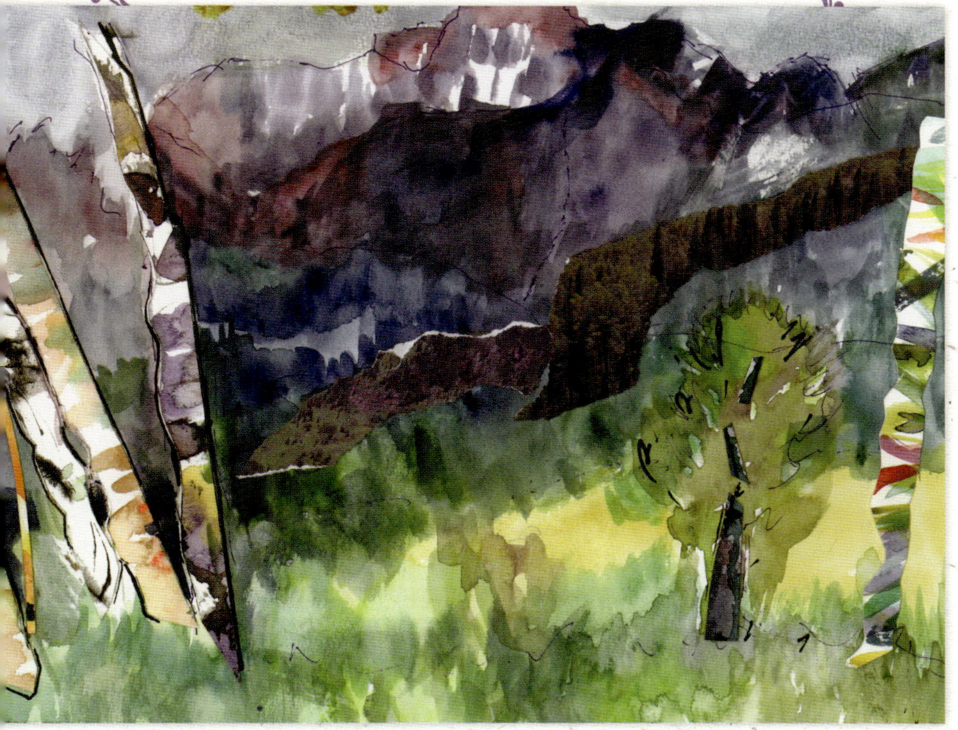

LONG'S PEAK AT BEAVER MEADOWS
Watercolor paint, strips of an original photo, 140-lb. (300 gsm) watercolor paper

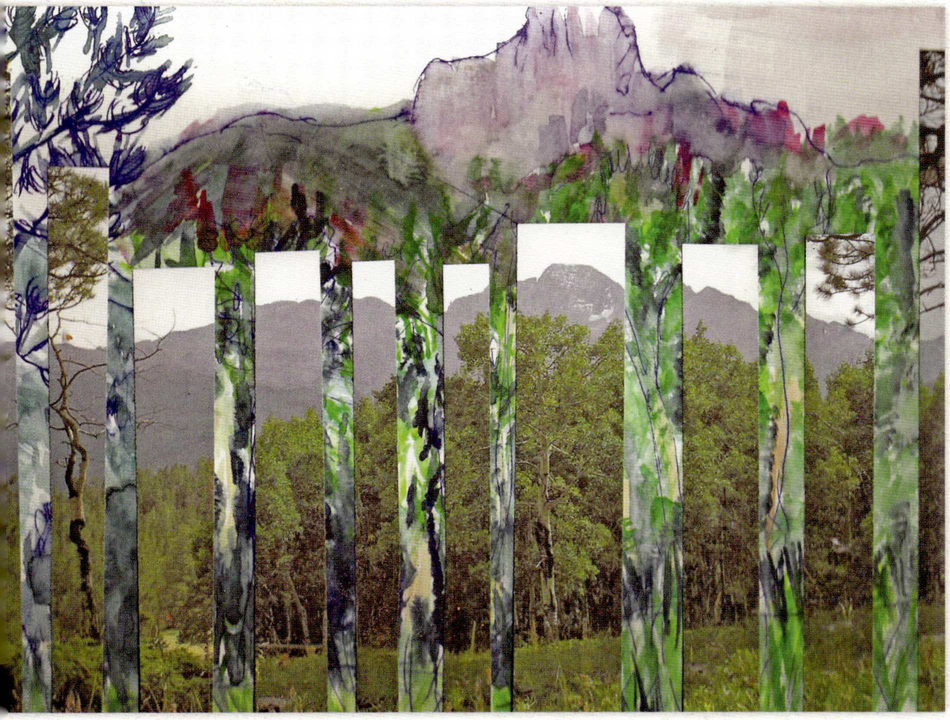

LONG'S PEAK #2
Watercolor paint, strips of an original photo, 140-lb. (300gsm) watercolor paper

What was your inspiration for *Bird in Hand*?

The inspiration for this piece came from my iconic love of ravens, hands and words imagery. I had recently acquired some old text pages at an estate sale and couldn't wait to turn them into a collage. I always have raven and hand stencils nearby, and once the papers were glued down, I began playing with watercolors and stencils, and this fun watercolor collage emerged.

What interesting or unique techniques did you apply to *Bird in Hand*?

No unique techniques. Just gluing down paper and watercoloring over it with stencils.

Are there any mixed-media artists who inspire you?

My mixed-media artist friend Marie Danti is my greatest inspiration. She has no fear of a blank page and sees tackling anything unknown as an exciting challenge.

Do you ever give yourself journal prompts?

I love using journal prompts and do so frequently, in both my art journals and my written journals—both of which have become interwoven over the last decade.

Do you have an art journaling process?

My art journaling process is really just to go with the flow of the moment. I always carry a camera with me, so a page might begin with a photo around which I create a page of color and art.

Teri Casper

What was your inspiration for this piece?

My inspiration was twofold: an article about map painting by Jacqueline Newbold and our annual trek to Arizona (we seem to collect maps from every state). Painting travel memories on the maps was a perfect idea.

Are there any mixed-media artists who inspire you?

A mixed-media artist who inspires me is Jacqueline Newbold.

Do you ever give yourself journal prompts?

I love prompts because they spark my muse to get creative.

When and why did you start art journaling?

I sketch every day and realized my sketches were a reflection of my life.

What tips would you give to fellow art journaling artists?

There are no art police around to criticize your work, so enjoy and try new things.

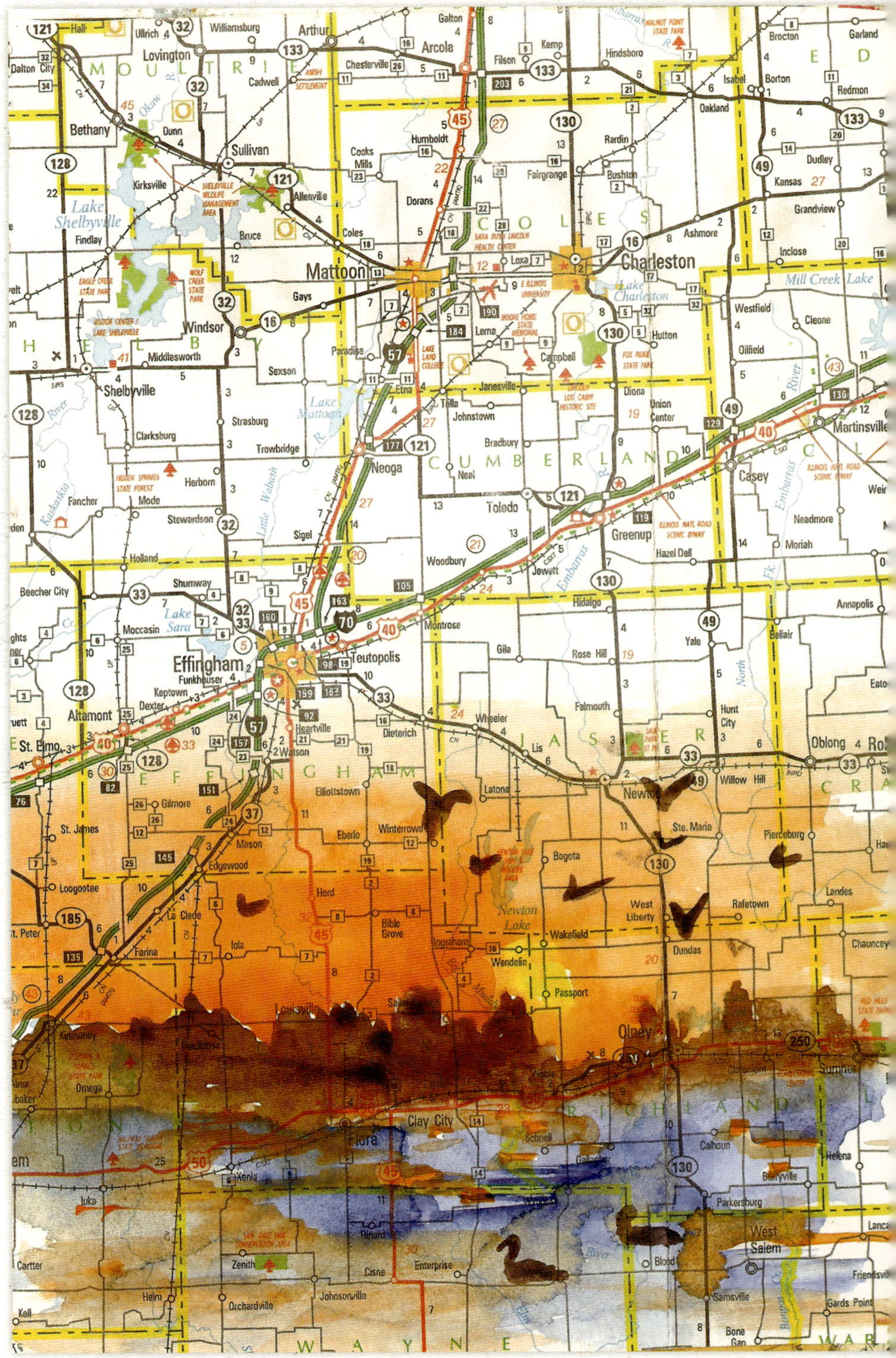

ALONG THE WAY
Map, thinned white gesso, watercolor

> “IF YOU OBEY ALL THE RULES, YOU MISS *all the fun.*”
>
> — AUDREY HEPBURN

Deb Versluis

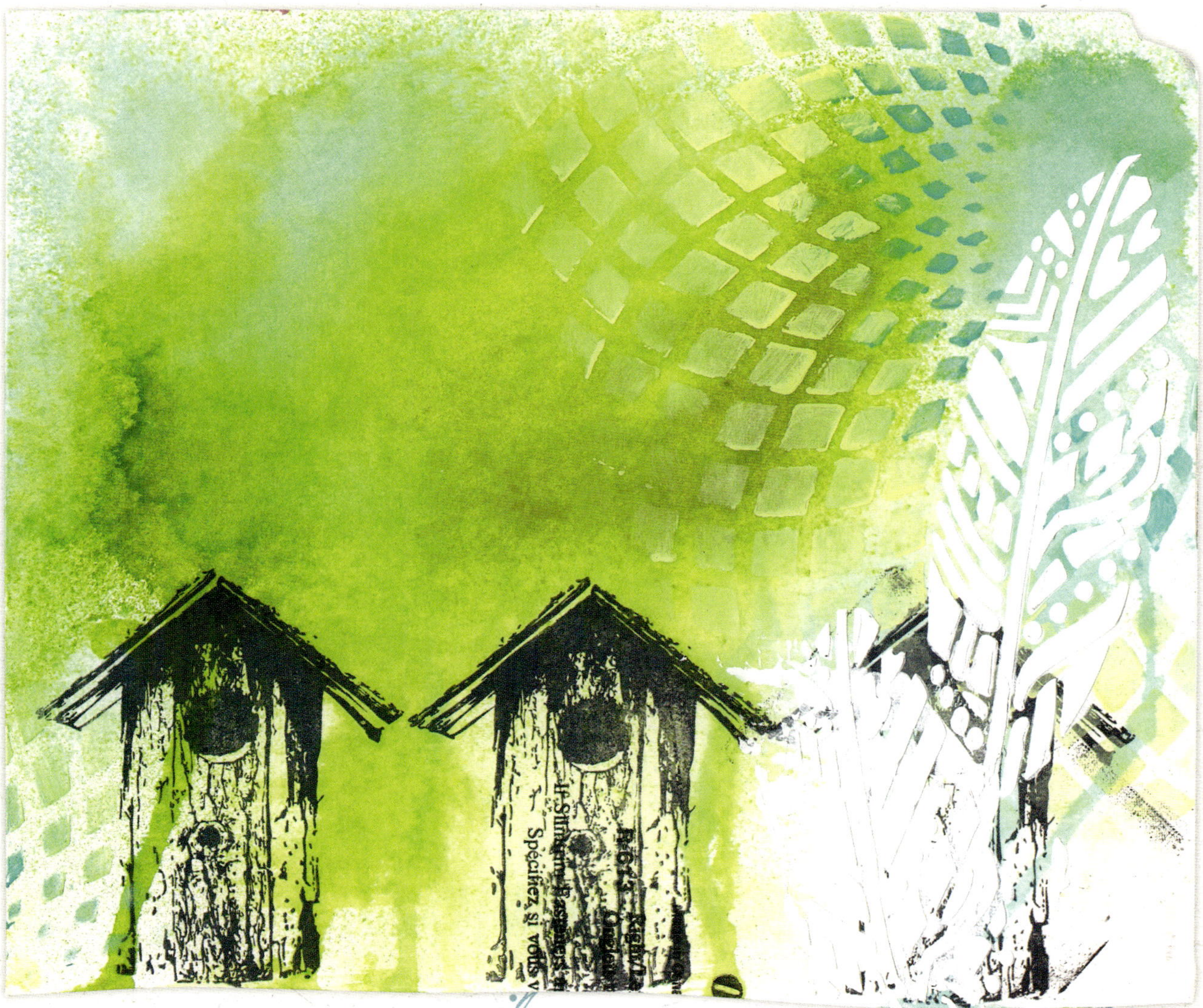

SONGBIRD HOME IN SPRING
Spray ink, stencils, acrylic paint, a bird house rubber stamp, Archival black ink, texture paste, manilla file folder

> "KEEP IT SIMPLE, IMAGINE AND DO! AND IF YOU GET STUCK, THEN DO FIRST, AND *imagine more.*"

What was your inspiration for this piece?

Inspiration always comes to me through nature. I love being outdoors, gardening and hiking. We've had a very long winter and I have been waiting, with very little patience, for spring to arrive this year. My page is inspired by the birds that visit our yard each year.

What interesting or unique techniques did you apply to this artwork?

This artwork is part of a series of pages that explored the effect of layering the same five products, each in a different order, on each page, and using the same colors and imagery each time. Also, it is created on a used manila file folder, for later binding in a book.

Are there any mixed-media artists who inspire you?

I have been inspired by Dina Wakley, Julie Fei-Fan Balzer, Dawn DeVries Sokol, Ronda Palazzari, Roben-Marie Smith, Pam Garrison and Mary Ann Moss.

Marianne Goodell

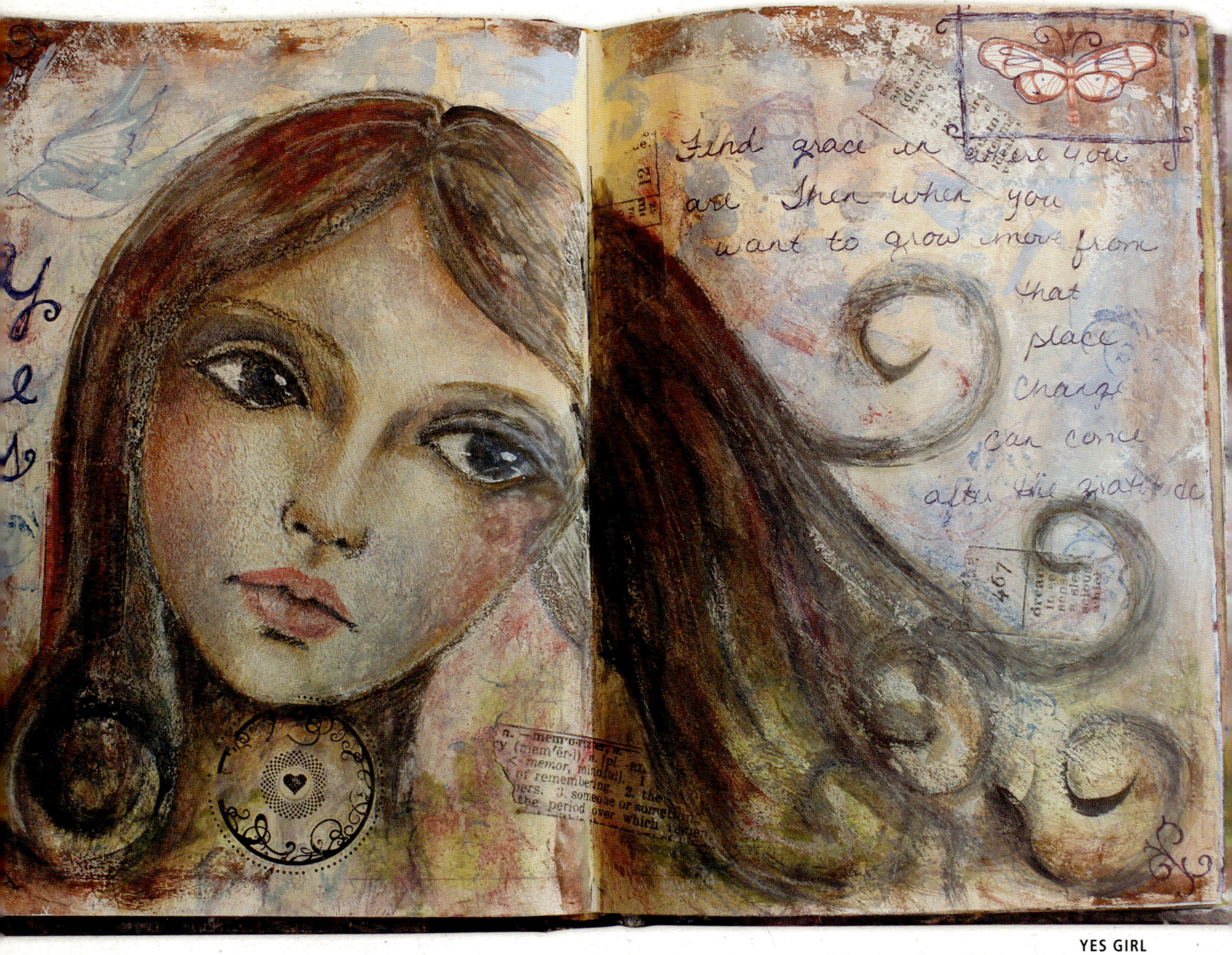

YES GIRL
Colored pencils, acrylic paints, glazing medium, credit card, embellishments

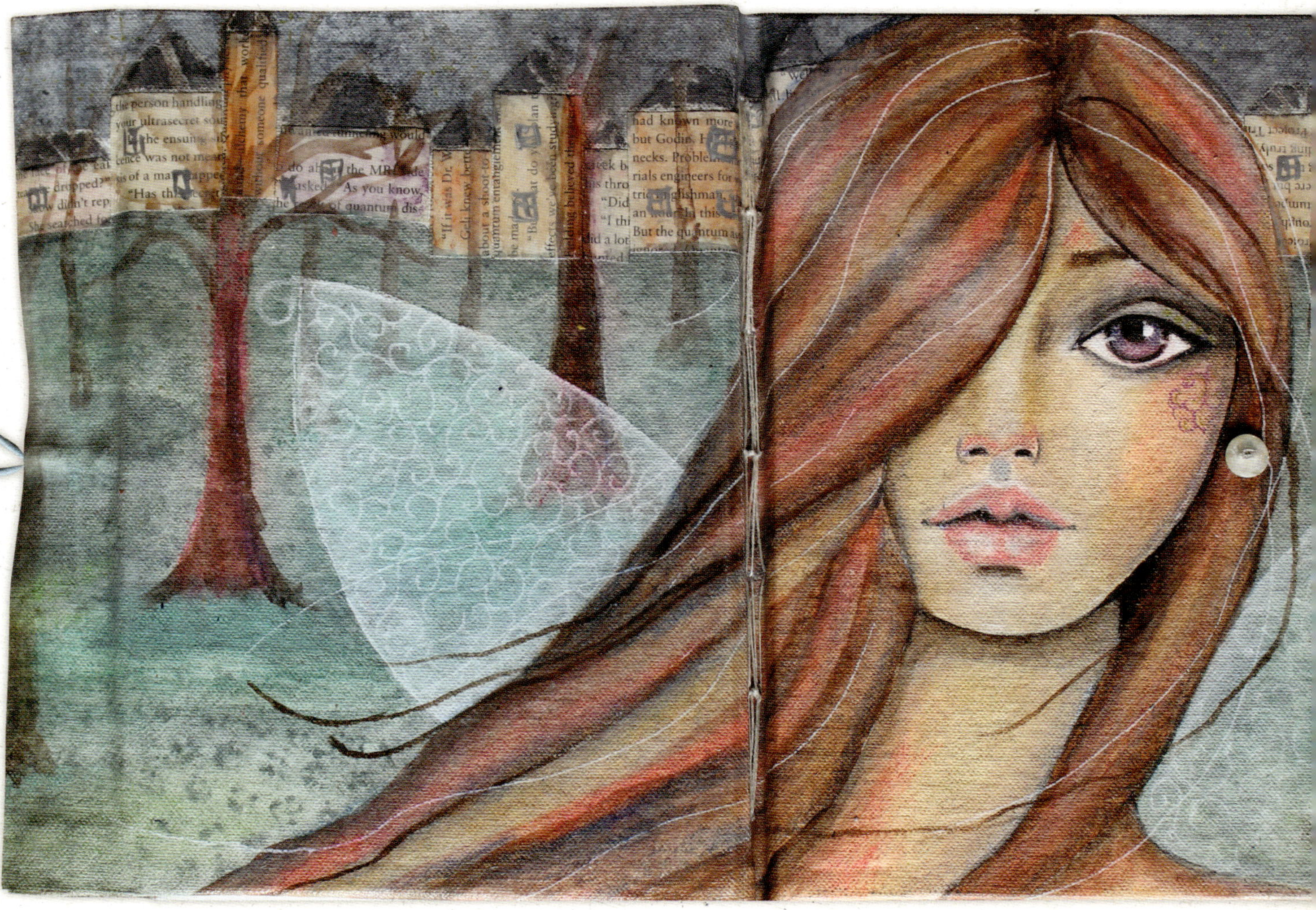

FAIRY JOURNAL COVER
Fabric, gesso, Prismacolor pencils, acrylic paints

What was your inspiration for your *Fairy Journal Cover*?

I love the idea of handmade journals. I have been exploring a variety of methods for creating journals by varying the type of stitches for binding, covers and the paper. I created my *Fairy Journal Cover* with the intention of exploring new art techniques on duck cloth canvas.

When and why did you start art journaling?

I have kept a writing journal for twenty years and an art journal for three. I started art journaling because I wanted to expand my artistic abilities. I love books, I love writing and I love art—art journaling became a natural progression.

I now have completed six journals and am working in three. Journaling is a centering ritual for me. I keep a journal next to where I sit and work in it when I sit down. I usually have several pages started and work on them randomly. It may take me several days to finish a single spread, but I have finally gotten to the point where I am free to let my pages unfold without judgment. If I ever get stuck, I just turn to artists who inspire me.

Are there any mixed-media artists who inspire you?

My painting inspiration comes from Kat McBride and Terra Sheridan.

What tips would you give to fellow art journaling artists?

I would advise any art journaler to explore and play with the curiosity of a child. Pure joy can be discovered this way.

Brian Kasstle

> "Believe in yourself.
> PRACTICE, PRACTICE, PRACTICE!"

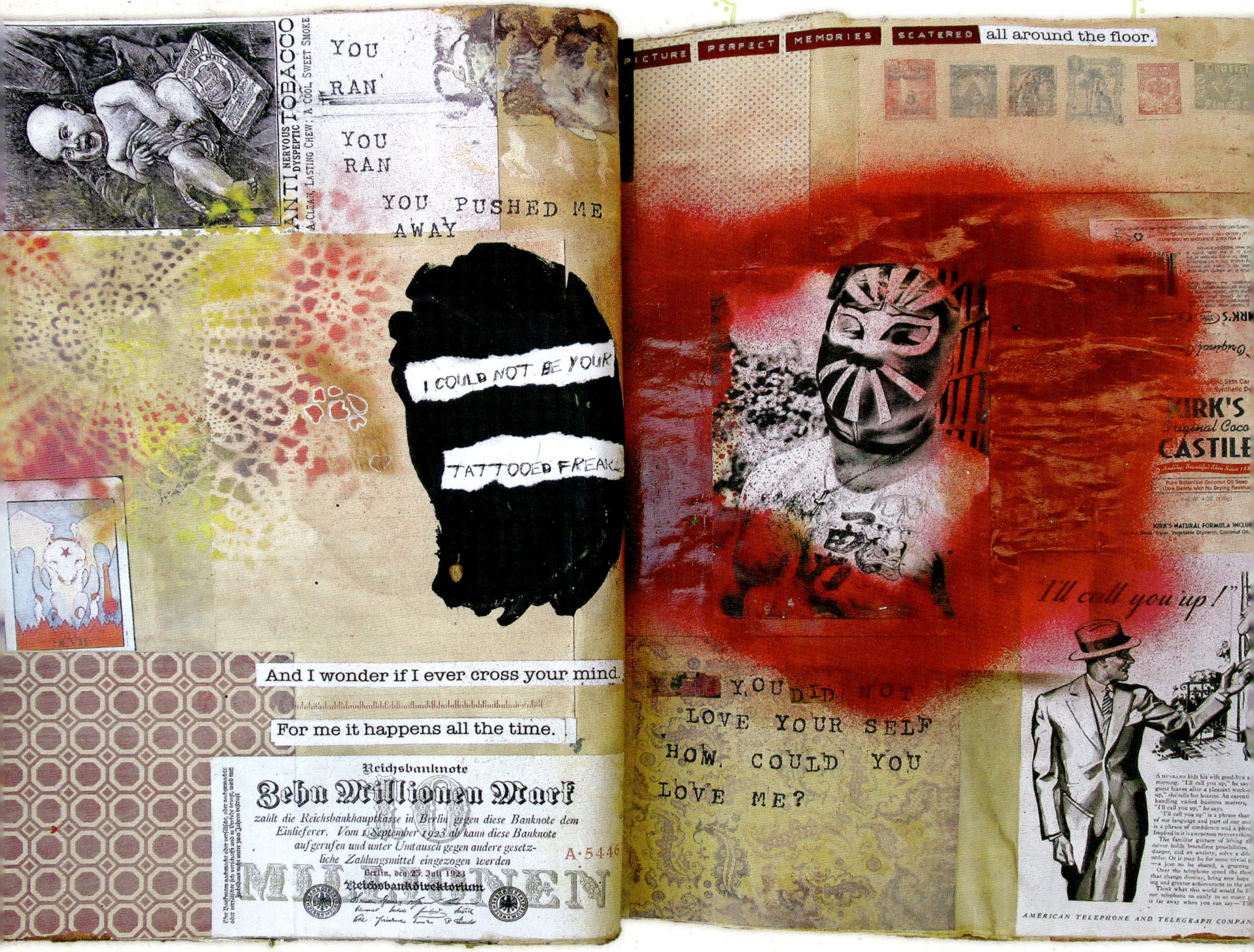

PICTURE PERFECT MEMORIES
Paper, matte medium, paint, a light wash, spray paint, stencils

What was your inspiration for *Enough*?

It was started during a class with Orly Avineri. Her classes are intense. I got home and it needed something more so the white gesso, on the top, was added.

Are there any mixed-media artists who inspire you?

There are so many. What I find inspiring now is watching folks who have never art journaled before, or unexperienced artists, who start and find their voice and their freedom in the process. It brings tears to my eyes.

How did you come up with the title for *Enough*?

It actually came to be about my process of creating. Layering, adding, subtracting, getting deep in thought. It is about the process of when you know you're done and the spread is complete—enough.

What tips would you give fellow art journaling artists?

Don't journal in isolation. Join a group, take a class, online or in person. Start a group. I tend to work a lot on my own, but I also enjoy working with other artists.

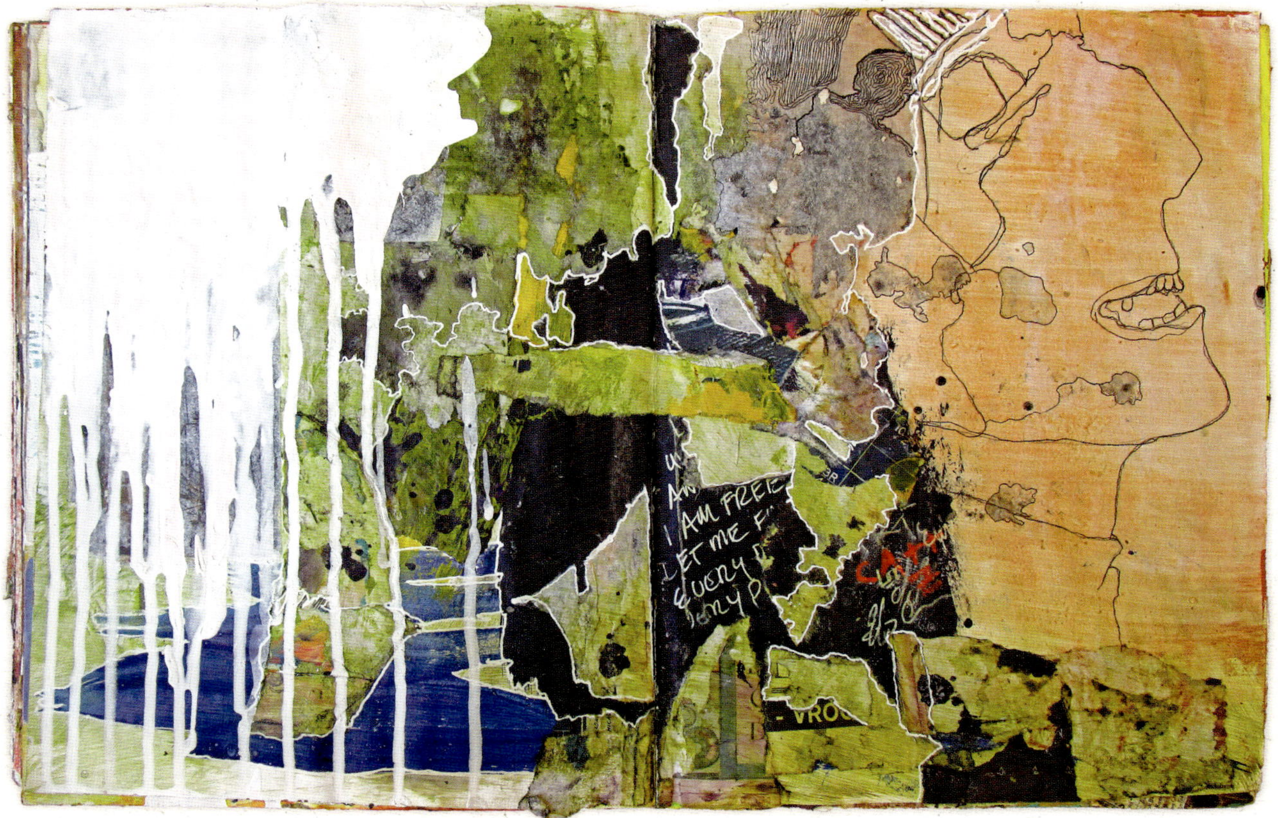

ENOUGH
Vintage and found papers, handmade papers, Signo white gel pens, Nova Color paints, white and black gesso

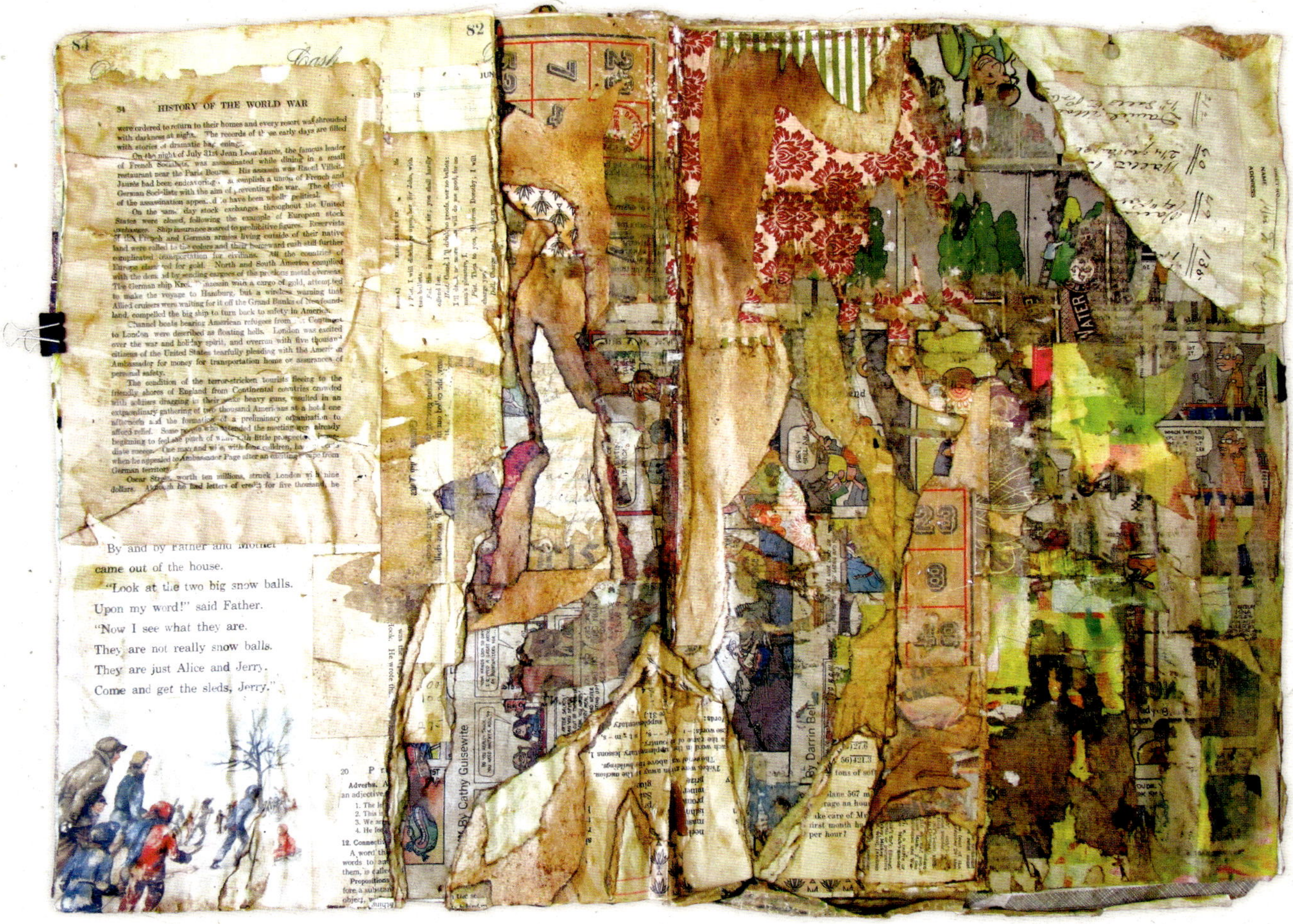

LAYERS OF LIFE
11" × 16" (28cm × 41cm) Moleskine, vintage and personal papers, comic book pages, Sunday funnies, ticket stubs, matte medium, Tim Holtz Distress Ink, matte varnish

Theresa Harrison

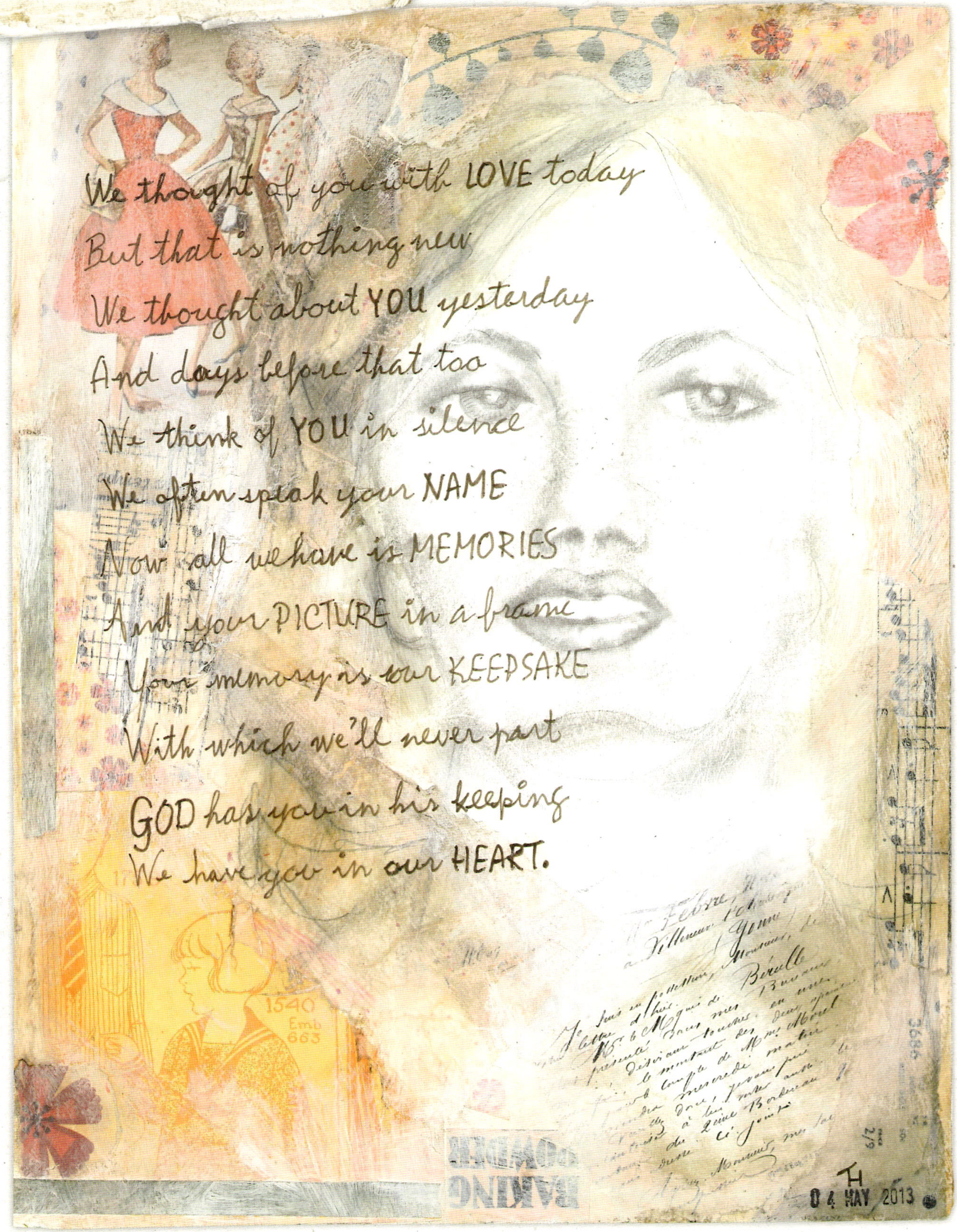

MoM (MEMORIES OF MOM)
Sheet music, sewing pattern paper, scrapbook paper, vintage graphics

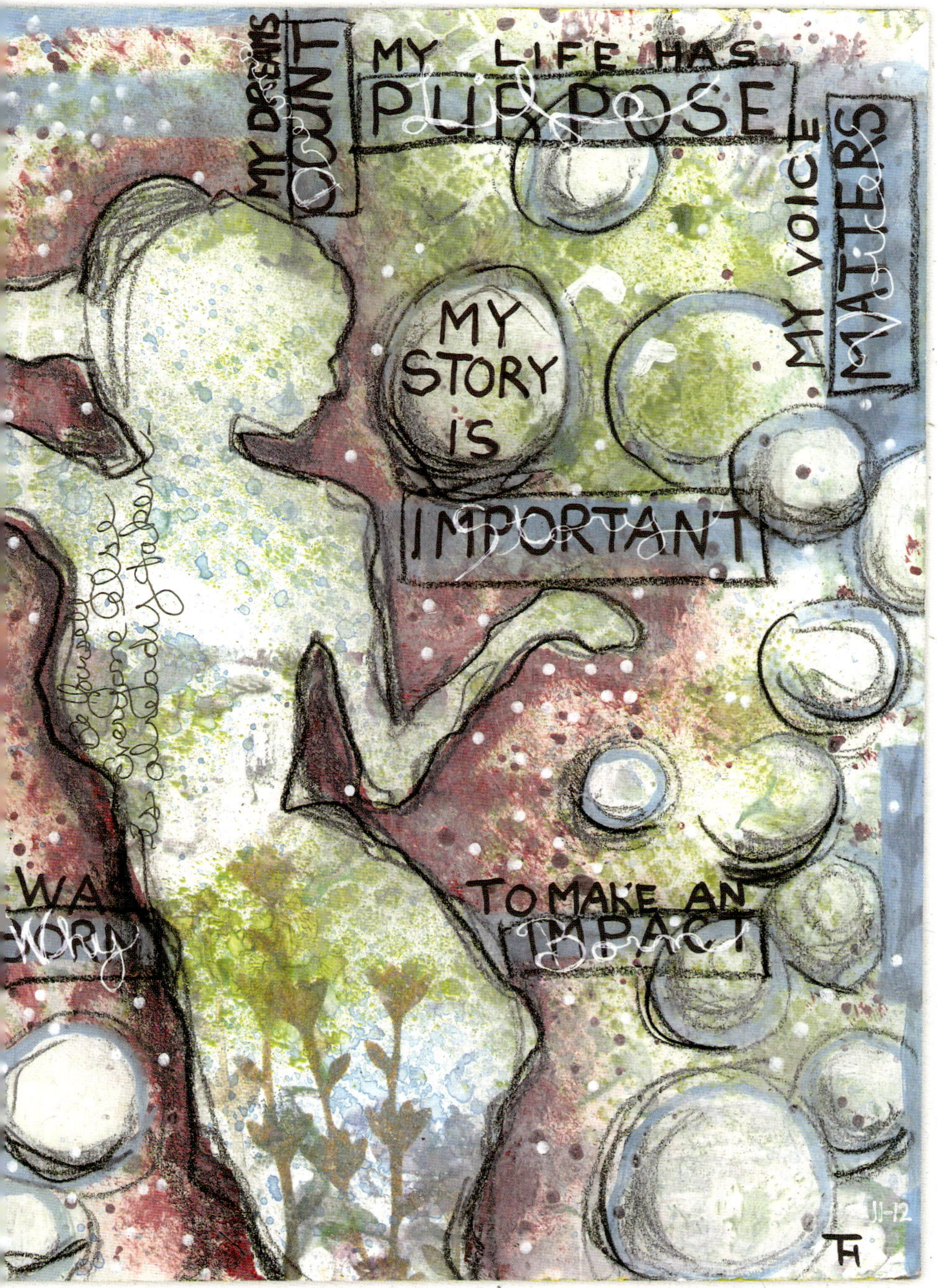

MY STORY
Gesso, acrylic paint, white gel pen, white paint pen, china marker, felt markers, Distress ink, my own flower stem stamp

What was your inspiration for *My Story*?

This piece was the result of an exercise in gaining a better insight into myself.

What interesting or unique techniques did you apply to *My Story*?

I wrote my thoughts on a blank journal page, made note of the important words and then painted over them to create a background. For the next layer, I dabbed paint over a silhouette mask cut from a magazine, blended everything together with gesso, then used a china marker to highlight the various shapes.

Are there any mixed-media artists who inspire you?

I'm inspired by Mary Beth Shaw.

Do you ever give yourself journal prompts?

I don't use journal prompts; rather I find inspiration all around me—a song, a quote, a color scheme, a pattern, an occasion, a thought or a new supply or technique.

What tips would you give to fellow art journaling artists?

I encourage fellow art journaling artists to journal every day, even if only for ten or fifteen minutes. Enjoy the process. There's no right way or wrong way. It's your journal—for you, made by you—and you don't have to share it with anyone.

Luis Montero

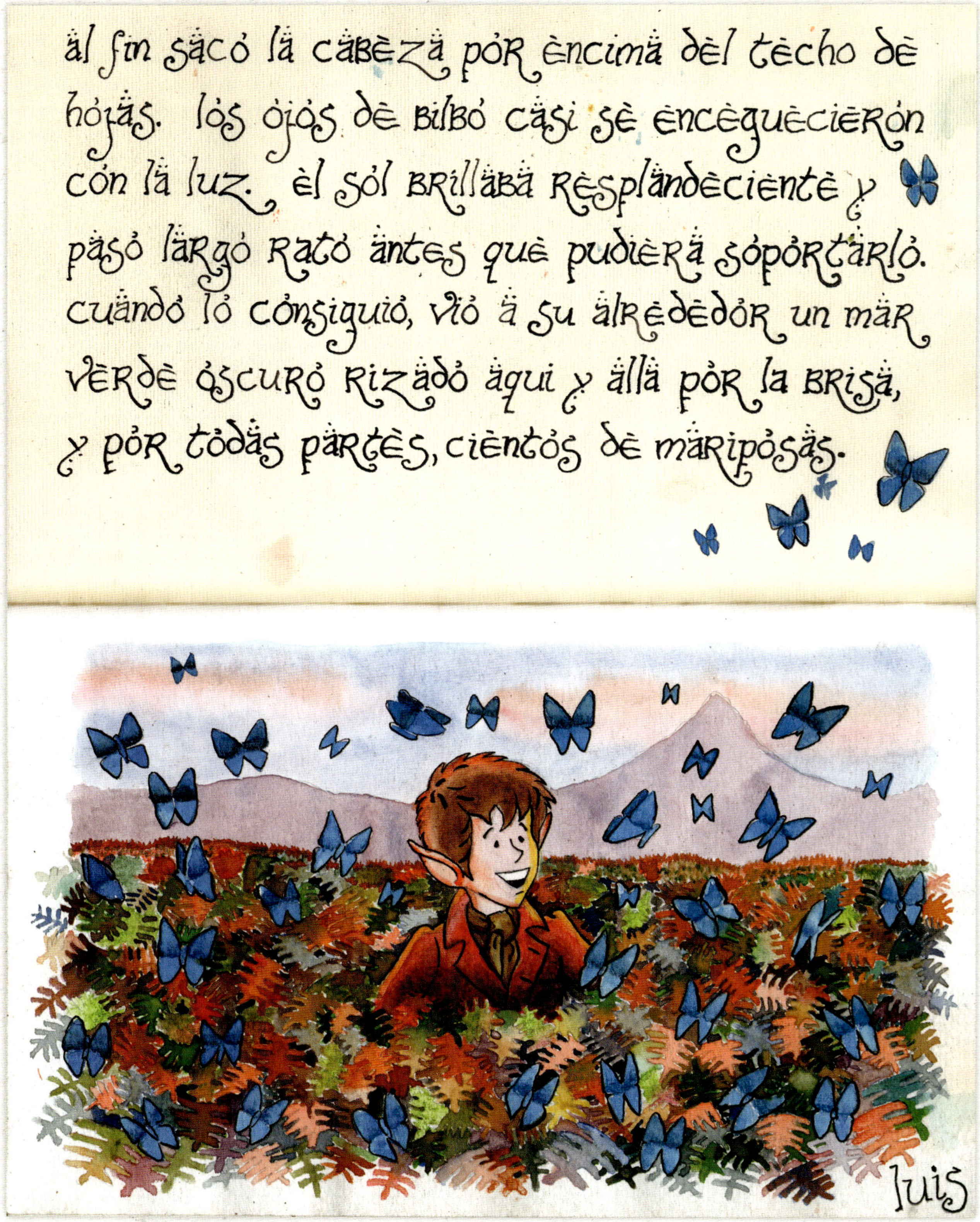

BILBO
Watercolor, colored pencils, china ink, brushes, quills, watercolor paper, Italian handmade paper

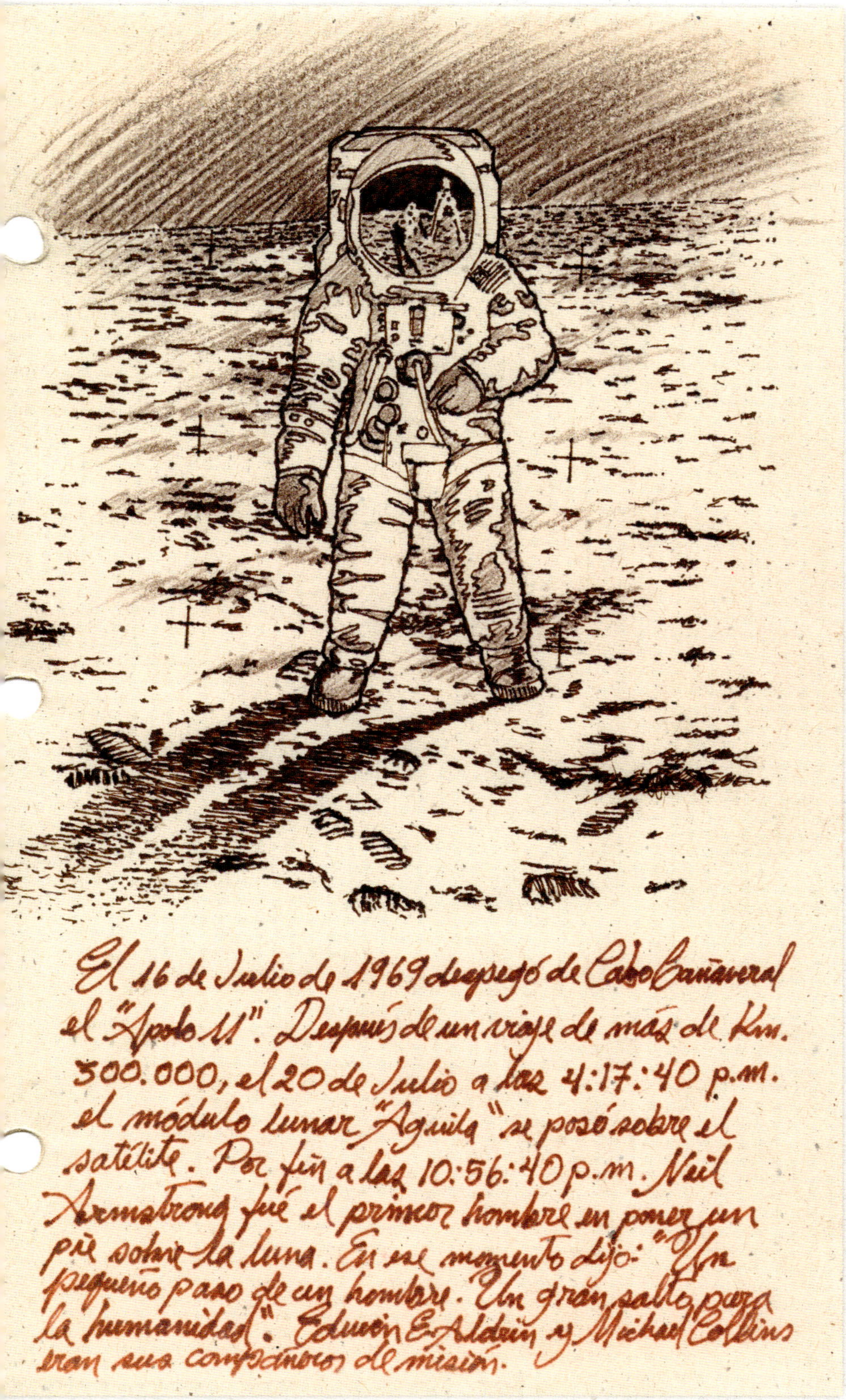

LEAP OF FAITH
Sepia china ink, sepia pencil, quill, banana paper

What was your inspiration for *Bilbo*?

Have you ever felt so much calm and peace after a very long and painful period in your life? This is what I felt while watching the scene when Bilbo climbs the oak tree. It was an inspiring moment due to the very personal meaning I shared with it.

What interesting or unique techniques did you apply to *Bilbo*?

I replaced Bilbo's face with my nephew Alberto's face.

What tips would you give to fellow art journaling artists?

If you want to live your own dream, then you have to be stubborn and never surrender when you feel fear—at those moments when apparently nothing's happening and your dream seems like it's not going to come true.

What was your inspiration for *Leap of Faith*?

In 1986 I worked as a graphic designer on a local newspaper. Don Jorge Brenes, the creative director, knew that I love *Star Trek*. So, one day, he came to me with one of several photos sent by NASA to the newspaper photo archive in 1969. He gave it to me saying, "I think you'll love to keep a piece of the real *Star Trek...*"

Traveling back in time, considering the powerful, very precise and almost unlimited technologies of the twenty-first century, I just can't imagine how those brave men could touch the moon in 1969. They deserve a little homage in the inside cover for my Astronomical Journal, so years later I copied it in my journal.

Cynthia Cole Russell

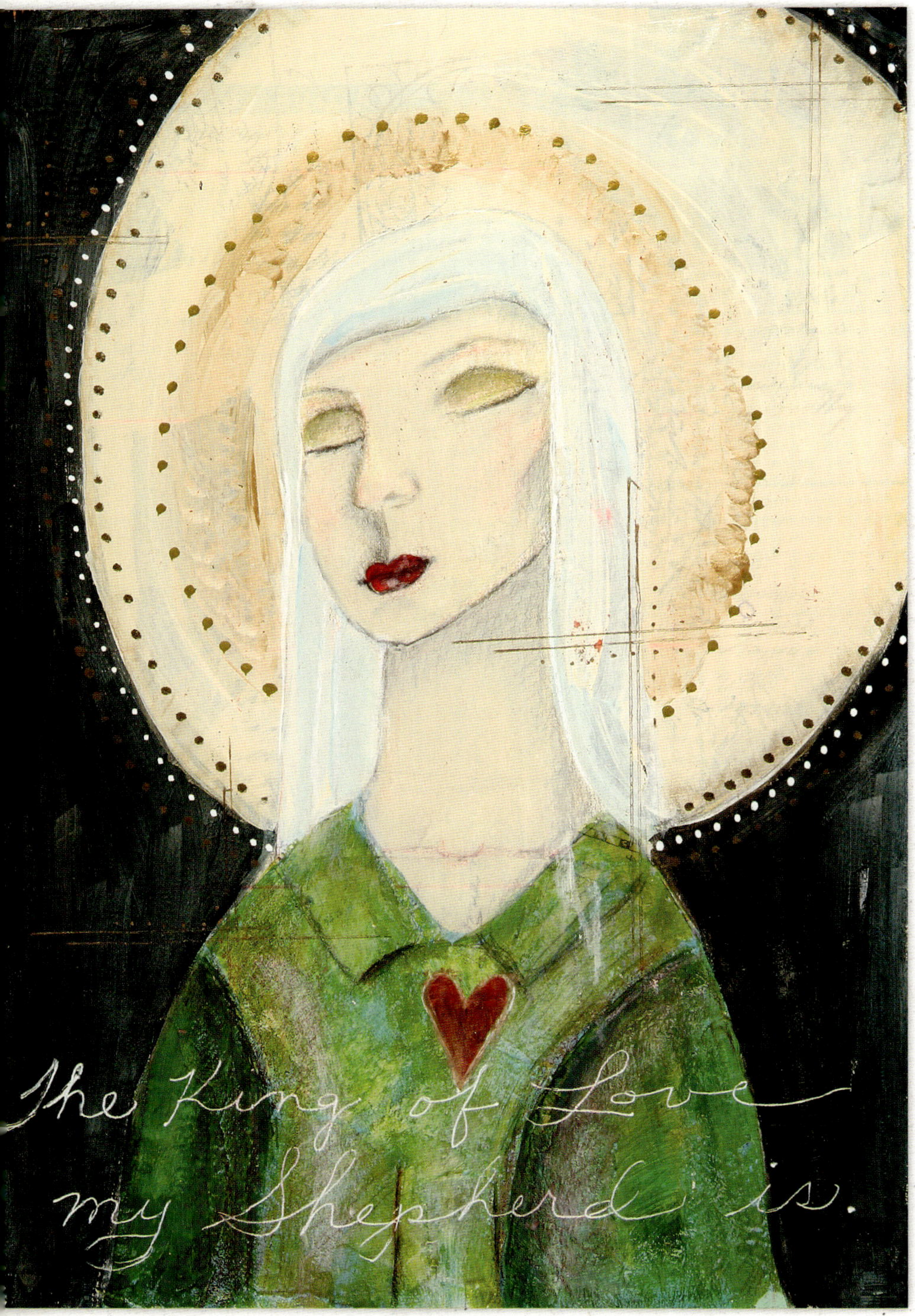

THE KING OF LOVE MY SHEPERD IS
Ballpoint pen, rubber stamps (hidden under final painting), craft paints, Prismacolor/graphite pencils, metallic and white gel pens

What was your inspiration for this piece?

The poems of Kabir.

What interesting or unique techniques did you apply to this artwork?

I started with a discarded appointment scheduling book.

Are there any mixed-media artists who inspire you?

I'm inspired by Suzi Blu and Pam Carriker.

When and why did you start art journaling?

Ten years ago my husband, Steve, handed me a book on collaging to change and guide life's journey. It began as a simple collage and emerged into full-blown mixed media.

Do you have an art journaling process?

I just start scribble journaling and see where it goes.

What tips would you give to fellow art journaling artists?

Make no excuses. Just do something in your journal every day—even if it is just gluing down one piece of paper.

Theresa T. Mirabile

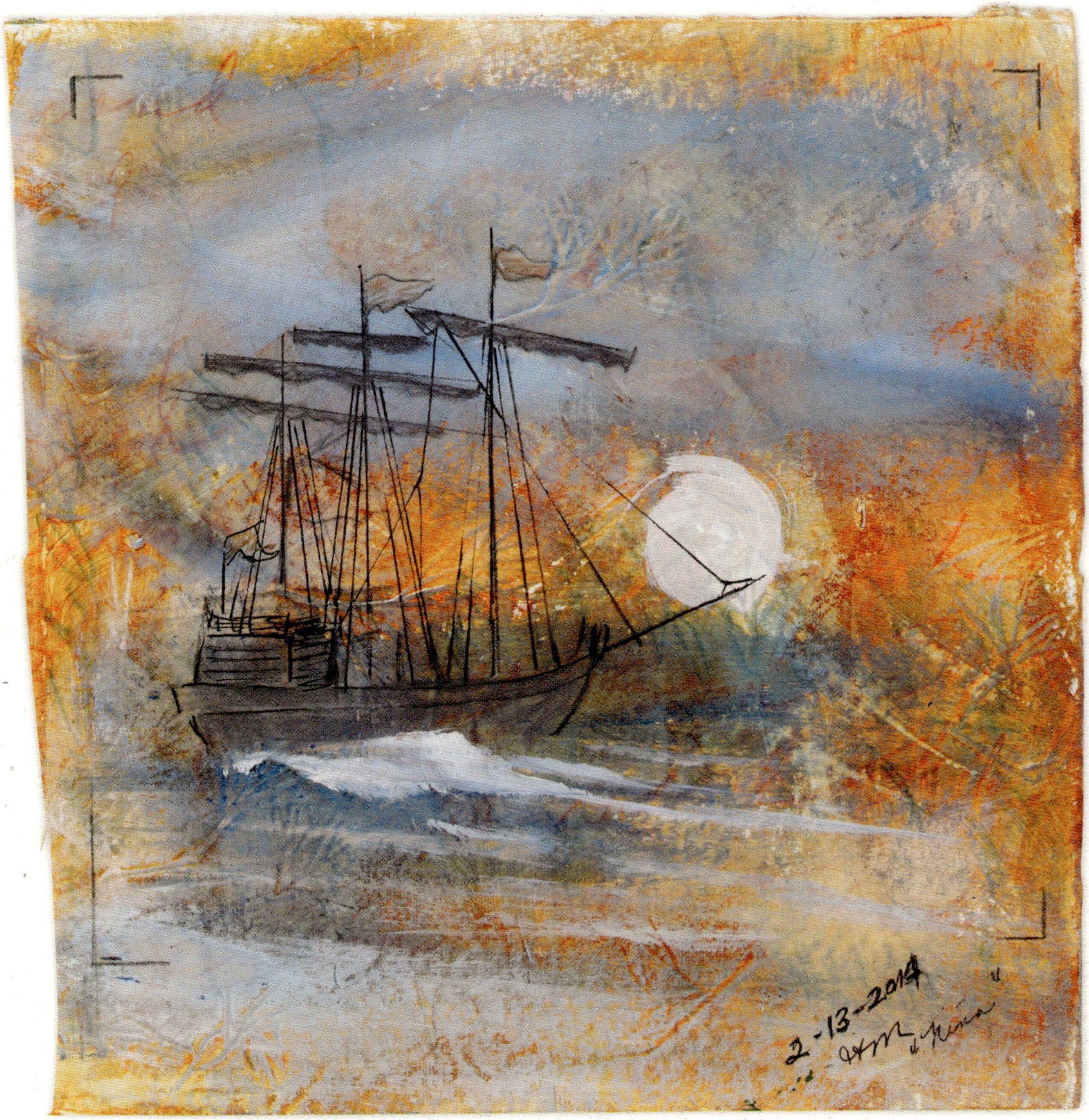

NINA
Acrylic glaze medium, pencil, black marker, pen

What was your inspiration for this piece?

Seeing the *Nina* and *Pinta* ship replicas was my inspiration.

What interesting or unique techniques did you apply to this artwork?

I used a mixture of Quinacridone Nickel Azo Gold and glaze medium to cover it with a thin gesso coat. Then using a sketching pencil, I drew the ship. The sky and sea were created with a mixture of Ultramarine Blue and gesso.

Are there any mixed-media artists who inspire you?

I'm inspired by Pam Carriker.

Do you ever give yourself journal prompts?

An interesting quote, word or a recent trip often triggers ideas.

When and why did you start art journaling?

Artist friends inspired me. I began mixed-media journaling in earnest a year ago.

"IT'S *only paper.*"
— FRED RAWLINSON

Maureen Craddock

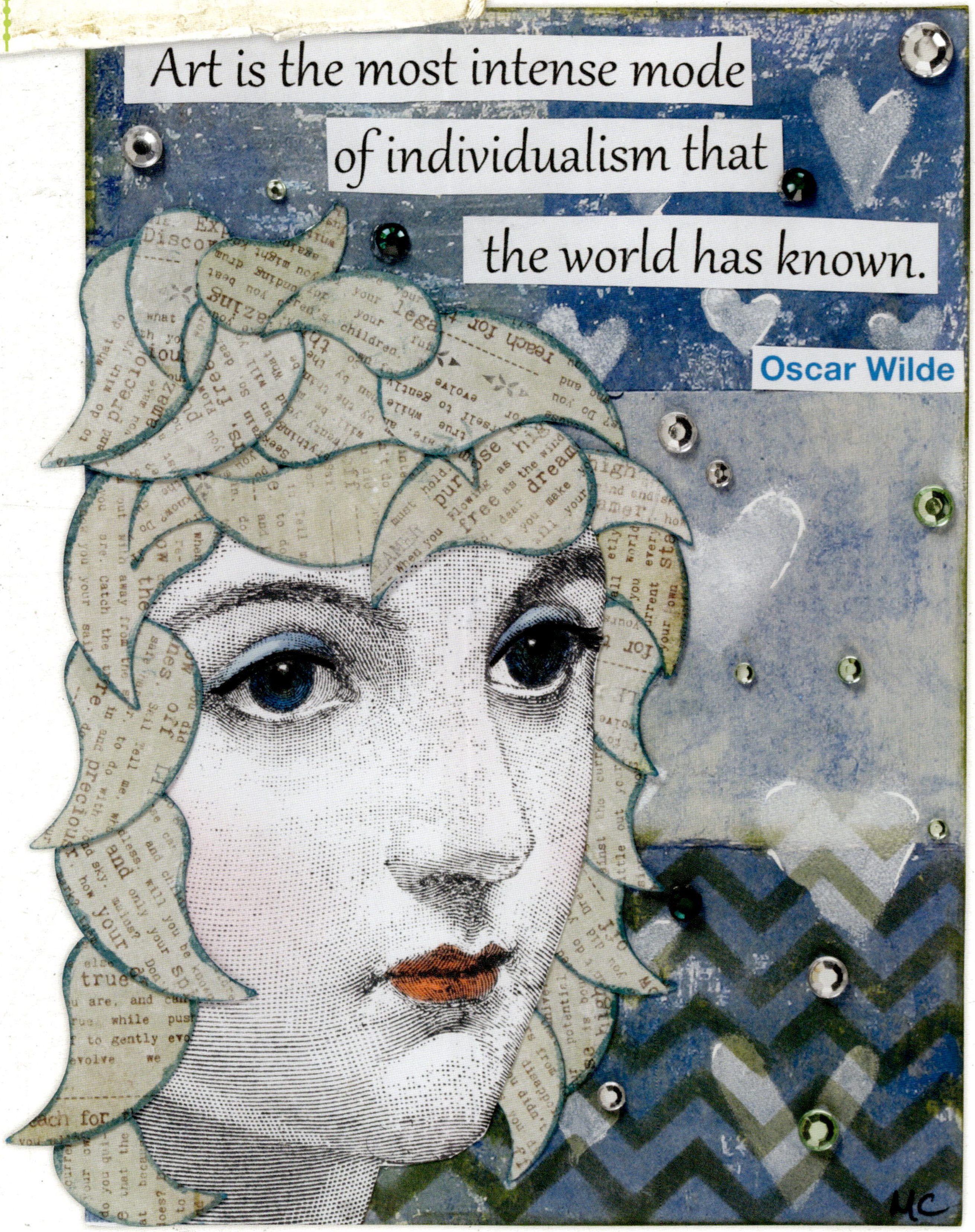

INTENSE MODE
Stampington & Company paper, Heidi Swapp stencil, heart stencil, face stamp, EK paper punch, assorted rhinestones, Copic markers, chalk pastels, Tim Holtz Distress Inks, Memento black ink stamp pad

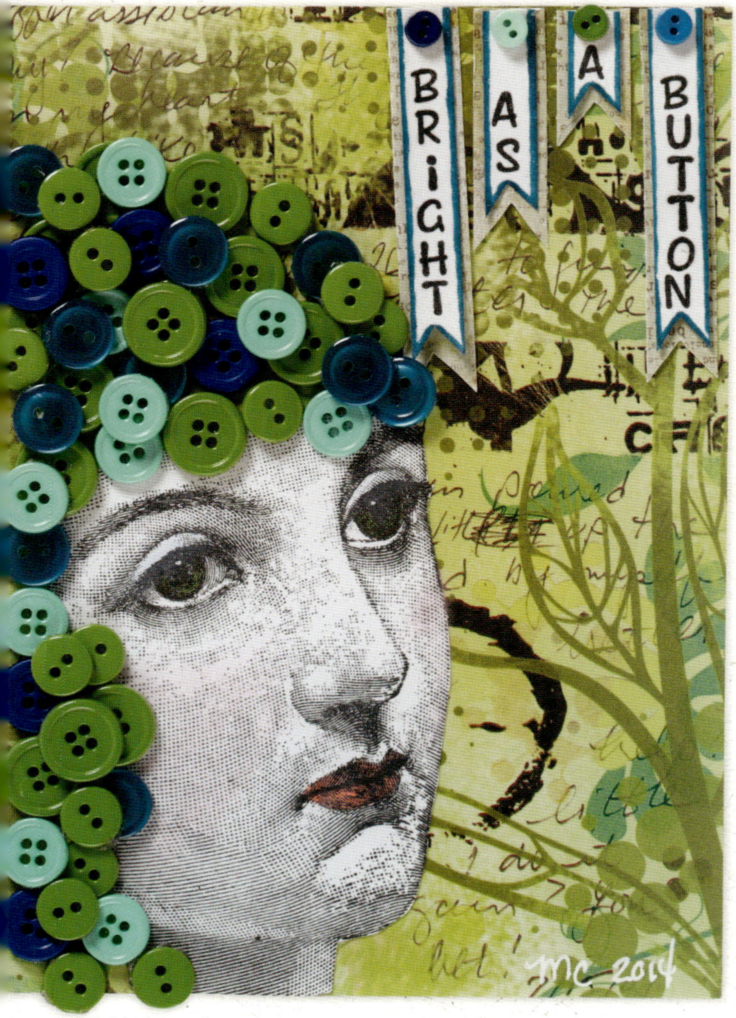

BRIGHT AS A BUTTON
Stampington & Company's paper, face stamp, Memento black ink stamp pad, Copic markers, chalk pastels, assorted buttons

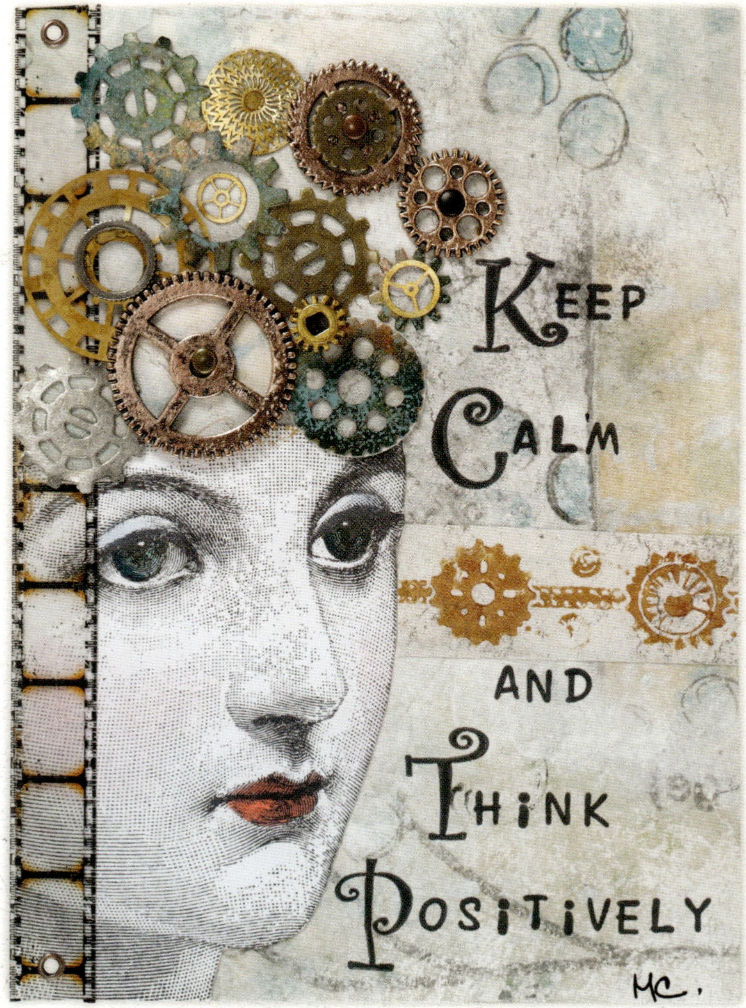

KEEP CALM AND THINK POSITIVELY
Stampington & Company paper, face stamp, Memento black ink stamp pad, Copic markers, chalk pastels, assorted gears, Inka Dinka Doo stamp, Studio G alphabet stamp set, Adirondack acrylic paint dabber, Tim Holtz ideaology film strip ribbon

What was your inspiration for *Intense Mode*?

The face stamp.

What interesting or unique techniques did you apply to *Intense Mode*?

I used the paper punch drops to create her hair.

Are there any mixed-media artists who inspire you?

So many mixed-media artists inspire me. Tim Holtz is one of my favorites, as is Christine Tomlinson, Traci Bautista and Suzi Blu—to name a few.

Do you ever give yourself journal prompts?

Not usually.

When and why did you start art journaling?

I belong to an online art group, The Art Colony, and there were members who encouraged me to try journaling.

Do you have an art journaling process?

I don't really have a process for my art journaling. It really comes from whatever happens to be inspiring me at the time.

What tips would you give to fellow art journaling artists?

Just have fun. Journaling is a place for you to express yourself. In art journaling, anything goes.

How did you come up with the title of *Keep Calm and Think Positively*?

As an artist, I find myself filled with doubt. I need to push away the negativity and focus on the positive.

Lynette Potts

Are there any mixed-media artists who inspire you?

I'm inspired by Tamara Laporte.

How did you come up with your title?

I was putting ideas down on paper from the theme "up, up and away." I came up with a silhouette floating, holding something. So I drew circles from a stencil around the silhouette and added a gold glow (gold is my favorite color). The words reminded me of my daughter, dreaming about her future: Live like you dance, be happy in life, love yourself first.

When and why did you start art journaling?

About two years ago, I wanted to give my daughters something personal from me. I started looking at different ideas on the Internet. Journaling was what I liked, with pictures and words, that also meant something to me.

What tips would you give to fellow art journaling artists?

Look around for ideas, create your own style and do workshops online or at a studio. Post to get feedback and always enjoy what you are doing.

"CREATING CAN BE THE *perfect moment in time.*"

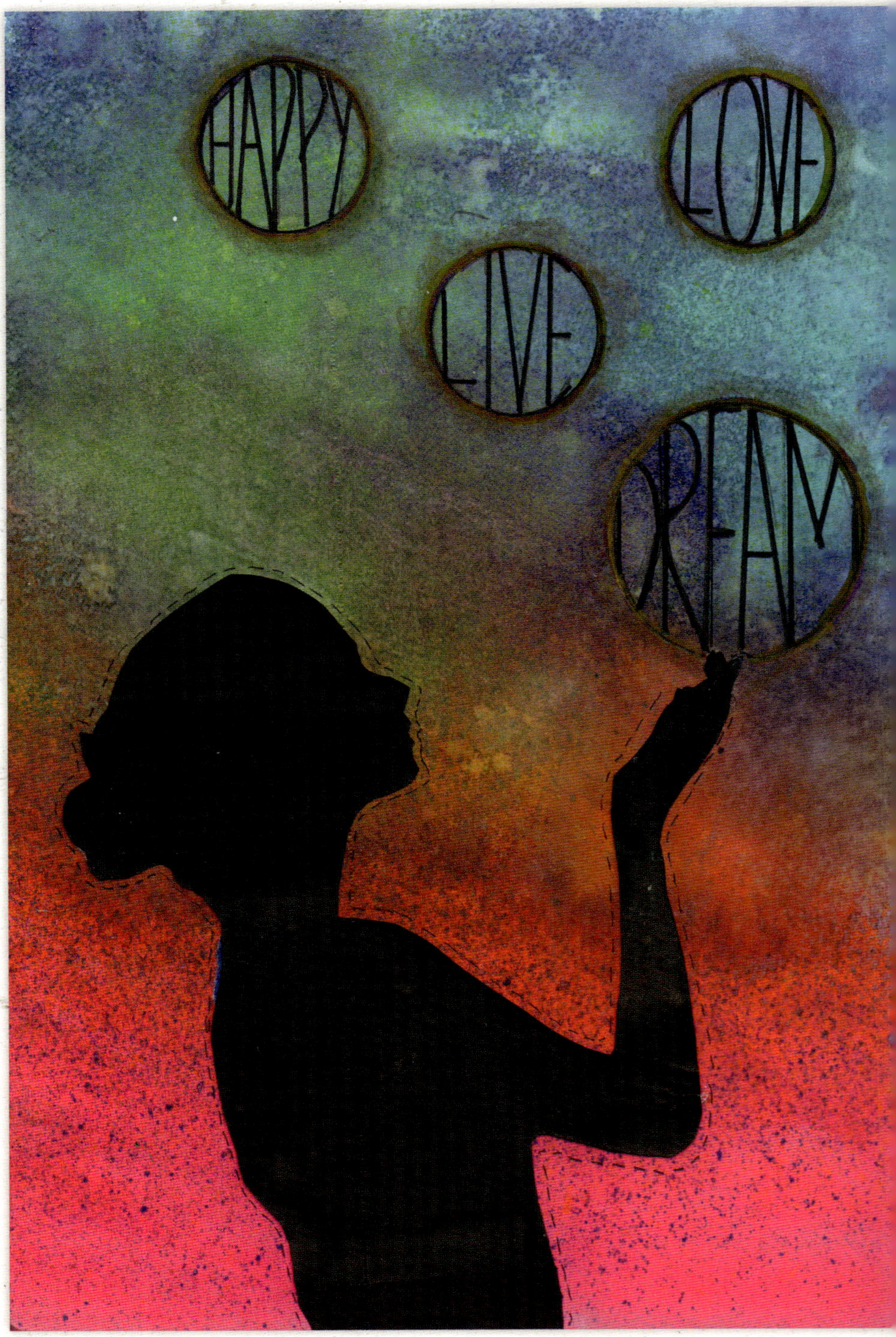

A DAUGHTER'S THOUGHTS
Dylusions ink, silhouette, Derwent gold water-soluble metallic pencil, gold and black pen, paper towel, water, Liquitex matte medium, gesso, Jasart, A4 blank paper, stencils

Jan La Follette

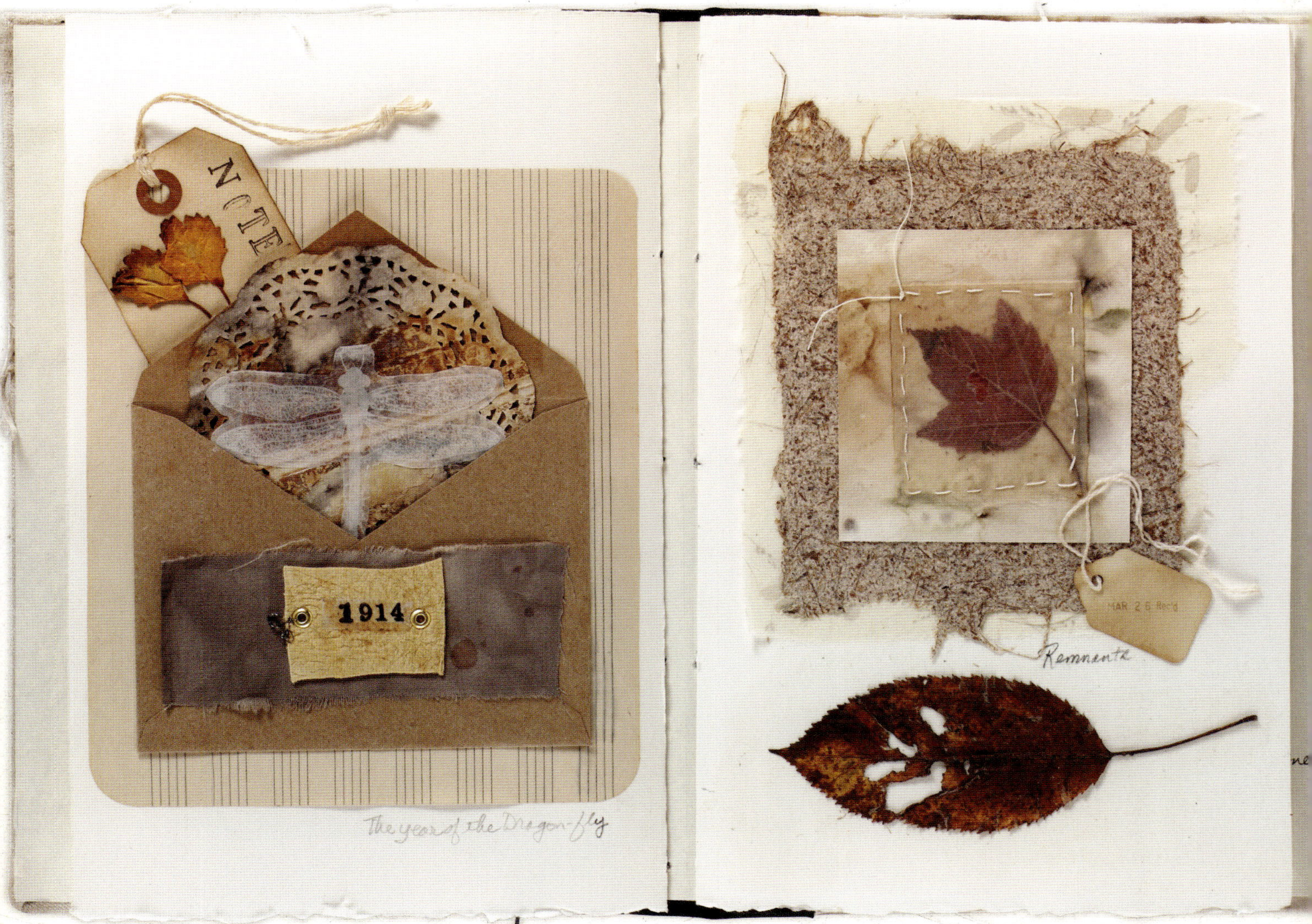

REMNANTS
Maple leaf, silk tea bag, handmade papers, fabrics

What was your inspiration for this piece?

I was inspired by nature and the desire to re-create my own version of a Victorian woman's herbarium, or nature diary. So I then began collecting bits and pieces of natural materials for this page.

For me, the joy of using collage in art journaling comes from collecting and creating the elements, natural and man-made, and combining them to tell a story.

What interesting or unique techniques did you apply to this artwork?

On this page, titled *Remnants*, I've used papers and fabrics that I ecologically dyed in a hot water bath with flowers and leaves. I preserved a single maple leaf in a recycled silk tea bag, then stitched it to handmade papers, adding a partially deteriorated leaf.

Are there any mixed-media artists who inspire you?

Roxanne Evans Stout, an Oregon mixed-media artist from whom I have taken classes, has been my nature art journaling inspiration. Her sensitive and thoughtful teaching methods have encouraged me to create art that comes from my heart.

Thomas LaBadia

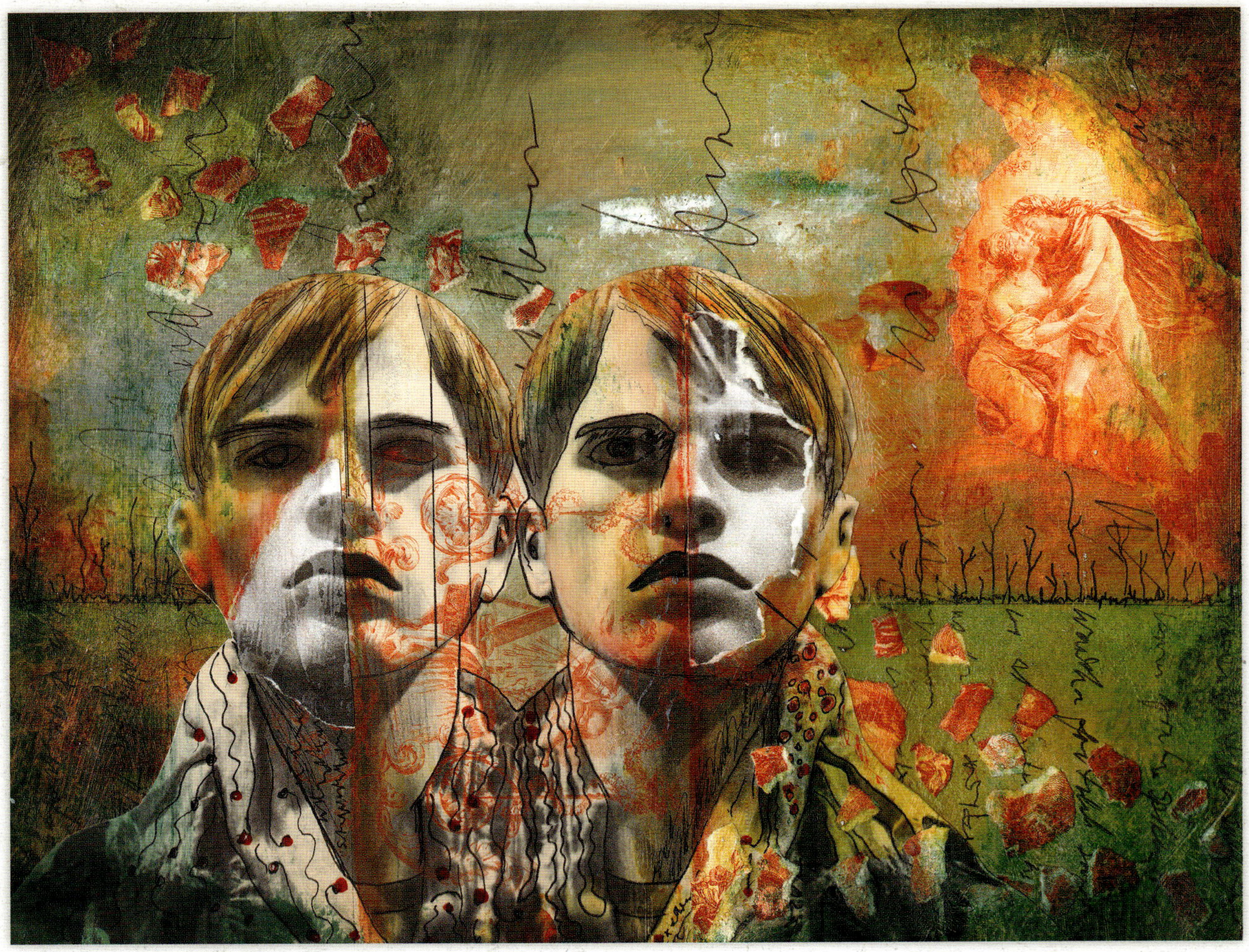

SEPARATED AT BIRTH
Strathmore mixed-media paper, Golden acrylics matte medium, pens, antique book pages

What was your inspiration for this piece?

This piece was created to visually communicate the essence of a profoundly deep friendship. A soulful connection unlike any other that occurred quite suddenly and most unexpectedly. The type of friendship that is unexplainable, yet requires no explanation. Two people seemingly sharing one soul, yet living in two different bodies ... separated at birth, but together again.

What interesting or unique techniques did you apply to this artwork?

If I were to pick one thing I consider unique, it would be the contrast of collage fodder scanned and printed on antique book pages, layered and mixed with the same image printed on thick new paper, then painted over. Mixing the old with the new seemed like an accurate representation of a new friendship that felt like one that has existed for hundreds of years.

Are there any mixed-media artists who inspire you?

I am inspired by so many mixed-media artists. It would be virtually impossible to list them all. A few are Brian Kasstle, Orly Avineri, John Arbuckle and Terry Garrett.

Do you ever give yourself journal prompts?

Never. I don't work well with guidelines or prompts. I try to work from the inside out. My professional work is all about guidelines (and deadlines), and I try to keep all of that out of my personal art.

Carrie Todd

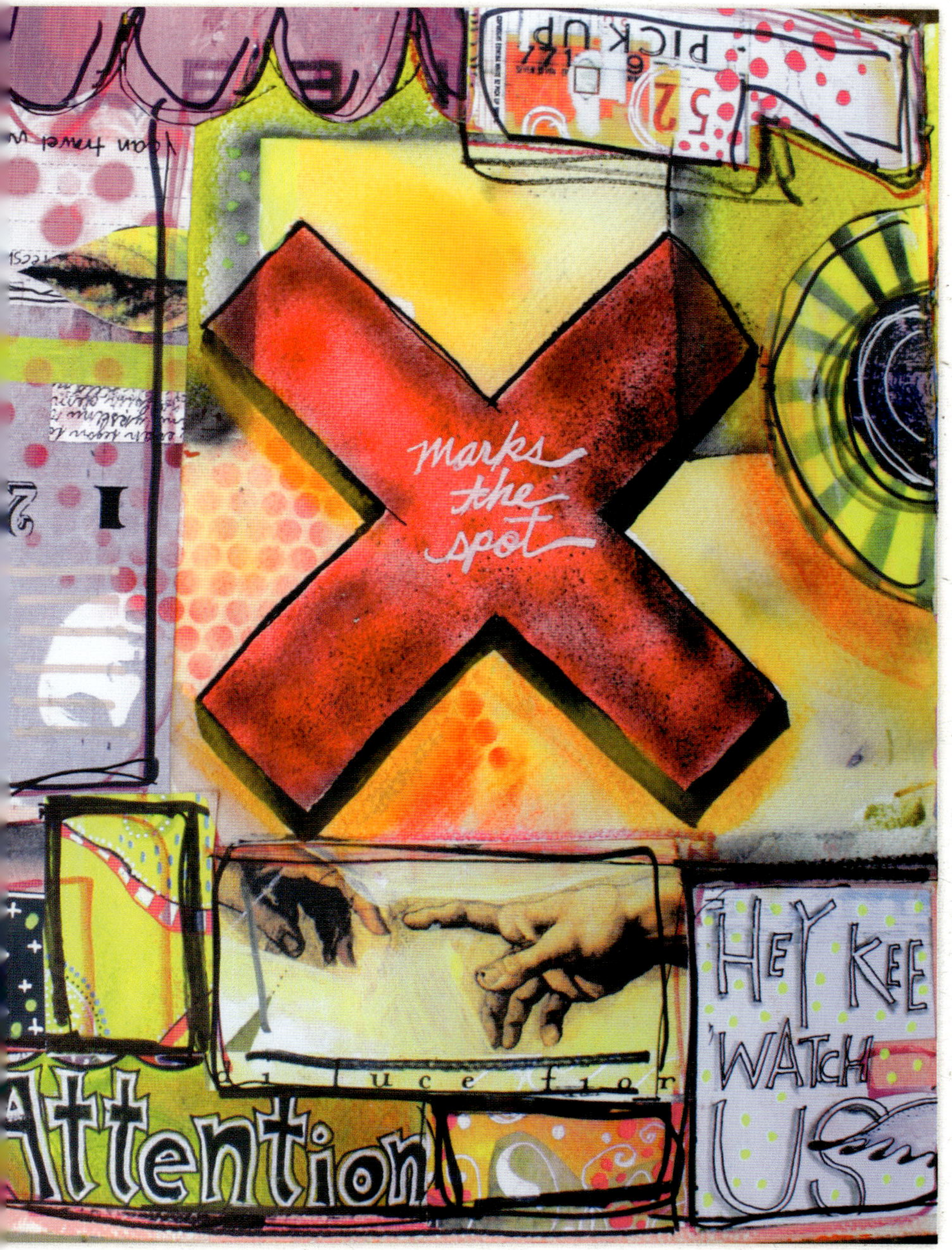

X MARKS THE SPOT
140-lb. (300gsm) watercolor paper, collage sheets, scanned journal pages, acrylic paint, stencils, markers

What was your inspiration for this piece?

The inspiration for this piece was a treasure map.

What interesting or unique techniques did you apply to this artwork?

Interesting techniques I applied to this piece were drawing with air-brush pens and using large stencils that were cut out of Mylar.

Are there any mixed-media artists who inspire you?

Mixed-media artists who inspire me are Pam Carriker, Flora Bowley, Teesha Moore and Jade Adams.

Do you have an art journaling process?

My process begins with making the journal. I love to hand-bind my own journals, and I feel like it makes it more mine somehow. I always paint the pages first, and then either sketch and paint a focal point, or use collage elements to frame the page, and save the journaling for later.

What tips would you give to fellow art journaling artists?

I would recommend to never stop learning, never stop experimenting and be fearless!

“NEVER THINK THAT YOU HAVE EVER LEARNED *all there is to know.*”

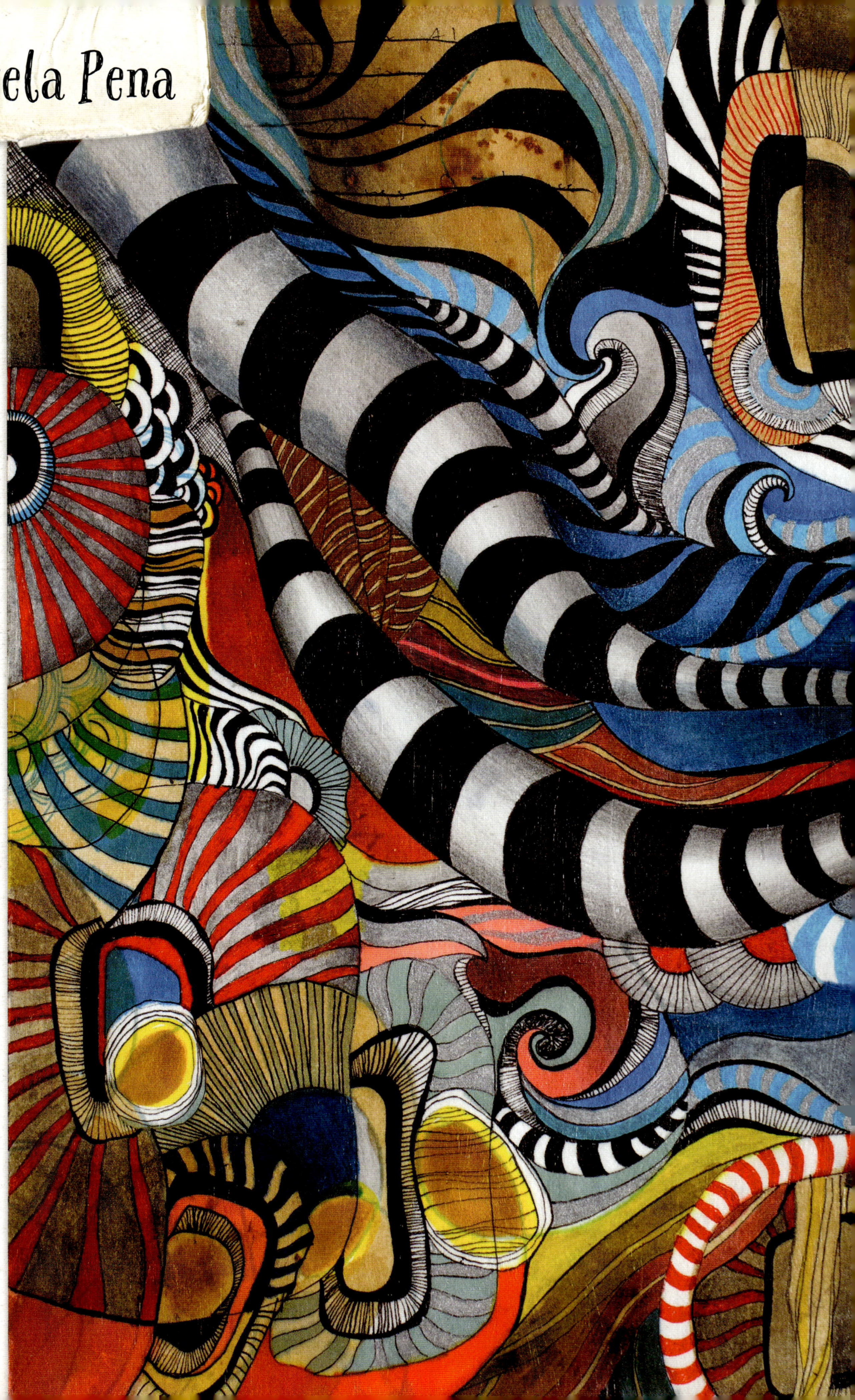

UNTITLED 1
Marker, coffee stain, ink, colored pencil, graphite, acrylic varnish

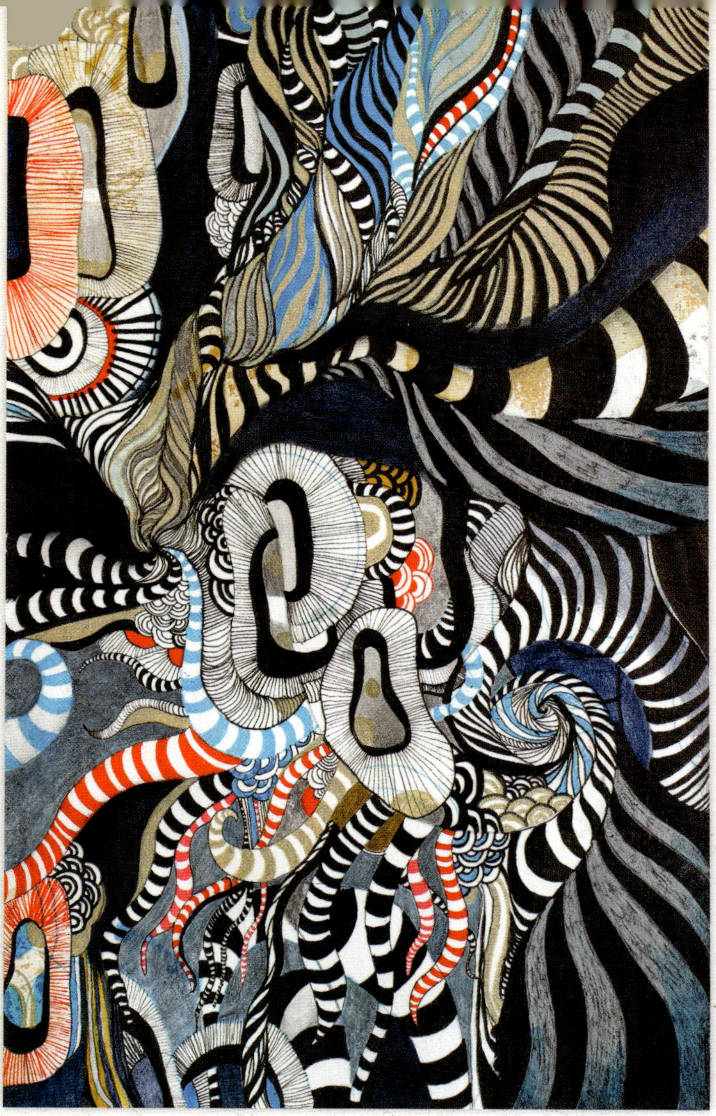

UNTITLED 2
Marker, ink, graphite, acrylic, acrylic varnish

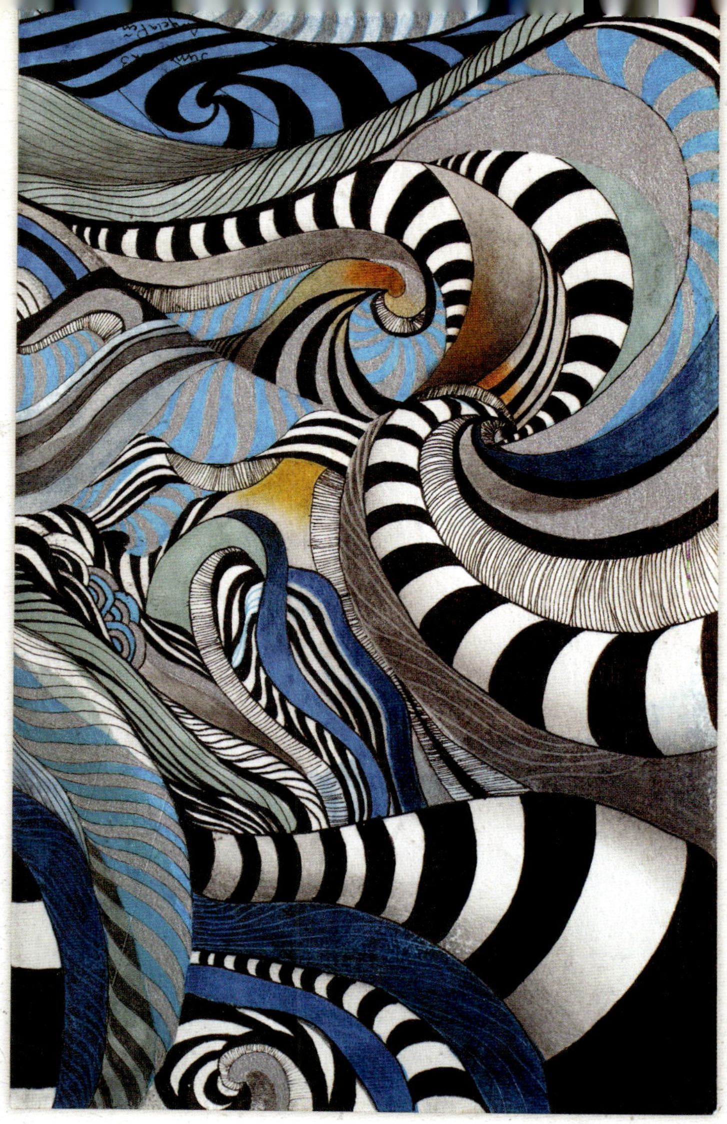

UNTITLED 3
Marker, ink, graphite, colored pencil, acrylic varnish

What was your inspiration for *Untitled 1*?

This piece was inspired by Zentangle and created by mixing markers, ink, colored pencils and graphite. I started with a pen doodle, then I stained parts of the page with coffee. After, I filled in the lines with colorful markers and inks. On top of the marker, I added colored pencils and graphite. I finished with a thin layer of acrylic varnish to enhance the colors.

Are there any mixed-media artists who inspire you?

My favorite mixed-media artists right now are Yellena James and Hollie Chastain.

Do you ever give yourself journal prompts?

When I need inspiration, I will go to the art supply store and try out some new materials. I use journal prompts to get ideas of what to draw and new techniques. For example, I recently bought a book about how to use wax and cheesecloth in your art. Messy, but fun!

When and why did you start art journaling?

My love for art journaling came with the discovery of Zentangle, which helped me to start drawing after a creative dry spell. Drawing for other people can be stressful, but art journals are just for you—there are no rules, you have total creative freedom!

It's also important because it provides a wealth of inspiration for later pieces. It can also be a way of learning new techniques, styles and experimenting. But most importantly, it's fun!

Jana Bodin

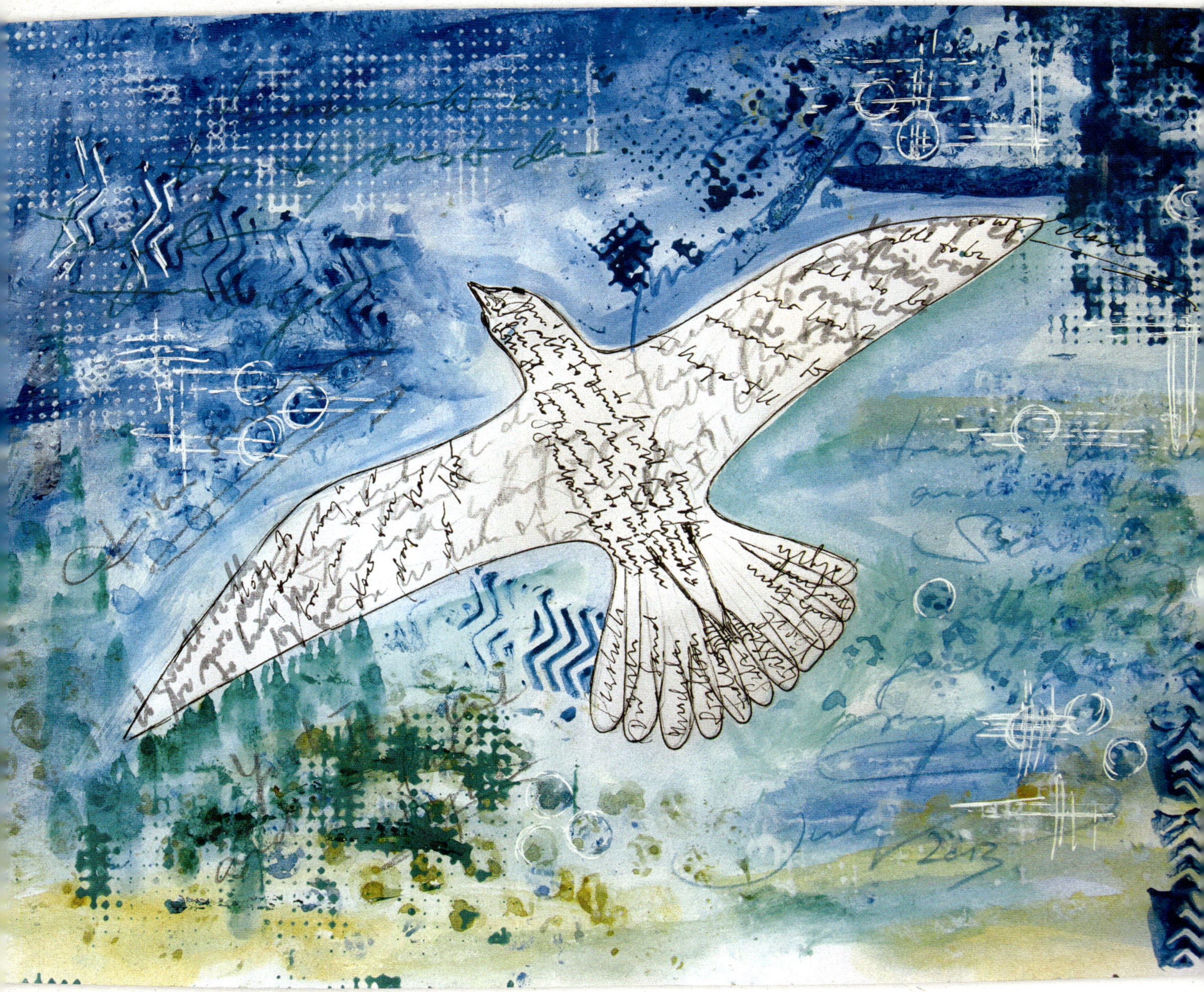

BY THE SEA
Generic mixed-media paper, acrylics, white and black ink, recycled material for stamping (e.g. a high heel sole for the zigzag pattern, plastic boxes from cookies for the grid pattern), fine liner

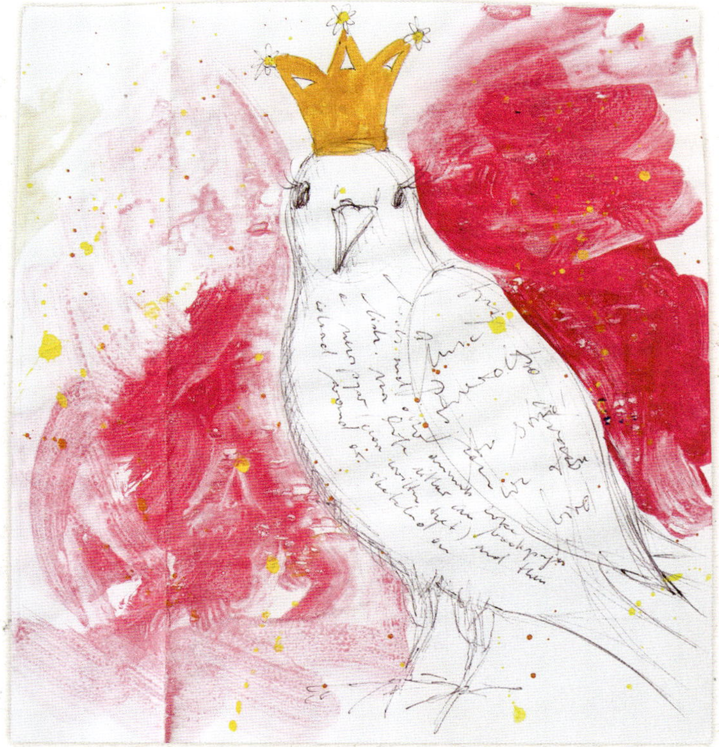

PINK AND PRINCESS
Paper from my scrap journal, ballpoint pen, watercolor

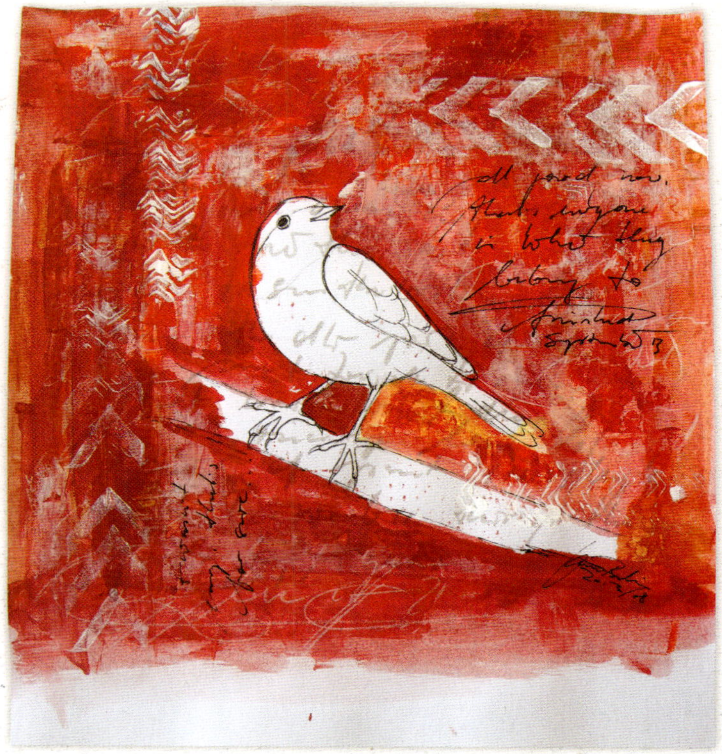

ALL IS WELL
Generic mixed-media paper, brush pen, acrylics, white ink, fine liner, hand-carved stamp

What was your inspiration for *By the Sea*?

Inspiration for this page came from our trip to the Netherlands. Besides visiting Amsterdam, we spent some time at the beach during that summer. Blue skies, seagulls, dunes … everything was just right.

What interesting or unique techniques did you apply to *By the Sea*?

This page was done with the negative painting technique in mind. It's negative because the object of interest is left untouched, and color or decorative matter surrounds it.

I use this technique when I don't feel the patience to work on details but want to capture a certain mood or color combination.

Are there any mixed-media artists who inspire you?

I'm inspired by Gabriele Langfeldt-Feldmann, Tammy Garcia, Mindy Lacefield and Dawn DeVries Sokol.

Do you ever give yourself journal prompts?

Usually I don't work with prompts. Most of the time I simply start with some kind of sketch or doodle that shows up in my mind, and everything else just evolves from there.

Do you have an art journaling process?

Sometimes a page is finished within a few minutes, but more often it takes several sessions. Meaning that I find myself adding onto the page, little by little, until I feel it's done.

What tips would you give to fellow art journaling artists?

Just get started. Don't overthink. There is no right or wrong when it comes to your art journal.

Lisa Maxwell Brown

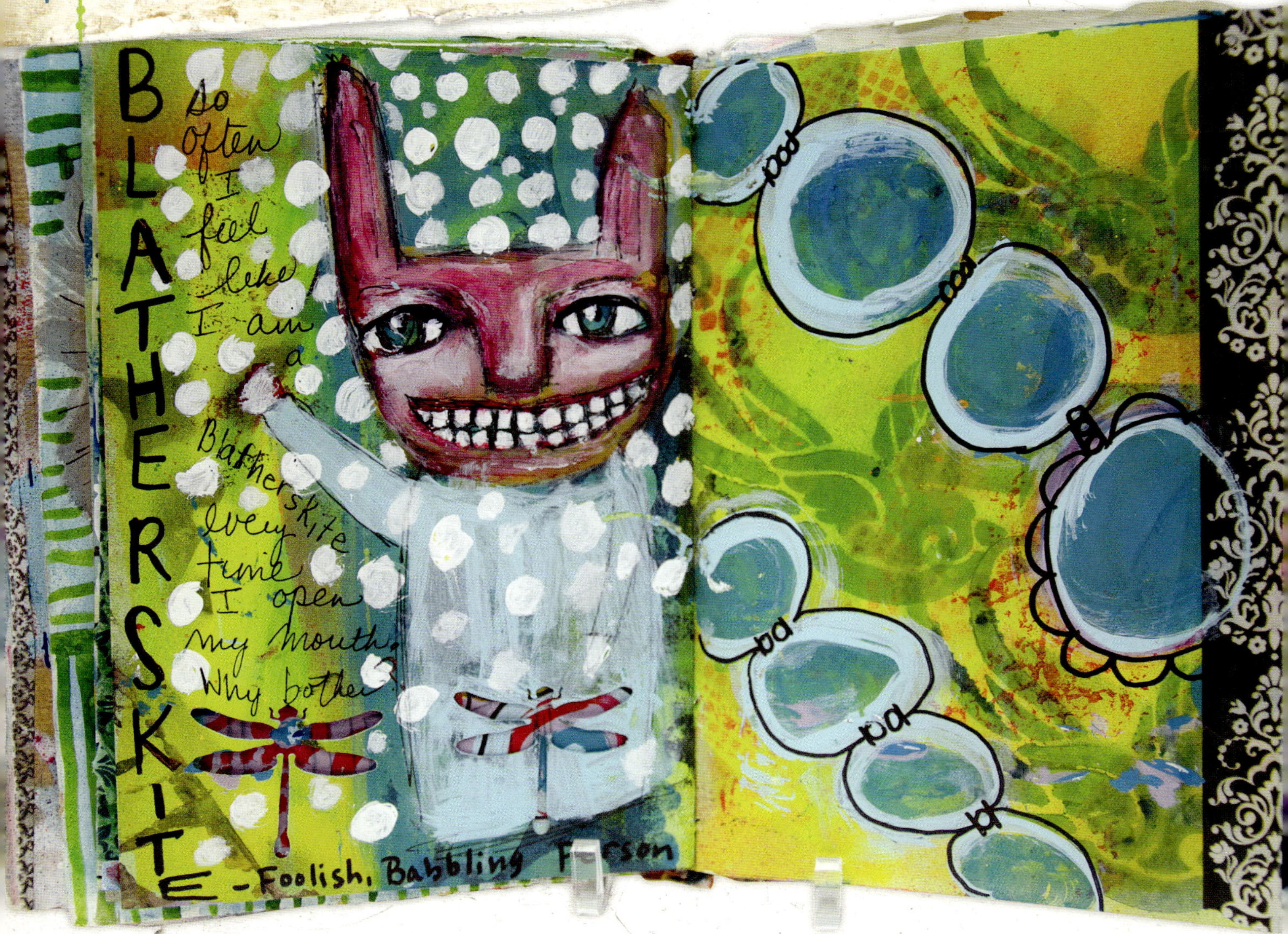

BLATHERSKITE
Patterned papers, magazine images, paints, inks, stencils

What was your inspiration for this piece?

I love to track down unusual words that have an interesting sound or meaning and write them in my art journal so I don't forget them (such as *blatherskite*: a foolish, babbling person).

Do you have an art journaling process?

My usual approach to journaling is to randomly paint pages using different techniques and often randomly collage materials, such as patterned papers, magazine images, etc. I keep working until eventually something emerges that has meaning to me. I often realize that I've demonstrated something about myself or my thoughts that I didn't realize was there until it appeared on the page.

What interesting or unique techniques did you apply to this artwork?

In this image, I painted a background and then sprayed inks randomly through stencils before painting the creepy bunny figure, which is a common figure in my journals, along with other anthropomorphized animals.

As the last step, I was looking through my journal of completed images with a list of words I had compiled to see where they would fit, and *blatherskite* seemed perfect for the page. I realized that I do often feel like a blatherskite when talking to people I don't know or in front of groups.

Amy Forsyth

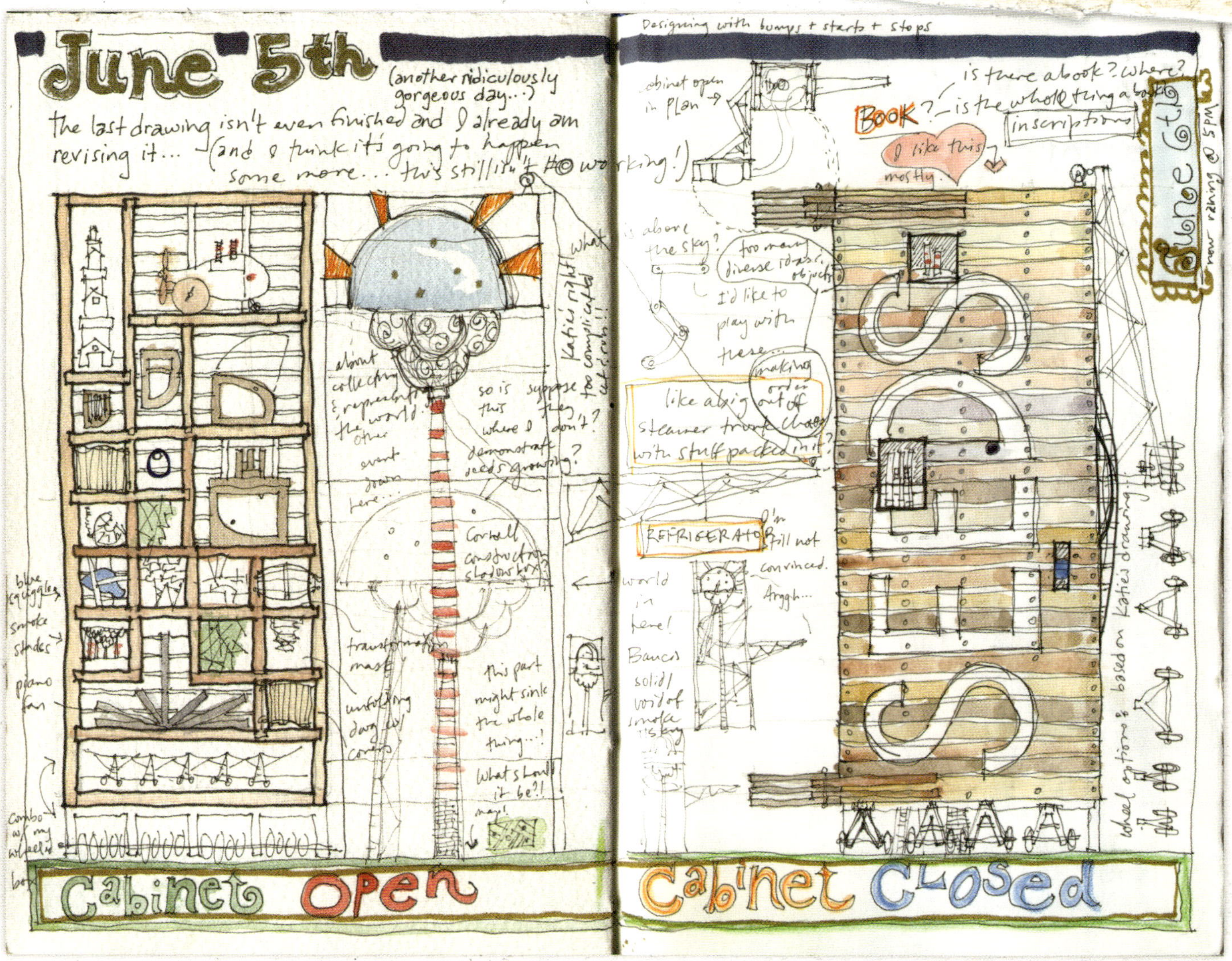

SEED CABINET
Watercolor, pencil, ink, colored pencil

What was your inspiration for this piece?

This sketch explores some design options for a cabinet piece I was building for an exhibition. The project was a collaboration with a friend in which we sent one another some drawings and small constructions to inspire one another.

How did you come up with your title?

Seed is metaphorical, because it describes something that contains possibilities yet to be germinated.

When and why did you start art journaling?

I started drawing in a sketchbook in my first year of architecture school and continue to this day—many years later.

Do you have an art journaling process?

I make my own sketchbooks. I bind them out of whatever papers I want to use during the upcoming months, and I carry one with me in my purse wherever I go. I find that if I don't draw or write something down immediately, I forget it. Drawing and writing about something makes you see it more clearly and remember it better.

> "*Make something* FIRST, INVESTIGATE IT SECOND. DO IT AGAIN AND AGAIN, AND THE WORK WILL IMPROVE."

Ingrid Dijkers

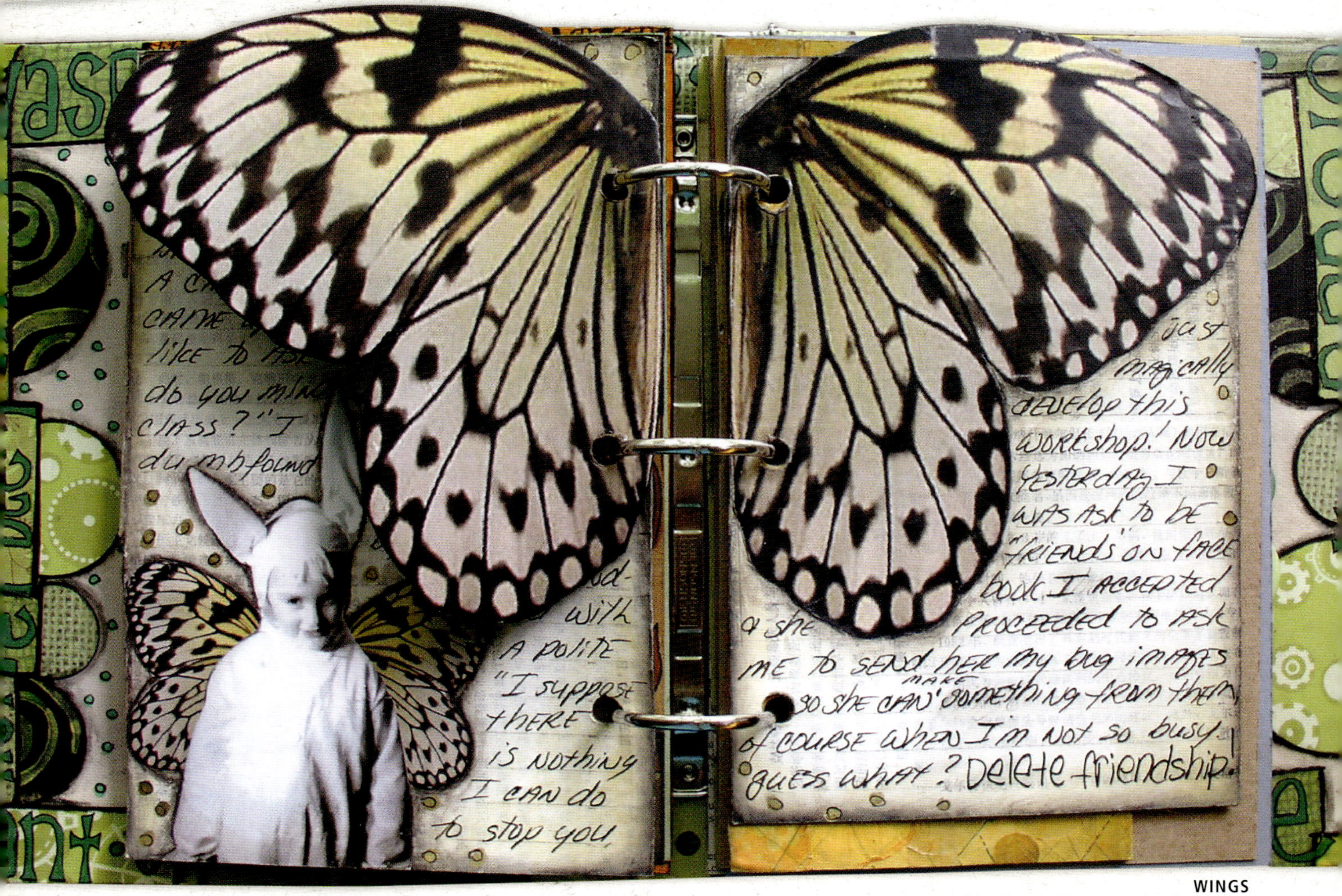

WINGS
Acrylic paints, collaged elements, color photo copy of a butterfly wing mounted onto boxboard

What was your inspiration for *Wings*?

The inspiration for this journal page was the small image of a butterfly wing I've had for several years.

What interesting or unique techniques did you apply to *Wings*?

I love adding shaped pages to my journals and ran into this beautiful image of a butterfly wing. So I enlarged the image, mounted it to boxboard, cut it out and punched a few binder holes in it, and it made for a stunning and unexpected page in my journal.

Do you ever give yourself journal prompts?

I can't say I really use or give myself journal prompts. I begin working simply on a background, and the page seems to take on a mind of its own. I just follow its lead.

When and why did you start art journaling?

I started about nine years ago, working with altered books, and my interests slowly developed into bookbinding and journaling.

Do you have an art journaling process?

I begin by laying color washes and collage material for a background. The page seems to slowly evolve on its own from there. A border and perhaps a focal image are included, then journaling and any final details are added.

What tips would you give to fellow art journaling artists?

I always suggest to keep it simple and uncomplicated. Start with supplies you already have and experiment.

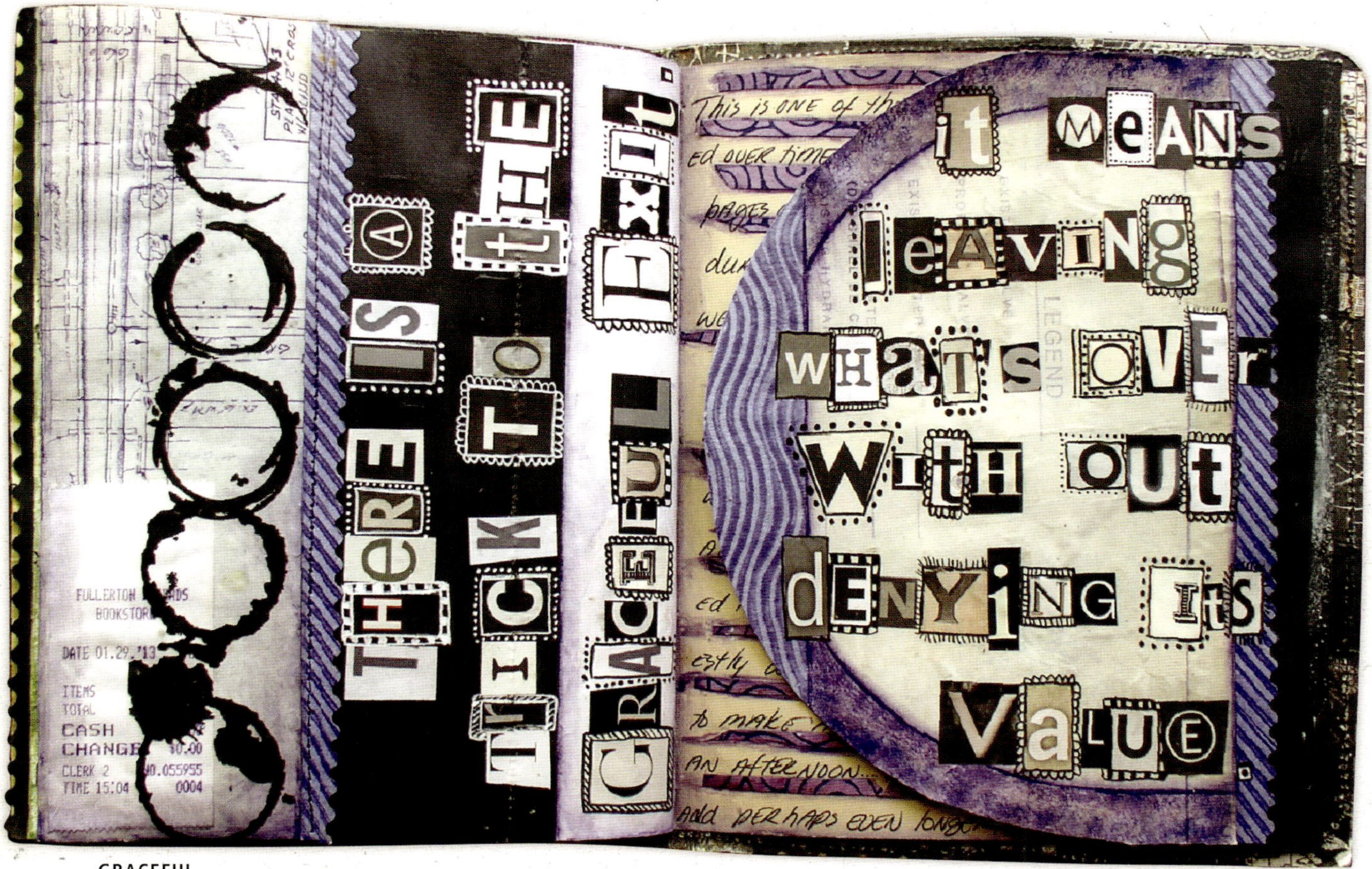

GRACEFUL
Tape, ransom lettering, acrylic paint, pen work

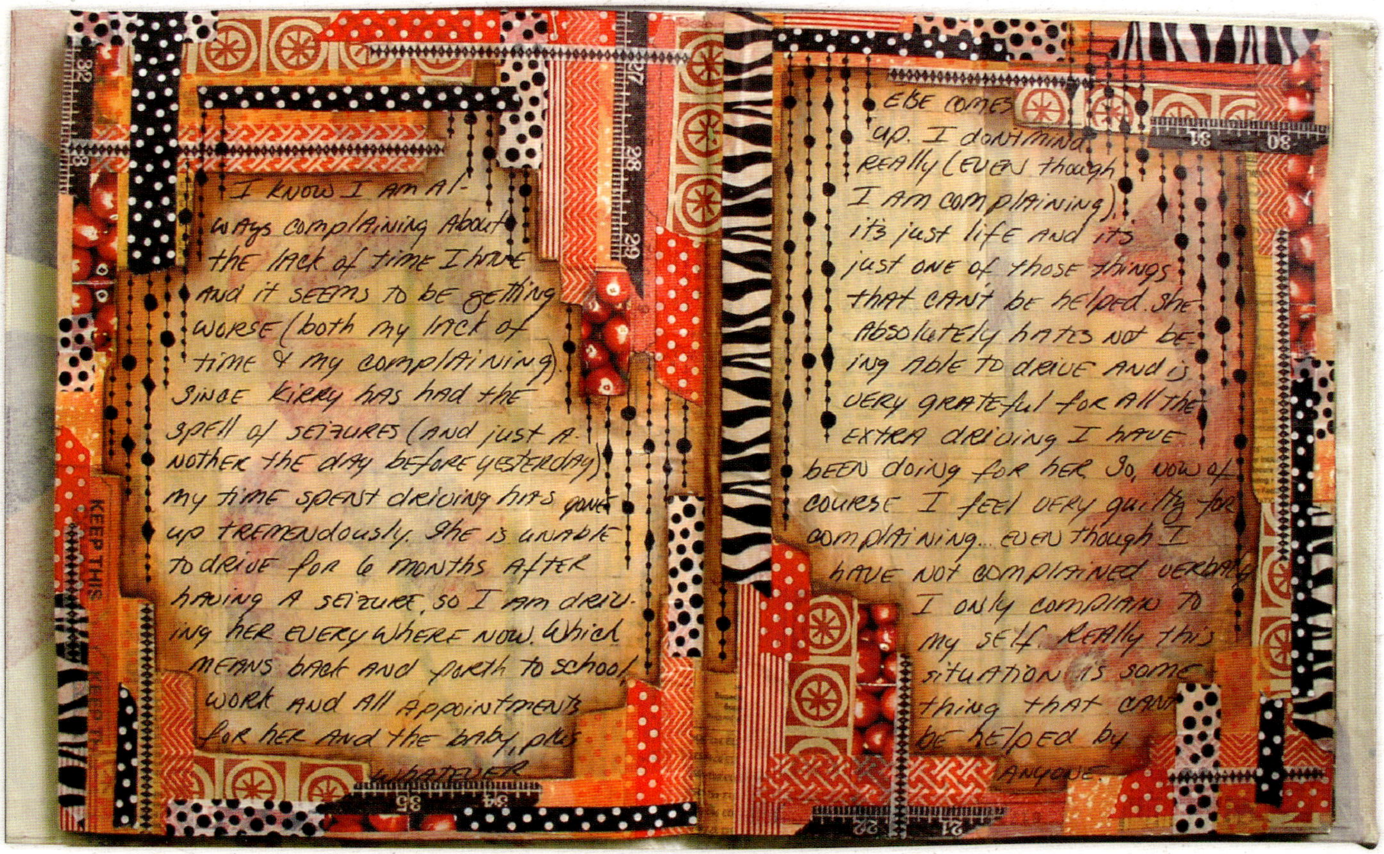

COMPLAIN
Various papers, washi tape, paints, journaling, pen work

Roxanne Coble

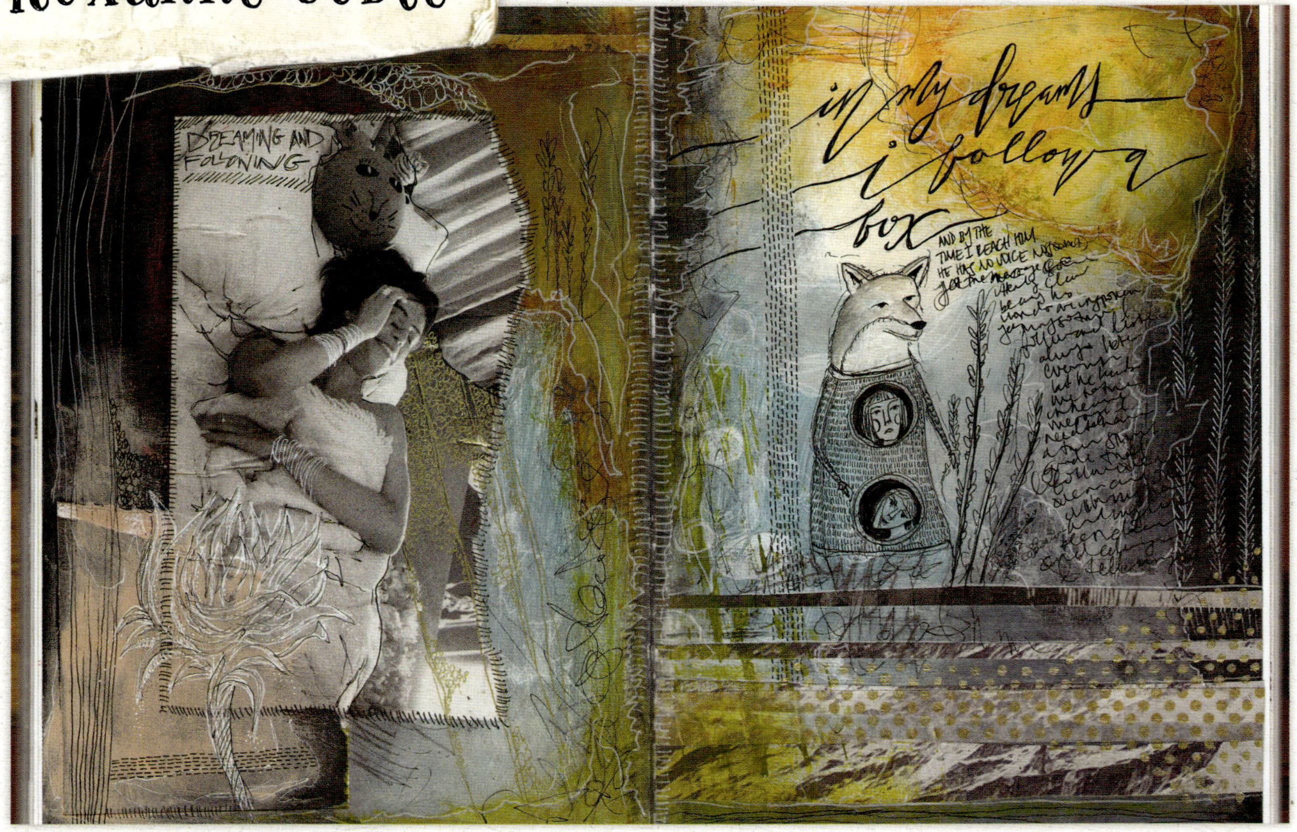

FOLLOWING FOXES
Standard acrylic paint, fluid acrylic, white and gold gel pens, black Pitt pens, white gesso, found ephemera, washi tape, graphite pencil

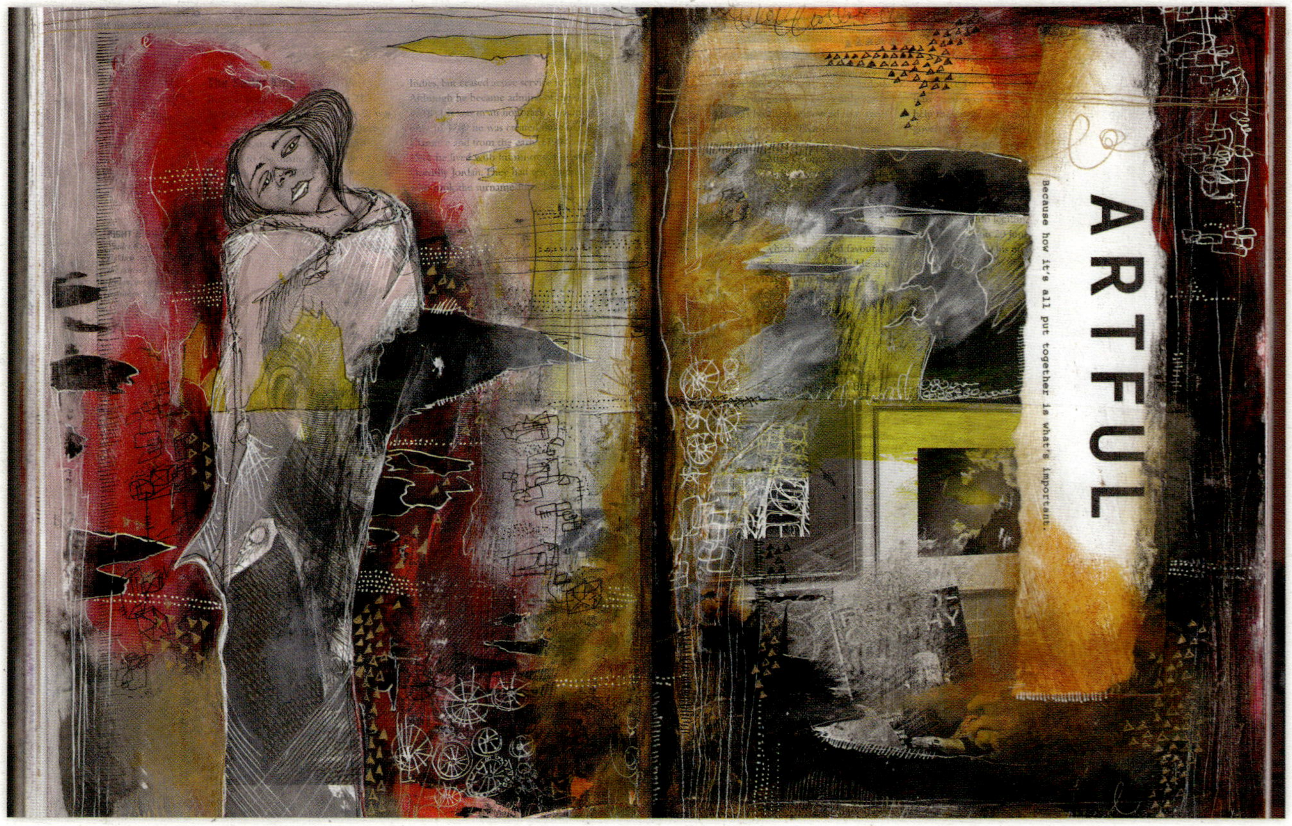

ARTFUL
Standard acrylic paint, fluid acrylic, white and gold gel pens, black Pitt pens, black and white gesso, found ephemera, sandpaper, graphite pencil

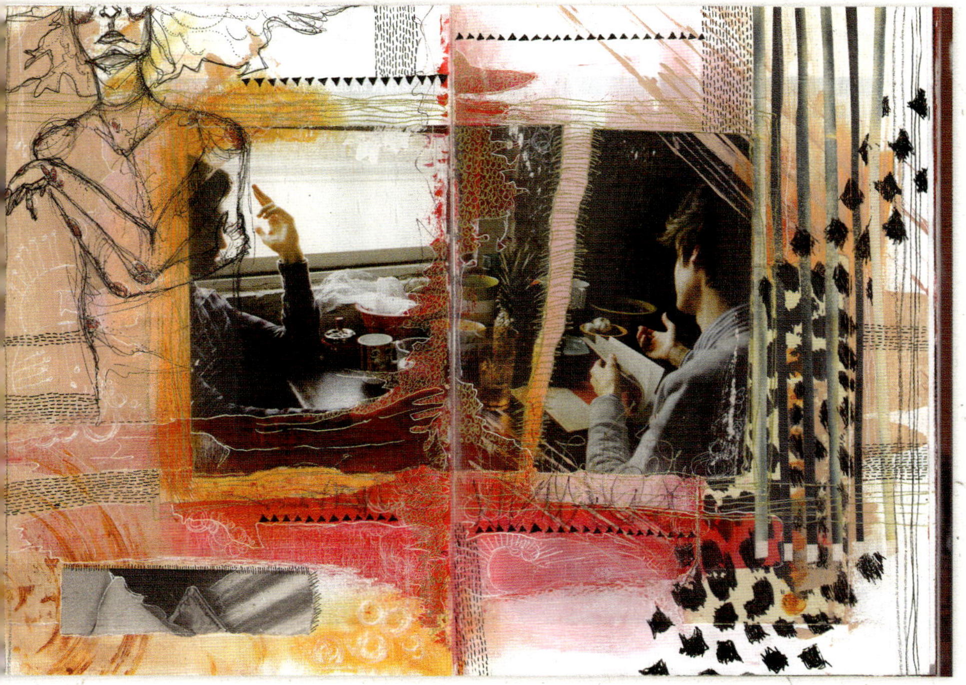

NO TEXT REQUIRED
Standard acrylic paint, fluid acrylic, white and gold gel pens, black Pitt pens, found ephemera, sandpaper, graphite pencil

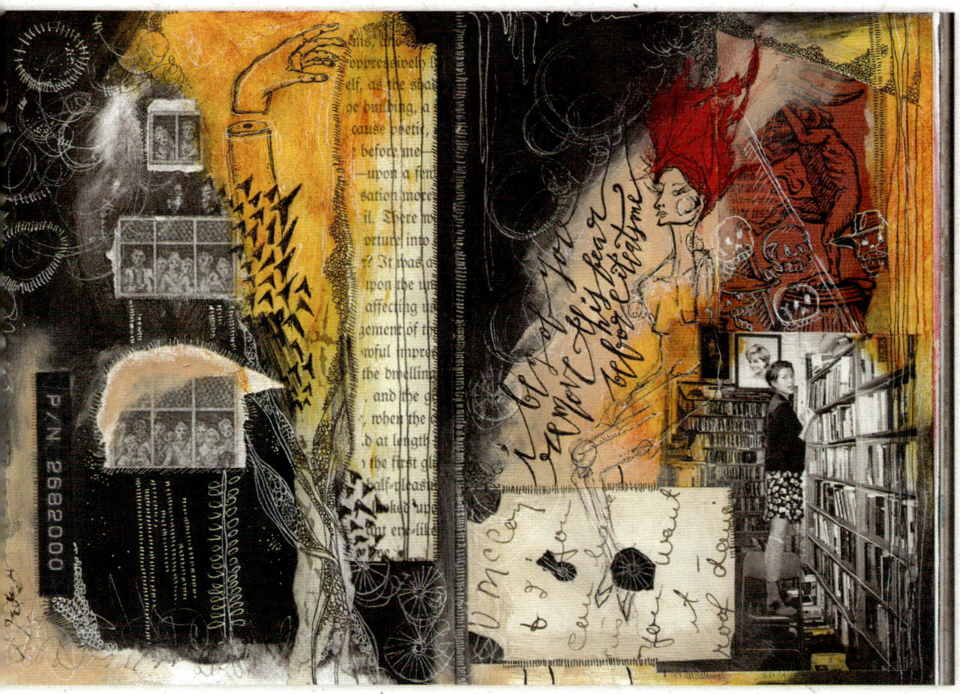

REMOVE THIS FEAR
Standard acrylic paint, fluid acrylic, white gel pens, black Pitt pens, found ephemera, sandpaper, graphite pencil

How did you come up with the title for *Following Foxes*?

Although I don't start with any ideas or themes when making a journal spread, this one evolved into something pretty personal. At the time, I had been going through a big transition in my life and found myself dreaming about foxes. After some research, I realized that they coincided with changes happening in real life. From that day forward, I've consider the fox as my personal spirit animal—something I trust and follow.

What interesting or unique techniques did you apply to *Remove This Fear*?

A bit of a secret about this page is the origins of the found ephemera. The black numbered label on the left was something I found in an alley while walking my dog. The red paper in the upper right is off of a wine bottle given to me by my in-laws. Lastly, the beige paper in the bottom center is actually the back of a vintage photograph. I thought it was fascinating—here was a photograph I bought at a swap meet, of people I don't know, with writing I can't quite comprehend—and yet, there was something so personal to it. To have something so foreign, yet so relatable, in this spread was just beautiful to me.

Are there any mixed-media artists who inspire you?

Taking a workshop with Orly Avineri opened up something greater within me—a Pandora's box of brilliantly vast and incredibly powerful art making. I remember coming home and sobbing after my first day of making art with her—I had felt my creative soul again.

Natasha White

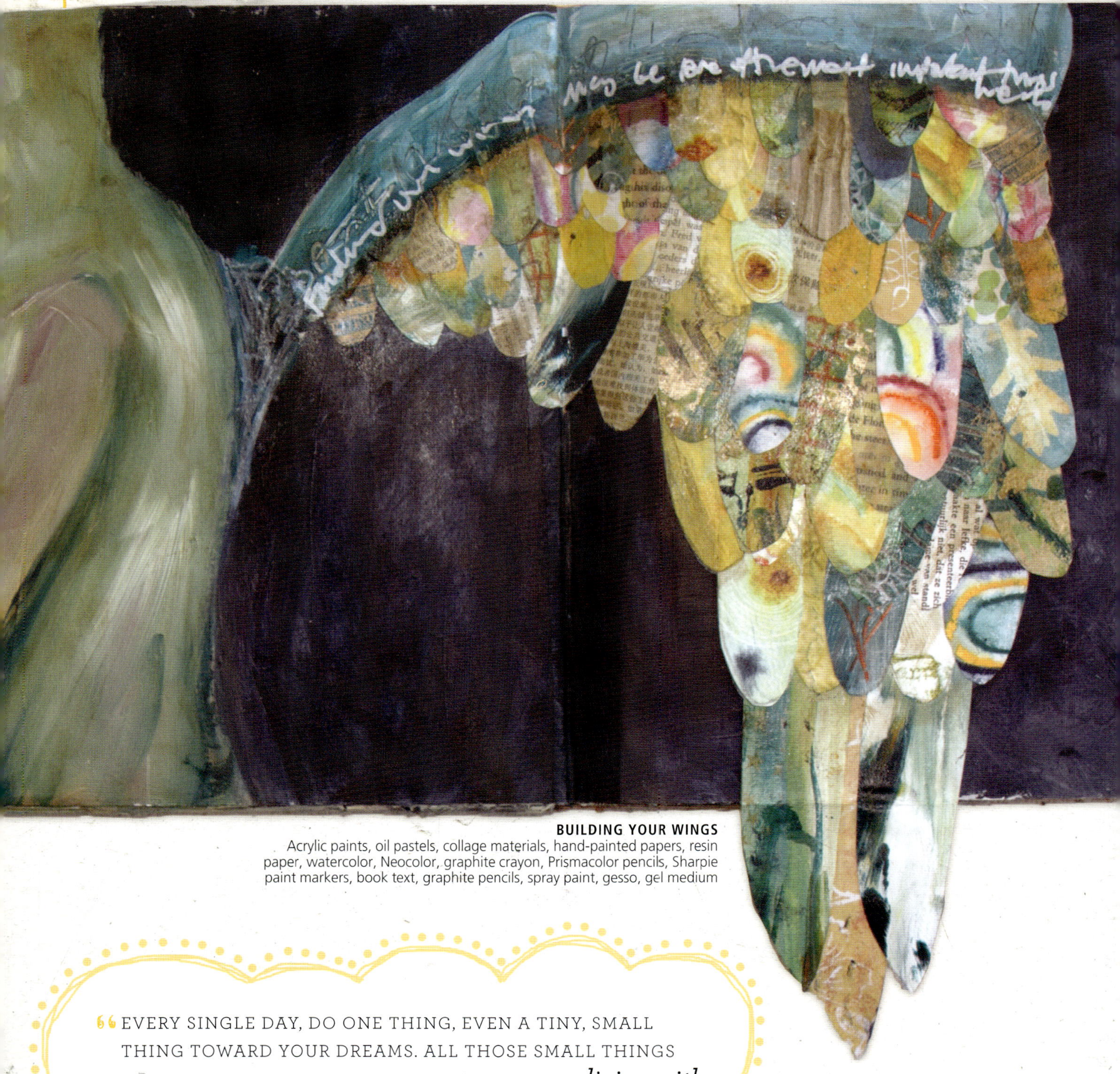

BUILDING YOUR WINGS
Acrylic paints, oil pastels, collage materials, hand-painted papers, resin paper, watercolor, Neocolor, graphite crayon, Prismacolor pencils, Sharpie paint markers, book text, graphite pencils, spray paint, gesso, gel medium

"EVERY SINGLE DAY, DO ONE THING, EVEN A TINY, SMALL THING TOWARD YOUR DREAMS. ALL THOSE SMALL THINGS ADD UP AND, BEFORE YOU KNOW IT, YOU END UP *living with your dream every day.* KEEP IT REAL AND MANAGEABLE. YOU JUST NEED TO SHOW UP AND KEEP SHOWING UP."

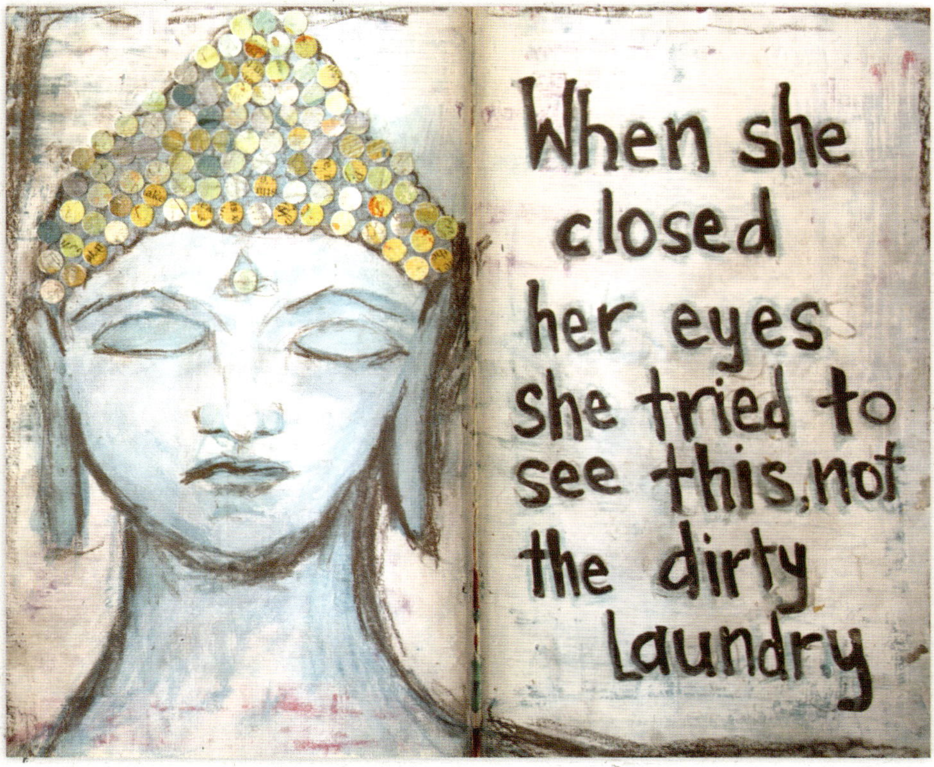

LAUNDRY ON HER MIND
Acrylic paints, graphite crayon, paint pen, hand-painted paper, gel medium

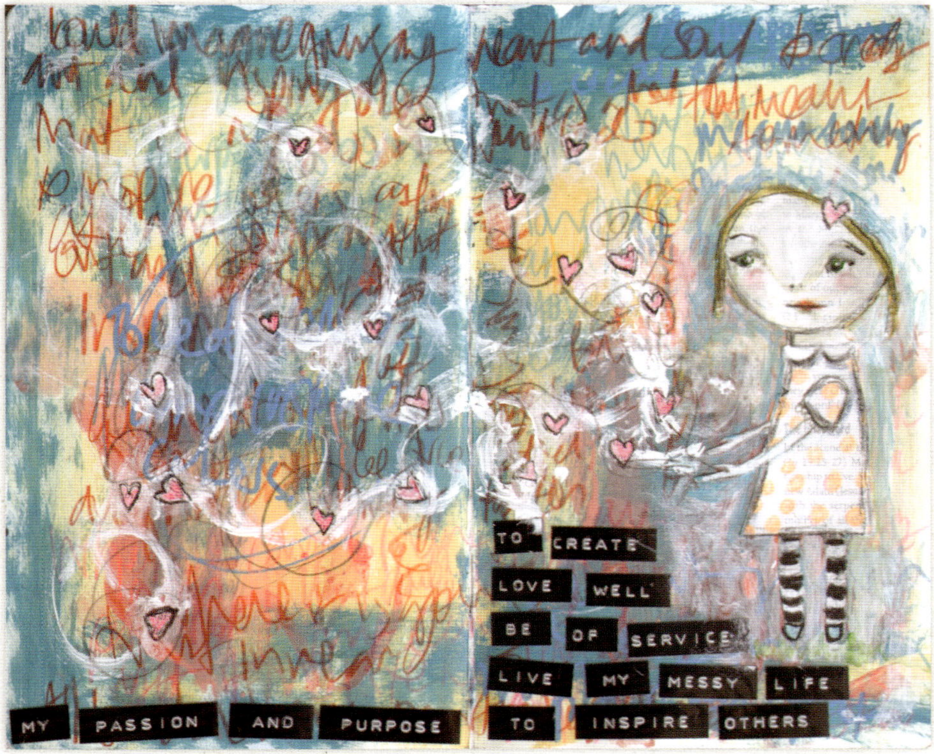

PASSION AND PURPOSE
Prismacolor pencils, pens, paint pens, graphite, acrylic paints, embossed tape, book text girl sketch, gel medium, book text hearts

What was your inspiration for *Laundry on Her Mind*?

I was working on this page, and I looked over at my never-ending laundry pile, then felt incredibly guilty at where I was spending my time. The quote popped into my head while I was in the middle of feeling guilty and seemed perfect—and a further justification to procrastinate on that task for a little while longer.

What was your inspiration for *Building Your Wings*?

I created a class for 21 Secrets Spring 2014 with Connie Hozvicka and this page was the result of my class. I had created journaling questions around dreams and what supports you and what lessons we need to learn. While working through the questions myself, I had the inspiration that the page should be about building our wings.

Before we can fly, we need to gather our resources and plan and practice—it all came together better than I imagined.

Are there any mixed-media artists who inspire you?

I'm inspired by Michelle Brown, Robert Rauschenberg, Line Juhl Hansen, Emare Karaka and Jesse Reno.

Do you have an art journaling process?

My art journaling practice is to turn up. Basically, I need to show up regularly to the page (as cheesy and trite as that sounds).

Honorata Chorąży-Przybysz

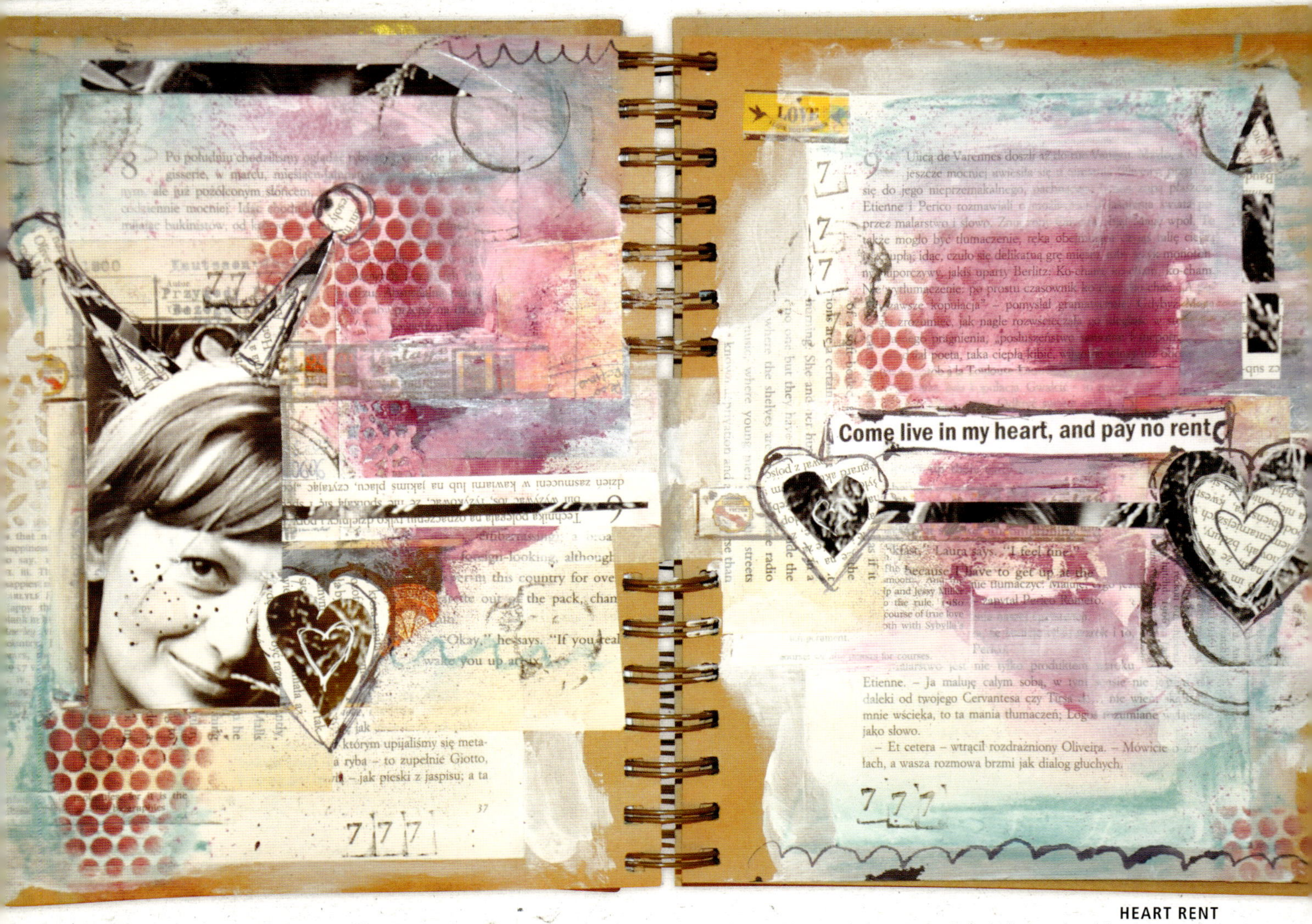

HEART RENT
Soft chalk pastels, white gesso, water

What was your inspiration for *Have Fun*?

The inspiration for this page was my desire to escape from the pressure of having to create high quality art.

What interesting or unique techniques did you apply to *Have Fun*?

I used thick layers of white gesso as a medium over plastic mesh to create strong texture. I also let ink splatters freely form stains by pressing two pages together.

Are there any mixed-media artists who inspire you?

I am inspired by British artist Kate Crane and Polish artist Czekoczyna.

How did you come up with the title for *Life Game*?

This page reflects my life philosophy, as I am very interested in cause-and-result relationships. I was inspired by watching a card game and thinking about how much in our life comes down to accidental choice.

When and why did you start art journaling?

I started art journaling in March 2013 but, in my heart, it was always there. It gives me full freedom to express my way of analyzing reality.

> "*Accept your imperfections* AND FREE YOURSELF FROM COMPARISIONS."

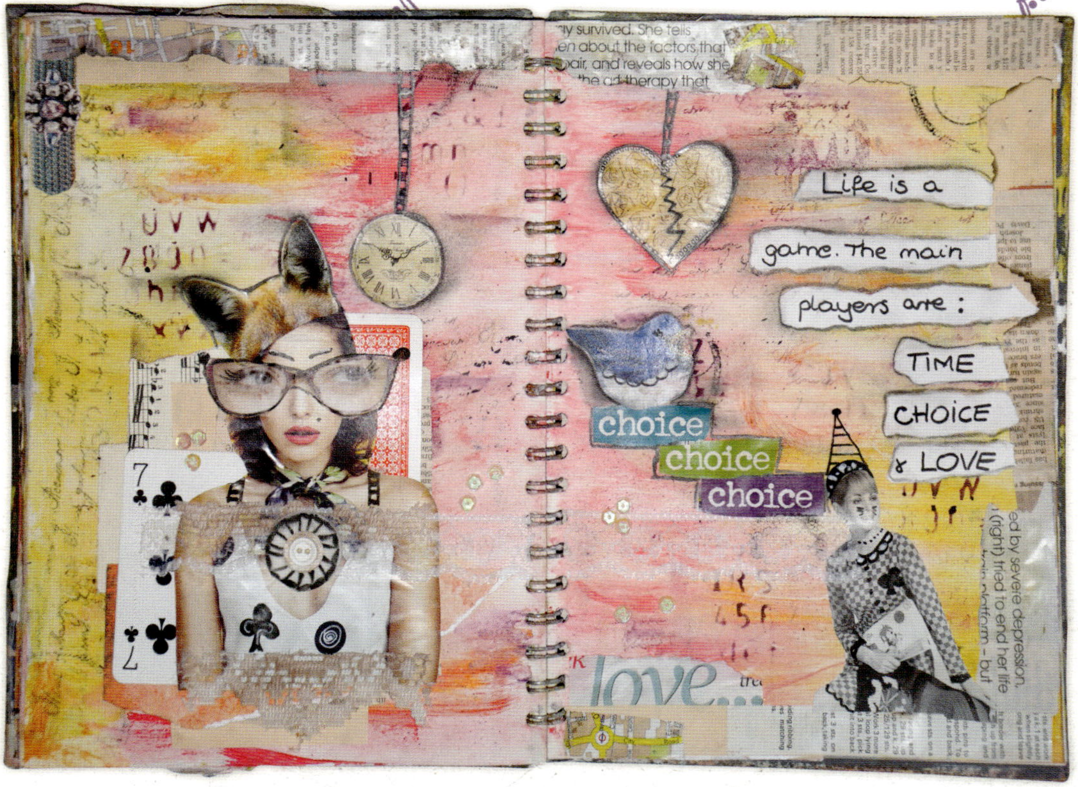

LIFE GAME
Newspaper, acrylic paint, toothbrush

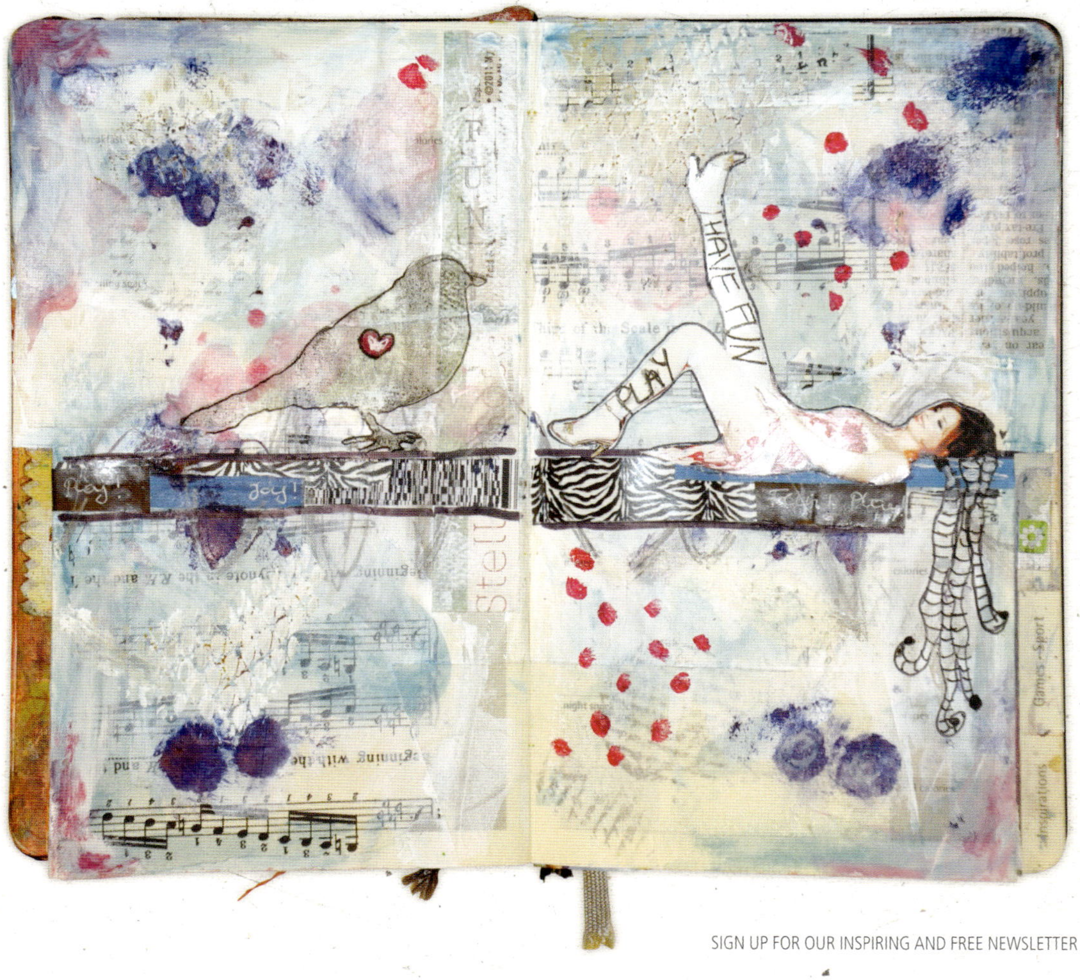

HAVE FUN
White gesso, bits of music notes, ink, marker, stamp, diluted acrylic paints and white pen

Jessica Sporn

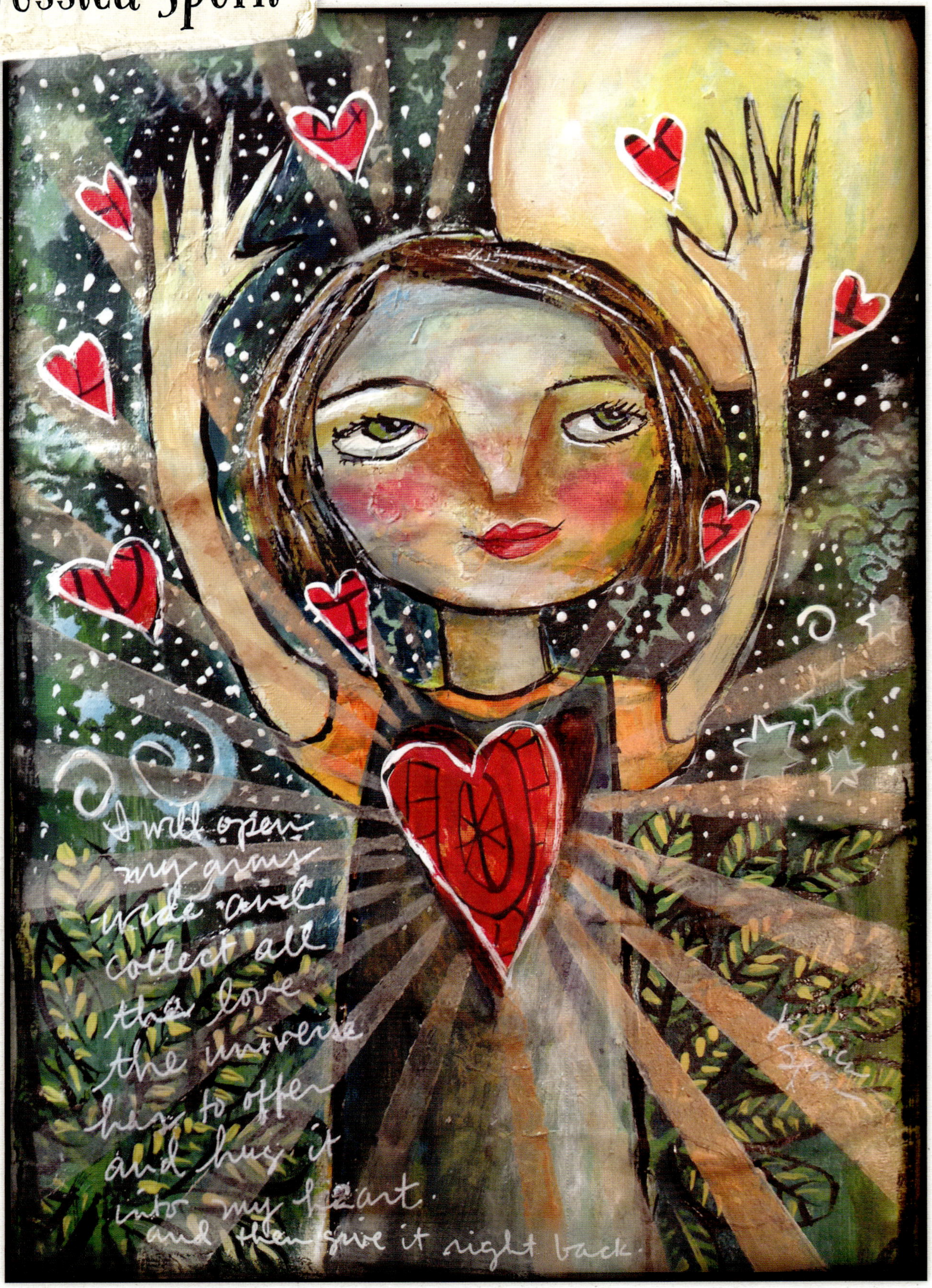

ARMS OPEN WIDE
Collage, gesso, acrylics, stenciling, Posca paint pens

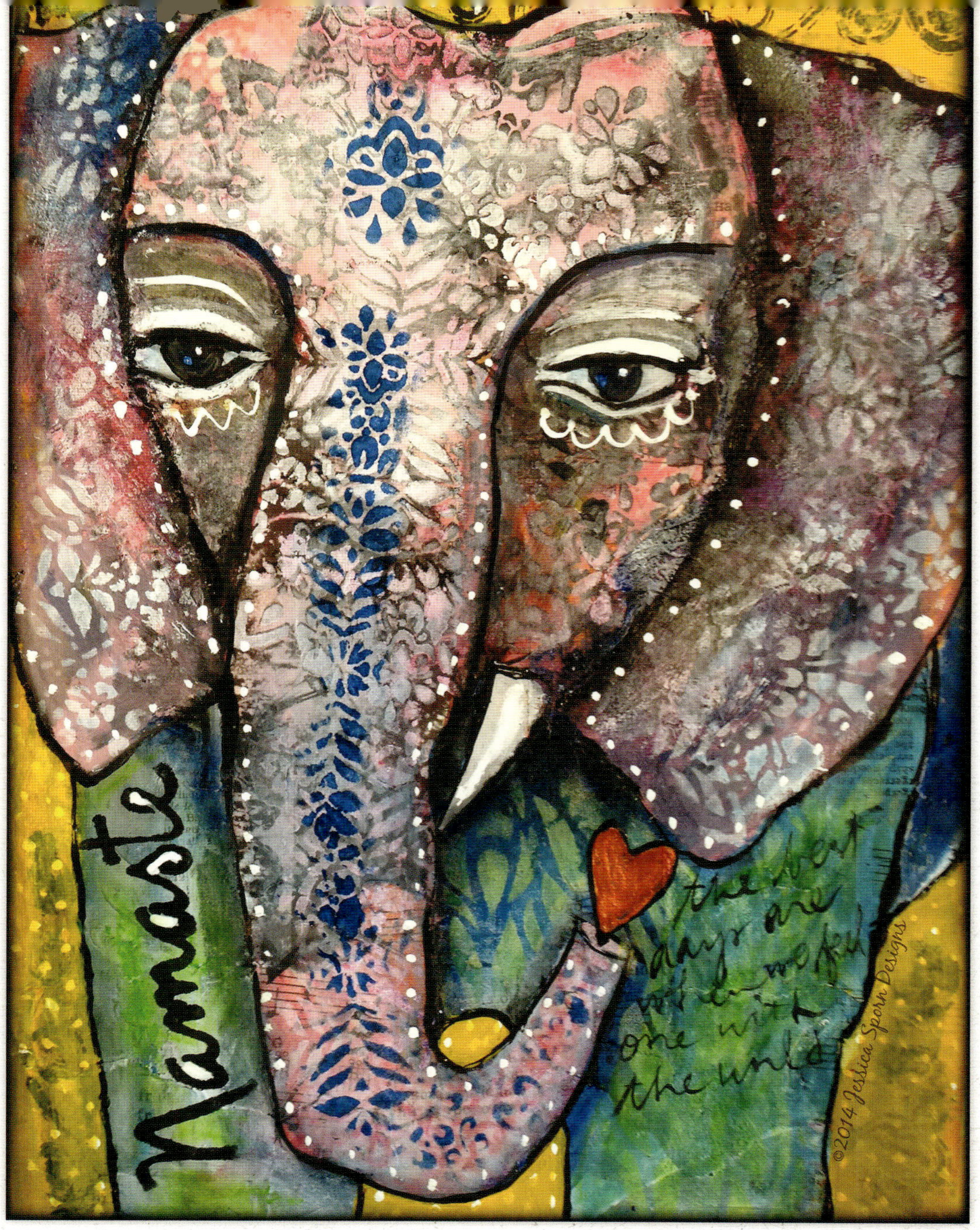

ELEPHANT NAMASTE
Collage, acrylic paint, Posca white markers

What was your inspiration for *Elephant Namaste*?

My inspiration for this piece came from playing with the Namaste stencil from StencilGirl Products. I had been using it in another project and wiping it off on top of a collaged page in my art journal. When I looked at it later, it looked somehow like an elephant—so I went with it.

Do you ever give yourself journal prompts?

The journaling here says, "The best days are when we feel one with the world." This is how I often feel when spending a lot of time in my studio. Often my prompts come from leftovers in my journal, but I am also inspired by online challenges and wonderful books.

When and why did you start art journaling?

I started art journaling a little over a year ago, after taking an online course with Julie Fei-Fan Balzer. It has provided a freedom to me that has been so liberating.

What tips would you give to fellow art journaling artists?

The biggest tip I have, and one that I try to give myself, is to be loose and nonjudgemental and to trust the process. It's not done until you feel it's done—which may be many layers away.

How did you come up with the title for *Arms Open Wide*?

It comes from the phrase, "I will open my arms wide and collect all the love the universe has to offer and hug it into my heart and then offer it right back."

Tina Walker

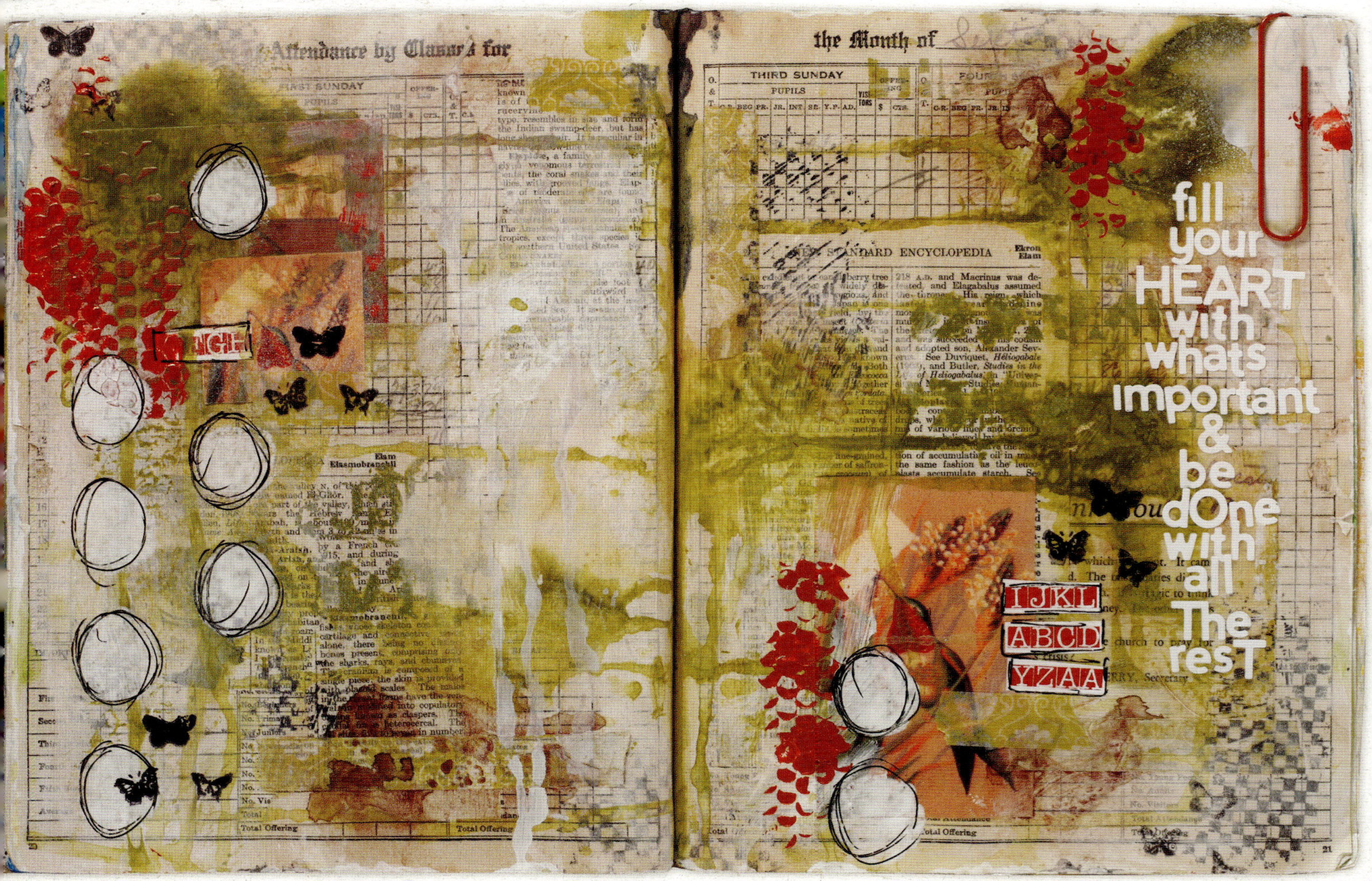

FILL YOUR HEART
Vintage ledger, Ranger Distress paint, Liquitex gesso, ARTchix ephemera, stamps, stickers, modeling creme, pens, StayzOn ink

Are there any mixed-media artists who inspire you?

I'm inspired by Dina Wakley, Ronda Palazzari, Julie Fei-Fan Balzer and Nathalie Kalbach.

Do you ever give yourself journal prompts?

Many of my journaling prompts originate from wanting to experiment with a certain product or technique. The page evolves from there.

Do you have an art journaling process?

Not really. My art journal pages can begin from multiple inspirations: a quote, a product, a color, etc.

What tips would you give to fellow art journaling artists?

Let go. Experiment. Keep trying. If all else fails, cover it in gesso and begin again.

What was your inspiration for this piece?

The inspiration for my piece started with using a specific product, Distress Paint. I love the transparent nature of Distress Paint, which allows the vintage ledger paper to still be visible behind splashes and drips of color.

What interesting or unique techniques did you apply to this artwork?

One of my favorite techniques when creating art journal pages is to allow the product to move across the page. Allowing drips both horizontally and vertically draws the eye across the page in a random, unique way.

Susan Goodell

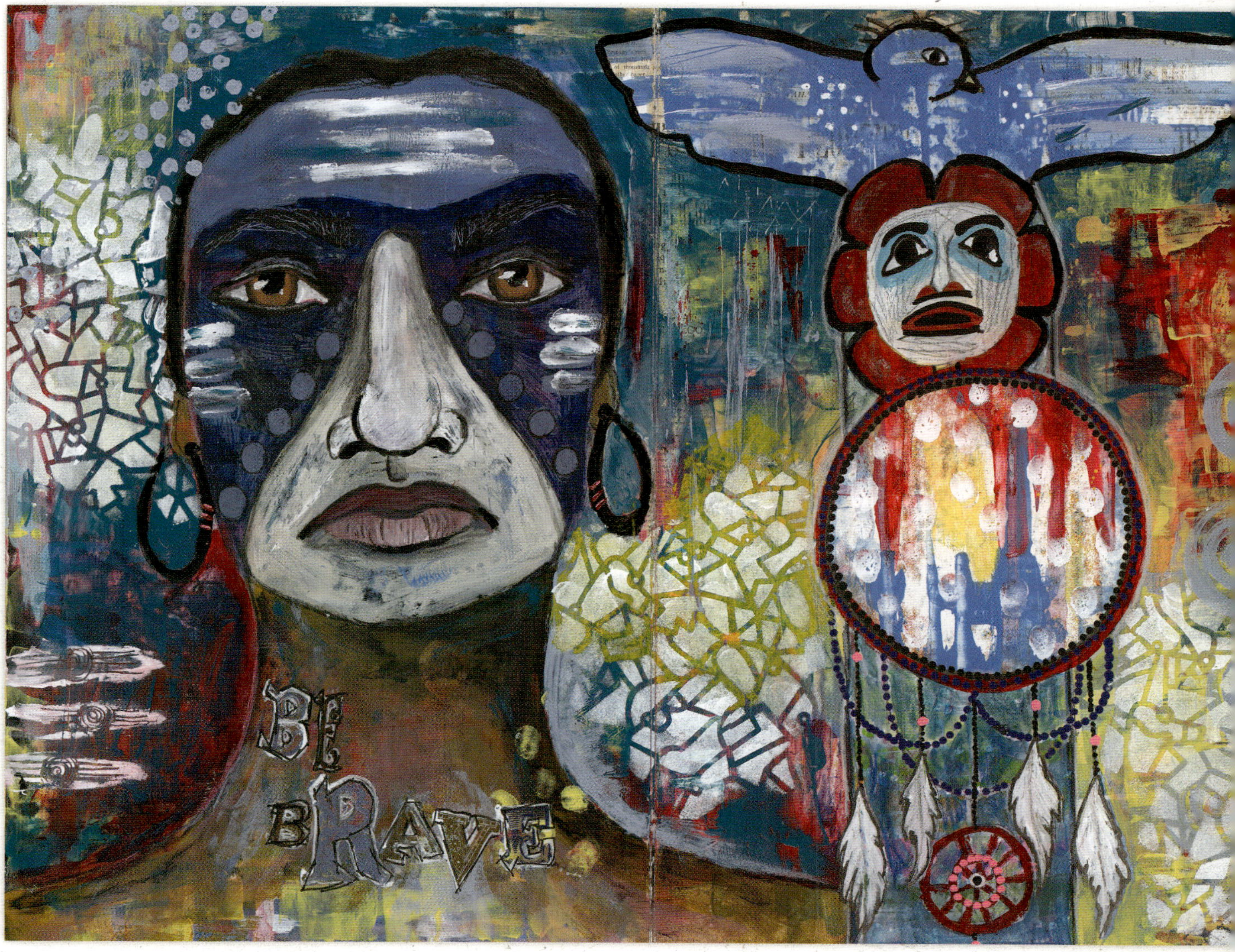

BE BRAVE
Acrylic paint, acrylic paint markers, stencils, rub-ons

Do you ever give yourself journal prompts?

I use paint and paper as journal prompts. I glue down a doodle or label or just clean off my paintbrush and that starts my journaling process.

Do you have an art journaling process?

My art journaling process is random. I usually work on several pages at once, coming back to each one as the desire strikes. I start with a label or a doodle or a few random strokes of paint and I just work intuitively, seeing where the feeling takes me.

What tips would you give to fellow art journaling artists?

Don't try to be perfect and make a pretty picture. Just paint and journal and let your feelings out on the page. You'll be surprised at what appears.

What was your inspiration for this piece?

The artwork was inspired by my many friends and family members who have bravely fought against cancer.

"TAKE A CHANCE, *it's only paper.*"

Agnieszka Anna Niedźwiecka

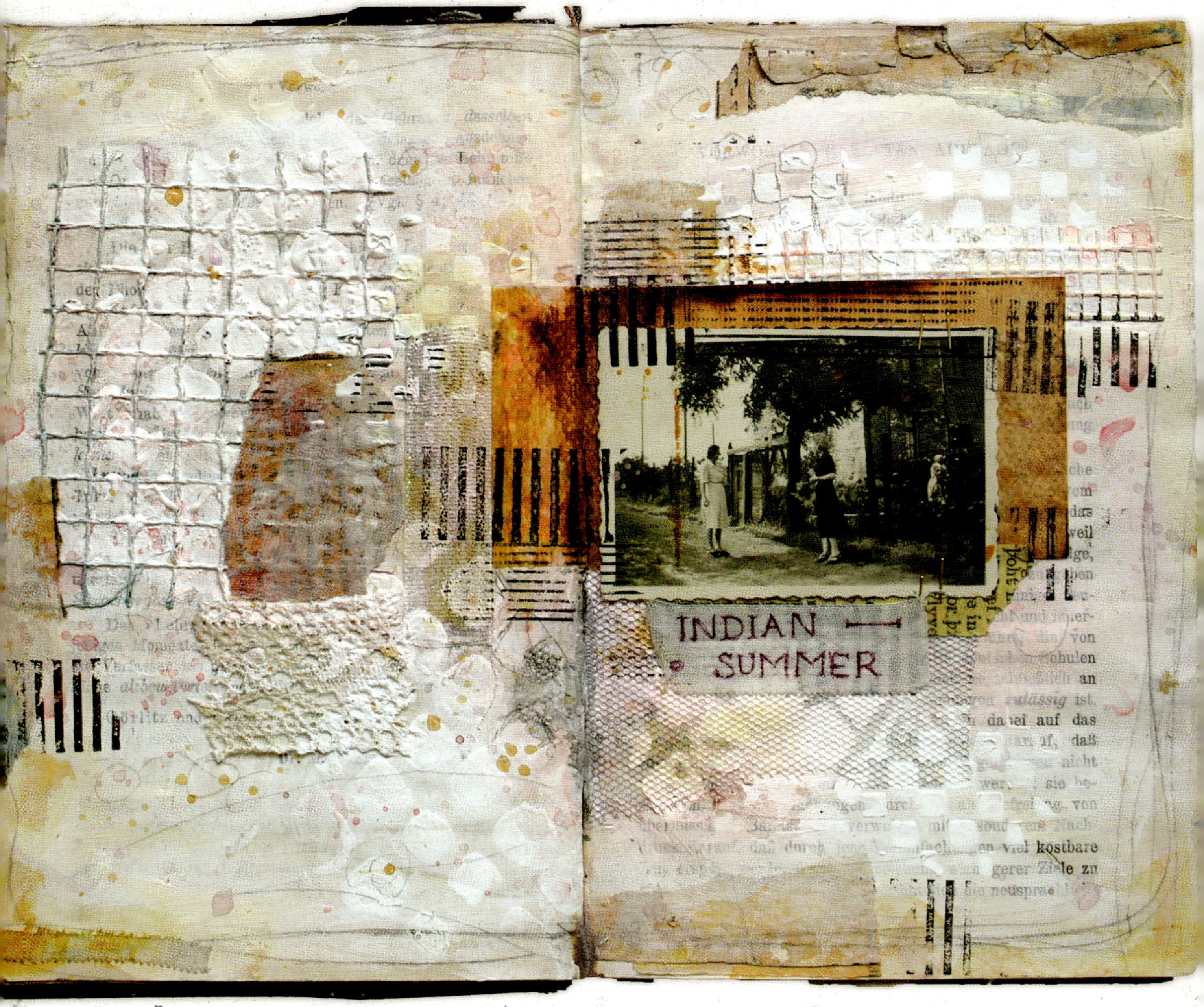

INDIAN SUMMER
Gesso, adhesive bandages, tea bags, fabric, photo, stamp, white liquid watercolor

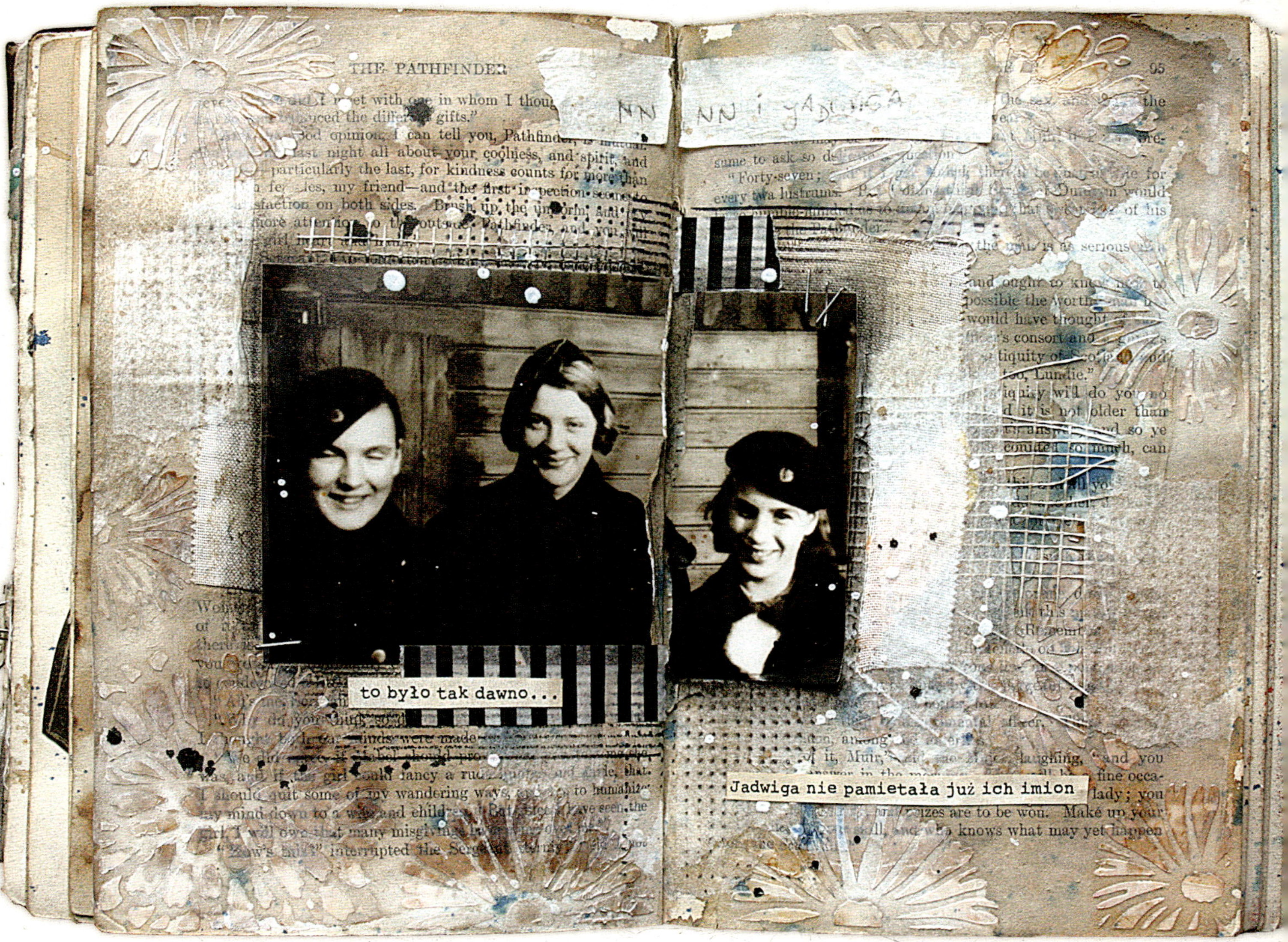

N.N.
Tea, Glimmer Mist, mask, flowers, gel medium, adhesive plasters, washi tape, black ink

What was your inspiration for *N.N.*?

I was inspired by an old photo. With its color and mood, a story was contained in it. Plus, the art journal's base was an old book, and I was challenged to use the images.

Are there any mixed-media artists who inspire you?

I love to observe famous mixed-media artists like Pam Carriker, Michael deMeng, Misty Mawn and Julie Prichard. I'm also often inspired by the works of completely unknown artists, accidentally found somewhere on the Internet.

Do you have an art journaling process?

When I have the blank page syndrome, I take a few pieces of paper and glue them onto a page and then the blank page disappears.

What interesting or unique techniques did you apply to *Indian Summer*?

First I primed my pages with gesso. When it dried, I painted it with a little more gesso using a mask. Next, I glued pieces of papers and fabric, bandages, tea bags and the photo of course. At the end I stamped and splashed the background with the white liquid watercolor Ecoline.

When and why did you start art journaling?

I first encountered art journaling when I decided to take part in a round-robin journal project. At the time, I didn't even know that it was called art journaling.

What tips would you give to fellow art journaling artists?

When I'm blocked and I haven't any idea, I put everything aside and rest. Then, with new strength, I go back to work.

Lelainia Lloyd

What was your inspiration for this piece?

I found this old photograph of Russian children in my stash. I have no idea where it came from or how long I've had it, but I wanted to use it as the jumping off point.

What interesting or unique techniques did you apply to this artwork?

When I am creating a background, I like to start by working on a large substrate and then when I am finished creating all the layers, I cut it down into smaller pieces to use as background. I like the randomness of how this works. I love to use old Letrasets in my artwork. I have letters and numbers in all kinds of sizes, colours and fonts and I like to mix and match when I use them. I don't care if the letters themselves are damaged (half missing) because that's what makes them more interesting to use.

Are there any mixed media artists who inspire you?

Yes! Currently, I'm inspired by Ann Patay, Diana Sudyka, Rebecca Sower and Sabrina Ward Harrison.

Do you have an art journal process? If so, please describe it.

I tend to save up a lot of small random bits of ephemera until the pile gets quite large and then I will dive in and work on several pages at once. I love to just glue things down as I go and see where it takes me—I don't tend to plan things out.

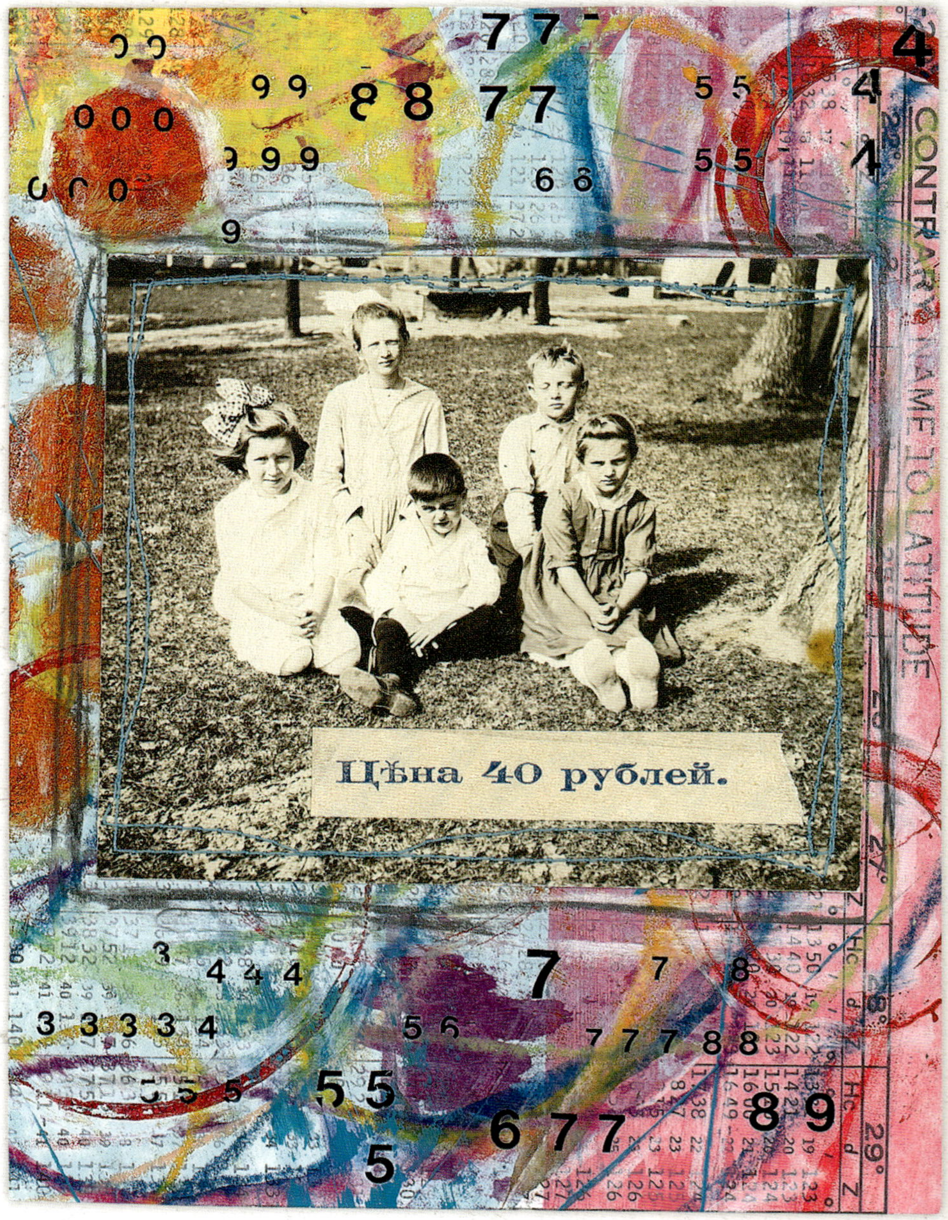

SUMMER IN LENINGRAD
Vintage ephemera, acrylic paints, stencils, Caran d'Ache crayons, vintage numeric Letrasets, pencil, sewing machine, aqua thread

"WHY DID SHE MAKE THINGS? WELL SHE ENJOYED IT OF COURSE; BUT IT ALSO SOMEHOW HELPED HER REMEMBER WHO SHE WAS AND *where she came from.*"

Joella Carson Russert

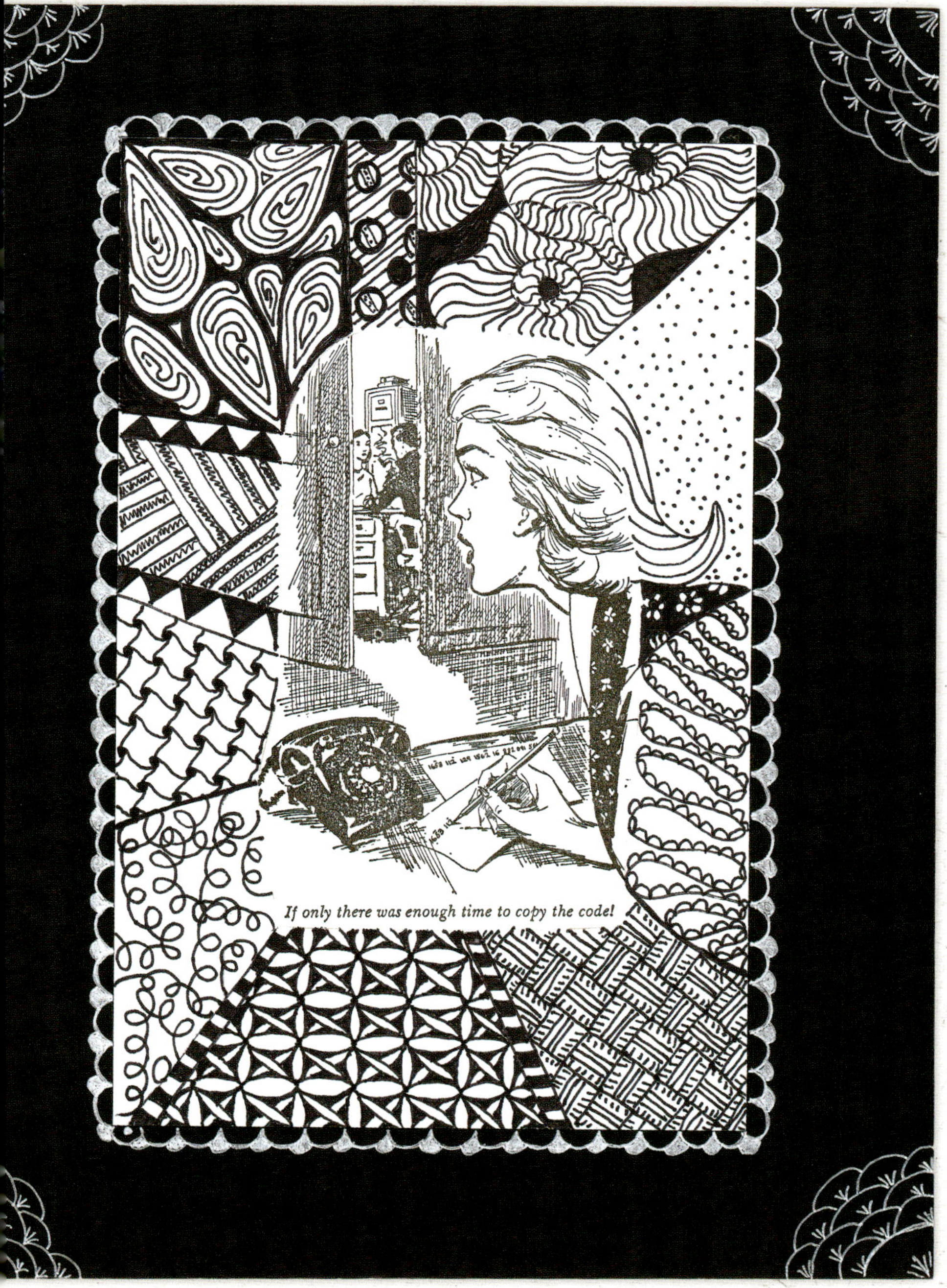

LOOKING FOR A CLUE
Mixed-media paper, black permanent marker, black paper, Signo gel pen

When and why did you start art journaling?

My adventures with art journaling began when I came across an old children's book that an artist had repurposed as a journal. Library book stores and second-hand bookshops became favorite stops for me.

What was your inspiration for this piece?

This artwork began with a picture from a Nancy Drew book mounted on white mixed-media paper.

What interesting or unique techniques did you apply to this artwork?

I used a black permanent marker to extend the scene from the book. That work was then mounted to black paper and framed with white doodles. I have found that a white Signo gel pen gives clean white lines on dark paper.

Krista Wells

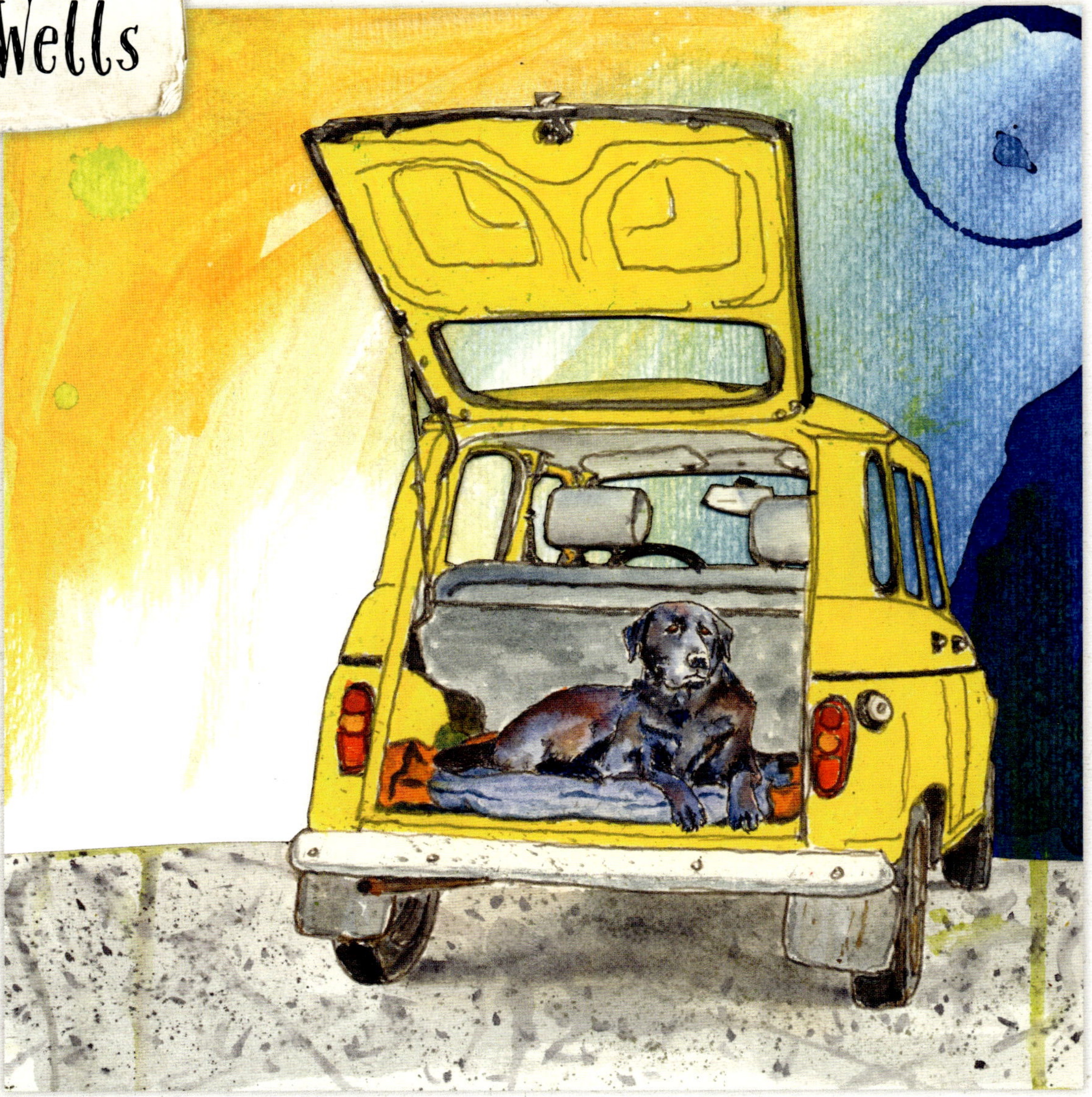

PATIENCE
Watercolor paper, Pitt artist pen, watercolors, ink, matte medium

What was your inspiration for this piece?

I walked by this dog in the back of a car and started to imagine what his life was like. The dog was happy to wait patiently, knowing that at the end of the day he would be treated to a ride in the countryside and he would hang his head out the window to smell the many messages in the wind.

> “WHEN WE SET OUT TO PLEASE OTHERS, IT MAY BE UNAPPRECIATED, BUT WHEN WE CREATE JUST FOR OURSELVES, THAT'S WHEN *we can make magic...*”

What interesting or unique techniques did you apply to this artwork?

When I first made this image, I added a green/gray/brown hillside in the background and really messed the whole thing up, but rather than toss it, I cut out the hillside and put the car on a page that I had previously splashed and smeared with color in an abstract way. The ring of blue in the corner feels a bit like a moon and the dark drip below it could be a cliff. Much better!

Are there any mixed media artists who inspire you?

I love the work of Nick Bantock and appreciate that he often creates his own ephemera, making it look like it actually had a life before he used it in his art. Also, Chris Sickels creates incredible worlds in which I would love to live.

Do you ever give yourself journal prompts?

I don't usually give myself verbal prompts, but often I begin a journal page with an image. I find flipping through my photos will spark an idea and a narrative will begin to take shape.

Jennifer Rogers-Daniels

What was your inspiration for this piece?

I completed this page during a workshop with Teesha Moore. Her journaling style and use of bright colors has always inspired me.

What interesting or unique techniques did you apply to this artwork?

The technique Teesha taught in this class was to use your own artwork to make collage sheets and then cut them up and use them in different ways on future pages as backgrounds or borders. I used Teesha's collage sheets on this page but was inspired to make color copies of my pages to reuse my own art.

Are there any mixed media artists who inspire you?

Teesha Moore inspires me in her use of magazine image collage and her Zetti-style people and creatures.

Do you ever give yourself journal prompts?

If I need a journal prompt, I look online, join a journal challenge or look at magazines or books. I have come up with journal prompts when I had a journal challenge on my blog or when I teach art journaling to kids in my summer art camps.

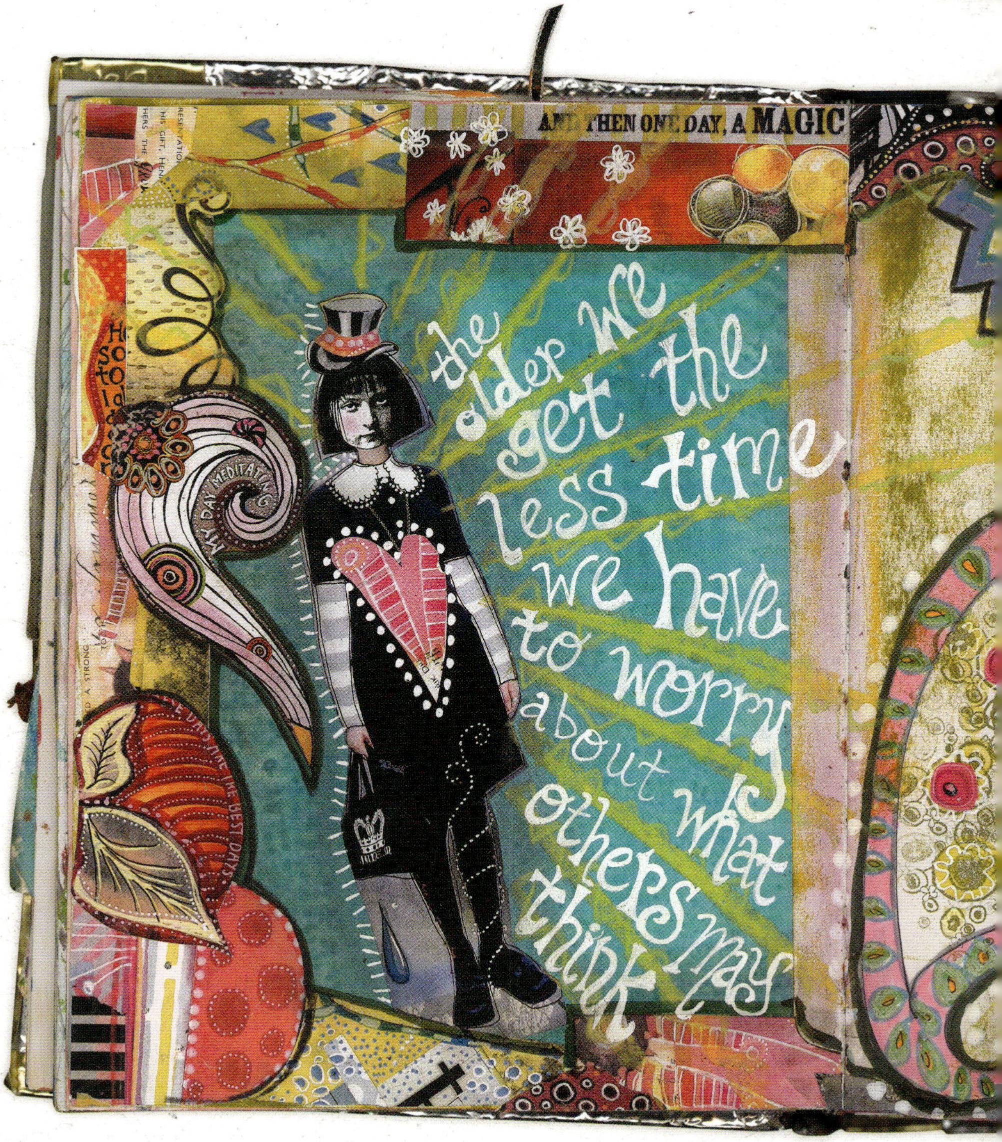

THE OLDER I GET...
Watercolor paper, paint, collage sheet images, watercolor crayons, white gel pen

"*There is a power to writing* DOWN YOUR ASPIRATIONS WITH COLOR, IMAGERY AND PERSONAL FLAIR. IT GIVES IDEAS A CONCRETE FORM AND ALLOWS YOU TO ARTICULATE EXACTLY WHAT YOU INTEND TO BRING ABOUT IN YOUR LIFE."

contributors

Molly Alexander
13134 S. 178th Ave.
Goodyear, AZ 85338
(602) 206-3349
molly@missmollysdesigns.com
www.missmollysdesigns.com

Denise Alloca
denibannon@gmail.com
denisealloca.blogspot.com

Cindy Angiel
rainbowelephant.com

Eila Anttila
eilaantt@gmail.com
saksetjaliimaa.blogspot.com

Seth Apter
New York, New York
shap97@gmail.com
sethapter.com

Joy Bathie
133 / 33-93 Spinifex Avenue
Tea Gardens, NSW 2324
Australia
0011 61 2 4997 9610
jvar@bigpond.com

Karen Bearse
karenbearse@gmail.com
karenbearse.blogspot.com

Nancy Belle
(949) 200-7335
planetnews8@gmail.com
artslant.com/global/artists/
show330233-nancy-belle

Cindy Blevins
Cindylouwho67@verizon.net
cindylovespaper.blogspot.com

Jana Bodin
jana.tangledpen@gmail.com
instagram.com/tangledpen
tangledpen.wordpress.com

Normajean Brevik
57 Dean Road
East Lyme, CT 06333
(986) 739-3032
seasew@yahoo.com
seasew.blogspot.com

Jeanne Brickman

Lisa Maxwell Brown
electablluesworld.blogspot.com

Bunk (Sarah Bunker)
bunk@artybunk.com
artybunk.com

Dianne Bishop Carey
dbcarey_2000@yahoo.com
artbeneaththecottonwoods.
blogspot.com

Darby Casey
darby@ymail.com
darbyart.com

Teri Casper
(608) 564-2359
painteddaisies@gmail.com
painteddaisies.blogspot.com

Sharen Chatterton
Gypsy Muse Studio
106 East Texas St.
Grapevine, Texas
sharen@gypsymusestudio.com
sharenchatterton.com
gypsymusestudio.com

Honorata Chorąży-Przybysz
hona@e-project.co.uk
facebook.com/honoratachorazy-
przybysz

Roxanne Coble
madebybun@gmail.com
bybun.com

Maureen Craddock
Long Island, New York

Julia Crucil
Comox, BC, Canada
jcrucil@yahoo.com

Lisa L. Cyr
Cyr Studio LLC
Artist member of the Society of
Illustrators NYC
lisa@cyrstudio.com
cyrstudio.com
lisalcyr.blogspot.com

Julia Antica Dean

Lea DeCosta
careandfeedingofartists.com

Sharon Denney-Parcel
Lees Summit, Missouri
mrsparcel@gmail.com

Tristina Dietz Elmes
Tarpon River Art Center
614 SW Flager Ave.
Fort Lauderdale, FL 33301
(954) 817-2042
multimediamaven@yahoo.com
multimediamavenart.com

Ingrid Dijkers

Carla Dixon
terarla1@msn.com
carladixon.blogspot.com

Teri Mezzo Flemal
Moderator of Blissfully Art Journaling
mackenzielo@aol.com
quinceberry.blogspot.com

Amy Forsyth
The Furniture Society
The Center for Art in Wood
amyforsyth.com

Terry Garrett
1137 Whisperwood Court SW
Bemidj, MN 56601
terrygarrett763@gmail.com
whisperwoodartworks.blogspot.com

Barbara Giller
Klamath Falls, Oregon
(541) 892-0921
b.giller.art@gmail.com
bgillerart.com

Marianne Goodell
illuminationsart99@gmail.com
illuminationsart.etsy.com
illuminationsart.wordpress.com

Susan Goodell
ladymojo99@aol.com
sgoodell@winstream.net
susangoodell.com

Joanna Grant
Summerland, BC, Canada
joannabanana@shaw.ca
facebook.com/joannagrantart
joannabanana.etsy.com

Paula Hagar
Denver, Colorado
phagar@mindspring.com

Penelope Harris
Vancouver, BC, Canada
pharris@direct.ca
radiantcrust.blogspot.com

Theresa Harrison
Winlaw, BC, Canada
mtharrison05@hotmail.com
terrystakeonart.blogspot.ca

Maz Hawes
mazhawes@mac.com
www.diving-for-pearls.com

Jill Hejl
124 W. 1st St.
Oglesby, IL 61348
(815) 488-8360
jillhejl@comcast.net
livedrawpaint.blogspot.com

Bernice Hopper
Bernice@hopper.uk.net
newlycreative.blogspot.co.uk

Dawn Howell
dhowell9000@yahoo.com

Deborah Hunter-Davis
(256) 653-9160
astridzhang@gmail.com
deborah@deborahhunter.info
deborahhunter.com

Melissa Johnson
Garden Ridge, Texas
(210) 573-7735
melissajohnson8@gmail.com
melsartjournal.wordpress.com

Kara LC Jones (MotherHenna)
kara@motherhenna.com
motherhenna.com

Amanda Judd
Pink Love Studio
pinklovestudio@gmail.com
pinklovestudio.com

Liubov Kadyrova
+353 (86) 3839283
lkadyrova@gmail.com
facebook.com/elevenforms

Brian Kasstle
bkasstle@icloud.com
apaperbear.wordpress.com

Colleen Mulligan Kline
cleenstar@yahoo.com
colleenmulligan.weebly.com

Jessica T. Kovan
ISEA, ISAP
jtkovan@gmail.com
jessicakovan.com

Thomas LaBadia
(954) 630-1909
tom@elusicemu.se
elusivemu.se

Jan La Follette
Hubbard, Oregon
dandelionanddaisy.blogspot.com

Abigail LaShomb
New Jersey
lashomab@gmail.com

Candace Lawlor
Newfoundland, Canada
Candace@saltonscovestudio.com
www.saltonscovestudio.com
etsy.com/shop/saltonscovestu-dio

Ruth S. Levy
Atelier Lerusho
Antwerp, Belgium
lerusho.wordpress.com

Ann Renee Lighter
Art Unstructured
A2nren2e@cfu.net
annreneelighter.blogspot.com

Lelainia Lloyd
Coquitlam, BC, Canada
tatterededge@shaw.ca
tatterededge.blogspot.com

Carol Marion
cmarion333@gmail.com
artjournalingwithcarol.blogspot.com

Jean Marmo
(616) 874-6309
mjmarmo@comcast.net
pagesintime.blogspot.com

Boo Giannini Martin
ellieandscoots@gmail.com
artjournalfeel.blogspot.com
stamplaughplay.blogspot.com

Sharon Mathis
heartfully.inspired.studio@gmail.com
flickr.com/photos/sharonmathis

Theresa T. Mirabile
Coastal Art Center of Orange Beach, Alabama
26389 Canal Road
Orange Beach, Alabama 36561
theresattm@mac.com

Jenny Moed-Korpela
jennymoedkorpela@yahoo.com
jennymoedkorpela.com

Jeanette C. Montero
jeanetics@jeanettemontero.com
jeanettemontero.com
Published art in the Sept./Oct. 2013 issue of *Cloth Paper Scissors* magazine.

Luis Montero
Moravia, San Jose, Costa Rica
Tool shop: 506 22412990
Cell phone: 506 88414329
luiscmontero@yahoo.com
eldiariodelosviajes.com

Tammy Murdock
tammy@embellishstudios.com

Gerit Nagel

Sara Naumann
Sopot, Poland
saracnaumann@gmail.com
saranaumann.com
youtube.com/user/saranaumann

Agnieszka Anna Niedźwiecka
a.a.niedźwiecka@gmail.com
Agnieszka-Anna.blogspot.com

Frieda Oxenham
friedaquilter@yahoo.com
friedaquilter.blogspot.com

Anna K. Pasquale
annak@annakoriginals.com
annakoriginals.com

Angela Pena
angelavelker@gmail.com
angelapena.squarespace.com

Kristin Peterson
323 W. Main St.
Luverne, MN 56156
alteredstatesstudio@yahoo.com
alteredstatesstudio.blogspot.com
HGS Gallery

Sherry Pollack
Columbia, Maryland
alittlecoloreveryday.blogspot.com

Lynette Potts

Gayle Price
pricepine@bigpond.com
blissandgesso.blogspot.com

Palma Rea
flickr.com/photos/palmarea

Kay M. Reist
reistcowell@comcast.net

Jennifer Rogers-Daniels
Palm Avenue Fine Arts Magnet School
San Bernardino, California
jenzfrenz3@yahoo.com
artisticallydesigneddiversions.blogspot.com

Cynthia Cole Russell
PaperWorks, Kaitlin's Creative Cottage
russell_c_@hotmail.com

Joella Carson Russert
Rancho Santa Margarita, California

Linda Sedgley
(206) 722-6387
lindasedgley@gmail.com
www.sedgleygroup.com

Stacy Spangler
Signature member of the Arkansas League of Artists, Arkansas Arts Council Registry
spanglerstacy@yahoo.com
sleepyheaddesignsstudio.com
stacyspanglerart.com

Belinda Spiwak
(630) 803-0259
crazyartgirl@sbcglobal.net
alteredbelly.blogspot.com

Jessica Sporn
jsdesigns@gmail.com
www.cciart.com/jessicasporn.html
www.jessicasporn.blogspot.com

Debra Ann Terry
nuleaf@comcast.net
learningtojustbreathe.blogspot.com

Carrie Todd
carrie@mystudio13.com
mystudio13.com

Stephanie Trice
ladymojo99@aol.com
stephaniesbirdandmixedmediapictures.blogspot.com
Journal Photographer: LaVena Wilder

Melinda Newlin Tshudy
mintsh15@yahoo.com
facebook.com/melindanewlintshudy

Mandy van Goeije
Tel: 0031-6-52680908
mandy@mandyvangoeije.com
www.illustrateyourlife.eu
mandyvangoeije.com

Patricia E. Van West
The Artery Studio
214 Williams Ave.
Port St. Joe, FL 32456
arterystudio.com

Deb Versluis
Prairie Scrapbooking
Beausejour, B, Canada
(204) 268-2637
memories@prairiescrapbooking.com
prairiescrapbooking.com

Tina Walker
7931 Madison Nan Dr.
West Jordan, UT 84081
(614) 551-5853
adogslife13@hotmail.com

Krista Wells
Art Lab Studios & Gallery
121 Main St.
Parrsboro, Nova Scotia
B0M 1S0
(902) 254-2972
krista@kristawells.ca
kristawells.ca

Natasha White
248 Waddington Drive,
Naenae, Lower Hutt 5011
New Zealand
006449761133
tarshw@gmail.com
defineyourjoy.com

Katherine Jeanne Wood
katherinejeannewood.com

Robyn Wood
purplesalt.net

Delfina Zapata
(419) 290-6269
mzfina@yahoo.com
etsy.com/shop/4creativechicas
facebook.com/4creativechicas

index

about the editor

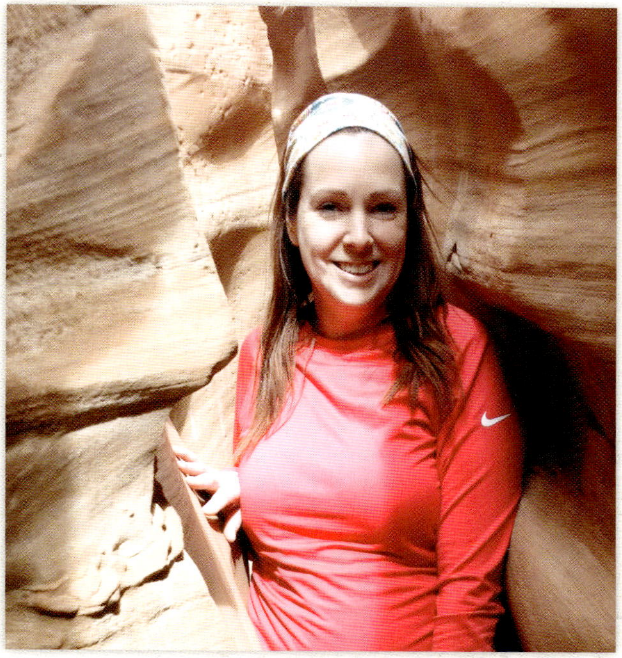

Kristy Conlin is manging editor for F+W Media's North Light art community. She has a degree in journalism and a minor in Spanish (which has imbued her with a serious crush on Mexican and South American art). Kristy has been surrounded her entire life by art and craftiness—her mom, dad, grandmother and brother are seriously artsy/crafty—and there is probably no medium she hasn't at least tried.

Encouraged and inspired by the authors she works with, Kristy currently dabbles in art journaling, acrylic painting and encaustic painting and is ready to tackle urban sketching. She is a convert to the wabi-sabi philosophy of honoring the aged, the humble and the oftentimes overlooked. When she's not at work, Kristy can usually be found reading, running, watching movies or writing. She lives in Cincinnati, Ohio, with her husband, dog and two cats.

 Published by North Light Books, an imprint of F+W, A Content and eCommerce Company, 10151 Carver Road, Suite 200, Blue Ash, Ohio, 45242. (800) 289-0963. First Edition.

Other fine North Light Books are available from your favorite bookstore, art supply store or online supplier. Visit our website at fwmedia.com.

18 17 16 15 14 5 4 3 2 1

DISTRIBUTED IN CANADA BY FRASER DIRECT
100 Armstrong Avenue
Georgetown, ON, Canada L7G 5S4
Tel: (905) 877-4411

DISTRIBUTED IN THE U.K. AND EUROPE
BY F&W MEDIA INTERNATIONAL LTD
Brunel House, Forde Close, Newton Abbot, TQ12 4PU, UK
Tel: (+44) 1626 323200, Fax: (+44) 1626 323319
Email: enquiries@fwmedia.com

DISTRIBUTED IN AUSTRALIA BY CAPRICORN LINK
P.O. Box 704, S. Windsor NSW, 2756 Australia
Tel: (02) 4560-1600; Fax: (02) 4577 5288
Email: books@capricornlink.com.au

ISBN 13: 978-1-4403-3701-7

fw a content + ecommerce company

Metric Conversion Chart

TO CONVERT	TO	MULTIPLY BY
Inches	Centimeters	2.54
Centimeters	Inches	0.4
Feet	Centimeters	30.5
Centimeters	Feet	0.03
Yards	Meters	0.9
Meters	Yards	1.1

EDITED BY:
Brittany VanSnepson & Kristy Conlin

DESIGNED BY:
Hannah Bailey

PRODUCTION COORDINATED BY:
Jennifer Bass

Ideas. Instruction. Inspiration.

Receive FREE downloadable bonus materials when you sign up for our free newsletter at CreateMixedMedia.com.

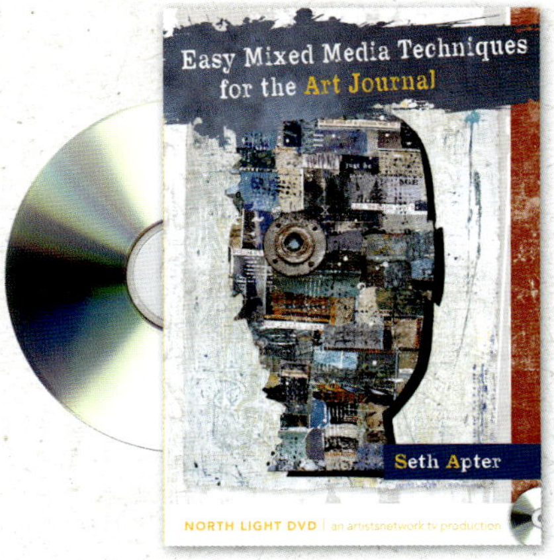

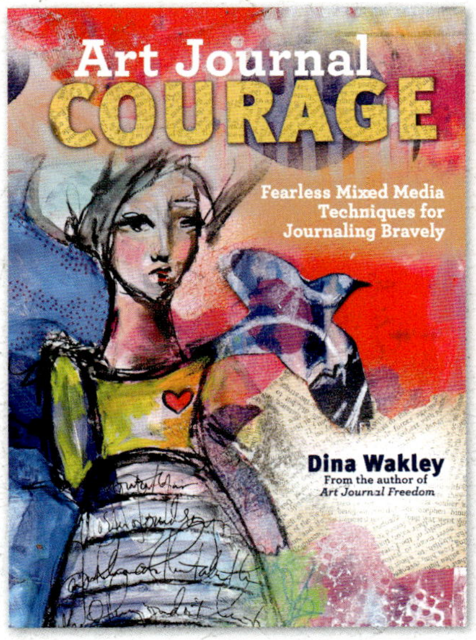

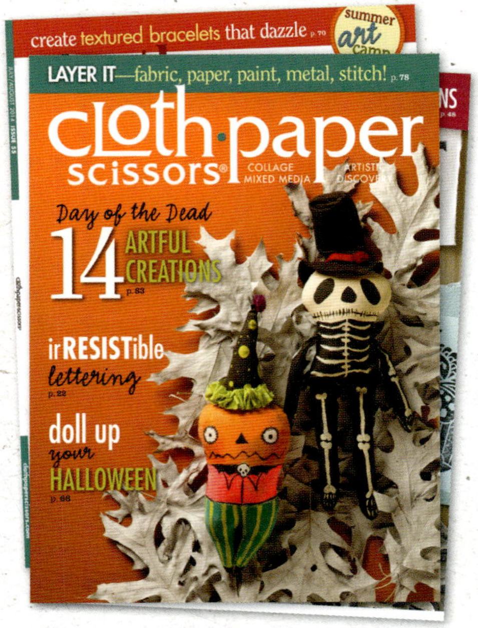

Find the latest issues of ***Cloth Paper Scissors*** *on newsstands, or visit ClothPaperScissors.com.*

These and other fine North Light products are available at your favorite art & craft retailer, bookstore or online supplier. Visit our websites at artistsnetwork.com, artistsnetwork.tv and CreateMixedMedia.com

Follow CreateMixedMedia.com for the latest news, free wallpapers, free demos and chances to win FREE BOOKS!

Visit CreateMixedMedia.com

- Connect with your favorite mixed media artists.
- Get the latest in mixed-media inspiration.
- Be the first to get special deals on the products you need to improve your mixed-media endeavors.

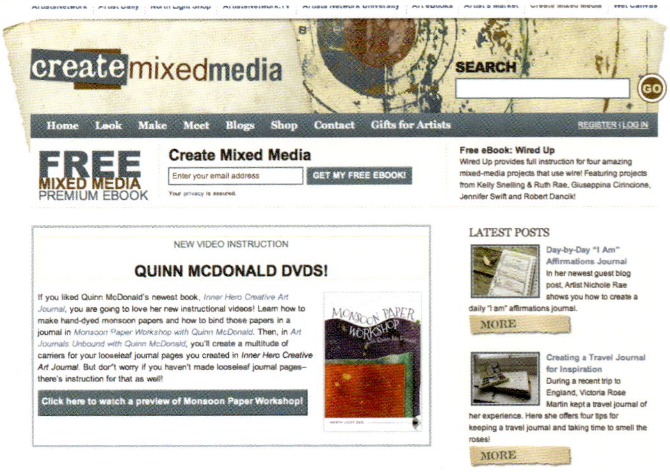